U0060373

The Fall of a President

Osman C.H. Tseng 曾慶祥

Printed in Taiwan, Republic of China
For information address:
Elephant White Cultural Enterprise Ltd. Press,
8F.-2, No.1, Keji Rd., Dali Dist., Taichung City 41264, Taiwan (R.O.C.)
Distributed by Elephant White Cultural Enterprise Co., Ltd.

A Self-Made Man
Also by Osman C.H. Tseng（曾慶祥）

ISBN: 978-626-364-254-6
Suggested Price: **NT$600**

For my late father,
Tseng Xian-huai
曾憲槐
And my late mother
Ai Jin-shiang
艾金香

Acknowledgments

I am particularly grateful to my partner and better half, Lei Yen-ming 雷燕鳴, for the unwavering support she has rendered over many years and her ability to put up with the numerous family sacrifices that allowed me to pursue my writing career. Without her support and understanding, it would have been impossible to overcome the challenges and difficulties I encountered along the way.

My thanks also go to my daughter Tseng Wen-yi 曾文儀 who helped me conduct research for The Fall of a President, and my son Tseng Wen-chieh 曾文傑 for his ready assistance in fixing the myriad problems I encountered when wrestling with my often uncooperative computer.

Furthermore, I want to thank my good friend and former colleague William Kazer for contributing the foreword to this book.

About the Author

Author Osman C.H. Tseng 曾慶祥 is a veteran journalist. Although he wrote for a leading Chinese-language newspaper in the early stage of his journalistic career, it was in English-language writing that he found a home. His career spanned over four decades, with journalistic roles ranging from reporter to city editor to editor-in-chief and editorial writer and commentator. Over the years, his commentaries graced the pages of several of Taiwan's general and specialized publications, making his views well-known to readers with a serious interest in political and economic developments in Taiwan. His long service in key positions in local news organizations gave him a unique vantage point for observing crucial events in Taiwan's modern history.

English is not his mother tongue. He began his association with this curious second language in his early 20s while serving in the army. At that point, he was a career soldier with a keen interest in English. His persistent efforts in understanding and applying that language eventually landed him a role as an army interpreter.

His skills in English writing and journalism came later, honed throughout his lengthy career. Like his English, his journalism was largely self-taught – or learning by doing. He never attended school but always found time to further his education and deepen his skills on his own. It was this unique life and work experience that prompted him to write his first book, an autobiography, A Self-Made Man.

Foreword

Chen Shui-bian is one of the most consequential -- and controversial -- politicians in Taiwan's modern history. The former lawyer who rose from a humble farming background was instrumental in Taiwan's transformation from authoritarian rule to the thriving democracy of today. It was Chen who broke the political grip of the ruling Kuomintang (Nationalist Party), winning the presidency in 2000 and paving the way for the first peaceful transfer of power to the opposition – the Democratic Progressive Party. But Chen, who was later convicted in four corruption-related criminal cases, was also responsible for inflicting great political harm on a young democracy and staining the office of the president. The lengthy court battles that ensued and the damaging testimony that emerged undermined his important accomplishments, convincing even some of his closest allies in the push for democratic reform to abandon him. Ultimately, Chen will be remembered as the first president of Taiwan to be sentenced to jail.

Chen's intriguing story deserves retelling, and veteran journalist Osman Tseng, author of The Fall of a President, is uniquely suited to the task. Tseng's journalistic career spanned more than four decades with the Chinese language China Times as well as English media outlets, the China Post, and the China Economic News Service (CENS), part of the United Daily News media group. This gave him a choice vantage point for observing Chen's political ascent and the dramatic legal battles of his eventual downfall.

Foreword

In The Fall of a President, the author draws on a wide range of research material, court documents, public statements, domestic and foreign news reports as well as his contemporaneous commentaries and editorials to assess the Chen presidency and its effects on Taiwan's political landscape. He offers his readers a detailed account of the twists and turns in the various court cases involving Chen and First Lady Wu Shu-chen, among others, stemming from actions taken during the eight years of the Chen administration. He also examines Chen's policies toward the mainland, which was long wary of what it perceived to be thinly disguised pro-independence objectives, and assesses the president's often strained interactions with the United States. The author traces how tensions flared in both of these critical relationships. His conclusions are instructive for readers today.

The Fall of a President provides insight into the career of one of the most perplexing actors on Taiwan's political stage. It is likely to be of significant value to historians, journalists, and all general readers with an interest in Taiwan's political development.

William Kazer
(William Kazer is a former correspondent for Reuters and the
Wall Street Journal as well as a CENS alumnus)

Contents

Preface

The Fall of a President is a work about Chen Shui-bian, Taiwan's charismatic but controversial former leader. Chen served as the president of Taiwan, officially known as the Republic of China, from 2000 to 2008, leaving behind a dizzyingly mixed legacy that ran the gamut from praise for his inspirational democratic ideals to vexation and condemnation for his crass and venal behavior. That legacy also included social and political divisions that are not fully healed today.

Several factors compelled me to write this book. First and foremost, the ex-president provides a classic example of how "power corrupts." In 2000, he came to office pledging to combat corruption and ensure clean government. But eight years later, after stepping down from office, he was prosecuted for taking bribes and money laundering in his official capacity, as well as obstruction of justice.

At the end of protracted court battles, Chen was found guilty and sentenced to a combined 20 years in jail. The charges against him and his wife were many. They were related to taking kickbacks in a land procurement deal, involvement in an office-buying scandal, soliciting payments related to an exhibition hall construction project, receiving bribes to smooth the way for the merger of two financial institutions, and money laundering.

Another convincing reason for undertaking this project was that Chen was an internationally known figure who managed to alarm friends as well as adversaries. This unique quality could be seen in many of the policies pursued during Chen's time in office and the controversies they created. I hope that my analysis will help future

Taiwan administrations avoid such disruptions in carrying out their duties.

In May 2000 when Chen Shui-bian began his first term as president, he famously pledged to the United States and the international community that he would not pursue independence for Taiwan while in office. Independence was – and still is -- the acknowledged "third rail" of Taiwan politics. China insists it is willing to wage war to prevent it. Chen's message seemed to be clear: he would not cross that thin red line.

But Chen abandoned those firm pledges throughout his presidency, bowing to a combination of greed and political expediency. In a speech in August 2002, Chen declared, "With Taiwan and China on each side of the Taiwan Strait, each side is a country." The following year, Chen announced he planned to draft a new constitution for Taiwan.

In his final year in office, from April 2007 to March 2008, Chen embarked on a series of political actions that were seen as the most controversial of his presidency. His applications for formal entry into the World Health Organization and the United Nations and his campaign to conduct a U.N.-related referendum prompted strong opposition from both Beijing and Washington. They saw these moves as aimed at promoting Taiwan as an independent country and changing its political status.

A look back at these and other related controversies surrounding Chen's tenure will provide insights into where Taiwan was heading politically, socially, and economically under his leadership. As I noted earlier, it also offers us valuable lessons that could apply to Taiwan's future political direction.

There is another personal reason behind my decision to write The Fall of a President. As a longtime journalist and newspaper editorial writer who regularly covered Chen Shui-bian and tracked his performance, I have abundant knowledge as well as a strong sense of the importance of recounting the events of his presidency and commenting on his legacy.

My views and the discussions on the following pages are supported by information collected from the former leader's statements, news releases by relevant government agencies, court documents, comments by Taiwan and international experts, and reports in authoritative newspapers, as well as the numerous editorials I wrote about the president during his time in office and afterward.

The Fall of a President consists of 11 chapters, with each one covering a specific topic, as listed below.

Chapter 1
Fall from Grace

Making History Twice

Chen Shui-bian made history twice in his remarkable political career. In March 2000, he successfully toppled the long-ruling Kuomintang (KMT) in a historic popular vote to become Taiwan's first president from an opposition party. That ended over a half-century of authoritarian KMT rule and ushered in a vibrant two-party political system in Taiwan, formally known as the Republic of China. His electoral victory at the head of the Democratic Progressive Party (DPP) earned him the adulation of many who had longed for a more open political system that truly reflected the will of the people. They saw Chen as a shining symbol of Taiwan's young democracy.

In November 2008, a few months after completing his eight years in office, Chen made history once again, albeit in a much less laudable fashion; he became Taiwan's first president arrested for suspected corruption. He was found guilty and sentenced to 17-and-a-half years in jail for taking bribes in a land procurement deal and as payment for an appointment to office. The sentence was later extended to 20 years -- the maximum prison time allowed in his case -- after he was found guilty on two more corruption charges, one involving the taking of bribes from a financial firm and another related to money laundering.

All four convictions also involved the president's wife, Wu Shu-chen. She was found guilty in a fifth and separate corruption case linked to a scandal involving kickbacks on the construction of the Taipei Nangang Exhibition Center, a conference and exhibition complex designed to showcase Taiwan's status in the global economy. Instead, it put on display Taiwan's murky nexus between business and politics. Despite the additional offense, Mrs. Chen was given the same 20-year sentence as her husband due to the legal limits on sentencing. She was also spared the ignominy of serving time in jail because of poor health and serious physical disabilities. She was wheelchair-bound after being run over by a truck some two decades earlier.

Around the world, it is not unheard of to have a top government leader charged with corruption after leaving office. Sometimes it is a matter of the wheels of justice turning slowly toward a righteous conclusion long after the transfer of power. At other times, particularly in less mature and more malleable legal systems, it is a matter of an incumbent using the powers of office to strike at a former political opponent. In the case of Chen Shui-bian, both claims were made as to the nature of the charges against him. But in the pages that follow, it is hoped that the reader will see that a fair analysis makes clear this was hardly a case of political persecution, despite the charges leveled by Chen's supporters as well as some prominent, neutral observers. It was, however, truly head-spinning that the former president was found guilty of so many separate instances of graft. His humble origin and stellar career made this a stunning fall from grace. This was a man born into a tenant farming family in the rural township of Guantian in southern Taiwan. In this largely agricultural area, traditional values, such as honesty and integrity, have long been instilled in homes and

Chapter 1
Fall from Grace

schools. It was true in 1951 – the year Chen Shui-bian was born. It still holds today, even in this somewhat more cynical day and age.

Chen Shui-bian obtained a bachelor's degree in commercial law from the prestigious National Taiwan University in 1974. He passed the bar exam during his junior year and entered the legal profession shortly after graduation. All of this might have pointed to the acquisition of a healthy respect for the law.

In his early years in the legal profession, Chen became a partner in Taiwan's Formosa International Marine and Commercial Law firm. He earned a reputation as a conscientious and promising young lawyer, specializing in maritime insurance.

He soon won acclaim as a "human rights lawyer" for his courage in defending a group of political dissidents charged in what became known as the Kaohsiung Incident in 1979.[1] His clients were activists arrested for organizing a rally in the southern Taiwan city of Kaohsiung on December 10 of that year to commemorate World Human Rights Day. But the event, aimed at giving democracy a peaceful push forward, ultimately turned violent as clashes broke out between police and demonstrators. Taiwan was still under martial law at the time, and some of those arrested were charged with sedition by military prosecutors. Chen lost the case but burnished his reputation.

---

1 The Kaohsiung Incident, also known as the Formosa Incident, occurred on December 10, 1979, in the southern Taiwan city of Kaohsiung, when a group of political activists held a rally to commemorate Human Rights Day and demand democratic reforms. The event, which turned violent, resulting in the prosecution and conviction of its organizers, was widely seen as a watershed in Taiwan's democratization. (Source: Wikipedia last modified on May 16, 2016).

According to Chen's account, the experience of defending the political activists implicated in the Kaohsiung incident spurred him to enter politics himself. He later recalled in conversations with friends that it was "during this period that he had come to realize the unfairness of the political system in Taiwan." In 1980, he joined the Tangwai movement, an informal grouping of opposition figures at a time when opposition parties were banned.[2] The following year, he ran and was elected to the Taipei City Council, a seat he held until 1985.

As democratization gathered pace in Taiwan, the Democratic Progressive Party was formed in 1986 despite the continuing ban on new political parties. Chen was among the founders of the party. The following year, Taiwan ended 38 years of martial law, and with that, the ban on new political parties was formally swept away.

In 1989, Chen was elected to the Legislative Yuan (parliament) as a lawmaker from the DPP and was reelected to another three-year term in 1992. In the lawmaking body, he concentrated his time and energy on attacking the KMT's culture of corruption, then referred to as "black gold" politics, in addition to targeting irregularities in the military.

During his four years from 1994 as mayor of Taipei, the rising political star of the DPP launched a series of high-profile "clean-up" campaigns, including efforts to drive illegal gambling and prostitution

---

2 The Tangwai movement was a political initiative in Taiwan from the mid-1970s to the early 1980s. Tangwai referred to politicians "outside the party," i.e. the KMT. Because opposition parties were still forbidden, many opponents of the KMT, officially classified as independents, ran and were elected to central and local representative bodies as members "outside the party." (Source: Wikipedia).

Chapter 1
Fall from Grace

rackets out of the city. His policy of levying heavy fines on polluters also earned him widespread support.

While campaigning ahead of the March 2000 presidential election, Chen vowed that, if elected, he would lead a clean government. Due largely to the popularity of his anti-corruption appeal, he triumphed at the polls. When he took the presidential oath of office, he formally committed himself to carrying out political reform and eliminating corruption at all levels of government.

Four years later in 2004, when Chen sought a second term, he ran on this popular platform once again. His reform policy proved popular once more, gaining him another four years.

Given Chen Shui-bian's repeated pledges to fight corruption and his impressive record carrying out his promises as a legislator, mayor, and president, many of his supporters found it hard to believe the accusations when the first whiffs of the scandal emerged. But the details of his family's numerous financial dealings ultimately came to light in the final years of his second term, thanks to the efforts of whistleblowers, prosecutors, and a determined local media.

But it is often asked how someone with such strong moral convictions could change so drastically after reaching the pinnacle of power. And how could someone with such a deep respect for the rule of law be accused of so many offenses? This brings to mind an old proverb, most famously linked to British historian Lord Acton: "Power corrupts, and absolute power corrupts absolutely." The experience of Taiwan's ex-president Chen Shui-bian appears to be a classic example of how morality weakens as power increases, or how power corrupts.

Chen Shui-bian and his wife were first convicted in December 2010 by the Supreme Court on charges of taking kickbacks and bribes. The defendants were sentenced to 17 and a half years in jail. Chen began serving his prison term though his wife was spared a prison term on health considerations.

Yet the 2010 convictions proved to be only the first of a series of final court verdicts handed down to him on a variety of corruption charges. In the following two years, 2011 and 2012, the couple each received an additional two-year sentence for money laundering and another 10-year jail term for taking bribes given by a young executive, Diana Chen (no relationship to Chen Shui-bian). The executive offered the payment in exchange for the first couple's help in getting a top position managing Taiwan's landmark building -- Taipei 101.

By late 2012, the jail sentences that the former president had received on the various convictions added up to nearly 30 years. However, a provision in Taiwan's criminal law limited jail terms to 20 years, except for cases where a life sentence could be imposed. Chen was therefore sentenced to a maximum of 20 years. (Although the maximum jail term had been extended to 30 years at the time of sentencing, the lower limit was in effect when the crimes were committed. The 20-year ceiling, therefore, applied to Chen.)

Even though the sentences Chen received far exceeded the maximum 20-year prison term, the former president still had other court cases pending. This raised a curious legal question as to whether these cases could potentially result in additional punishments for the ex-president.

Chapter 1
Fall from Grace

But that hypothetical question was never asked. A year later in December 2013, the Taipei District Court granted an application filed by Chen's lawyers, asking on health grounds for permission to suspend their client's trial in two other cases -- one involving "charges of corruption" and one concerning "unauthorized retention of confidential government documents."

The district court cited a medical report--presented by the lawyers and verified by a group of court-commissioned medical experts--as saying that Chen was suffering from a string of ailments, making him unable to attend hearings. The court at the same time ordered that the trial suspension would remain effective until the defendant was able to attend hearings and answer questions. [3] However, many critics questioned the credibility of the medical report, contending that the medical group consisted of members sympathetic to Chen.

Over more than two years until April 2016, Chen also successfully won court approval for the suspension of other court proceedings. One approval was given by the Taipei District Court and three by the Taiwan High Court. The four cases were about charges of embezzling "state affairs" funds, laundering money obtained from bribes, and perjury.[4]

---

[3] Richard Chang, Taipei District Court Suspends Chen Shui-bian Trial Over Health Concerns, Taipei Times, December 21, 2013.

[4] Lin Chih-han, Tsai Mong-yu, Chen Shui-bain Granted Application for Suspension of Trials on Health Reasons, United Daily News, April 22, 2016.

Developing Health Problems in Prison

Chen Shui-bian, while serving time in prison, developed health problems and his condition reportedly deteriorated rapidly. Chen's family and supporters blamed his rapid physical decline on poor treatment in prison. "From the start, Chen's defenders presented him as a victim of his political enemies. They raised questions about the fairness of his trial and criticized conditions in prison, where at first, he was held in a small cell without a bed and permitted only an hour of exercise per day."[5]

Such a defense strategy helped Chen win sympathy and support, particularly from world human rights organizations and some influential politicians in the United States. U.S. Human Rights Action Center founder Jack Healey, for example, condemned Taiwan's prison authorities for "neglecting Chen's right to medical treatment, causing the deterioration of his health conditions."[6]

In an open letter in 2012 to Chen's successor, President Ma Ying-jeou, Healey wrote: "Mr. Chen has served over four years since his conviction and has spent twenty-three hours per day in a cell shared with another prisoner that is only six feet by ten feet. He was permitted only an hour per day out of his cell. Mr. Chen's health is not good. His access to the hospital was finally allowed, and the medical care he received was helpful but unable to fully survey his medical needs... In

---

5 Austin Ramzy, Taiwan Debates Medical Parole for Ex-Leader, the New York Times, July 21, 2013.
6 News Release, Agency of Corrections of ROC Justice Ministry, December 27, 2012.

Chapter 1
Fall from Grace

the United States, we have prosecuted and convicted politicians from the most local to national offices, but we do not systematically deny those people access to health care due to political differences."[7]

Healey thus appealed to President Ma to free Chen before "he dies in prison" and to work to heal political polarization.

During a visit to Taiwan in August 2012, Ramsey Clark, a former U.S. attorney general and a renowned human rights advocate, called for "an immediate release of former President Chen Shui-bian," adding that the Taiwanese government would be viewed as Chen's murderer if his health deteriorated further."[8] Speaking of his one-hour meeting with Chen in Taipei Prison, Clark said the former Taiwan leader was of clear mind and expression but was "obviously weak" and was kept in a condition that would further undermine his health.

On a May 2013 visit to Taiwan, Steven Chabot, chairman of the U.S. House of Representatives Subcommittee on Asian and Pacific Affairs, and his fellow congressional member Eni Faleomavaega met with Chen at Taichung Prison's Pei De Hospital. During the meeting, they said Chen's hands were shaking visibly and he stuttered when he spoke. "As Chen's friends, we were worried about his situation," Chabot said, adding that "U.S. representatives cannot tell Taiwan what to do, but we think there is a humanitarian way to resolve the situation, and we would like to see that happen."[9]

---

7 Jack Healey, an Open Letter to Taiwan's President Ma Ying-jeou, Huffington Post, updated September 19, 2012.
8 Chris Wang, Rich Chang, Clark Says Chen Facing 'Murder' by Parole Denial, Taipei Times, August 23, 2012.
9 Jake Chung, U.S. Politicians Concerned About A-bian, Taipei Times, May 3, 2013.

Chen Shui-bian's supporters in Taiwan continued to criticize his prison conditions and medical care, which they said had contributed to the former president's failing health. They kept up the pressure on the government of President Ma Ying-jeou to grant Chen medical parole.

The criticisms both at home and abroad put considerable pressure on the Ma government, forcing it to repeatedly clarify how Chen Shui-bian was treated during his incarceration. In a statement, the Ministry of Justice said: "We treated Chen Shui-bian as both a convict and a former president." The statement went further to explain why he could not be granted medical parole or pardoned, as requested by his supporters and sympathizers. But foreign and domestic pressure persisted, and the ministry felt obliged to regularly publish updates on Chen's life in prison and his health.

President Ma spoke repeatedly on the issue of Chen Shui-bian's incarceration. He used his meeting with visiting U.S. Senator Lisa Murkowski (R-AK) in January 2013 to state the case for keeping the former president in prison.[10]

During the meeting, the U.S. senator expressed serious concerns over Chen's treatment in prison and enquired about the possibility of granting him medical parole. In response, Ma pointed out that "Mr. Chen was convicted on multiple charges of corruption. He was not jailed as a political prisoner or a prisoner of conscience," as some of his supporters contended. Ma also told his visitor that "while Chen Shui-bian has been convicted and sentenced in four corruption cases,

---

10 Minutes of the Meeting between President Ma Ying-jeou and U.S. Senator Lisa Murkowski, Ministry of Justice of the Republic of China (Taiwan), January 17, 2013.

he is still facing trials in three other cases and, additionally, is being investigated for another charge against him."

Ma went on to say: "Out of deference to the former head of state and former chairman of the largest opposition party, however, the government has been providing Mr. Chen the most preferential treatment within the scope of the law during his incarceration."

As for Murkowski's question about medical parole, President Ma stated, "In Taiwan, medical parole is possible only when adequate medical treatment cannot be provided at the prisoner's current prison, or a hospital under guarded escort, or at a prison hospital. At present, Mr. Chen is receiving comprehensive medical care at a hospital under escort."

Ma was long known to be opposed to pardoning Chen. During Ma's eight years in office (2008-2016), Chen's supporters repeatedly called on the president to grant a pardon. High-profile appeals came from the DPP's caucuses in the Taipei and Kaohsiung city councils on the eve of Ma's departure from office. In their appeal, DPP councilors said: "Pardoning Chen by President Ma before his second term ends on May 20, 2016, would go a long way toward achieving reconciliation between Taiwan's two major rival political forces, the pan-blue and pan-green camps."

Why Ma Ying-jeou Refused to Pardon Chen Shui-bian

Ma responded swiftly. In a statement issued through his office, he said: "Presidential pardon is an issue that can be considered only after final court verdicts on all of the charges against Chen have been reached.

23

But the fact is that several other criminal cases implicating the former president are still going on."[11]

Earlier, when asked whether he would consider pardoning Chen Shui-bian during his time in office, Ma had cited one other reason why he was unwilling to grant a pardon: "Chen had never admitted to the various crimes he was convicted of, and he never expressed remorse."

Comparatively speaking, the public discussion of the ex-president's prison treatment and medical care was far more impassioned; so impassioned that it blinded both his supporters and critics to two hard facts: Chen's critics failed to notice that during his years of prison life, the former president had developed health problems, some of which worsened rapidly.

Similarly, his supporters failed to recognize that Taipei Prison, in response to pressure from home and abroad, did make significant efforts to improve Chen's jail conditions and arrange top-quality medical care based on the recommendations of medical experts.

During the more than four years of incarceration in Taipei Prison -- from December 2010 to January 2015 when he was granted medical parole – Chen received treatment at four different hospitals -- Taoyuan General Hospital, Linkou Chang Gung Memorial Hospital, Taipei Veterans General Hospital, and Taichung Prison's Pei-de Hospital. Such hospital visits and treatments did not include Chen's numerous in-prison doctor visits.[12]

11 Stacy Hsu, Renewed Call to Pardon Chen Shui-bian Rejected, Taipei Times, April 9, 2016.
12 Report on the Human Rights in Prison of Former President Chen Shui-bian, Ministry of Justice Agency of Corrections, November 16, 2012.

Chapter 1
Fall from Grace

According to an October 2012 special report prepared by the Ministry of Justice for delivery before the judicial committee of the Legislative Yuan, the former president had since his admission to Taipei Prison repeatedly complained of acute headaches, chest tightness, chest pains, fatigue, irregular bowel movement and shortness of breath.[13] Whenever it learned of Chen's complaints, Taipei Prison would quickly arrange for him to be examined and treated in prison by physicians invited from the nearby Taoyuan General Hospital or by prison-retained doctors. After such treatments, Chen's condition stabilized.

The same report said that in late February 2012, Chen, for the first time, filed an application with prison authorities for out-of-prison medical treatment. Following initial in-prison examinations, Chen was soon escorted to Taoyuan General Hospital, one of the hospitals contracted to provide medical services, for further medical examination.

Chen underwent the following tests: prostate gland sonography, liver sonography, echocardiography, electrocardiogram, colonoscopy, gastroscopy, cardiac nuclear medicine test, and blood and urine tests. Preliminary results of these examinations found Chen showing cardiovascular stenosis and a lump in his urinary system; no other symptoms were noted.

A cardiac catheterization examination performed on him, however, verified that Chen's left cardiovascular stenosis was a congenital

---

13 Special Report on Medical Treatment of Former President Chen Shui-bian, Ministry of Justice, October 4, 2012.

condition. Thus, balloon angioplasty or installation of a vascular stent was not essential since his condition could be treated through medication. Still, he continued to complain of shortness of breath, leading his attending physician to recommend hospital confinement for observation. But a new round of examinations at the same hospital, including a bronchoscopy and a cerebral CT scan, found everything normal.

However, according to the Justice Ministry report, a urology examination in April of that same year showed a new development: a suspected lump mass. To find out more about the condition, physicians came to the prison to explain to Chen that a biopsy was necessary, but he had some misgivings about the diagnosis of Taoyuan General Hospital and was unwilling to accept the proposal.

To dispel Chen's doubts, Taipei Prison called Chang Gung Memorial Hospital--another hospital contracted to provide medical services to prisoners -- to arrange diagnostic procedures and treatment for him. Upon conclusion of a new series of examinations at Chang Gung, the hospital's deputy administrator and 14 physicians in charge of the various medical tests for him personally read the results to Chen, his son Chen Chih-Chung, and his friends Ko Wen-je and Kuo Chang-feng. Both of these friends are physicians.

In a series of physical examinations conducted at the same Taoyuan General Hospital in September of that year, however, Chen was found to show some explicit health problems. He seemed to be suffering from bladder dysfunction while displaying speech problems and complaining of headaches and related discomfort. More seriously, a lesion measuring 0.4 cm was noted on the right lobe of his brain that was suspected to be an old cerebral ischemia condition.

Given these findings, Taoyuan General Hospital concluded that Chen Shui-bian needed to undergo further neurological and psychiatric examinations. However, the hospital did not have the equipment needed to perform those examinations. Taoyuan General Hospital recommended to Taipei Prison in September 2012 that Chen be transferred to a well-equipped medical center for further tests.

After careful study and consultations with medical experts, Taipei Prison decided to transfer the former president to Taipei Veterans General Hospital (TVGH) for further examination and treatment. According to the same special report of the Justice Ministry, the choice of the TVGH was based on the following considerations: the TVGH has a complete range of the required medical equipment and greater professional expertise. The hospital also specializes in the treatment of neurological disorders, such as stroke, Parkinson's disease, migraine, Alzheimer's disease, and hereditary degenerative disorders.

Taipei Prison in the report also cited the lack of hospital space as an important factor in deciding to transfer Chen to the TVGH. A sizable police force was needed to ensure the security of the ex-president during his escorted hospital treatment and confinement. This meant that a hospital selected to treat Chen needed sufficient space. The TVGH met that criterion, too.

According to a news release issued by the TVGH, Chen Shui-bian became feverish after his admission to the hospital and was diagnosed with a urinary tract infection.[14] Medication was prescribed to treat that illness, and soon after, he was transferred to a special ward of the TVGH for treatment of "severe depression." To provide the best possible treatment for Chen openly and transparently, the TVGH invited 10 outside psychiatry specialists, as well as its professional personnel, to form a joint team to examine Chen's condition and devise a treatment plan for him.

TVGH Releases Details of Chen's Medical Condition

Chen was hospitalized at the TVGH for seven months until April 2013, when he was released and transferred to Taichung Prison's Pei-de Hospital. Months before the transfer, the TVGH had drafted a report on the discharge of the former president with a detailed description of his medical situation. The report was delivered to the Ministry of Justice's Agency of Corrections, which is responsible for prison matters, on December 19, 2012.[15] The findings of the report were summarized by the Ministry of Justice as follows:[16]

"...Psychiatry Diagnosis: Severe depression and severe sleep apnea. After treatment, his symptoms are slowly improving.

---

14 News Release on the Status of Mr. Chen Shui-bian's Health, Taipei Veterans General Hospital, October 2, 2012.

15 An Update on the Status of Mr. Chen Shui-bian's Health, the Agency of Corrections, Ministry of Justice, December 25, 2012.

16 News Release: Transfer of Mr. Chen Shui-bian from the TVGH to Taichung Prison's Pei-de Hospital, the Ministry of Justice, April 19, 2013.

Chapter 1
Fall from Grace

"...Neurology Diagnosis: Stuttering speech disorder, non-typical Parkinson's disease, and mild brain atrophy. After treatment, his stuttering speech disorder has not worsened, and the noticeable tremor of his (right) hand appears to have stabilized and improved, and ought to be tracked over the long term.

"...Other major physiological symptoms. Difficulty urinating: His urinary tract infection has been cured, and his enlarged prostate is being treated with drugs. Bleeding hemorrhoids: Surgery has been performed and he has made an excellent recovery. Nasal septal deviation and nasal passage blockage: Surgery has been performed and the nasal passage blockage has been completely alleviated. His sleep apnea symptoms have also improved."

The TVGH discharge report further pointed out that while "preliminary improvement of Chen's conditions has been achieved, he continues to manifest residual symptoms of severe depression, poor sleep quality, and general fatigue." The TVGH recommended "continued administration of medicine, occupational rehabilitation therapy, and an appropriate settlement" for the former president after his release from the Taipei Veterans General Hospital.

The report went on to say, "Since depression is an illness that relapse could easily occur due to uncongenial emotional and social factors and that he is still harboring the idea of death, it would not be suitable to immediately send Chen back to Taipei Prison following his TVGH release. This would be so even though prison authorities had enlarged his prison cell space and prison treatment."

The TVGH also said that, after Chen's release, an improvement of his surroundings, support from family members, and the selection of an appropriate location for convalescence were extremely important in improving Chen's health and reducing the risk of recurrence. Therefore, the TVGH recommended three options: home convalescence, a general hospital with a psychiatric ward, or a psychiatric hospital.

However, this was a big challenge for the Justice Ministry as it had to strike a balance between respecting medical expert recommendations and observing the law. [17] Due to this balancing consideration, the ministry ruled out the possibility of granting Chen either "home convalescence" or "medical parole."

Under the Prison Act, a ministry official explained, "The executing of a sentence or detention shall take place within a prison except where the law provides otherwise." This meant that there was no legal basis for "using an inmate's private residence as the locale to serve his or her prison sentence," he added.

More fundamentally, the official pointed out, "Chen's symptoms do not warrant medical treatment on bond or medical parole." If the former president were to be granted medical parole, it would violate the principle of "penal equality." The official noted that as of March 2013, there were 445 inmates in Taiwan's prison system suffering from depression.

"Chen's illness could be treated at a hospital facility under guarded escort," the ministry official said. He invoked an alternative suggestion contained in the TVGH discharge report that

---

17 News Release: Home Convalescence Does Not Accord with the Law, the Ministry of Justice, April 19, 2013.

Chapter 1
Fall from Grace

"hospitalization in a psychiatric ward would also be appropriate for Chen."

After weighing up Chen's continued medical treatment and care needs as well as existing legal constraints, the Justice Ministry finally decided to transfer Chen, upon his release from the Taipei Veterans General Hospital to the Medical Treatment Special Quarter of Taichung Prison's Pei-de Hospital in central Taiwan. According to the ministry, the Pei-de Hospital was the most appropriate facility for Mr. Chen to continue receiving medical treatment and care while serving his sentence.

The ministry listed the following reasons for its decision: First, Pei-de Hospital, backed by the prestigious China Medical University Hospital, operates 20 different specialized clinics, including psychiatry, neurology, otolaryngology, orthopedics, surgery, and urology, among other things. In a word, that facility was capable of providing the in-prison medical services that Chen needed. The ministry pointed out that the Pei-de Hospital was originally established as an institution for psychiatric treatment; it is not just part of a prison.

Moreover, Pei-de Hospital has physicians and nurses on duty 24 hours a day. It also hired special registered nurses' aides to provide the former president with home-like care around the clock. To create a warm and homey atmosphere and reduce the stress of imprisonment, the ministry said, "Pei-de Hospital had rebuilt its medical treatment quarter into a garden-like care facility before Chen was moved in. The (treatment) quarter features a spacious setting with green spaces, flower gardens, and an arched gate. It is enclosed by low walls, secluded and quiet. Chen's prison cell measuring 9.2 pings (30.4 square meters) was outfitted with a single-person bed, desk, chair, bookcase, and a storage cabinet, as well as a private bathroom."

In line with the TVGH special medical team's recommendation to place Chen in an environment where he would have family support and accompaniment so his recovery would be speedier, Taichung Prison adopted a flexible policy regarding Chen's requests to receive friends and relatives. And the frequency of visits by his family members was not limited.

"This kind of prison treatment is unavailable to other convicts and is unprecedented in our nation's prison history," said the Ministry of Justice in the news release. During a press conference, President Ma Ying-jeou went out of his way to comment on his predecessor's new confinement environment. Ma said, "Chen's confinement in Taichung Prison's Pei-de Hospital, as it looks now, could hardly be taken as prison life."[18]

But less than one and a half months into his new environment of "garden-style" prison, Chen made news again, this time by attempting to commit suicide in his bathroom on June 3, 2013. "But he was treated quickly and did not appear to have any significant condition," the Justice Ministry said in a statement.

After an investigation, the ministry concluded that Chen tried to kill himself because he was distraught after authorities, instead of allowing him to return home for convalescence, as recommended by

---

18 Shann Hou-chih, Chen's New Confinement Environment Can No Longer Be Called Prison Life, United Daily News, April 20, 2013.

Chapter 1
Fall from Grace

his medical team, transferred him to Taichung Prison from Taipei Veterans General Hospital.[19]

According to Vice Minister of Justice Chen Ming-tang, the former president also mentioned to prison workers his distress over difficulties in rejoining the DPP, the party that he helped found. As noted earlier, Chen Shui-bian resigned from the DPP in 2008 to take responsibility for the party's defeat in both the legislative and presidential elections that year. Chen was also said to have complained of "judicial injustice." He told prison personnel that he was disappointed that a new revision of the Accounting Act made to deregulate the use of the "special public funds" failed to include the item of "state affairs funds." One of the many charges against Chen involved the misuse of such funds. "It is unfair (to) me to have been prosecuted for using 'state affairs funds' to support diplomatic programs, while others now can even spend 'special public funds' on buying drinks in hostess bars, free from judicial prosecution."

Chen's complaints prompted an immediate response from the Ministry of Justice. "Former President Chen is serving a 20-year sentence for taking bribes and money laundering in four separate cases. None of these cases have anything to do with the one of him being charged with abusing 'secret state affairs funds,' which is still under deliberation at the Taiwan High Court, following appeals."

Moreover, the "secret state affairs funds" and "special public funds" are not the same, said Vice Minister Chen Ming-tang. "So the

---

19 Rich Chang, Chris Wang, Chen Shui-bian Stable After Suicide Attempt, Taipei Times, June 4, 2013.

recent law revision to decriminalize 'special public funds' was irrelevant to his case, posing no question of doing him an injustice, as he alleged." Special public funds refer to allowances of certain officials while the state affairs funds apply to funds used by the office of the president, including for confidential diplomatic purposes.

Chen's attempted suicide polarized public opinion. Chang Chung-hsiung, who was twice appointed premier by the former president, said the ex-president's attempt to hang himself from a shower fixture "only proved his medical team to be right in recommending that he be granted medical parole."[20]

But his critics did not see it that way. Antonio Chiang, a political columnist who served as a national security official under the Chen administration, for example, argued that the public was tired of the former president's complaints. "Now Chen's news is in the newspapers every day -- some (people) are sympathetic, but more are simply annoyed, as they feel a disgraced politician and convicted criminal ought not to make such nonstop political moves," he told the New York Times. "They feel that Chen is like a political ghost who refuses to die."[21]

20 Chen Jie-liang, Hung Rong-chih, Mrs. Chen Shui-bian Comments on Her Husband's Suicide Attempt, the China Times, June 5, 2013.
21 Ex-President of Taiwan Attempts Suicide in Prison, The New York Times, June 3, 2013.

Chapter 1
Fall from Grace

Political Trends Take a Turn in Chen Shui-bian's Favor

In November 2014, the DPP -- the party that Chen once headed -- won big in Taiwan's mayoral and county chief elections, handing a major setback to the governing KMT. The DPP's big win at the local government level lent momentum to the party's long-running campaign to win Chen's release.

In January 2015, a little more than one month after the local elections, the former president was released on medical parole. The Ministry of Justice moved quickly to deny public speculation that the ruling KMT's electoral defeats played a role in the government's decision to grant Chen medical parole. Chen had served over six years of his 20-year sentence at the time of his release.

Vice Minister of Justice Chen Ming-tang (no relation to the former president) said at a press conference that "the decision to release Chen was based on the recommendation of a panel of medical experts that the former president's failing health could be better treated at home." Taiwan law allows for medical parole if suitable treatment cannot be received in prison, he added.

The Ministry of Justice's Agency of Corrections stated at the press conference about Chen's release. [22] "Former president Chen's neurodegenerative condition has deteriorated since mid-2014, and this deterioration is simultaneously present in several different brain

---

22 Chen Shui-bian Granted Medical Parole, News Release, Agency of Corrections, Ministry of Justice, January 5, 2015.

areas….," it said. "This proves that the effectiveness of his current treatment is limited, and… that this is most likely because there is no way to alleviate the mental pressure on former president Chen in the [prison] environment."

Vice Minister Chen also pointed out in the statement that the former president's parole "will be contingent on his medical condition and will be subject to monthly health check-ups" by prison authorities.

The ailing former president, then nearly 64 years old, was seated in a wheelchair pushed by medical personnel as well as his son, Chen Chih-chung. Sporting a baseball cap with English letters reading "Free A-bian, Free Taiwan" – referring to his nickname - he got up and walked with the aid of a cane to a black sedan waiting outside Taichung Prison. He waved to dozens of cheering supporters who shouted: "A-bian is not guilty" and "Go, A-bian." He was then driven to a family home in southern Taiwan.

Judging from his outward appearance, he seemed to have lost much of the energy of old. Perhaps this reflected his years in prison. Perhaps it reflected the deflated perception of the former head of state in the eyes of the public; whenever Chen was mentioned in the international media, he was routinely referred to as Taiwan's "disgraced former president." The descriptions of him as a shining symbol of Taiwan's democracy and acknowledgments of his past role in the island's transformation from authoritarian rule were few and far between.

Living outside the prison on medical parole, Chen Shui-bian continued to be a center of controversy. He frequently violated rules set by Taichung Prison governing his parole, and his behavior aroused

Chapter 1
Fall from Grace

much heated discussion. Under what was called the "four noes" rule, the ex-leader was banned from appearing on stage, making public speeches, accepting media interviews, and discussing politics. Yet in the years following his release on medical parole, he violated those regulations repeatedly. Some noted examples:

In May 2018, Chen Shui-bian attended a politically sensitive fundraising dinner for the pro-Taiwan independence Ketagalan Foundation, ironically with permission from the Taichung Prison. A senior prison officer later apologetically explained: "Since being released on medical parole, Chen has consistently asked the Taichung Prison for permission to attend various public political events."[23]

In September 2018, Chen Shui-bian granted a high-profile interview to the Japanese newspaper Sankei Shimbun. He called on President Tsai Ing-wen to promote the use of a referendum on independence to counter pressure from Beijing and let the world know that Taiwanese people were unwilling to be a part of China.

In January 2021, Chen launched a radio show in his home city of Kaohsiung. The program, with Chen as host, was aired on Sunday mornings on a radio station called Smile Taiwan. He told reporters that the program would not focus on politics. When the press questioned whether Taichung Prison approved his radio show, Chen replied he had "communicated with the prison authorities."[24]

More recently, in the November 2022 local government elections, the former president actively campaigned for his son Chen Chih-chung,

23 Attending a fundraising dinner, Taiwan's Central News Agency, May 4, 2018.
24. Chen Shui-bian Hosts Radio Show, Taipei Times, January 4, 2021.

who was running for a seat on the Kaohsiung City Council. Chen Shui-bian's activities were conducted in open defiance of government restrictions against him from attending political events.[25]

The Taichung Prison authorities had in the past repeatedly stressed that if there was convincing evidence of Chen Shui-bian breaching major regulations, his parole would be revoked. Many in the public believed the prison was turning a blind eye to Chen's repeated parole violations, due to political considerations. As an ex-president and former leader of the ruling DPP, many senior government officials would find it hard not to demonstrate some level of support.

According to Taichung Prison, Chen's parole was a temporary release granted on medical grounds. Chen needed to return to prison to resume serving his time once his health stabilized. However, he could apply for an extension of his parole if his condition warranted it. However, he needed to accompany his application with an authoritative medical evaluation to prove his case. Each extension remained valid for only three months.

Over the years following his release, prison authorities, with no exception, routinely approved Chen Shui-bian's request to have his medical parole extended. The reason cited was almost always the same: "The former president's condition is complicated and difficult to control, which is why it cannot be treated while he is in prison."

But the countless parole extensions were taken by Chen Shui-bian's political opponents and others as amounting to a de facto pardon

---

25 Campaigning for His Son, The United Daily News, November 23, 2002.

Chapter 1
Fall from Grace

for his crimes. At that point, Chen had served less than one-third of his 20-year sentence.

A detailed account of the multiple corruption charges, prosecutorial probes, the ensuing indictments, and the final verdicts handed down by courts, will be given in the following segment, Chapter 2.

Chapter 2

An Examination of Chen Shui-bian's Multiple Graft Cases

Criminal Probes after Losing Presidential Immunity

Chen Shui-bian was placed under investigation for corruption immediately after the transfer of presidential powers to his successor Ma Ying-jeou on May 20, 2008. Once the power transfer was completed, Chen no longer had immunity from prosecution.

Chen was served an investigation notice issued by the Special Investigation Division (SID) of the Supreme Prosecutor's Office while he was riding home in a government limousine after leaving the presidential building, where he had spent the past eight years as head of state.

In the notice, a lead prosecutor from the SID informed the former president that he was barred from leaving the country, pending the completion of probes into a range of corruption allegations against him.

The SID at the time was investigating four alleged bribery and corruption cases implicating Chen Shui-bian and his wife Wu Shu-chen. These were allegations of embezzlement of state affairs funds, taking bribes in a land procurement deal as well as bribes related to the Nangang Exhibition Center construction project, and money laundering.

In the fund embezzlement case, Chen and his wife were suspected of using fraudulent invoices to claim reimbursements from the president's "special state affairs funds." The ex-first couple was accused of illegally claiming NT$14.8 million (about US$448,000) from the special fund with false receipts during the period from July 2002 to March 2006.

Mrs. Chen, who allegedly collected invoices from friends and relatives, had already been indicted in November 2006 by what was then known as the Public Prosecutor's Office of the Taiwan High Court on charges of embezzling public funds and forging documents.

In the 2006 indictment of his wife, Chen Shui-bian was listed as a suspect. "But the president had the protection of the constitution against criminal charges. He could be prosecuted only after leaving office," said Chang Wen-cheng, a spokesman for the prosecutor's office.[26]

Since her indictment, Mrs. Chen had been summoned by the Taipei District Court 16 times to attend hearings, but she repeatedly refused to appear, citing poor health. As a result, the trial of Mrs. Chen in the false invoices case ground to a halt.

But the investigation had been reactivated by the Supreme Prosecutor's Office, which had taken over the embezzlement case from its predecessor agency, the Public Prosecutor's Office. The SID sought to interview the former president to determine his role in the case. (The SID was a relatively new prosecutorial organization that was created exclusively to combat corruption among top-level government officials.)

---

26 Taiwan's Chen in Corruption Case, BBC News, November 3, 2006.

Chapter 2
An Examination of Chen Shui-bian's Multiple Graft Cases

In the months following the revival of the embezzlement case, the SID obtained crucial new evidence against Chen and his wife. This was supplied by the former first family's bookkeeper, Chen Cheng-hui, who turned over a personal mobile hard disk as part of a plea-bargaining arrangement with prosecutors. On the disk, she kept a detailed record of all reimbursements applied for from the president's special state affairs fund as well as other related information.[27]

In addition to the allegation of embezzling funds from the president's special state affairs fund, Chen and his wife were also investigated by the SID for allegedly taking a NT$300 million (US$10 million) bribe in an industrial land procurement deal in Longtan and another NT$90 million (US$300,000) in connection with the construction of the Nangang Exhibition Center in Taipei.

Investigation Takes a Dramatic Turn

The SID investigation into the former first family's corruption scandals soon took a dramatic turn. On August 14, 2008 -- less than three months after Chen Shui-bian had stepped down -- the ex-president called a surprise press conference. He made a stunning confession: His wife had wired what he called his "leftover campaign funds" from his eight years of office abroad. This was done without his knowledge, he assured his listeners, without specifying how much money was

---

27 Chen Shui-bian's ex-Treasurer Pleads Guilty in Graft Trial, AFP, Taipei, February 20, 2009.

involved. The tally would not stay secret for long. It was an eye-popping US$21 million.

"My conscience has told me that I cannot continue to lie to myself or others. I have, in the past, committed deeds that are against the rule of law, and I am willing to apologize to the people," Chen said in a prepared statement. By "leftover campaign funds," Chen implied that the funds his wife had sent overseas were not obtained illegally.

The timing of the ex-president's confession came one day after his family's secret overseas bank accounts had been revealed by Next magazine, a Chinese-language news weekly known for its exclusive accounts of political and social scandals. And it came only hours after a KMT lawmaker had revealed more information on the Chen family's secret overseas assets. Legislator Hung Hsiu-chu told reporters that an official Swiss judicial document alleged that Chen Shui-bian's family members had opened four secret bank accounts in Switzerland, with combined deposits totaling US$32 million. She backed up her revelations with an excerpt from the document, which was in the possession of authorities in Taiwan.

Chen's August 14 confession, however, proved that his previous statements on the family's assets were false. In the past, there had been rumors that his family had assets hidden abroad, but he routinely brushed them aside. He maintained that all of his assets had long been placed in a trust and there was "nothing left for me to hide."

Chen's admission to having large amounts of money secretly deposited overseas provoked outrage from across the political spectrum, including the ruling DPP. Asked by a reporter about the movement of family funds offshore, Tainan Mayor Hsu Tien-tsai, a

Chapter 2
An Examination of Chen Shui-bian's Multiple Graft Cases

DPP stalwart, said: "A politician moving huge amounts of money abroad – this kind of behavior is unacceptable and unforgivable."

Chen's vice president, Annette Lu, exploded, "If I had not heard it with my ears, I would not have believed it; I am still in disbelief. Any politician who genuinely loves Taiwan would not wire contributors and taxpayers' money overseas."

Wang Chien-shien, a ranking KMT politician and head of the country's highest civil service watchdog, told reporters: "I just wanted to kick my TV when I watched Chen Shui-bian confess that he had large sums of money stashed away in foreign banks. These people always say that they love Taiwan, but in fact, they are doing shameful things like this."

Former DPP heavyweight Shih Ming-teh told a reporter that he was eating dinner while watching a TV news report about Chen's overseas accounts. He said he became so angry that he threw his chopsticks on the floor in disgust. Shih's anger was understandable. In 2006 -- about two years into Chen Shui-bian's second four-year term -- Shih Ming-teh had led a months-long, anti-corruption campaign aimed at forcing the president to step down. The movement was dubbed "One million voices against corruption, President Chen must go."

Amid widespread public anger, Chen Shui-bian and his wife resigned from the ruling DPP the following day. In a statement, Chen said: "Today I have to say sorry to all of the DPP members and supporters. I let everyone down and failed to meet your expectations. My acts have caused irreparable damage to the party. I love the DPP deeply and am proud of being a DPP member. To express my deepest regrets to all DPP members and supporters, I announce my withdrawal from the DPP immediately. My wife Wu Shu-chen is also withdrawing from the party."

Legislator Hung told reporters she had obtained a copy of an official Swiss document and that was the source of her information about the former first family's bank accounts in Switzerland. She did not give details on how she obtained the information but stated that Swiss prosecutors suspected former President Chen and his wife had used the names of their son Chen Chih-chung and daughter-in-law Huang Jui-ching to launder money in Switzerland. Such financial activities had broken Swiss laws and were being investigated by Swiss authorities, she said.[28]

According to the lawmaker, the younger Chens had moved US$21 million in total from Singapore to Switzerland in a short period in 2007 using shell companies and multiple bank account transfers.[29] The SID investigators later said the funds originated in Taiwan and were from bribes taken by the older Chens from private companies while in office.

---

28 Chen Chih-chung and Huang Jui-ching's financial activities were alleged by the Swiss Office of Attorney General to have broken Switzerland's laws against money laundering, organized crime, terrorist financing and economic crime. The allegations were made based on a report filed by the Federal Police's Money Laundering Reporting Office (MROS) of Switzerland, a member of the Ottawa-based international anti-money laundering Egmont Group.

29 The Swiss judicial document, serial number EA II.07.0186-OTE, was issued by the Office of Attorney General of Switzerland with investigation conducted by two federal prosecutors Edmond Ottinger and Luc Leimgruber.

Chapter 2
An Examination of Chen Shui-bian's Multiple Graft Cases

The Swiss document referred to by the KMT legislator was real. About two weeks earlier Taiwan had received a letter from the Office of the Attorney General of Switzerland, informing Taiwan that Chen Shui-bian's son and daughter-in-law had some US$21 million deposited in the Geneva branch of what was then Merrill Lynch Bank (Suisse) SA and an arm of the former Royal Bank of Scotland's office in Zurich.[30]

Swiss federal prosecutors also stated they suspected that those bank deposits were illegal funds laundered by the Chen family through Singapore. They requested that information on Chen and his family members, including their roles in Taiwan's ongoing corruption cases, be provided to Switzerland to facilitate that country's investigation into alleged cross-border money laundering.

The Swiss judicial document, together with Chen's own August 14 confession, gave a major boost to the SID's investigation of the corruption and money laundering cases involving the former president and members of his family. Shortly after receiving the judicial assistance request from Switzerland, the SID decided to shift its emphasis from investigating the allegations of bribe-taking by the Chen family to overseas money laundering activities. With the shift of emphasis, the SID first moved to ascertain the sources of the US$21 million deposited by the Chen family at the two foreign financial institutions, as revealed in the Swiss document. The SID believed this information would facilitate its probe of the alleged bribery.

---

30 Jiang Hui-tseng, Liang Hung-pin, Switzerland Requests Assistance in Probing Chen Family's Swiss Bank Accounts, China Times, August 15, 2008.

The Ministry of Justice dispatched Chief Prosecutor Ching Chi-jen of the Taipei District Office to Switzerland in August 2008.[31] She had two main objectives: One was to respond to requests from Swiss judicial authorities and deliver information about the Chen family members and the suspected corruption. The other was to acquire additional details about the US$21 million deposited with the two financial institutions in Switzerland and negotiate the return of those funds. The money had been frozen by Swiss authorities in January 2008.

Ms. Ching returned from Switzerland more than a week later but soon was on her way to Singapore to examine questionable financial transactions there that also involved the Chen family. With the help of judicial authorities in Singapore, the prosecutor found several suspect bank accounts held there by the former first lady, her brother Wu Ching-mao, and their friends.[32]

While placing greater emphasis on looking into the Chen family's questionable overseas bank accounts, prosecutors did not ease up in their quest to probe suspected corruption by the first couple and their illegal financial transactions in Taiwan.

Prosecutors questioned the former first lady at her home two days after her husband's press conference where he stated his wife had remitted funds to Switzerland during his presidency without his knowledge. During the interview, investigators focused on the role

---

31 Jimmy Chuang and Loa Iok-sin, Prosecutor Investigates Chen Family's Accounts, Taipei Times, August 16, 2008.
32 Taiwan Prosecutor Heads to Singapore in Chen Probe, AFP, August 27, 2008.

Chapter 2
An Examination of Chen Shui-bian's Multiple Graft Cases

played by the former first lady in the family's overseas financial transactions, as well as the extent of illegal payments to the Chen family during Chen Shui-bian's presidency and who made the payments.

A day after questioning Chen Shui-bian's wife, prosecutors and investigators searched the former president's offices and the couple's residence in southern Taiwan. Also searched was the home of Mrs. Chen's brother Wu Ching-mao, who allegedly assisted the Chen family in moving funds out of Taiwan and depositing them in banks in Singapore. Investigators removed numerous documents from these locations.

SID prosecutors also questioned the former first couple's son and daughter-in-law. Following these interviews and searches, the SID formally listed Chen Shui-bian and his wife, as well as their son and daughter-in-law as defendants in a money laundering case.

Raids and interviews continued in the weeks that followed, as prosecutors widened the scope of their investigation into the couple's alleged corruption. In these subsequent actions, prosecutors detained more than half a dozen former administration aides, senior bankers, and family friends on charges of either giving bribes to the Chens or helping them conceal funds and wire them into overseas bank accounts.

Two Startling Discoveries

As the probe deepened, investigators unexpectedly made two important discoveries. One was that of hidden wealth belonging to the Chen family at the Cathay United Bank in Taipei. The former first lady was found to have rented a large vault in the bank to store what she claimed were "political donations." To keep the vault confidential, all incidental paperwork was put in the name of Chen Chun-ying, the first lady's sister-in-law. Chen Chun-ying later admitted in court to having provided dummy accounts for use by the former first lady to wire money abroad.[33]

At the time of the discovery -- about two months after the SID expanded its probe into the Chen family's corruption scandals -- the amount of money stored in the bank vault stood at NT$740 million, or about US$25 million. Mrs. Chen Shui-bian confessed that the vault contained as much as NT$1.1 billion, or US$34.38 million, in cash at one point. She insisted, however, that the money was from contributions from businesspeople and other supporters.[34]

More damaging testimony was obtained from Chen Cheng-hui, the bookkeeper in the office of the former president and a key witness in the case. She told investigators during questioning that she "was often required by Mrs. Chen Shui-bian to make cash deliveries to the vault and report on the cash on hand to the first lady."

The NT$740 million remaining in the Cathay United Bank vault was later moved to a basement vault in the private residence of Yuanta Financial Group's chief executive officer Ma Wei-chien. This was done at the direction of the former first lady. Yet the funds were parked there only briefly before the lion's share -- amounting to NT$540 million

33 News Staff, Chen's Request to Take out Deposits from Vault Rejected, China Post, June 22, 2010.
34 Judge Norman K. Moon, Memorandum Opinion, U.S. District Court for the Western District of Virginia, Civil Action, No. 3: 10--cv-0037.

(US$18.2 million) – was transferred to Wegelin, a private Swiss bank, via a shell company registered in the British Virgin Islands. Prosecutors said Wegelin was the third bank in Switzerland in which the Chen family was found to have deposited large amounts of money, in addition to the Geneva branch of Merrill Lynch Bank (Suisse) and the Zurich branch of what was then the Royal Bank of Scotland.

The task of moving so much money across national borders using deceptive ownership structures and multiple bank accounts was aided by Yuanta's CEO, who could draw on his professional wealth management experience to assist the first family. (See Chapter 3: How the Chen Family Laundered Large Sums around the World to Evade Official Probes)

Another important discovery was that the head of Taiwan's Investigation Bureau, which has a role similar to that of the F.B.I. in the United States, had repeatedly covered up intelligence about the Chen family's overseas financial transactions. Yeh Sheng-mao, a trusted confidant of the former president, served as director of the Investigation Bureau for all of Chen's eight-year presidency. SID prosecutors discovered he had twice held up information from the Egmont Group, an international organization that plays a key role in global anti-money laundering efforts and leaked it to Chen Shui-bian. The Egmont Group's confidential intelligence was about the Chen family's suspicious overseas money transfers.

In December 2006, the Investigation Bureau chief had deliberately suppressed a confidential document from authorities on the Island of Jersey, also a member of the Ottawa-based Egmont Group. The document advised the Taiwan bureau, which has a section dealing with money laundering crimes, that Chen Shui-bian's wife was suspected of having used accounts belonging to her brother Wu Ching-mao, his wife Chen Chun-ying, and family friends to wire large sums of money to Singapore via Jersey.

However, no sooner had Yeh received the confidential document than he passed on the information to the president, who in turn advised his wife that the family's bank deposits in Singapore were being monitored by international anti-money laundering watchdogs.

In early 2007, Mrs. Chen called an emergency family meeting, where she directed her son and his wife to shift their US$21 million in deposits in Singapore to Switzerland, according to investigators. The relocated funds were put into accounts opened with the two Swiss arms of Merrill Lynch and the Royal Bank of Scotland. The bank accounts, however, were registered in the names of shell companies domiciled in third areas, including the Cayman Islands, with son Chen Chih-chung and daughter-in-law Huang Jui-ching being the real owners.

The secret Swiss bank deposits were again detected by the Egmont Group, as well as Swiss authorities, less than one year after they were transferred from Singapore. In January 2008, the Cayman Islands, also an Egmont group member, notified Taiwan that the first couple's son and daughter-in-law used a Cayman Islands-registered shell company to transfer large amounts of money to Switzerland.

But Yeh Sheng-mao, the Investigation Bureau director, once again blocked the information from distribution to other law enforcement officials. As in the earlier instance, Yeh held up the confidential intelligence from the Cayman Islands, disclosing it only to his boss, Chen Shui-bian, a potential target of any official probe.

Chapter 2
An Examination of Chen Shui-bian's Multiple Graft Cases

The Cayman Islands had alerted Taiwan to the suspicious fund transfers by the younger Chens months ahead of the Swiss authorities. The Office of the Federal Attorney General of Switzerland did not inform Taiwan of the matter until some six months later. This was even though it had frozen bank accounts believed to be linked to the illegal transfers as early as January – around the same time as the Cayman Islands anti-money laundering agency notified Taiwan of its intelligence.

Years later, the director of Taiwan's Investigation Bureau paid a price for his repeated suppression of the explosive information on the first family's money laundering activities. In 2012, he was sentenced to one year and four months in jail after he was found guilty of concealing the intelligence from the Cayman Islands on the Chen family's money laundering activities.

In the case related to the intelligence from Jersey, Yeh initially was cleared by the Taipei District Court of the alleged crime. But after the case was taken to the Taiwan High Court, the acquittal was overturned and Yeh was sentenced to one year in prison, later commuted to six months and served concurrently with Yeh's other conviction. Yeh gave up his right to appeal to the Supreme Court and the high court ruling was final.

Despite the reputational damage to the Investigation Bureau and the delays in the official probes linked to the first family, the cover-up ultimately made an important contribution to determining the role of Chen Shui-bian in the family's illegal activities. Yeh's leaks of confidential intelligence about the family's offshore financial transactions proved to be solid evidence for the SID in refuting Chen's claims of innocence, upending his defense that he "knew nothing about his family's overseas bank deposits."

A Historic Moment: Chen Shui-bian Arrested on Bribery Charges

The SID's sweeping investigations culminated in the early hours of November 12, 2008, with the arrest of former President Chen Shui-bian on multiple corruption charges, including taking bribes and embezzling special state affairs funds.

The previous morning, Chen had been summoned to appear before the SID for a fifth round of questioning amid much media speculation that it would be the final interview and that an arrest would follow. Chen left his office in the early morning and walked to the SID, just a few hundred yards away. A crowd of DPP lawmakers, supporters, and journalists trailed behind him. Chen stopped at the main entrance of the SID offices for a brief press conference where he accused President Ma Ying-jeou and his government of pursuing "political persecution" and "judicial persecution." Alerting his supporters to the possibility of his imminent arrest, the former president said with a dramatic flourish, "I'm going to Taiwan's Bastille. They can lock up my body, but not my heart."

Inside the SID office, a team of eight prosecutors awaited the ex-president's arrival. At this point, they still needed answers to crucial questions before deciding whether to indict Chen and his wife. The eight prosecutors took turns asking him questions about a wide range of issues. After nearly seven hours of interrogation, the prosecutors pressed ahead with what would prove to be a political earthquake: the former president was arrested on bribery charges.

Chen was handcuffed and led away by court police to the nearby Taipei District Court for a detention hearing. Outside the SID gates, he paused briefly before cameras, raising his cuffed hands into the air and shouting defiantly: "Fight against judicial injustice, long live Taiwan independence!"

But the political drama that day was hardly over; moments after he shouted his slogans, Chen claimed that he had been roughed up by police officers. That caused a further delay as Chen was taken to a hospital next door for a medical examination. The medical team found no sign of injuries from what Chen described as rough handling by the police.

By the time Chen was escorted to the Taipei District Court for his detention hearing, it was already in the early hours of November 12. After a review of the SID's detention request, a panel of three judges of the district court agreed without dissent to hold Chen in custody. The detention capped a six-month investigation into the former president and his family over a string of corruption allegations. In the process, more than half a dozen other suspects had been placed in custody by the SID. More would join them later.

Mixed Public Reaction to Chen's Detention

It was hardly surprising that the public reaction to the detention of the controversial ex-leader was deeply divided. Senior members of Chen Shui-bian's Democratic Progressive Party condemned his arrest and detention, denouncing it as "politically motivated." Many DPP members and supporters, already dismayed by the devastating electoral defeats, saw Chen's detention as an attempt by the Ma Ying-jeou government to "thoroughly crush the opposition" under the guise of upholding democracy and justice.

The angry accusation, while understandable, was hardly true. It was understandable because Chen's arrest came shortly after the DPP suffered two devastating electoral defeats -- first in the legislative elections in January 2008 and then in the presidential race in March. The successive setback at the polls forced the DPP to yield both legislative and presidential power to the KMT. Now, less than a year after the DPP was driven into the political wilderness, its former party chairman Chen Shui-bian had been arrested and detained on corruption charges.

DPP chairwoman Tsai Ing-wen, speaking at a press conference, condemned the detention of the former president as "shoddily administered" and an "abuse of power." "The methods used in investigating Chen's case had made many people feel sad, angry, and humiliated," Ms. Tsai said. She called on judicial authorities to abide by the law and respect Chen's human rights.

But some critics of the former president reacted with glee, clapping their hands and shouting: "Long live the Taiwanese judiciary!" In the countryside, some people even set off firecrackers to show their delight over Chen's detention.

Many independent-minded people, though, saw this in a very different light; they viewed the Chen case from the perspective of Taiwan's judicial development. They were impressed by the fact that the judiciary dared to probe an ex-leader who, although tainted by corruption scandals, still enjoyed a great deal of support at the grass-roots level. This was viewed by them as a further sign of strengthened judicial independence in Taiwan.

As to the DPP chairwoman's charge that Chen Shui-bian's detention and arrest was "shoddily administered" and an "abuse of power," were these accusations well-founded? A review of the pre-detention questioning provides a somewhat different picture.

During the nearly seven hours of questioning immediately preceding his arrest, the president was quizzed on a range of issues, including the eventual formal charges: embezzling state affairs funds, taking bribes in connection with a land procurement deal and a construction project, as well as forgery and offshore laundering of illegally obtained funds.

Throughout the interrogation, Chen consistently denied any wrongdoing. But according to the description given by a SID spokesman at another news briefing, prosecutors refuted Chen's denials one by one and backed up their charges with witness testimonies and documentary evidence. These included an information-rich personal digital assistant device (PDA) used by Chen's office bookkeeper as well as false receipts, money transfer records, copies of remittance invoices, and contracts that revealed irregularities in the Longtan land procurement deal and the Nangang Exhibition Center construction project.

At the end of their interrogation, the eight prosecutors discussed the charges against the former president, assessing the allegations and the laws that would be applied in pursuing the government's case. At the heart of the matter was their judgment as to whether it was necessary or justifiable for the prosecution to take a former president into custody. Ultimately, they concluded that Chen Shui-bian had indeed broken the country's laws and there was sufficient evidence for the following charges: embezzlement, fraud, taking bribes, forging documents, and illegally remitting funds abroad. Each of these violations carried a minimum penalty of five years of imprisonment.

Detention and Possible Flight Risk

This meant that the crimes Chen had allegedly committed were grave ones, prompting the prosecution to detain him as a possible flight risk. The discussion raised a further reason for having to place Chen in custody: Several additional cases filed against Chen and his family members, including a complex money laundering charge, were still under investigation. Investigators feared that Chen – if released on bail -- could tamper with evidence and collude with other accomplices. The eight prosecutors unanimously decided to seek court permission to keep Chen in detention.

Under Taiwan law, prosecutors may apply to a court for approval of pretrial detention of an unindicted suspect for a maximum of two months, with one possible two-month extension. Prosecutors may request pretrial detention in cases in which the potential sentence is five years or more and when there is a reasonable concern the suspect could flee, collude with other suspects or witnesses, or tamper with or destroy material evidence.

Chapter 2
An Examination of Chen Shui-bian's Multiple Graft Cases

In Chen's case, he was first ordered detained at a suburban Taipei Detention Center on November 12, 2008, though a month later, following his indictment, a Taipei District Court judge ordered his release without bail. But he was placed in custody once more after a new panel of three judges of the same Taipei District Court accepted an SID appeal. He was confined in the detention center for more than two years as his two-month detention period was repeatedly extended at the request of the SID, despite numerous appeals to higher courts by Chen and his lawyers.

In total, he was held in custody for 734 days -- or just over two years -- before he was transferred to Taipei Prison in December 2010. The transfer followed his conviction and sentencing by the Supreme Court to 17 and a half years in jail for taking kickbacks and bribes.

Throughout the litigation process -- from the day Chen was taken into custody to the time he was transferred to Taipei Prison to begin serving his lengthy sentence -- the SID had insisted at detention hearings that the defendant be kept in custody. The arguments it used in both the district and appeals courts were essentially the same – besides possible flight risk, there was the potential for witness tampering and collusion. These arguments were convincing as far as the presiding judges were concerned. The judges used those same arguments in their own opinions as to why Chen had to be kept in detention.

A striking example of this is given below. In the summer of 2010, Chen twice appealed to the Supreme Court after the Taiwan High Court had repeatedly ruled to extend his detention period.[35] The Supreme Court responded positively to Chen's first appeal, as it urged the Taiwan High Court to review its ruling on extending his detention by holding a second hearing to see if the reasons it had cited were appropriate.

To comply with the Supreme Court's request, the Taiwan High Court held a second detention hearing, but in the end, it again ruled that Chen should be remanded in custody. Yet a defiant Chen still found the high court's new detention ruling unacceptable and he appealed to the Supreme Court once again.[36] This time, however, the highest court rejected Chen's appeal, saying that the reasons given by the Taiwan High Court for keeping him in custody were sufficient.

The reasons given by the high court were virtually the same as the ones raised by the SID from the outset, as it sought Taipei District Court permission to detain Chen. Below are the major arguments of the SID, which were upheld by presiding judges of courts at all levels:

First, the former president was implicated in several cases. While Chen was indicted in some of them, he still faced investigations in others. Under such circumstances, if Chen was granted bail, this could pose a risk of his tampering with evidence or colluding with other alleged accomplices.

Second, the charges filed against Chen mostly were "serious crimes." By law, people charged with committing grave crimes must

---

35 Ku Liang-chieh and Yang Shu-mei, Chen's Detention Extended by Two More Months on Flight Concerns, China Times, June 19, 2010.
36 Lin Ho-ming, Chen Protests Detention Extension, Court-Appointed Lawyer to Appeal, the United Daily News, July 15, 2009.

be placed in detention to prevent them from fleeing. As Chen had already been sentenced by the Taiwan High Court in June 2010 to a 20-year jail term for embezzling state affairs funds, he was seen as a flight risk.

Third, with the advantage of being a former president, Chen – if released on bail -- had more overseas connections and private channels through which to escape from the country than ordinary defendants.

And fourth, the Chen family was found to have more than US$21 million in bribe money deposited in two banks in Switzerland. Yet as of June 2010, only about US$11 million was returned to Taiwan at the request of the SID.[37] The remaining deposits left in the two accounts in Switzerland, plus other questionable funds allegedly secreted in other Swiss banks, would be sufficient to provide a comfortable life overseas for Chen and his family. In short, the ample funds hidden abroad by the Chen family provided another potential incentive for the former president to flee the country.

Anger Over Chen's Unending Detention

But Chen's lengthy detention became a focus of constant criticism by his supporters ranging from human rights activists to legal experts and political commentators at home and abroad.

From the start, Chen Shui-bian's lawyers attacked the custody of the ex-president as a serious infringement of his legal and human

---

37 Ku Liang-chieh and Yang Shu-mei, Chen's Detention Extended by Two More Months on Flight Concerns, China Times, June 19, 2010.

rights, undermining his constitutionally protected right to a fair trial. They continued to protest against Chen's detention and argued for his release.

At a court hearing in July 2009, Chen's court-appointed public defender Tseng The-rong maintained that "it was no longer necessary to keep the former president behind bars when a prosecutorial investigation into cases allegedly involving him had already been concluded."[38]

In November of the same year, after the Supreme Court rejected an appeal of a high court ruling once again extending his detention, Chen's lawyer Shi Yi-ling stated with evident frustration: "We will soon call for the Council of Grand Justices to rule on the constitutionality of a clause in the Code of Criminal Procedure that does not limit the number of times courts can extend detention periods for defendants of serious crimes."[39]

Chen Shui-bian continued to insist that the handling of his case, particularly his prolonged detention, was purely "judicial prosecution" and a "political vendetta." In Chen's view, the government of his successor, President Ma Ying-jeou, was trying to punish him for his efforts in pursuit of Taiwan's independence while he was in office. (Note: Ma Ying-jeou and the KMT are traditionally opposed to Taiwan pursuing independence and favor improving relations with the Chinese mainland).

---

38 Lin Ho-ming, Chen Protests Detention Extension, Court-appointed Lawyer to Appeal, the United Daily News, July 15, 2009.
39 Shelly Huang, Supreme Court Rejects Chen Appeal against Detention, Taipei Times, November 6, 2009.

Chapter 2
An Examination of Chen Shui-bian's Multiple Graft Cases

Momentum had been building for setting limits on detention since Chen's lawyer Shih Yi-ling's called for a review of the constitutionality of the criminal code applying to defendants in cases of serious crimes. The following are from two reports by the French news agency Agence France-Presse:

"Taiwan's top judicial body said in February 2010 that it was planning to limit the time a defendant can be kept in custody amid concerns over ex-president Chen Shui-bian's lengthy detention," AFP reported. "According to Lin Jiun-yi, an official at the Judicial Yuan, the authorities intended to impose a maximum 35-month detention period for those charged with felonies such as murder and corruption. Currently, Taiwan courts can lock up indefinitely those accused of serious crimes that carry a minimum 10-year jail term. Those suspected of lighter crimes can be held for 23 months." [40]

Parliament quickly followed with legislation setting limits on detention. "Taiwan's parliament on April 23, 2010, passed a bill to limit the time a defendant can be held in custody," the news agency reported. "A spokesman for the Legislative Yuan said a maximum eight-year detention period will be imposed on those charged with serious crimes such as murder and corruption after the new rule takes effect within 10 days." [41]

---

[40] Taiwan May Change Rules amid Chen Detention Controversy, AFP, February 23, 2010.

[41] Taiwan Changes Detention Rules amid Chen Controversy, AFP, April 23, 2010.

In late June of 2009 – a time when Chen Shui-bian had been detained for more than 200 days -- **Tsai Ing-wen**, chairwoman of the DPP and a future president of Taiwan co-signed a joint statement with a group of 10 academics, lawyers, and human rights activists in Taiwan denouncing the unlimited detention. The statement called for the reform of the detention system, the protection of human rights in the administration of justice, and an immediate end to the detention of the former president.

Separately, Ms. Tsai, in an open letter to "our international friends," had this to say: "I am worried that the prolonged and unjustified incarceration of President Chen during the investigation period and trial is sowing the seeds of long-term public unrest and division. We are appealing, therefore, for President Chen's human rights to be respected by the Judiciary and for his immediate release." [42]

She continued: "As friends of Taiwan and observers of developments in Taiwan, you must be aware that since former President Chen's arrest and incarceration incommunicado on November 12 last year, he has been detained for more than two hundred days. The signatories and I believe that his continued detention is unjustified and in violation of President Chen's basic rights."

In conclusion, she said: "I also urge our international friends, especially those of you who have stood with us in the past through the

---

[42] Open Letter by Tsai Ing-wen on Chen Shui-bian's Detention, Democratic Progressive Party, June 30, 2009.

Chapter 2
An Examination of Chen Shui-bian's Multiple Graft Cases

more difficult years of fighting for democracy and freedom in Taiwan, to continue to stand with us, as we demand a fair and just legal system."

Jerome A. Cohen, a respected law professor at New York University and a specialist in the legal systems of Taiwan and the Chinese mainland, also expressed his concern over Chen's detention. Professor Cohen was visiting Taiwan in mid-September of 2009, shortly after the Taipei District Court announced its verdict in the Chen case. Chen and his wife had been found guilty of embezzlement and taking bribes and were initially sentenced to life in prison.

"If (Chen) appeals, I would prefer to see him released as it would be difficult for him to prepare his case while in detention," said Cohen, who was a mentor to then-President Ma Ying-jeou when he studied at Harvard Law School.

Cohen continued, "You need to punish corruption, but you also have to protect human rights. The power of custody needs to be used carefully because it is an instrument that can have huge effects [on the defendant involved]." [43]

SID's 'First Round' of Corruption Charges Against Chen and His Family

On December 12, 2008, the SID of the Supreme Prosecutor's Office indicted Chen Shui-bian, his wife, their son and daughter-in-law as well as 10 non-family members for their offenses in one or more of

---

[43] Jimmy Chuang, Chen Should Be Released during Appeal: Ma's Mentor, Taipei Times, September 12, 2009.

four different corruption cases.[44] The indictments announced at a press conference came exactly one month after the former president was arrested and placed in custody on charges of taking bribes while in office.

The four cases as contained in the SID indictment statement were: 1) embezzling money from the presidential state affairs fund, 2) illegally remitting millions of U.S. dollars to Switzerland via Singapore, 3) taking kickbacks in a land acquisition deal involving the Longtan branch of the government-operated Hsinchu Science-Industrial Park, and 4) taking bribes on a construction project related to the Nangang Exhibition Center in Taipei.

The SID in the statement pointed out that the bribes allegedly taken by the former first couple in the above cases totaled NT$495 million, or about US$16.4 million. They included NT$105 million from the special state affairs fund, NT$300 million from the Longtan land acquisition deal, and another NT$90 million from the exhibition center construction project. The SID said the vast majority of the illegally obtained funds had been remitted abroad by the Chen family.

The former first lady was named a defendant in all four cases, while the ex-president was named in the first three. The couple's son and daughter-in-law were charged in the money laundering case.

The SID requested the "most severe punishment" for Chen Shui-bian because "he showed no remorse and obstructed the prosecutorial investigation." The term "most severe punishment" could mean life

---

44 An Indictment Statement on the Chen Family's Four Cases, Special Investigation Division of the Supreme Prosecutor's Office, December 12, 2008.

Chapter 2
An Examination of Chen Shui-bian's Multiple Graft Cases

imprisonment for the former president, SID spokesman Chen Yun-nan told a press briefing. Heavy punishments were also suggested for the former first lady as well as her son and daughter-in-law.

As for the 10 non-family defendants in the four corruption cases, the indictments called for lenient punishments for them because they either confessed their involvement, offered to negotiate plea-bargaining agreements, or played only minor roles.

Chen's lawyers responded swiftly, contending that all charges filed by the SID simply were not true and that all the defendants were innocent. "The indictments in nature were a political persecution against the officials of the former government," the lawyers said in a statement issued to the news media.

Yet despite the protests from Chen's lawyers, the high-profile indictments of December 2008 represented only what the SID described as the first charges against the Chen family. The SID would continue to pursue other possible cases, and indeed, it followed its initial indictments with more investigations into the Chen family, eventually yielding significant results.

In the following years, SID prosecutors lodged second and third rounds of new indictments against Chen, his wife, and a long list of other suspects, including top corporate bosses.

Among the new indictments were charges against the former first couple for accepting bribes from Diana Chen, a business executive who allegedly made payments in exchange for help in obtaining the chair position of Taipei 101 Financial Corporation; allegations of bribery in two separate bank merger cases in connection with the Chen government's pet project, a program billed as the "second-phase" of financial reform; the alleged misuse of confidential diplomacy funds; and the mishandling of classified government documents.

Chen's Failing Health Hinders Probes and Court Proceedings

As the SID prosecutors continued their efforts to probe other possible corruption related to the Chen family, a fresh concern arose: the ex-president's failing health could threaten their investigations if he could not attend court hearings and answer questions.

This was not a hypothetical issue. In December 2013, the Taipei District Court was forced to suspend Chen's trial for unlawful possession of confidential government documents due to health concerns.[45] The court decided at the request of his lawyer, who had filed a motion to suspend Chen's hearings, citing his poor health.

Before granting the request, the Taipei District Court had commissioned the deputy administrator of Kaohsiung Chang Gung Memorial Hospital Dr. Chen Shun-sheng to organize a medical team to assess Chen Shui-bian's physical and mental health. Upon completing its assessment, the court-commissioned medical team concluded that Chen "lacks sufficient capacity for legal action and is unable to appear in court." Based on the health assessment, the Taipei District Court agreed in December 2013 to postpone hearing Chen's case until he was able to appear in court.

---

45 Lan Kai-cheng, Taipei District Court Suspends Trial of Chen's Document-Seizing Case Over Health Concerns, United Daily News, December 21, 2013.

Chapter 2
An Examination of Chen Shui-bian's Multiple Graft Cases

To deflect criticism of its decision, the Taipei District Court added that the suspension of Chen's hearings had a "temporary status." According to a legal expert, the term "temporary status" has two meanings. First, the hearings could not be postponed indefinitely and second, the postponement order would be valid only for the case in question. This would mean the ruling would have no binding effect on Chen's other cases.

But ironically, shortly after the Taipei District Court judges made their ruling, hearings on four more cases involving President Chen were also suspended with the approval of the same district court and the court of appeals. In all of those cases, health concerns were cited as the reason.

The four additional suspended cases were as follows: 1. embezzling money from the state affairs fund and laundering payments in the Nangang Exhibition Center construction project. 2. a scandal involving Cathay Financial Holdings' acquisition of United World Chinese Commercial Bank in the "second phase" of financial reform. 3. perjury. 4. laundering money from payments made by Diana Chen. [46] These suspended cases generated heated public debate (These will be discussed in detail in the latter part of this chapter).

Court hearings on these cases were never resumed because of the severity of Chen's illnesses. [47] The ailments included severe

---

46 Lin Chi-han and Tsai Meng-yu, Court Grants Chen's Request to Suspend Hearings on His Role in Embezzlement Case, United Daily News, April 22, 2016.
47 Chen's Current State of Health, Ministry of Justice Agency of Corrections, November 16, 2012.

depression, severe sleep apnea, and a speech disorder with mild anomia. Chen's declining health, combined with his former political party's overwhelming local election victories in 2014, forced the government of President Ma Ying-jeou to release Chen Shui-bian on medical parole in January 2015.

But even if it was possible for the judicial system to resume Chen's suspended cases and he was found guilty and given new sentences, it would carry no substantive meaning in terms of imprisonment. That was so because the sentences handed down previously had already far exceeded the legally allowable maximum jail time of 20 years.

A review of the various legal battles fought by the ex-president at all levels of the judicial system shows that he had lost five cases in total, while winning only two as of December 2013.[48] This was a time when the Taipei District Court ruled Chen did not have to attend hearings in all of his other cases because of health concerns.

Chen's defense proved successful in a case where he was charged by the SID with taking bribes from Jeffery Koo Jr., a major shareholder of CTBC Financial Holdings. In July 2012, the former president was acquitted of corruption by the Supreme Court which ruled the payments which Koo made to Chen were political donations. The other case where Chen's lawyers prevailed was an acquittal on a charge of "embezzling secret diplomatic funds." The exoneration came in

---

48 An Overview of Legal Cases Involving Former President Chen Shui-bian and Their Verdicts, Attachment II, Ministry of Justice, January 17, 2013.

Chapter 2
An Examination of Chen Shui-bian's Multiple Graft Cases

November 2010 after the Supreme Court rejected the embezzlement charge filed against him by the SID.

Five Cases of Corruption

The five corruption cases that the former first couple lost in court included the scandal surrounding the Nangang Exhibition Center project. The president was not a defendant in this case which involved only the former first lady. (Note, in relating these cases, emphasis will be placed on the charges that were brought against the former first couple, what crimes they were convicted of, and what penalties were meted out. All such relevant information and data were taken from the respective final decisions. These documents were made available to the press at news conferences announcing the verdicts.)

The Five Convictions

---Case one was about a charge of taking kickbacks in a land acquisition deal in connection with the Hsinchu Science-based Industrial Park, which is owned and managed by the government. In this case, Chen and his wife were each sentenced to 11 years in jail by the Supreme Court in November 2010 for taking NT$300 million (about US$9.9 million) in kickbacks in 2004 from a private company called Dayu. The law invoked was an anti-corruption act. Under this act, abusing one's official position to extort bribes is considered a grave crime.

The kickbacks were paid in exchange for Chen's help to Dayu in selling a plot of land to the Longtan branch of the industrial park. According to the Supreme Court's decision, Chen kept his word after taking the commission. He instructed then National Science Council Chairman Wei Che-ho to allow the industrial park to procure the land in question. He advised the park's chairman, a ministerial-level official, to use a "first rent and then buy" scheme to circumvent an existing government policy against using state funds to make the purchase. The deal was brokered by Tsai Ming-che, whose close connection with Mrs. Chen Shui-bian enabled him to play the role of a middleman in the kickback scandal.

---Case two: This was about a "money for office" scandal. In this case, Chen and his wife were sentenced by the Supreme Court in 2010 to eight years in jail for taking NT$10 million (US$330,000) from business executive Diana Chen. She gave the money to the first couple in return for being appointed to a high-profile position as chair of the Taipei Financial Center Corp. The allure of that position was that it gave its holder the authority to operate and manage Taiwan's landmark building Taipei 101 -- the world's tallest structure until the opening of the Burj Khalifa in Dubai in 2010.

In court, Diana Chen consistently denied that the money she paid to the former first couple was a bribe. Instead, she claimed, it was a "political donation" meant for the president's ruling Democratic Progressive Party. But evidence presented by the prosecution suggested otherwise, according to the prosecution. The payment, made in seven checks, was delivered to Mrs. Chen Shui-bian through a close friend of hers.

The payments were made weeks after the March 2004 presidential election, in which Chen Shui-bian won a second term. Prosecutors said the money soon found its way into the Chen family's overseas secret bank accounts. Diana Chen was later charged and convicted of perjury, accompanied by a 10-month prison term, which was commuted to three years' probation.

Chen Begins Serving a Prison Sentence

Since the above two convictions and sentences were final, Chen was soon transferred from the Taipei Detention Center to a state prison in Taoyuan County to begin serving his sentence. The Taiwan High Court ruled that Chen should serve his two sentences concurrently. This meant Chen would have to serve a total of 17 years and six months in state prison as punishment for taking bribes in the land procurement deal and the office-buying case.

Mrs. Chen, who is paralyzed from the waist down, was spared from serving her two sentences of eight and 11 years in jail on health grounds. Instead, she was granted treatment similar to medical parole but was confined to her home and prohibited from traveling freely.

---A third conviction related to a charge that the Chens laundered proceeds from the bribes they took in the Longtan land procurement deal. In the underlying land procurement deal itself, Chen and his wife had already been found guilty in November 2010 of taking kickbacks. They were both given an 11-year sentence. In this derivative money laundering case, the Supreme Court in June 2012 upheld the Taiwan High Court's judgment and added another two-year sentence for moving the NT$300 million (US$9.9 million) taken from Dayu -- the private company that offered the bribe in exchange for a government purchase of its land -- to overseas bank accounts.

In its decision, the Supreme Court rebuked Chen for his claim of "knowing nothing" about his family's overseas bank accounts and financial transactions. The court drew attention to Chen's high-profile confession in August 2008. In that confession, Chen admitted that his family had remitted some US$21 million to banks in Switzerland via Singapore during his eight-year presidency "without his knowledge."

However, the new evidence that emerged from investigations proved the opposite. The Supreme Court, quoting a string of prosecutorial findings, said that the former president not only had long been aware of his family having large amounts of money concealed in Singapore and elsewhere but had discussed plans with his wife to relocate the funds. The discussion took place after he had been alerted by the Investigation Bureau chief of the Egmont Group's discovery of money sent to Singapore through Jersey. The plan devised by Chen and his wife was implemented by their son Chen Chih-chung and daughter-in-law Huang Jui-ching. The younger Chens, according to the court, transferred the family's Singapore funds to Switzerland via shell companies domiciled in one of the world's favorite tax havens, the Cayman Islands. Briefly, it worked in this way: Chen Chih-chung and Huang Jui-ching first used the names of the shell companies to open new bank accounts in Switzerland before making the fund transfers. But the paper firms were registered in their names. It was the younger Chens who owned the Swiss bank deposits and had the real authority to manage those funds.

Chapter 2
An Examination of Chen Shui-bian's Multiple Graft Cases

"Upon learning that his family's overseas financial transactions had been tracked by the Jersey intelligence center of the Egmont Group," the court verdict said, "Chen should have moved immediately to end such unlawful activities." Instead, he continued to flout the law by ordering his children to move the money from the Longtan land procurement deal to Switzerland to escape detection and prosecution. In doing so, the court said, Chen had managed to entangle "almost all of his family members involved in the money laundering scandal, resulting in them facing prosecution and court trials ultimately."

---A fourth case, in which Chen and his wife were both convicted of corruption by the Supreme Court, involved a bank merger scandal. In this case, Chen and his wife were charged by the prosecution with receiving NT$200 million (US$6.67 million) in bribes paid by Yuanta Financial Holding in exchange for the couple's help in its bid to acquire a smaller financial firm, Fuhwa Securities. The highest court, in a final decision handed down in December 2012, upheld the Taiwan High Court's conviction of the Chens for corruption. Chen was sentenced to 10 years in prison for this crime, and his wife received an eight-year sentence.

The First Lady's Consent

In court hearings on the Yuanta-Fuhwa merger scandal, Ma Wei-chien, chief executive officer of Yuanta, admitted to having made the payment. But he quickly defended himself by saying that it was impossible for him not to do so. "It is common knowledge that if government help was sought in a bank merger deal like ours, consent from Madam was needed," referring to the former first lady.[49]

Asked why NT$200 million was needed for that help, Ma's answer was that was the "going rate." According to Ms. Tu Li-ping, a Yuanta executive who acted as a go-between in the arrangement, the Yuanta CEO described the demand for payment as "nothing less than extortion." Still, Ma Wei-chien insisted that the money Yuanta paid to the Chens was a "political donation" and not a bribe. Ultimately, the Supreme Court rejected Ma Wei-chien's argument, accepting the prosecution's charge that the corrupt financial deal between Yuanta and the Chens was a typical form of "negotiated bribery." In effect, Yuanta paid a bribe to the Chens, and they, in turn, used their influence to help the firm's merger bid succeed over that of a rival firm.

Harsh as it was, the latest sentencing of Chen Shui-bian and his wife to another 10 and eight years, respectively, had only a very limited effect on the convicted in the sense of jail term as a penalty. Consider this: Before Chen received the most recent jail term of 10 years, he had been serving three sentences concurrently -- 11 years for receiving commissions in the Longtan land procurement scandal, eight years for taking bribes in the appointment of Diana Chen as chair of the Taipei 101 Financial Corporation, and two years for laundering the bribe money paid to the couple in the Longtan land purchase scandal. The above three sentences, after commutation by the Taiwan High Court, added up to a total of 18 and a half years in prison.

---

49 Ku Liang-chieh, Ma Chih-ling Says He Was Forced to Donate NT$200 Million to the Chens, China Times, October 14, 2011

Chapter 2
An Examination of Chen Shui-bian's Multiple Graft Cases

With the addition of the newest 10-year sentence, Chen's total jail time was extended by only one year and six months to meet the legally allowable maximum prison sentence of 20 years. In other words, Chen's new 10-year sentence in the Yuanta merger scandal had only a net effect of an additional one and a half years in jail.

Here, some background information is needed on the Yuanta case. This bribery charge was split from a broader corruption case stemming from a 2009 indictment filed by the SID of Chen and his wife. In that indictment, the SID accused the Chens of using a program called the "second phase of financial reform" to extort money from Yuanta and another financial firm, Cathay Financial Holdings. Both companies had made acquisition bids and turned to the government for support. The two financial firms were also accused of helping the first family illegally transfer money out of Taiwan.

Yet after the whole case was appealed to the Supreme Court by both the defense and the prosecution, the highest court split the case into three parts as they made their final rulings. In the first part, they upheld the Taiwan High Court's bribery conviction against Yuanta Financial and the Chens. But at the same time, the Supreme Court created a second part regarding Yuanta's money laundering role and a third part concerning the allegations of Cathay Financials' payments to the Chens and the storing of illegal funds. These were sent back to the Taiwan High Court for retrial.

In short, the former first couple and the Yuanta financial firm's legal troubles originating in the 2009 indictment did not come to an end with the Supreme Court's 2012 bribery conviction against them. Chen and his wife were still facing trials for laundering tens of millions of U.S. dollars, allegedly obtained as bribes from the two financial firms, Yuanta and Cathay.

Similarly, Yuanta still had to face retrial on a charge of helping the Chens launder their bribe money to Switzerland through shell companies established in Hong Kong and the British Virgin Islands. Cathay Financial Holdings also faced a retrial by the Taiwan High Court for bribing the Chens and helping them engage in unlawful financial transactions.

But the high court's trials of Yuanta on a money laundering charge and Cathay Financial on bribery and money laundering charges were suspended in 2013 at Chen's request for health reasons, as were several other cases mentioned in previous pages.

---A fifth case in which a final verdict was given by the Supreme Court in 2012 related to a bribery scandal in connection with the construction of an exhibition center next to Taipei's Nangang metro station. Unlike the previous four cases, this one involved the first lady alone. Her husband was not implicated.

The First Lady's Jail Terms

In the case of the Nangang Exhibition Center construction scandal, Mrs. Chen was sentenced to nine years in prison for taking an illegal NT$90 million (approximately US$2.73 million) payment from Kuo Chuan-ching, chairman of Leader Construction Co. In return for the money, according to court documents, the president's wife helped Kuo win a contract for construction work on the government-funded Nangang Exhibition Center.

Chapter 2
An Examination of Chen Shui-bian's Multiple Graft Cases

Mrs. Chen used her influence as first lady to instruct then Interior Minister Yu Cheng-hsien to leak to the contractor in question the names of members of a screening committee responsible for selecting the most eligible candidate for building the exhibition hall. With the names of the committee members in hand, the construction company chairman presented most of the committee members with a bribe of NT$1.5 million (about US$50,000) each. Under Taiwan law, the identities of people chosen to screen bids for public work construction projects must be kept secret.

Seven out of a total of nine committee members received a payment. They too were convicted of corruption and given jail terms. Yu Cheng-hsien, the former interior minister who supplied the names of the committee members to the contractor, was given a suspended sentence of three years. A Supreme Court spokesman said Yu was treated leniently because he revealed the names of the committee members under "tremendous pressure from a powerful first lady."

In addition to her conviction in the Nangang Exhibition Center construction scandal, the First Lady was also convicted of crimes in two other cases that did not implicate the president. One was the crime of pressuring presidential office staff to lie to investigators in an alleged embezzlement case. For that crime, she was given a nine-month prison sentence. The other crime was related to laundering the funds received in the "money-for-office" scandal. In this separate money laundering case, Mrs. Chen was sentenced to seven months in jail.

Adding them all together, Mrs. Chen was convicted of corruption in a total of seven cases -- three more than her husband. On its face, this made her jail sentence much longer than that of Chen Shui-bian.

But as noted earlier, the longer jail sentence she received for the three additional corruption charges made no difference to her at all. Like her husband, she benefited from an old criminal law that limited an individual to a maximum sentence of 20 years, in cases that did not involve a life sentence. A new and stricter law was in effect at the time of sentencing, but the Chens could not be given longer sentences because the older and more lenient law was in effect when the crimes took place.

Second, it had already been determined that Mrs. Chen should not be required to serve time in jail.

In the previous pages, the focus was on various graft cases in which Chen Shui-bian and his wife were found guilty and sentenced by the Supreme Court, as of December 2012.

What follows are the five charges in the cases where proceedings were suspended due to Chen Shui-bian's incapacity to attend hearings. Although suspended, the five are worth recounting as they all aroused heated debate, not just between the prosecution and the accused but also among the judges in courts of different levels. A review of these suspended charges will provide insights into the various legal disputes involved as well as the underlying charges themselves.

---Suspended Charge 1: Abetting False Testimony by Presidential Staff

The last development in this false testimony case -- before proceedings were suspended by the court -- was the Supreme Court's rejection of the Taiwan High Court decision to clear Chen Shui-bian of a perjury charge. In its decision of December 2012, the Supreme Court also called for a retrial by the High Court, which only four months earlier had acquitted Chen on a perjury charge, contending that Chen had not instructed his staff to give false testimony to investigators looking into allegations of embezzlement by the former first couple.

The case arose from allegations that then-President Chen and his wife had used invoices obtained from others to claim reimbursements from a "special state affairs fund." This was 2006 and the anti-corruption division of the Taiwan High Prosecutor's Office, which had not yet been replaced by the SID and was still in charge of corruption investigations, was looking into the allegations. The president had learned in advance that prosecutors were planning to interview his aides, including Presidential Office Director Lin Teh-hsun, about the case. He allegedly called Lin and several other aides into his office to instruct them to make two untruthful statements.

One was that the president "had truly used the special state affairs funds to support secret diplomatic operations, rather than siphon off them into the first family's pockets." The other was that the invoices used to claim reimbursements from the special state fund account were "provided directly to them by the president himself, not by the first lady or her friends."

These statements, however, were later found to be untrue by prosecutors investigating the embezzlement case. Consequently, Chen Shui-bian was indicted in February 2010 -- nearly two years after he left office -- for instructing his aide Lin Teh-hsun to lie to investigators.

The perjury indictment was first filed with the Taipei District Court. The district court decided in favor of the prosecution, agreeing that Chen Shui-bian had indeed coached Lin and senior presidential aide Ma Yung-chen to lie to investigators in the embezzlement case. It sentenced the former president to four months in jail.

However, the conviction at the district court level underwent a reversal after the lawyers for the defendants appealed to the Taiwan High Court. A panel of three high court judges overturned the lower court's ruling, acquitting Chen Shui-bian on the charge that he directed his aides to give false testimony.

Why did the high court reverse the district court's views on the perjury charge? The presiding judges offered the following explanation. "In defining what constitutes a perjury offense," they said in a statement, "a primary consideration should be whether the things on which a false testimony was given are closely related to the underlying case itself."[50]

In the embezzlement case, the high court statement said, the most relevant points that needed to be examined were whether Chen Shui-bian had truly "carried out his stated secret diplomatic operations and whether the money he got from the state affairs fund was used to finance those operations." Examined from this angle, the statement said, Lin's testimony on who provided the invoices and how this was carried out should not be taken as evidence in deciding whether or not to convict Chen or his wife of embezzlement.

Moreover, the high court statement pointed out that the prosecutors, before questioning Lin Teh-hsun, had failed to inform the accused that he had the right to refuse to testify. Under such

---

50 Su Wei-rong, High Court Clears Chen Shui-bian of Instigating False Testimony, United Daily News, August 18, 2012.

circumstances, Lin should not have been convicted of perjury even if he had given untrue testimony during questioning. "If what Lin had testified could not be construed as legitimate testimony, then there were no grounds for the district court to convict Chen Shui-bian of telling his staff member Lin Teh-hsun to give false testimony," the court said.

The prosecution appealed to the Supreme Court. After months of deliberation, the Supreme Court found the high court's judgment unconvincing. A spokesman for the Supreme Court said: "The false statements made by a former member of the presidential staff Lin Teh-hsun bore a close relationship to the Chens' embezzlement and forgery convictions. But the high court did not bother to identify such a relationship ...before deciding to acquit Chen Shui-bian of instigating perjury."

The Supreme Court annulled the Taiwan High Court's ruling and ordered a retrial of the perjury case.[51]

---A Second Suspended Charge: Seizing Classified Documents.

In May 2012, the SID under the Supreme Prosecutor's Office filed a fresh indictment against Chen Shui-bian, this time accusing the former president of illegally seizing thousands of confidential documents from the Presidential Office before he stepped down in May 2008.

Months before filing the indictment, SID prosecutors had raided Chen's Taipei offices, carrying away boxes of what were alleged to be secret government files. The raid came after Chen's aides failed to

---

51 Lin Wei-xin, Supreme Court Overrules High Court's Acquittal of Perjury Against Chen, China Times, December 14, 2012.

answer a summons to submit requested documents. "We decided to search Chen's offices because of a pressing need to preserve evidence," SID spokesman Chen Hung-ta told reporters.

In the new indictment, Chen was charged with instructing his aides to pack up and transport 17,375 documents from the Presidential Office to his personal offices on the eve of his retirement. About 3,400 of those papers were alleged to be classified documents, belonging to the Presidential Office, the National Security Council, the Ministry of National Defense, and the Ministry of Foreign Affairs.

The SID prosecutors speculated that Chen had decided to keep the documents for several purposes: To use them as a reference in writing his memoir, to help him in preparing a defense in his numerous legal cases, and to find potential material from those files that could be used against his political opponents after he left office. Investigators also said they found no evidence that Chen had leaked any of those confidential government documents. The former president was indicted for violating the National Security Information Protection Act. If convicted, the former president could have been given a sentence of up to seven and a half years in prison.

However, the case remained stalled in the Taipei District Court since December 2013 when the court announced a suspension of Chen's trial on the charge of illegally seizing and possessing confidential government documents.[52] As noted earlier, the district court move was prompted by concerns about Chen's health and made

---

52 Lan Kai-cheng, District Court Rules Suspension of Hearings on Chen's Case of Seizing Confidential Government Documents, United Daily News, December 21, 2013.

Chapter 2
An Examination of Chen Shui-bian's Multiple Graft Cases

at the request of Chen's lawyers who maintained the former president's "deteriorating health had made him incapable of attending court hearings without worsening his health problems."

A medical report prepared by a team of doctors commissioned by the Taipei District Court pointed out that the former leader was suffering from an array of ailments, including severe depression and non-typical Parkinson's disease. The report warned that Chen's health might be put at risk if he had to spend time traveling to court and attending lengthy hearings.

According to Article 294 of the nation's Code of Criminal Procedure, the trial of a defendant who is unable to attend court hearings due to illness should be suspended until the defendant can fulfill such legal obligations, a court official said.

The district court also went out of its way to explain that its order to suspend Chen's trial "referred only to the state of the proceedings involved being temporarily suspended." It should not be taken as a permanent suspension of the trial in question and applied only to the case of the alleged seizure of confidential government documents.

--- Third Suspended Charge: Embezzling Special State Affairs Funds

In September 2009, the Taipei District Court handed down a life sentence to the former first couple for a variety of corruption charges, including embezzling state affairs funds.

The Chens appealed to the Taiwan High Court and won lighter sentencing, as the high court in June 2010 reduced their life sentence to 20 years in prison. Yet the couple still contested the result and appealed once again, this time to the Supreme Court. At the highest trial institution, their cases took a further surprising turn. The Supreme Court ordered the Taiwan High Court to retry the high-profile charge of embezzling state affairs funds while handling down lenient penalties on the other charges.

The embezzlement case took a further twist after it was returned to the Taiwan High Court for retrial. This time the high court in August 2011 acquitted Chen and his wife of misusing state funds. The acquittal was a surprise to the SID, which then took the embezzlement case to the Supreme Court. In July 2012, the highest court overturned the lower court's acquittal and ordered a retrial on the embezzlement charge.

But Chen's embezzlement case was stalled at the Taiwan High Court despite the Supreme Court's instructions. No action was taken until April 2016 when the high court decided to suspend further trials on the charge in response to a request from Chen's lawyers who cited a hospital diagnosis of the ex-president. Once again Chen's lawyers maintained their client was physically unfit to attend court hearings and answer questions.

So the embezzlement case remained unsettled a decade after prosecutors first launched their investigation and brought charges against Chen and his wife. But the many surprising twists and turns in the embezzlement case merit examination in more detail.

As mentioned in earlier pages, the embezzlement scandal arose in 2006 when Chen was in the middle of his second term. In the summer of that year, the now-defunct anti-corruption center of the Taiwan High Prosecutor's Office was tipped off that the First Lady was suspected of illegally using invoices and receipts obtained from family members,

Chapter 2
An Examination of Chen Shui-bian's Multiple Graft Cases

friends, and others to claim reimbursements from the "special state affairs fund," a budget legally created for spending by the president.

After months of investigation, Prosecutor Chen Jui-ren of the same anti-corruption center filed an indictment against Mrs. Chen in November of the same year on charges of embezzling NT$14.8 million (about US$450,000) from the special fund and forging documents. Chen Shui-bian was named as a co-suspect in the case, but presidential immunity shielded him at the time.

But once Chen had stepped down and no longer had his constitutional protections, SID prosecutors reopened the investigation. In a terse statement issued almost immediately after presidential powers were transferred to Chen's successor, the SID announced: "We have formally named the ex-president, Chen Shui-bian, as a suspect in an embezzlement case, and started an investigation into his involvement." By this time the SID had already informed Chen that he had been barred from leaving the country, pending judicial investigation.

In addition to the embezzlement case, the SID also launched probes into Chen and his wife amid a series of bribery allegations. The expanded probe reached a climax seven months later, as the SID brought indictments against the former first couple on four broad charges: embezzlement, taking bribes in multiple corruption cases, laundering illegally obtained funds, and forging documents. The SID suggested "the harshest penalties" for Chen and his wife.

Regarding the alleged misuse of funds, the indictment accused Chen and his wife of embezzling a total of NT$104 million (roughly US$3.43 million) from the special fund account during his eight years in office from 2000 to 2008. This figure was considerably larger than the NT$14.8 million (US$489,000) cited in 2006.

In the indictment, the SID charged that the first couple routinely used false invoices and receipts to claim reimbursements from the state affairs fund. The items listed on such receipts, according to investigators, included various kinds of private expenses of the first family, ranging from expenses for the weddings of the president's son and daughter, their health insurance bills and overseas travel expenditures, and even payments for dog food.

Besides using deceptive invoices and receipts to claim reimbursements, the former president was also found by investigators to have used dozens of so-called "secret special diplomatic missions," many of which were non-existent, to demand payments from the state affairs fund.

Prosecuting Counsel Ms. Lin Yi-chun, speaking at the closing session at the Taipei District Court on the embezzlement case, had this to say: "Fortunately, investigators had discovered a personal digital assistant (PDA) at the home of former presidential accountant Chen Cheng-hui. Using the electronic device, the accountant detailed each expense reimbursed from the state affairs fund." The prosecuting counsel went on to say: "Had this information-rich device not been found, the prosecution would have never been able to discover the Chen family's blatant misappropriations of the state affairs fund."[53]

---

53 Wang Ji-yu and Kou Liang-chieh, Appropriation of Public Funds for Private Use, China Times, July 29, 2009.

Chapter 2
An Examination of Chen Shui-bian's Multiple Graft Cases

Accountant Chen Cheng-hui was listed by the SID as both a defendant and witness.

Chen Shui-bian Denies Any Wrongdoing

Throughout his embezzlement and bribery trials that began in March 2009, Chen Shui-bian consistently denied any wrongdoing. He rejected all accusations of irregularities as politically motivated. The following are the main answers he gave during questioning at the district court.

On the corruption charges, he claimed all of the funds he received during his years in office were political donations, not bribes as prosecutors sought to portray them. On the charge of embezzlement, he argued that existing rules governing the use of the presidential state affairs fund were vague, without clear stipulations of what the money could and could not be used for. Regarding the accusation of money laundering, Chen maintained his position that his wife had kept him in the dark when she wired his "leftover campaign funds" abroad.

Chen's complaint about vague rules governing the use of the presidential fund was not without some foundation. Legal experts like Liu Wen-shi, an adviser to the Chen administration on laws and regulations, took this view. In a newspaper commentary, Liu pointed to "a major grey area in existing laws and rules concerning the use, verification, and reimbursement of the presidential state affairs fund."[54]

---

54 Liu Wen-shi, the Legality of the State Affairs Fund, Taipei Times, November 20, 2006.

Nevertheless, Chen's arguments failed to persuade the presiding judges. On September 11, 2009, the Taipei District Court concluded trials on the Chen family's four broad corruption cases, dubbed the "trial of the century" in the local media, and announced its verdicts.

Chen Shui-bian was sentenced to life in prison after he was convicted of embezzling state affairs funds, taking kickbacks from a landowner, bribes from the chairwoman of Taipei 101, and laundering money. He was fined NT$200 million (US$6.59 million).

Mrs. Chen, as a co-defendant, also received a life sentence. Yet in addition to the same four convictions, she was found guilty of receiving money from a construction company executive who had been seeking a contract on a government project to build an exhibition center in Taipei. She was fined NT$300 million (US$9 million).

The couple's son and daughter-in-law were convicted of helping their parents conceal and move funds offshore illegally. The son was sentenced to two and a half years in prison, while his wife received a sentence of 20 months in jail with five years' probation.

But the judicial rulings on the embezzlement and corruption charges against Chen Shui-bian and his wife took stunning twists and turns, as appeals by the defense and prosecution went to the Taiwan High Court and the Supreme Court.

The first such twist took place in June 2010 when a panel of three judges at the Taiwan High Court reduced the district court's sentence of the former president from life to 20 years in prison. His wife, who was also sentenced to life in prison by the lower court, also saw her sentence cut to 20 years. Their fines were sharply reduced to a

Chapter 2
An Examination of Chen Shui-bian's Multiple Graft Cases

combined NT$370 million (US$12.21 million) from the NT$500 million (US$16.5 million) originally imposed by the district court. The key factor in the high court judges' decision was they were more lenient with the couple in trying the embezzlement case. They accepted Chen's arguments in his use of the state affairs fund--a specially budgeted fund for use by the president which consists of two different accounts: "secret" and "non-secret."

During the embezzlement trial at the district court, judges there accepted the prosecution's charge that Chen and his wife had embezzled more than NT$20 million from the "non-secret" account by using improper invoices and receipts collected from their relatives and friends.

However, after the case went before the Taiwan High Court judges, they ruled in Chen's favor, accepting his argument that all the money he got from this account was spent on "matters that had to do with performing his presidential duties." Chen Shui-bian and his wife were cleared of the charge of embezzling money from the "non-secret" account.

But since Chen and his wife were still found guilty of "using other people's invoices and receipts" to demand refunds from the "non-secret" fund account, they were convicted of committing forgery instead, a crime which carries a much lighter penalty.

On the "secret" fund account dispute, the judges at the high court also supported Chen's contention that the vast majority of the NT$80 million he obtained from this account was used to help fund "secret diplomatic" missions and "public service" activities. In the end, the judges concluded that the actual sum of money the couple embezzled

91

from the state affairs fund amounted to only some NT$14.9 million, far less than the NT$107 million they were originally accused of misappropriating.

It was due largely to this conclusion that the Taiwan High Court agreed to reduce the prison terms. The reduced sentence also took into account the penalties imposed on the couple for the kickbacks in a land procurement scandal and bribes from a business executive looking for an appointment.

A Snub of the Supreme Court

The state fund case took yet another head-snapping turn in August 2011, when the Taiwan High Court, after retrying the Chens on the embezzlement charges, announced an acquittal of the two defendants. The decision was seen by many as a snub of the Supreme Court which had overturned the high court's 2010 ruling on the same embezzlement and corruption charges and called for a retrial.

For the general public, the Taiwan High Court's decision to acquit Chen and his wife outright was difficult to understand. The not-guilty ruling stood in sharp contrast with the 20-year sentence imposed earlier by the same high court in the same case. The disparity was even greater when compared to the sentence of life imprisonment set by the Taipei District Court after the first trial.

The Taiwan High Court's acquittal triggered an outpouring of criticism. "There never has been a legal case in Taiwan's judicial history that is a better demonstration of how unpredictable our court decisions can be," commented Shih Ming-the, former chairman of the DPP.

As noted earlier, Shih had led a public drive to force his former ally to step down in 2006. The pressure campaign was launched in response to a series of allegations and formal indictments of Chen's wife, their son-in-law, and several senior presidential aides. This reflected a wave of public anger aimed at Chen, who at the time still had two more years in office.[55]

Some critics angrily condemned the high court's ruling as the "death of justice in Taiwan." KMT Legislator Chiu Yi slammed the presiding judges for "selling their souls to the devil." Chiu, an outspoken critic of the president, demanded that the KMT administration "purge the former president's hidden sympathizers from the judicial system." By "hidden sympathizers," he meant that some judges currently serving in Taiwan's three-tiered trial system remained loyal to the corruption-tainted former president, often letting their personal preferences influence their decisions.

Unsurprisingly, the SID appealed to the Supreme Court. "The decision by the Taiwan High Court to acquit Chen of corruption charges in its retrial of the case fell far short of public expectations," said a SID spokesman. "It was a complete reversal of the life sentence handed down by the Taipei District Court. This was just too wide a gap in sentencing to be acceptable to the general public."

---

55 "One Million Voices against Corruption, President Chen Shui-bian Must Step Down," en.wikipedia.org/ (from August to November 2006).

The Supreme Court, after months of deliberation, overturned the acquittal of the Chens and returned the case to the Taiwan High Court for a second retrial. In an accompanying statement, the Supreme Court said: "Be they 'secret' state affairs funds or 'non-secret,' the use of such budgeted government funds must have something to do with the execution of presidential duties. This is to say that if there is evidence that the state affairs funds were appropriated for private uses that had nothing to do with their prescribed purposes, such behavior constituted a criminal offense: embezzlement."

The Supreme Court statement also cited the personal digital assistant obtained by prosecutors as proof that Chen and his wife had indeed misused the special presidential budget to cover private expenses. As noted earlier, the former accountant in the presidential office had recorded details of the use of special state affairs funds to pay Chen's family expenses.

"But the Taiwan High Court in its retrial of the case completely ignored the PDA-recorded evidence, without giving any reason," the Supreme Court said. By refusing to recognize hard facts, it went on to say, the high court judges had been" blind to a universal legal and moral norm that public funds cannot and should not be spent on one's own personal or family expenses."

Instead of taking into account the evidence presented by the prosecution, the high court adopted Chen's arguments against the embezzlement charge. One of his key contentions was that during his eight years as president, he had undertaken 21 diplomatic and other secret projects entailing a total cost of NT$130 million (US$4.28

million), far exceeding the NT$104 million (US$3.43 million) which the prosecution had accused him of embezzling.

But the Supreme Court refuted that argument too, saying that only nine of the 21 diplomatic projects could be considered as having any links with other countries or territories. All of the remaining 12 projects -- such as funding mass demonstrations, giving gifts, and issuing bonuses – had no connection with diplomacy. Moreover, the Supreme Court went on to argue that there was no reason for those projects to be carried out in secret. The Supreme Court asked," Why weren't there any legitimate expense-related receipts to apply for reimbursements from the state affairs fund (and why) use falsified invoices that ran the risk of forgery charges?"

The judges of the highest court also raised the following questions: Why were the state affairs funds sent to the president's private residence, instead of being kept in the presidential office? Why was it necessary for the state affairs funds to go through Mrs. Chen before being transferred back for use by the president and why did the first lady handle invoices and receipts, when she had no role in implementing the so-called 21 diplomatic projects?

Exactly where was the Taiwan High Court thought to have gone astray in the retrial of the embezzlement case? The answer, as given by the Supreme Court, was that the presiding judges of the high court did not bother to delve into the questionable behavior of the Chens. Instead, they arbitrarily dismissed corruption charges based mainly on the former president's argument that he spent far more during his presidency than the amount he was accused of embezzling.

The embezzlement case, suspended in 2016 because of Chen Shui-bian's poor health, did indeed provide a classic example of how unpredictable Taiwan's court decisions could be.

(Note: Former President Chen Shui-bian was granted exemption from the charge of embezzling state affairs fund many years later in July 2022 as a result of an amendment to the Accounting Act. The amendment, which was pushed through by the DPP (Chen's former party)-controlled Legislature Yuan, retroactively cleared Chen of both criminal and civil liability for the alleged improper use of the fund when he served as president from 2000 to 2008. The exemption is not equivalent to "not guilty," however, as Chen still faces other charges, including bribery, corruption, and abuse of authority, according to a report published in the English-language Taiwan News (2022/7/15). Trials on the other charges have been suspended for years because of the former first couple's health problems. The exemption was also applicable to Mrs. Chen and others involved in the fund embezzlement case.)

Judicial Uncertainties – Judges Have Their Biases

Two major uncertainties made predicting the outcome of court cases in Taiwan more complicated. One concerned a non-judicial matter -- a judge's potential political affiliation. Generally speaking, judges in Taiwan remain politically neutral, thanks to decades of reform and democratization. And judges, with their constitutionally protected freedom, can perform their duties independently of political interference.

Chapter 2
An Examination of Chen Shui-bian's Multiple Graft Cases

But like their fellow citizens, judges have emotions, personal biases, and political preferences. But when these factors are allowed to play a role in determining the outcome of a case, the system that dispenses justice can be undermined, resulting in decisions that fall short of public expectations. The Taiwan High Court's acquittal of Chen Shui-bian and his wife on embezzlement charges, in the view of many, was a clear example of the situation.

In the nearly four decades of significant democratic development, politics has become polarized, with the formation of two camps associated with the colors of blue and green. The blue camp supports the KMT while the green camp identifies with the DPP -- the party which former President Chen helped found.

As a consequence of the political divide, public issues, legal cases included, have often been assessed along these lines. This was widely believed to have contributed to the convoluted path of the embezzlement case.

Another uncertainty in predicting the outcome of a court case, particularly a complicated one, is that the law in this country sets no limit on the number of times the Supreme Court can legitimately overturn a lower court's rulings. This means that the Supreme Court judges can reject a high court's decision on a given case and call for a retrial over and over again until they find a decision that is in line with their own views. Apparently, something needs to be done here to check and balance the power of the Supreme Court justices to prevent them from abusing their overruling authority.

---A Fourth Suspended Case: Taking Bribes from Cathay Financial Holdings

In this case, Chen Shui-bian and his wife were indicted in October 2009 for allegedly taking hundreds of millions of Taiwan dollars from Cathay Financial Holdings and Yuanta Financial Holdings in two separate bank merger scandals. The October 2009 indictment was a fourth batch of corruption charges filed against the former first couple by the SID since December 2008.

This indictment followed months of investigation focused on allegations the couple had been using the program known as the "second phase" of financial reforms -- launched in late 2004 shortly after the start of Chen's second four-year term -- to extort money from big financial firms.

Under this reform program, Chen claimed he wanted to achieve four goals during his new term: To have three big financial institutions each with a domestic market share of at least 10 percent; to halve the number of state-owned banks to six; to reduce the number of financial holding companies to seven from 14; and to have at least one domestic financial institution run by a foreign entity or listed on an overseas market.

However, critics contended this program had serious pitfalls. They said the government policy tended to spawn corruption when you pushed for financial firms to be merged within a prescribed time and for their numbers to be reduced to below the state-designated level. Yet Chen Shui-bian defended his financial reform program, dismissing criticism as intended to derail his policy.[56]

---

56 Ko Shu-ling, Chen Defends Second-Phase Financial Reform Program, Taipei Times, May 24, 2007.

Chapter 2
An Examination of Chen Shui-bian's Multiple Graft Cases

In the October 2009 indictment, the SID charged Chen and his wife with taking NT$300 million (US$9.83 million) from Cathay Financial Holdings and another NT$200 million (US$6.55 million) from Yuanta Financial Holdings. Prosecutors said the bribes were given by the two firms as payments to win the couple's support in their separate bank merger bids.

In addition to the bribery charges, Chen Shui-bian and his wife were also accused of laundering money they obtained from the two financial firms and others, into overseas bank accounts, mainly in Switzerland.

Also indicted by the SID in the latest round of prosecutions were the former first couple's son and daughter-in-law as well as 17 others, including Chen's former presidential aides and top executives in the private sector. They were charged with either giving bribes to the Chens or helping them to conceal their illegally obtained funds and transfer them abroad.

As with the state affairs fund embezzlement case, the more recent bribery case which involved the former first couple and the two financial firms, Cathay and Yuanta, also underwent sharply different judicial decisions at different levels of the nation's court system.

One example of the clash of opinion was the Supreme Court review of the financial bribery case. This case had already encountered opposite decisions at lower court levels. As noted in earlier pages, the Supreme Court convicted Chen Shui-bian and his wife of taking bribes from Yuanta Financial in 2012. But it also returned the portion involving alleged bribes from Cathay Financial to the Taiwan High Court for retrial. This, however, led to the indefinite suspension of court proceedings. Also ordered to be retried was the charge that the Chen family secretly sent money obtained as bribes from the two financial firms and other suspected sources to overseas financial institutions.

The following is a closer look at the dramatic differences in the conclusions of the courts in Taiwan's three-tiered trial system regarding bribery charges.

After more than a year of court battles related to the bank merger scandals, the Taipei District Court in November 2010 rejected the charges lodged by the SID against the Chens and their co-defendants. In his ruling, Presiding Judge Chou Chan-chun of the district court acquitted Chen and his wife of taking bribes from Cathay and Yuanta and laundering the proceeds through overseas transfers of funds. The other defendants involved in the case were also cleared of their alleged offenses.

At a press conference announcing the acquittals, Judge Chou, the head of a three-judge panel, said the not-guilty rulings were based on his view of the Constitution concerning presidential powers. "Nowhere in the constitution is there a specific provision that empowers the president to oversee bank merger matters," he said.[57]

Without such authority, Judge Chou inferred, it was unlikely that Chen Shui-bian as president could have been bribed by the two financial firms, Cathay and Yuanta, in exchange for presidential help in their respective bank merger bids, as the prosecution alleged.

---

57 Richard Chang, Chen Shui-bian Found Not Guilty in Bribery Trial, Taipei Times, November 6, 2010.

Chapter 2
An Examination of Chen Shui-bian's Multiple Graft Cases

But the acquittals triggered an avalanche of criticism, with some suggesting Judge Chou was biased toward the former first couple. The most controversial part of the rulings was Judge Chou's view on the president's constitutionally prescribed powers.

But if Chen was not guilty of taking bribes as charged by the SID, then what were the large payments made to him and his wife for? In this regard, Judge Chou unreservedly accepted the arguments made by Chen, his wife, and his former presidential aide, Ma Jung-chen, who testified as both a co-defendant and witness.

During the trial, Chen Shui-bian insisted that he was innocent, maintaining his defense that he was unaware of his wife's actions while his wife maintained the funds were political donations, not bribes.

About his decision to clear the Chens of the alleged money laundering, the reason given by Judge Chou was that the prosecution "failed to back up its accusation with sufficient evidence."

But the judge ignored the solid evidence provided by the SID, which included the defendants' confessions about a big bank vault that the Chens rented to secretly store large sums of cash, as well as how the funds were moved to a second location before they were transferred abroad. Similarly damaging was Mrs. Chen's explanation to prosecutors that she decided to move the huge amount of cash from the Cathay Financial Bank vault because several people had discovered where the money was kept.

SID prosecutors, in their indictments and court testimonies, unequivocally accused Chen and his family of sending large amounts of money overseas via complex bank account transfers using paper companies devised to escape detection.

They said that much of the money wired abroad by the Chen family originated in a huge vault rented in the Taipei-based Cathay United Bank. To evade unwanted attention, investigators said the bank vault was rented in the name of Chen Chun-ying, the wife of Mrs. Chen Shui-bian's brother Wu Ching-mao.

Receiving Political Donations

As noted earlier, Mrs. Chen acknowledged to investigators that the vault contained upwards of NT$1.1 billion (about US$34.38 million) at one point. According to prosecutors, Mrs. Chen admitted that in 2006 she had NT$740 million secretly moved from the Cathay United Bank vault to the basement of the residence of Ma Wei-chien, chief executive officer of a financial firm, Yuanta, "because several persons had learned about the money and its location."[58]

The relocation of those funds, Mrs. Chen confessed, was carried out with the help of her son and daughter-in-law as well as her brother Wu Ching-mao and his wife Chen Chun-ying -- the woman whose name was used by Mrs. Chen to rent the storeroom of the Cathay United Bank.

However, Mrs. Chen did not confess one other alleged offense of importance: The funds were parked in their new location only briefly, before being quickly moved abroad and deposited in overseas bank accounts at her request.

---

58 Liu Jun-koo, Mrs. Chen Shui-bian Acknowledges Upwards of NT$700 Million Stored in Bank Vault, United Daily News, December 19, 2008.

Chapter 2
An Examination of Chen Shui-bian's Multiple Graft Cases

Several months after the funds were transferred from the Cathay vault to Yuanta CEO Ma Wei-chien's private residence, Mrs. Chen told him that she wished to move the funds into the banking system and invest them overseas. The message, according to the 2009 indictment, was conveyed through her friend Ms. Tu Li-ping, also a senior Yuanta official. Mrs. Chen directed the Yuanta CEO to take NT$540 million (about US$17.99 million) out of the total of NT$740 million and send it abroad for that purpose.

The Yuanta chief executive officer complied with Mrs. Chen's request and wired the funds overseas. This was done via about a dozen false bank accounts and a paper company registered in the British Virgin Islands, to avert detection by regulatory authorities. The funds remitted overseas through these complex channels ended up in Switzerland.[59]

But the prosecution's account of how the former first family secretly moved so much cash from Cathay United Bank to the Yuanta CEO's residence, and of how the vast majority of the funds were ultimately shifted to Switzerland all failed to convince Judge Chou of the Taipei District Court. "Still, you gave no evidence to prove that the NT$740 million the Chen family had originally stored in Cathay United Bank were financial gains derived from criminal activities," the judge said in his assessment of the prosecution's case.

---

59 Both Ma Wei-chien and Tu Li-ping pleaded guilty in court in February 2010 to helping the former first family launder the money they helped move from Cathay United Bank.

In sum, the Taipei District Court's opinions on the financial scandal case were: One, the president constitutionally had no specific powers to set and oversee banking policy. That meant the accusation that Chen used his presidential authority to influence bank mergers to acquire financial gains was unlikely to be true. Two, the NT$300 million and NT$200 million Chen took from Cathay Financial Holdings and Yuanta Financial Holdings were campaign donations, not bribes as alleged by the prosecution. And three, there was no proof that the entire NT$740 million, originally stored at Cathay United Bank, was unlawfully obtained by Chen and his wife.

It was based on these opinions that Judge Chou of the Taipei District Court dismissed the SID's charges of corruption and money laundering against Chen and his wife in the financial reform scandal and acquitted them of both crimes.

The acquittals by the district court, however, shocked the prosecution. A dismayed SID found Judge Chou's rulings unacceptable and appealed to the Taiwan High Court. The SID appeal was accepted.

Following a year of trial and deliberation, the high court reversed the Taipei District Court's not-guilty decision in the financial bribery case. It sentenced Chen and his wife to 18 years and 11 years in prison, respectively, for taking bribes and laundering money.

Dispute over the President's Constitutional Powers

The high court in a statement refuted the district court's opinions—point by point.[60] On the opinion that the constitution provides the president no responsibility for supervising bank mergers, the high court dismissed that as untrue. Chang Chuan-li, the head of a three-judge panel at the high court, conceded that the constitution did not include anything that would oblige the president to oversee bank mergers. But the power of the president, following a series of constitutional amendments over the past few decades, had expanded considerably to make it more appropriate to the role as the nation's highest democratically elected leader.

"Specifically," the statement said, "the president now, as a result of the expansion of powers, has been able to fulfill his election campaign platforms and to influence virtually all aspects of government policy, through his authority to appoint or fire his premier."

Judge Chang invoked past constitutional amendments that considerably enhanced the power of the president and, as a result, made it easier for the leader to influence government policy. He also cited two fresh decisions by the Supreme Court that demonstrated how Chen Shui-bian had employed his presidential authority to sway government decisions to obtain financial gains.

---

60 Wang Ji-you, Mrs. Chen Shui-bian admits to having taken NT$200 million from Yuanta Financial Holdings, China Times, June 10, 2010.

The judge pointed to Chen's use of presidential authority to instruct James Lee, director of the government-run Hsinchu Science-based Industrial Park, to buy a piece of land from a private company in violation of the law. This created an opportunity for Chen to earn hundreds of millions of Taiwan dollars in kickbacks. Chen was convicted of receiving kickbacks and sentenced to an 11-year jail term for this offense by the Supreme Court.

He also cited the former president's use of his enhanced powers to instruct Taiwan's finance minister to appoint a business executive as chairperson of a government corporation that managed Taiwan's landmark tower, Taipei 101. In this case, Chen was sentenced to eight years in jail by the Supreme Court for receiving NT$10 million (more than US$300,000) in bribes from the executive.

In addition to overturning the district court's judgment about presidential powers, the high court also dismissed the defense's argument about the source of money in the Chen family's possession as "political contributions," not bribes. But the high court refuted that account as a one-sided story. It instead accepted the prosecution's evidence as demonstrating that bribes were offered and paid. The evidence included confessions and testimony from witnesses.

In the instance of Cathay Financial Holdings, the high court quoted prosecutorial evidence as proving that the company's chairman Tsai Hong-tu had reached an agreement with then-President Chen in its bid to merge with the former United World Chinese Commercial Bank. "Under this agreement, Cathay Financial would pay the former leader NT$300 million (about US$9.755 million) over three years in exchange for his help to win its merger bid," the high court said.

Chapter 2
An Examination of Chen Shui-bian's Multiple Graft Cases

And the two sides indeed made good on their promises, according to the indictment filed by the SID in 2009. The payments were made in cash and in three installments, each of NT$100 million. In return, Chen pressured a rival bidder for the bank to drop out of the contest. Chen sent his trusted aide Ma Yung-cheng to deliver a warning to Fubon Financial Holding to end its quest for a merger.[61]

The approach taken by Yuanta Financial Holdings in search of political favors from the Chen family was somewhat different from Cathay Financial strategy. Yuanta executives believed that the best way to win presidential support for their acquisition bid was to go through the First Lady.

According to court documents, Ma Chih-ling, founder of Yuanta, dispatched board director Tu Li-ping to call on Mrs. Chen at her home. At the meeting, Ms. Tu briefed the first lady on the firm's desire to merge with a smaller financial holding company, Fuhwa, and hoped to gain support for its bid from her husband.

After telling the first lady the purpose of her visit, the emissary asked how much compensation the Chens might want in exchange for their help. Mrs. Chen made no reply, instead extending two fingers of her right hand. The visitor immediately understood what her hostess meant, but wanted to be sure that she got the message correctly. She asked Mrs. Chen if she meant NT$200 million. At this point, Mrs. Chen nodded with a smile and then gave an assurance that Yuanta would receive full support for its plan to merge with Fuhwa.

---

61 Ma Yung-cheng was convicted by the Taiwan High Court of conspiring with the former first couple to take bribes and was sentenced to eight years in prison.

As a result of the meeting between Mrs. Chen and Ms. Tu, according to court documents, a deal was struck between Yuanta and the Chens. In late 2004, Yuanta fulfilled its promise to deliver NT$200 million, all in cash and stuffed in six big cardboard boxes, to the private residence of the first couple. The president and his wife, for their part, also kept their word to help Yuanta push through its merger bid uncontested.

The Shortest Route to the President

The ability of Mrs. Chen to help Yuanta finalize its merger with Fuhwa Securities by persuading a rival suitor to drop its bid appeared to confirm a rumor circulating in Taipei business circles at the time that the most effective way to lobby President Chen and his government was with the aid of the first lady.

Many top executives of big local corporations, knowing that Mrs. Chen was open to discussing business proposals, liked to visit her at the presidential residence. During such private meetings, the visitors told Mrs. Chen that they would be happy to make donations if their requests were granted.

The list of indictments and convictions of corporate leaders found to have bought government favors via the First Lady ran long. It included Leader Construction Corp president Kuo Chuan-ching,, Taipei 101 chair Diana Chen as well as Yuanta Financial founder Ma Chih-ling. Many business executives were willing to pay a hefty price to approach Mrs. Chen and establish a connection with her because they knew she had a powerful influence on the president and his government's policies.

At the end of the trial of the two bank merger scandals, the Taiwan High Court accepted the prosecution's evidence. "Negotiated bribery terms" were indeed reached between the first couple and the two financial firms, Cathay and Yuanta. The high court, therefore, reversed the Taipei District Court's acquittals and sentenced Chen Shui-bian to 18 years in prison and his wife to an 11-year jail term for money laundering and taking bribes.

The high court also sentenced the former first couple's son Chen Chih-chung to one year in jail and his wife Huang Jui-ching to six months for their roles in helping their parents wire money overseas via multiple bank account transfers and paper companies registered in foreign lands.

Ma Yung-cheng, the presidential aide who twice helped his boss take bribe money from Cathay Financial and persuaded a rival financial house to bow out of a bank merger contest, was given an eight-year jail term on charges of corruption as a co-defendant.

In other developments, the high court upheld the Taipei District Court's position acquitting 11 other defendants of their alleged crimes. Among them were Cathay Financial group's vice chairman Tsai Chen-yu and Yuanta Financial group's founder Ma Chih-ling, both of whom had been charged with paying bribes to the Chens. One other high-profile figure among the acquitted was presidential adviser Wu Li-pei, who was indicted for using his foreign-based bank accounts to help Chen conceal some two million U.S. dollars in "illegal funds."

Ironically, the main reason cited for the acquittals of the 11 defendants suspected of bribing the first couple or helping them launder money was "a lack of proper penalty provisions" set in the criminal code at that time.

Judge Chang Condemns the Chens' Corrupt Behavior

Before announcing the penalties, Chang Chuan-li, the presiding judge of the Taiwan High Court, condemned the former president and first lady for their corrupt behavior. The judge first accused Chen of "using his presidential powers as a profiteering tool to obtain financial gains," breaching the trust of the people. He then criticized the former leader for his repeated attempts to "conceal evidence of wrongdoing," his practice of "shifting the blame onto others" during the investigation, and for showing no sign of repentance.

Judge Chang also rebuked Mrs. Chen for "departing from traditional functions such as taking part in charitable and other public-spirited activities," as expected of a first lady. The judge lamented that she allowed herself to "socialize with wealthy corporate leaders and peddle influence with them, staining her prestigious position as wife of the head of state."

Mrs. Chen's influence-peddling business was so brisk that it led Judge Chang to compare the former president's official residence to a "financial trading center" where money could be offered in exchange for political favors.

The Taiwan High Court's decisions in the bank merger scandals were not final, however. Chen Shui-bian and his wife appealed the rulings to the Supreme Court. But the highest court at the end of a year-long trial delivered a verdict that caught many observers by surprise.

The Supreme Court broke the case into three parts. Part one concerned Yuanta's acquisition of Fuhwa while part two was related to the merger of Cathay Financial with Overseas Chinese United Commercial Bank. Part three was about the allegations of money laundering by the Chen family.

Regarding the Yuanta-Fuhwa case, the Supreme Court upheld the Taiwan High Court's view regarding presidential powers. It agreed that the president of the country indeed had the final say in the appointment of Cabinet ministers. "Possessing such 'final say' authority, once the president was determined to intervene in the making of a certain policy, including financial policy, this would surely have a decisive influence on the outcome of that policy," said Judge Hua Man-tang, a spokesman for the Supreme Court.

"The Chens, after receiving NT$200 million from Yuanta, were found to have pressured a rival bidder, Angelo Koo of China Trust, to drop his bid," said Judge Hua, adding that such government intervention made in return for payments was a typical form of "negotiated bribery."

In the Yuanta case, the Supreme Court convicted the Chens of corruption, supporting the SID's charge that Chen had used his presidential power and influence to obtain financial gains from Yuanta. The Supreme Court sentenced the former president to 10 years in prison and gave his wife an eight-year jail term. The sentence was final.

The other two parts of the bank merger-linked corruption case -- the allegation of Chen Shui-bian receiving bribes from Cathay

Financial and the charge that he and his family laundered ill-gotten gains abroad -- were returned to the Taiwan High Court for retrial. The reason cited was that the Taiwan High Court had failed to demonstrate evidence it found to prove that Chen Shui-bian and Cathay Financial had reached the alleged bribery agreement. The Supreme Court spokesman asserted that instead of resorting to hard evidence and a logical rationale, the Taiwan High Court "based its conviction merely on a sort of hypothesis."

---The Fifth Suspended Charge: In this case, the ex-president and his wife were accused of laundering NT$500 million (about US$15.8 million) received as bribes from the two financial holding companies and transferring the funds abroad.

The money laundering case, along with the bank merger scandal in connection with Cathay Financial Holdings, was returned to the Taiwan High Court for retrial in December 2012. The Supreme Court gave two reasons explaining why it wanted a retrial on this particular money laundering case.

One was that the high court did not specify which portion of the Chen family's NT$740 million -- originally stored at the Cathay United Bank vault and later frozen by the prosecution -- was derived from bribery activities. The other reason was that the high court gave no clear information on how the family's allegedly illegal funds were laundered.

The proceedings on the money laundering charge, as with four other bribery charges described in the previous pages, were ordered suspended by the court because of the ex-president's poor health. Whether hearings would be resumed depended, according to court explanations, on whether the former president regained his health. But Chen Shui-bian's multiple medical conditions prompted the Ministry of Justice to release him on medical parole in January 2015.

The suspended proceedings and the absence of a final verdict from Taiwan's court on the money laundering case put at risk the ability of the SID to recover the remainder of the funds, wired to banks in Switzerland by the Chen family and still frozen by Swiss judicial authorities.

According to a September 2015 report in the China Times newspaper, the Chen family originally had some US$17 million in the now-defunct Swiss bank, Wegelin. The SID had asked Switzerland to freeze these funds in late 2008 because they were bribes obtained from sources in Taiwan, including Cathay Financial Holdings and Yuanta Financial Holdings.[62]

For the SID to get those funds back to Taiwan, however, it needed to present the Swiss judicial authorities with legitimate court documents to prove the deposits involved were bribe money obtained in Taiwan.

In 2012, Taiwan's Supreme Court, after convicting Chen Shui-bian and his wife of corruption in the Yuanta-Fuhwa merger case, sentenced the couple to lengthy jail terms and ordered the confiscation of the NT$280 million (US$6.4 million) received from bribes. With court papers related to those convictions, the SID successfully obtained the agreement of the Swiss Prosecutor's Office to return to Taiwan the

---

62 Liu Chih-hsien, Switzerland Returns to Taiwan US$6.5 Million as Bribe Money Linked to Yuanta Bank Merger Case, China Times, September 5, 2015.

Yuanta-related portion of the funds that the Chen family secretly deposited with Wegelin. The Swiss bank ceased operations after it agreed to pay US$57 million in cumulative fines to U.S. authorities for allowing more than 100 American citizens to hide US$1.2 billion from the Internal Revenue Service of the U.S. for almost 10 years.[63]

As of 2016, the SID was still negotiating with Swiss authorities for the return of the remaining US$10 million from the Wegelin bank deposits. Now that the Cathay-United Bank merger bribery case has been stuck in the Taiwan High Court as a result of Chen Shui-bian's medical conditions, it remains to be seen whether the SID will be able to retrieve those funds. No new developments have since been reported in the SID's efforts to recover those frozen Wegelin bank deposits.

Separately, Swiss authorities had already returned to Taiwan over US$21 million, which the Chens had deposited in four other Swiss bank accounts under the names of their son and daughter-in-law. These deposits were alleged by the SID to be illegal funds derived from the Longtan land procurement deal, the Nangang Exhibition Center construction scandal, and the special state affairs fund.

Switzerland allowed the return of those deposits to Taiwan, in part because the Supreme Court had convicted Chen Shui-bian and his wife in three corruption cases and in part because the younger Chens had agreed to remit the money to Taiwan under a plea-bargaining arrangement with the SID.

---

63 Richard Andoh, Swiss bank Wegelin to Close after U.S. Tax Evasion Fine, RAK Offshore Company, August 4, 2016.

Chapter 2
An Examination of Chen Shui-bian's Multiple Graft Cases

The following segment, Chapter 3, will be devoted to describing how the Chen family secretly moved large amounts of illicit funds outside Taiwan and used methods to deceive regulators and mask their true ownership in what at least one regulator called "textbook money laundering techniques."

Chapter 3
How the Chen Family Laundered Money across the Globe

Chen Shui-bian's Most Embarrassing Day

On August 14, 2008, former President Chen Shui-bian publicly admitted that his family had secretly wired abroad what he called his "leftover campaign funds." At first, he didn't specify how much "leftover" money was involved. He conceded it was about US$21 million only the following day. He made this grudging confession under intense scrutiny from the media, new information from a political opponent, and disbelief from the general public. Chen knew he could no longer maintain the fiction that neither he nor his family had bank deposits abroad.

Chen Shui-bian's supporters and many others less kindly disposed to him found this public admission of moral failure hard to believe. It was true that Chen laid the blame elsewhere – with his wife, vague regulations, and similar behavior by other politicians. He also claimed the money was obtained legally as donations from supporters. Eventually, the money trail would be portrayed as part of helping to promote Taiwan's diplomatic relations or a Taiwan identity. Chen would maintain that the government's investigations were a partisan effort to curry favor with Beijing, which was adamantly opposed to independence for the island and saw Chen as a "troublemaker."

These points would be examined closely in court in the lengthy legal battle that ended with convictions for Chen, his wife, their son, and others, including Mrs. Chen Shui-bian's brother and sister-in-law. But Chen Shui-bian's first public admission of wrongdoing was a devastating blow, not only to his political party but to the national psyche of this young and promising democracy. Chen was a symbol of a new Taiwan that was no longer satisfied with years of one-party rule. He was a politician who had claimed to be a fighter for democracy and someone who loved Taiwan dearly. But no matter how you viewed politics, stashing away large sums of money in foreign lands was surely not the best way to express the love of a country.

Yet the truth was even more unsettling than it appeared at that point. Prosecutors eventually discovered that the two-term former president had far more wealth concealed abroad than the US$21 million he had publicly acknowledged.[64]

The prosecutors uncovered an additional NT$540 million (approximately US$17 million) hidden in Switzerland and about US$2 million more deposited in Singapore. Aside from the secret bank deposits, the Chen family was also found to have two expensive properties in the United States, both of which were suspected of having been purchased with bribe money, according to U.S. government

---

64 Chen Chih-chung and Huang Jui-ching's financial activities were alleged by the Swiss Office of the Attorney General to have broken Switzerland's laws against money laundering, organized crime, terrorist financing, and economic crime. The allegations were made based on a report filed by the Federal Police's Money Laundering Reporting Office (MROS) of Switzerland, a member of the Toronto-based international anti-money laundering Egmont Group, according to Legislator Hung.

investigators.

Chen made his public confession at a hastily called press conference, his first such meeting with the news media since he stepped down as president three months earlier, transferring power to his newly elected successor, Ma Ying-jeou of the KMT.

When notified by Chen Shui-bian's office that the former president would make an important announcement, many reporters assumed he would use the occasion to loudly proclaim his innocence amid mounting allegations of bribery and other forms of corruption.

But Chen surprised the assembled reporters by admitting that he had broken the law by failing to fully declare his past campaign funds, and more explosively, some of the money from supporters had been transferred to bank accounts abroad. He said in a statement: "My conscience told me I must not continue to lie to myself or the public. I have, in the past, committed deeds that are against the rule of law."

In the past year or so, there had been persistent media reports alleging that Chen and his family had large sums of money concealed overseas, though these reports had never been verified by authorities. Chen routinely denied any suggestion that he or any of his family members had secret deposits parked offshore.

He took no questions after reading his statement, leaving quickly once he had delivered the desired message. Just one day before, Chen had dismissed as "totally unfounded" a report carried by Next, a weekly news magazine, that his family held massive bank deposits overseas. The report said that the money was kept in foreign banks in the names of his son Chen Chih-chung and daughter-in-law Huang Jui-ching. In a rebuttal of the magazine story, released by his lawyer, he claimed to have all of his assets in a trust and there was "nothing left to hide."

In his dramatic confession, he insisted that it was his wife who moved the funds offshore and he was unaware of this until months after the fact. The funds were to be used for "diplomatic purposes" after his retirement.

While he acknowledged that he had underreported his campaign funds, he excused himself by suggesting he was not alone. "Underreporting campaign money was a common problem for people of all political stripes at a time when a whole set of relevant regulations was lacking." In other words, if he were to be prosecuted for failing to fully declare election funds, other politicians with similar violations ought to be prosecuted as well. More importantly, Chen wanted to stress that the funds his wife had moved offshore were political donations, not bribes. A bribery conviction would mean much harsher punishment.

What Prompted Chen to Make His Confession?

The real reason for Chen Shui-bian's confession was not his conscience; it was the arrival of a document sent by Swiss authorities to Taiwan weeks earlier. The document was from Switzerland's Office of the Attorney General, informing Taipei that Swiss prosecutors suspected the Chen family of engaging in money laundering activity in Switzerland. The Swiss authorities requested judicial assistance as they looked into the case.

The main contents of the document were leaked to a KMT legislator who quickly called a press conference of her own on the morning of August 14 to break the news. She told media representatives that the Chen family was being investigated by Swiss prosecutors for engaging in suspicious financial transactions in that country. The legislator, Hung Hsiu-chu, gave a detailed description of the Chen family's questionable financial activities in Switzerland, which included unusual fund transfers, the opening of multiple bank accounts, and the use of several shell companies.

The legislator told reporters that all of her information came from a confidential Swiss judicial document sent to Taiwan's Ministry of Foreign Affairs. Excerpts from the document, including its serial number, were printed in all of the island's major newspapers the following day.

Now with his overseas illegal financial transactions exposed before the eyes of the public, Chen Shui-bian knew he had little choice but to admit wrongdoing and try to contain the damage. This was why Chen hurriedly called a news conference to confess that his family had secret bank accounts abroad. The former president's meeting with reporters took place just a few hours after the KMT legislator broke details of the financial scandal.

Legislator Hung told reporters that Swiss prosecutors suspected former President Chen and his wife had used the names of their son and daughter-in-law to illegally transfer funds to Switzerland. Such financial activities had broken Swiss laws and, therefore, were being investigated by Swiss authorities, she said.[65]

---

65 The Swiss judicial document, coded with serial number EA II.07.0186-OTE, was issued by the Office of the Attorney General of Switzerland with the investigation conducted by two federal prosecutors Edmond

According to the legislator, the younger Chens, by the use of shell companies and multiple bank account transfers, had moved US$21 million in total from Singapore to Switzerland in a short period in 2007. [66] This same amount of money was later found by SID investigators to have originated as bribes that the former first couple took from private companies in Taiwan while Chen Shui-bian was in office.

The cross-border money laundering operation run by the younger Chens was described by international bankers as "sophisticated" and "professional." According to the Swiss judicial document, Huang Jui-ching began her money laundering activities in Switzerland in February 2007 by using her name to open two personal accounts with an office of Merrill Lynch Bank (Suisse) in Geneva.

Follow the Money

The following steps were taken by Chen's family members, and they involved transfers of tens of millions of U.S. dollars to Switzerland. The road map described below is based on published excerpts from the Swiss judicial document.

Within two weeks of the opening of the two Merrill Lynch Bank (Suisse) accounts, remittances of US$20.94 million and US$140,000

Ottinger and Luc Leimgruber. Also see news analysis, Switzerland requests Taiwan's judicial assistance…Kuomintang official website, 2008/8/15.

66 Lin Cheng-chun, the Leftover Campaign Fund Claim by Chen Is a Barefaced Lie, the United Daily News, August 15, 2008.

Chapter 3
How the Chen Family Laundered Money across the Globe

were wired to those accounts from an unidentified sender via a Credit Suisse private banking office in Singapore.

Three months later, in May of that same year, Huang Jui-ching entrusted the Geneva arm of Merrill Lynch Bank with setting up Bouchon Ltd., a company registered in the Cayman Islands. She was listed as a proprietor, while her husband Chen Chih-chung was a signatory on the account. But it soon became clear that the Cayman Islands company was created to provide a legal entity for parking family funds -- a step taken to increase the difficulty of laundered money being detected by regulatory authorities.

With the establishment of Bouchon, Ms. Huang transferred the US$21 million – originally from Singapore and deposited in her personal Merrill Lynch bank accounts -- into the accounts of the new company. When she applied to set up Bouchon, she had at the same time used the name of this shell company to open two corporate accounts, also with Merrill Lynch. One was a savings account and the other was for investment purposes.

In late November of 2007, Huang transferred into the Bouchon accounts an additional US$10 million, which she had just taken out of the bank accounts of a company called Galahad Management Service set up by her husband. Galahad's accounts were with the Zurich office of RBS Coutts Bank AG -- a private bank and wealth manager wholly owned by what was then known as the Royal Bank of Scotland. Before the funds reached the Bouchon account there was an additional step in the process as the funds were routed through the corporate accounts at Merrill Lynch Bank (Suisse).

With the addition of the new deposits into Bouchon's accounts, the shell company's total assets at Merrill Lynch appeared to be more than US$30 million. However, Swiss investigators were not sure they had a complete picture of the money trail. In the judicial letter sent to Taipei, they indicated it was unclear whether the fresh remittance of US$10 million from Galahad Management was a net increase in assets for the new company Bouchon.

The Swiss investigators suspected the money in question may have been a portion of the original US$21 million placed in the Bouchon accounts but had been transferred into Galahad Management sometime earlier. Such mutual inter-bank fund transfers were a classic tactic used by money launderers to mislead regulators. So Swiss investigators didn't rule out the possibility that it was purely for the sake of deceiving investigators that Huang had moved the US$10 million between Bouchon and Galahad.

Complex Money Transfers Arouse Suspicion

The complicated financial maneuvers of the younger Chens did not escape detection by the international anti-money laundering organization Egmont Group and financial intelligence authorities in several locations. In addition to Switzerland, these included Jersey, Singapore, the Cayman Islands, and the United States.

On January 9, 2008, the Swiss Office of the Attorney General gave orders to freeze all assets held by Huang Jui-ching and her husband Chen Chih-chung in the accounts of the shell company Bouchon.

The Chen family's suspected money laundering activities in

Chapter 3
How the Chen Family Laundered Money across the Globe

Switzerland were investigated by two federal prosecutors, Edmond Ottinger, and Luc Leimgruber, according to the Swiss document sent to Taipei. The two prosecutors asked Taipei's Ministry of Justice for assistance in providing all relevant information about Chen Chih-chung, his wife, and the elder Chens. They suspected Taiwan's first couple had used their son and daughter-in-law's names to launder bribe money that was eventually parked in Switzerland.

The suspicions of the Swiss prosecutors were reasonable, not only because of the complex money transfers, according to analysts. By the time the prosecutors made their request for more information, the former president and his wife were on trial for a series of corruption charges. Taiwan's investigators were also trying to follow the money trail.

Also, the younger Chens, both fresh from university, had never been formally employed, and it was unlikely that they had accumulated so much wealth on their own. It was the above considerations that led the Swiss federal prosecutors to conclude that the younger Chens' deposits in Switzerland were illicit funds linked to their parents.

In Taiwan, the KMT legislator's revelations of Switzerland's investigation into the Chen family's suspicious financial bank accounts in that country were given extensive media coverage, exerting considerable pressure on Chen Shui-bian. This pressured him to be more specific about his overseas wealth. He quickly issued his supplementary news release, adding something he had omitted in his confession one day earlier. "The funds that my family had remitted abroad during my eight-year presidency added up to somewhere around US$21 million," he said in the news release.

But Chen's statement referred only to the money that was then public knowledge. He made no mention of another NT$540 million (US$17 million), which his family had deposited in the private Swiss bank Wegelin, known for helping foreign citizens dodge taxes through confidential accounts. Those funds were uncovered by the SID months later.

Chen also failed to disclose US$1.9 million that had been deposited at a Singapore branch of the Dutch bank ABN AMRO. Those funds, when detected by investigators later, had already been moved by the former first lady into four Goldman Sachs bank accounts provided by Chen's former presidential adviser, Wu Li-pei. Investigators believed the funds were relocated to avoid being traced, as the money transfer took place just weeks after the Swiss government froze the Chen family's Bouchon Ltd. bank accounts.

Chen Shui-bian's public confession also made no mention of his family's two properties in the U.S., allegedly purchased with money from bribes paid to him and his wife. One property was in a trendy section of Manhattan in New York City and the other was in Keswick, Virginia, a popular location for expensive second homes near the scenic Blue Ridge mountains. The properties were registered in the name of the former president's son Chen Chih-chung and had a combined value of US$2.1 million. These investments were eventually uncovered by U.S. authorities.

At the time of the press conference, there were no clear signs that these properties had become targets of investigators, and the Chen family may have concluded that there was no need to draw attention to them. But Chen's slow and evasive responses to the exposure of his family's overseas assets only added to the public's anger and contempt toward him and his family.

After listening to his public confession, Hung Hsiu-chu, the KMT legislator, heaped scorn on the president, pointing to his past denials of having any funds offshore. When caught in the act of hiding large amounts of money abroad, he gave a limited acknowledgment, she noted, describing Chen's strategy as "to admit to what was discovered and to continue to deny whatever was not yet uncovered."

The KMT legislator was particularly incensed by Chen's shifting of the blame to his wheelchair-bound wife. Hung, a teacher-turned-politician, said of this contemptuously: "No true gentleman would act in such a hypocritical and unethical way."

A Turning Point

The Swiss document marked a turning point for the SID in the investigation of the former first family's money laundering scandal. First, the document, which detailed the suspicious financial transactions of the younger Chens, provided strong evidence that the family had secretly transferred large sums of money abroad. Second, it forced the ex-president to publicly admit for the first time to having hidden wealth overseas, and this would make it more difficult for Chen to maintain his claims of innocence on the multiple charges of bribe-taking in future court hearings.

The Swiss request for legal assistance from Taiwan also helped foster closer cooperation between the two countries in probing the Chen family's complex cross-border money laundering activities. For

Taiwan, this mutual judicial assistance would also prove helpful in the future in retrieving at least some of the money that the Chen family had secretly moved to Switzerland.

The SID responded swiftly to Switzerland's judicial assistance request. Within a week of Chen Shui-bian's August 14 confession, Prosecutor Ching Chi-jen of the Taipei District Prosecutor's Office was dispatched to Switzerland to "help Swiss judicial officials in their investigation into the former president's son Chen Chih-chung and daughter-in-law Huang Jui-ching's questionable financial activities in their country."[67]

During her stay in Switzerland, the Taiwan prosecutor also asked Swiss judicial authorities to provide more details on the younger Chens' Swiss bank accounts. The request was met. Thanks to Switzerland's assistance, the SID found that Chen Shui-bian's son played a key role in the family's overseas financial activities. He made decisions on matters such as where money was to be transferred to, how bank accounts were opened, and establishing shell companies.

Initially, Chen Chih-chung insisted that he and his wife were innocent of any criminal role in the alleged money laundering scandal. In reply to press questions upon his return from the United States in August 2008, he said: "My mother has been handling the money. We did exactly as our mother instructed and didn't ask any questions." The younger Chens, who left for the United States before the money laundering scandal broke, were summoned by the SID to return to

---

67 Probe into Taiwan Ex-President Leads to Singapore, AFP, August 21, 2008.

Chapter 3
How the Chen Family Laundered Money across the Globe

Taipei to face questioning.[68]

In a critical development, the SID succeeded in securing Switzerland's agreement to return to Taiwan the full amount of the US$21 million deposits held in the names of the younger Chens, once Swiss authorities were presented with court papers by Taiwan to prove those assets were obtained through illegal means.

As noted earlier, on return from Switzerland, prosecutor Ching was sent to Singapore to gather information on the Chen family's financial activities in that country. According to the United Daily News, the Chen family had allegedly transferred funds to Switzerland via the Singapore bank accounts of Chen's brother-in-law Wu Ching-mao.

The information-rich document from Swiss authorities also inspired the SID to place more emphasis on investigating the Chen family's money laundering case -- one that involved not only Chen and his family members but also a dozen or so others. Up to this point, the SID had been focusing on probing a series of bribery and corruption allegations against the former first couple.

With the aid of the new leads from the Swiss document, together with Chen's public confession, the SID moved to expand the investigation into money laundering. The expanded probe began with an interview of the former first lady, who was suspected of directing the family's fund transfers both at home and abroad. Investigators not only wanted to know the role she played in the money laundering case. They also intended to obtain from her the answers to two central questions: how much money had the family acquired from bribes and

---

68 Taiwan Investigates Alleged Money Laundering, AP, August 25, 2008.

129

where had the funds been concealed?

The questioning of Mrs. Chen came a day after Chen Shui-bian publicly admitted that his wife had remitted some of his "leftover campaign funds" abroad without his knowledge. After questioning Mrs. Chen, prosecutors and investigators scrambled to search Chen's offices and the couple's homes in Taipei and the southern city of Tainan, taking away boxes of documents. At the end of the search and questioning, the SID listed the former president and his wife as well as the couple's son and daughter-in-law as defendants in the money laundering case.

Raids and interviews continued in the weeks that followed. SID prosecutors detained more than half a dozen former administration aides, senior bankers, and family friends, for their roles in the money laundering scandal. The sweeping investigations climaxed in November of 2008 with the detention of Chen Shui-bian.

Unsurprisingly, Chen's detention made headlines around the world. The man detained on corruption and money laundering charges was not just a former president; he was also a champion of democracy in Taiwan and his years of dedication to this cause contributed greatly to the island's transformation from decades of authoritarian rule.

Moreover, he was an ardent advocate of Taiwan's independence from China. As president, he was willing to risk the ire of Beijing as well as the United States, Taiwan's principal partner on the global political stage, in his pursuit of this ambitious goal. For many people, the sharp contrast between his strong democratic and political convictions and staggering moral weakness was hard to fathom.

The worldwide attention paid to the Chen case also had much to do with the former Taiwan leader's style. Chen was a populist

Chapter 3
How the Chen Family Laundered Money across the Globe

politician with a knack for winning voter sympathy and support. This skill in winning public sympathy, honed over his numerous election campaigns in the past, was now applied to his battle against corruption and money laundering charges.

From the moment the SID launched an investigation into his many suspected offenses, Chen portrayed himself as the victim of persecution. He railed against the KMT, the new ruling party, accusing it of pursuing a political vendetta against him and his family.

In the eyes of many international observers and political activists, Chen's legal problems were indeed a source of concern. They were alarmed that the arrest of this champion of democracy came so soon after power was transferred to the KMT -- the party that Chen had defeated in two fiercely contested presidential elections.

With Chen Shui-bian taken into custody, the SID decided to bring its wide-ranging investigations to a temporary halt so that its prosecutors could focus on drawing up what they called a first round of indictments against the former leader and others. An SID spokesman explained that indictments needed to be filed in stages because the cases implicating the former first family were numerous and complex.

In December, one month after Chen's arrest, the SID filed its first batch of indictments against him, his wife, and more than a dozen others. The indictments contained four broad charges: embezzling state affairs funds, taking bribes, forgery, and money laundering. In many ways, these cases were interrelated, significantly complicating the task of investigators.

Cover-up by Bureau of Investigation Director

After filing its first series of indictments against the Chens, the SID
went on to investigate the still-unfolding money laundering scandal.
Discoveries quickly emerged. Two of them were remarkable for their
audacity.

One discovery was a finding that Chen Shui-bian's Bureau of
Investigation Director Yeh Sheng-mao had covered up the Chen
family's overseas money laundering activities. The cover-up severely
delayed the progress of the investigation by prosecutors probing the
scandal.

Another jarring discovery was that the Chen family was found to
have far more assets hidden abroad, in addition to the deposits of
US$21 million with the Geneva office of Merrill Lynch Bank (Suisse)
and the Royal Bank of Scotland (Switzerland) that Swiss prosecutors
had frozen in January 2008.

Yeh Sheng-mao, the man who served as Chen Shui-bian's director
for almost all of Chen's eight-year presidency, was found to have twice
concealed documents given to his office by the Egmont Group -- an
international organization that shares information on suspicious
financial activities around the world. The Egmont Group had informed
Yeh's bureau that Chen Shui-bian's wife, their son and daughter-in-law,
and other relatives were suspected of laundering funds through the use
of bank accounts created overseas.

But the man in charge of the bureau focused on national security
and combatting serious crimes, concealed the Egmont documents,
effectively quashing any possible investigation. On both occasions,

Chapter 3
How the Chen Family Laundered Money across the Globe

Yeh personally submitted copies of the confidential Egmont documents to the president, a prime suspect in the money laundering case. Yeh tipped off his boss that some of his family's secret offshore bank accounts had been targeted by the anti-money laundering watchdog, and that he needed to make new arrangements to avoid regulatory scrutiny.

Yeh's behavior was incomprehensible. An official at the Ottawa-based Egmont Group, when approached by a Taiwanese reporter for comment, expressed shock that the confidential information could have been passed on to the party involved in the case. The official, who spoke on condition of anonymity, said: "The organization has never experienced a scandal like this since its creation in 1995."

In December of 2006 -- midway through Chen Shui-bian's second and final four-year term -- the Investigation Bureau received its first Egmont document about alleged money laundering by the Chen family. The document raised suspicions that Taiwan's first lady had used the name of her brother Wu Ching-mao to wire money to Singapore via trust bank accounts opened in a third area, the island of Jersey.

Instead of forwarding the financial intelligence for investigation, according to court documents, Yeh rushed to Chen's residence and personally handed the president a copy of the document. Chen immediately passed on the information to his wife, telling her that the funds she sent to Singapore under her brother's name had been tracked by the financial intelligence center in Jersey, a member of the Egmont Group.

Alarmed that family bank accounts in Singapore had been targeted by financial watchdogs, investigators said, Mrs. Chen held an emergency meeting with her son and daughter-in-law to discuss a response. The funds were soon withdrawn from Singapore and transferred to a new and presumably safer place.

"To this end, I instructed my son Chen Chih-chung to retain the services of a U.S. lawyer, asking him or her to help us open new bank accounts and establish paper companies in places outside Singapore," Mrs. Chen later told investigators. Why did Mrs. Chen want to make that "admission?" As one investigator explained to reporters: "She wanted investigators to believe that she made all the important decisions in the money laundering case and that her son played only a passive role."

Funds on the Move

With expert advice, the family finally chose to transfer funds to Switzerland, a country long known for its banking secrecy.[69] Huang Jui-ching, the younger Chen's wife, acted as the front person in moving the funds this time. She opened two bank accounts with Merrill Lynch Bank (Suisse) in her own name. Huang later told investigators that she did so at the request of her husband, a statement widely reported by the

---

69 The expert was widely reported in the local media to be a senior financial advisor from Bank of America Merrill Lynch in the United States, who flew into Taipei in late December 2006 to advise the Chen family on ways to relocate its massive deposits in Singapore. Chen Shui-bian's son Chen Chih-chung arranged the Taipei trip for the unidentified Merrill Lynch officer during a brief visit to New York. But the younger Chen denied he had made the arrangement during court hearings on his role in the money laundering case.

local media.

According to the information contained in the document given to Taiwan by the Swiss judicial authorities, the younger Chens made the first transfer of funds from Singapore to Switzerland in mid-February 2007. The initial remittance was made two months after Chen Shui-bian was tipped off by his Investigation Bureau director that the first family's suspicious financial transactions in Singapore and Jersey had aroused the interest of the anti-money laundering watchdog.

Several more transfers of Chen family funds were made to Switzerland in the following weeks. Altogether, a total of US$21 million was shifted to that country between February 15 and March 5 in 2007. All of those funds were deposited in Huang Jui-ching's newly opened bank accounts with Merrill Lynch Bank (Suisse).

Judging from the timing of the movement of the funds, prosecutors concluded that Yeh Sheng-mao's leak of the Jersey financial intelligence to Chen Shui-bian was indeed the main reason behind the family's decision to shift funds from Singapore to Switzerland.

Even with the funds placed in a new home, the Chen family was still concerned that they were not necessarily free from detection. So the younger Chens decided to make further account transfers with the US$21 million to ensure that the money could be more securely concealed. Unlike their previous money transfers that moved across national borders, these were made within Switzerland.

According to the same Swiss document, the first such new account transfer was made about two months later in May following the establishment of a shell company called Bouchon Ltd. The paper company was registered under Huang Jui-chung's name and domiciled in the Cayman Islands. Huang's position at the company was proprietor, while her husband was an authorized signatory.

What was Huang going to do with the creation of Bouchon Ltd.? First, she used the company to open two new bank accounts, also with the Merrill Lynch Bank (Suisse). Then she moved the US$21 million -- which up to this point had been kept in her personal Merrill Lynch Bank accounts after their relocation from Singapore -- into the two newly opened accounts in the name of Bouchon.

One major purpose of setting up the shell company and having the money transferred into its bank accounts was to create a corporate link for the laundered funds, making the money look like legitimate trade-generated income. By having the US$21 million transferred one more time from Ms. Huang's personal Merrill Lynch bank accounts to those of the shell company, the family intended to add to the difficulties in tracing the funds to their original sources, experts observed.

For the same reasons, her husband asked the Zurich branch of the Royal Bank of Scotland to help establish a second shell company called Galahad Management, shortly after the creation of the Cayman-registered Bouchon. With the new dummy company in place, the younger Chen emailed Merrill Lynch Bank (Suisse), instructing it to take US$10 million out of his and his wife's Bouchon accounts, and have the money transferred into the accounts of their new company, Galahad Management.

The younger Chens continued to play a money transfer game thereafter, according to the Swiss document. In November of the same year, Huang Jui-ching wrote to the Royal Bank of Scotland with a request to withdraw the US$10 million that her husband had deposited at the bank in the name of Galahad Management more than a month earlier. Huang instructed the Royal Bank of Scotland to transfer the money back into Merrill Lynch Bank accounts held in the name of Bouchon Ltd.

The transfers of the US$10 million between Merrill Lynch Bank and the Royal Bank of Scotland aroused the suspicion of Swiss authorities, including federal prosecutors. They suspected that the interbank fund transfers were money laundering activities designed to avoid scrutiny.

Refusing to Reveal Fund Origins

The reluctance of the younger Chens to provide details about the funds they transferred back and forth between the two shell companies reinforced that suspicion. As a result, on January 9, 2008, Swiss federal prosecutors moved to freeze the accounts of both Bouchon and Galahad, pending further investigation. At the time, the accounts had combined deposits of US$21 million.

Ironically, the efforts by Chen Chih-chung and his wife to make their funds more difficult to track had achieved the exact opposite effect.

From the very beginning, the younger Chens appeared to be intent on hiding the identities of the former president and first lady when wiring the family's funds abroad. In opening foreign bank accounts and establishing shell companies, the younger Chens used their names, instead of their parents. The reason was obvious: Their parents were widely known figures and would more easily attract attention.

Switzerland took its time informing Taiwan of its decision to freeze the younger Chens' bank accounts and its suspicions about possible money laundering. Taiwan learned of the case six months after its authorities received the request for judicial assistance from the Office of the Attorney General of Switzerland, as recounted in earlier pages.

It was the Cayman Islands' financial intelligence unit that immediately notified Taiwan of the Chen family's suspicious financial activities, making use of the anti-money laundering facility of the Egmont Group. The Cayman notification came just one week after Switzerland froze the younger Chens' bank accounts.

In a secret document delivered to Taiwan's Bureau of Investigation, according to investigators, the Cayman Islands' financial intelligence unit expressed its concern that Chen Shui-bian and his wife were laundering money through a number of bank accounts created in the names of their son and daughter-in-law. The money laundering tip provided by the Cayman Islands would have helped Taiwan's judicial authorities wrap up their probe into the Chen family's corruption and financial scandals much sooner had it not been for a second cover-up by Chen Shui-bian's loyal ally, Bureau of Investigation Director Yeh Sheng-mao.

As related earlier, it was Yeh's suppression of intelligence regarding Mrs. Chen's financial activities in Singapore that had slowed a judicial probe of the first lady, giving her time to relocate funds to Switzerland. The cover-up unfolded as follows:

The Investigation Bureau has a section devoted to combating

Chapter 3
How the Chen Family Laundered Money across the Globe

money laundering. It was this office that first saw a copy of the Cayman Islands intelligence. Acting on the information, officials from that key section wrote a report intended for delivery to the Supreme Prosecutor's Office recommending that investigative action be taken against the Chen family.

But Yeh thought otherwise. He did not want the money laundering intelligence from the Cayman Islands to be forwarded to the Supreme Prosecutor's Office, as this would certainly lead to a probe of his boss – the president – and the first lady. Both of them had already come under investigation by the SID for a series of bribery allegations.

Yeh used a seemingly legitimate reason to hold up his subordinates' reports. He explained to the bureau's anti-money laundering section chief Chou You-yi, according to a Taipei District Court paper, "the matter was so confidential and sensitive that it had to be handled with great care."

Yeh requested that the report be handed over to him so that he could personally pass it on to Chen Tsung-ming, then director of the Supreme Prosecutor's Office. But Yeh never acted on this assurance. Prosecutor General Chen Tsung-ming recalled in a subsequent prosecutorial interview: "I never received the kind of report Yeh mentioned."

Asked by investigators why he had not relayed the intelligence from the Cayman Islands, Yeh replied he was busy with national security work. By "busy with national security work," Yeh may have been referring to Taiwan's presidential election campaign, then in full swing.[70] While term limits prevented Chen Shui-bian from running again, the president had a keen interest in who would succeed him.

But what about the document from the Cayman Islands? Asked where it went, Yeh replied that he had lost it, but a search of his home by investigators yielded a photocopy. "The fact that Yeh was careful to keep a photocopy of the Cayman document at his home proved untrue his claim that he was so busy as to completely forget about the matter," the Taipei District Prosecutor's Office said in its indictment of the Investigation Bureau chief. Yet the whereabouts of the original copy remained unknown. Chen Shui-bian had also consistently denied having received any such document from Yeh.

What was also unimaginable was that the suppression of information on the Chen family's unusual fund transfers failed to come to light until August 2008. This was seven months after the Cayman Islands informed Taiwan that Chen Shui-bian's son and daughter-in-law were suspected of using shell companies to launder money to Switzerland, and 20 months after Jersey authorities notified Taiwan that the first lady had used the island as a transit point for moving large

---

70 Investigation Bureau Chief Yeh Sheng-mao's cover-up of the Cayman money laundering intelligence took place at a sensitive time in Taiwan's politics. First, Chen Shui-bian's DPP party had just lost the 12 January 2008 legislative elections to the opposition KMT in a devastating defeat--only days before Yeh's bureau received the Cayman document. Second, a more crucial presidential election was due in two months in March, but opinion polls had since the opening of the year continued to show the KMT's Ma Ying-jeou well ahead of DPP candidate Frank Hsieh. It was against such a background that Yeh, in his words, "had completely forgotten to act on the Cayman intelligence report."

sums of money to Singapore.

Yeh Convicted in Intelligence Cover-up

The cover-up scandal broke only following a special investigation ordered by the Ministry of Justice. The order was prompted by the judicial document from the Swiss Office of the Attorney General, which asked Taiwan to help investigate the suspicious US$21 million deposited in bank accounts in Switzerland, as recounted earlier.

After studying the document's description of how the younger Chens laundered the tens of millions of U.S. dollars to Switzerland, the ministry raised two questions. One, how was it possible for such large sums of money to have been sent out of Taiwan without being discovered by regulatory authorities? Two, why hadn't Taiwan, as a member of the Egmont Group, heard anything about the Chen family's cross-border money laundering activities?

On closer examination, investigators finally realized that the Bureau of Investigation had twice been informed by the Egmont Group -- once in December 2006 and again in January 2008 -- that Chen Shui-bian and his family were suspected of laundering money through offshore bank accounts and that none other than the bureau's director had concealed the information on both occasions.

As a result of the findings, Yeh was placed under investigation by prosecutors of the Taipei District Prosecutor's Office. It took little more than a week for investigators to complete their probe. The speedy cracking of the cover-up scandal reflected the fact that the evidence was explicit and easy to obtain – once authorities knew what to look for. In the indictment, prosecutors proposed a two-and-a-half-year sentence for Yeh on a charge of "covering up the Cayman Islands' money laundering intelligence implicating the Chen Shui-bian family."

During his first trial at the Taipei District Court, Yeh was sentenced to eight and a half years in jail, a far harsher sentence than the prosecution had proposed. Judges invoked different law provisions and found him guilty of "benefiting others," or graft, in the Chen family's money laundering case.

Three years later in 2011, Yeh was indicted for concealing intelligence from Jersey and leaking it to Chen Shui-bian.[71] Yet in this case, the Taipei District Court acquitted Yeh of the crime. After appeals in both cases, the high court ultimately shortened Yeh's sentence to 16 months on a charge of "concealing documents," dropping the other allegation of "leaking information." The verdict was final since neither the prosecution nor the defendant lodged a further appeal this time.

Commenting on the verdict, a spokesman for the high court condemned the former intelligence chief for his criminal behavior, saying this "had seriously damaged Taiwan's image and, in particular, the credibility of its judicial institutions." However, the spokesman added, "Because Yeh Sheng-mao has pleaded guilty and shown deep remorse for his misconduct, the high court panel decided to give him a lighter jail term of one year and four months."

Despite all of the reputational damage from the leaking of Egmont intelligence to Chen Shui-bian, there was one positive footnote to this

71 An investigation into the Jersey case was launched belatedly in 2011 only at the request of the Taiwan High Court, and not at the initiative of prosecutors.

Chapter 3
How the Chen Family Laundered Money across the Globe

sorry episode: The discovery of Yeh's cover-up helped prosecutors refute Chen Shui-bian's claims that he had no knowledge of his wife's money transfers and that his family had no funds kept secretly in overseas bank accounts. Yeh's offenses were later cited by the SID as a crucial part of the evidence against Chen Shui-bian and his family members in deciding to indict them for corruption and money laundering.

A Major Challenge for the SID

The task of finding out exactly how much money the Chen family had transferred abroad and where the money was concealed was a significant challenge for the SID, especially in the initial stages of the investigations. Chen Shui-bian had consistently denied any wrongdoing and was unwilling to cooperate in the SID probe.

To be sure, Chen had admitted in his high-profile August 2008 confession that his wife had wired money abroad "without his knowledge." But he made the admission only after the news broke that funds in Switzerland had already been frozen by Swiss federal prosecutors. In other words, his willingness to cooperate emerged only when he was caught in the act.

However, the bank deposits of US$21 million frozen by Switzerland were not the only assets hidden abroad by the Chen family. New evidence that surfaced in subsequent investigations confirmed that the family had held considerably more, including two expensive properties in the United States.

As mentioned earlier, the SID decided to shift its focus in the

143

investigation from Chen's corruption cases to his money laundering activities soon after it received the document on the Chen family's questionable financial transactions in Switzerland. The shift in emphasis meant that the SID would spend more time and energy from then onward on detecting the overseas assets of the former president. It wanted to find out how much more money his family had moved abroad--beyond the large sum already frozen by Swiss federal prosecutors—and where any such funds were concealed.

To this end, the SID sought law enforcement cooperation from foreign countries, mainly Singapore, Switzerland, and the United States. These countries were called on for help as they were seen as the most likely places that the Chen family might have chosen as safe destinations for hiding its wealth.

This strategy soon proved fruitful. In the following months, the SID discovered that the Chen family had more secret bank accounts in Singapore and Switzerland than those already exposed. Additionally, the SID also learned of the properties in the U.S. These properties were suspected of having been bought with bribe money received from a company in Taiwan, in this case, Yuanta Financial.

The SID's success in uncovering these additional assets held secretly offshore was due largely to the assistance from the judicial authorities of the three countries cited above.

As described in earlier pages, Mrs. Chen transferred US$1.9 million from her brother Wu Ching-mao's accounts at a Singapore branch of the Dutch bank ABN AMRO into four accounts at Goldman Sachs' London and Hong Kong offices. This was in late February of 2008, about three months before Chen Shui-bian stepped down.

Chapter 3
How the Chen Family Laundered Money across the Globe

The four Goldman Sachs accounts, as investigators later learned, were provided by Wu Li-pei, a senior presidential adviser to Chen Shui-bian and a fellow advocate of Taiwan independence. The money was transferred in four separate transactions to avoid arousing regulatory suspicion, investigators said.

The SID had failed to detect the February 2008 cross-border money transfers until more than a half year later. Significantly, this was a time when Singapore had just responded positively to the SID's request for law enforcement assistance. The response included giving information on as many as 10 secret bank accounts opened and owned by Mrs. Chen Shui-bian and her relatives in that country.

A Major Coup for the SID

Getting Singapore's cooperation was a major coup for the SID. The agency's spokesman Chen Yun-nan gave credit to Singaporean authorities at a press conference, saying that the "bank account information given to us by the government of Singapore was quite helpful in our ongoing investigation into the Chen family's illegal overseas financial transactions."

As a result of that help, the SID quickly placed Wu Li-pei, Chen Shui-bian, and Mrs. Chen under investigation for their roles in the cross-border transfers of the US$1.9 million in question. SID prosecutors noted that amount was the balance in the family's bank accounts in Singapore after the US$21 million was moved to

Switzerland in early 2007.[72]

Wu Li-pei told investigators that while he provided the four bank accounts to Chen Shui-bian, none of them bore his name. "I only had access to those accounts," Wu said. But then why did Wu agree to these banking arrangements? His reply to investigators was that he did so out of respect for Chen Shui-bian's steady efforts to raise Taiwan's international profile.

"I was invited by the former president to his official residence for a meeting with him on February 3, 2008. At the meeting, President Chen said to me that he was willing to provide some capital to help promote Taiwan's diplomatic relations," Wu told prosecutors. "I was so moved by his love for Taiwan that I immediately agreed to do what I was asked," referring to providing the Goldman Sachs accounts.[73]

Chen Shui-bian's invitation to Wu Li-pei to discuss his intention to transfer "some capital" to the latter's accounts to promote Taiwan's international relations came shortly after Switzerland moved to freeze the US$21 million in that country.[74] The timing of Chen's decision to move the US$1.9 million elsewhere led investigators to reach the following conclusion: The former president withdrew the remaining

---

72 The US$21 million which Huang Jui-ching transferred from Singapore to Switzerland in early 2007 was confirmed by both Taiwan and Swiss investigators to be the same money as was frozen by the Swiss judicial authorities 11 months later in January 2008.

73 Rich Chang, Wu Li-pei Brought in for Questioning on Wire Transfers, Taipei Times, October 12, 2008.

74 Note: The intended use of the controversial US$1.9 million varied in media reports. Some news reports also quoted Chen Shui-bian as saying that the said money was meant for use by him to promote Taiwan's diplomatic relations after his retirement.

Chapter 3
How the Chen Family Laundered Money across the Globe

deposits from Singapore out of concern that Switzerland's freezing of the family's bank accounts there could result in the discovery of the funds by Taiwan's judicial authorities.

Throughout the probe, Wu Li-pei emphatically denied that he had personal relationships with any member of the Chen family. "I neither knew his wife, his son nor his daughter personally," Wu said. That statement was probably true, but he omitted one vital element in his ties to Chen Shui-bian. The relationship between them went beyond that of a president and his political appointee. The two shared political values and objectives. Both strongly advocated a fully independent Taiwan and spent long years working toward that goal. Such a special relationship might help to explain why Wu Li-pei could be so easily convinced of Chen Shui-bian's claim that he needed additional bank accounts to hide money for use in Taiwan's "diplomatic affairs," according to political analysts.

But Wu Li-pei could not hide his disappointment in Chen for divulging his help in arranging the bank accounts used in transferring the US$1.9 million. "I was surprised that Chen disclosed my identity in the case since this was certain to bring problems for me and my corporate business," newspapers quoted Wu Li-pei as saying. He was speaking to reporters outside the SID office, where he was summoned for questioning about his role in the offshore fund transfers.

Wu Li-pei later was indicted for helping the Chen family launder money. But he was acquitted of the charge by an appeals court, as were a dozen or so other businessmen who were also on trial for aiding the Chen family's unlawful financial activities. The acquittals by the Taiwan High Court did not mean the court found them guiltless. Rather, it was due to a legal technicality - because of a lack of "adequate provisions" in the law to impose punishments on them, according to a high court spokesman.

It is unclear whether Wu Li-pei, a veteran banker with intimate knowledge of cross-border financial transactions, had ever asked himself whether the Chen family money that passed through his bank accounts had come from bribes, particularly at a time when Chen Shui-bian had already been tarred by numerous allegations of corruption.

The Origin of a US$1.9 Million Deposit in Singapore

A key point that Taipei District Court judges trying the case of Chen's questionable US$1.9 million deposit in Singapore wanted to ascertain was the legitimacy of the money in question. The judges first asked Chen the question of why his wife wanted to transfer a sum of US$1.9 million from their accounts at ABN AMRO bank in Singapore to the Goldman Sachs offices in London and Hong Kong in February 2008.

His reply was as follows: "My wife told me we still had some US$1.9 million in an ABN AMRO branch in Singapore, which had not been frozen [by judicial authorities]. The money, she explained to me, was intended for use in promoting Taiwan's international diplomacy after my retirement. I then urged her to apply the full amount of the money to that purpose now, rather than wait until after I left office. So I consulted with a Taiwanese elder of some repute about my idea. He responded positively. Then my wife remitted the money, in four transactions, into the four bank accounts he designated."

When questioned about the origins of those funds, Chen used his standard defense that these were leftover election campaign funds. He insisted that the US$1.9 million was similar to the US$21 million that was deposited in Switzerland and later frozen by Swiss federal prosecutors. They were not illegal funds, he insisted.

Lee Ying-hao, the head of a three-judge panel, asked: "If their sources were legitimate, then why did you want to move the funds around through multiple account transfers and into several specially created bank accounts? Such remitting arrangements cost considerably more than normal banking procedures. Isn't that right?" Judge Lee also asked: "Why was it necessary for you to deposit the US$1.9 million abroad if it was meant for use in promoting Taiwan's international relations?" Chen gave no convincing answers to either of the two questions, according to media reports on the hearings.

Still, when questioned if his transfers of money from Singapore to Goldman Sachs' offices were prompted by an attempt to escape tracking by investigators, Chen protested. "This was a trumped-up charge against me. I must reaffirm that the money under investigation was truly set aside by me for use to support Taiwan's diplomatic work and other public affairs after my retirement."

During the investigation, SID prosecutors refuted Chen's argument that the US$1.9 million was intended for diplomatic purposes.[75] They came to that conclusion based on the testimony of Yeh Ling-ling, a witness in a separate case who testified that Mrs. Chen insisted that the funds belonged to her when she opened the account

---

75 Supreme Prosecutor's Office News Release, issued by the Special Investigation Division, September 16, 2011.

and were to be left for use by their son and daughter-in-law.

A Third Money Laundering Scandal Brought to Light

New money laundering cases by Chen's family members emerged after Chen departed from office in May 2008. A third case was filed in November of that year after SID prosecutors learned from witnesses that Chen Shui-bian and his wife had in 2007 transferred a separate NT$540 million (about US$17.6 million) into the private Swiss bank Wegelin.[76]

The most recent discovery of the Chen family having more secret bank accounts in Switzerland came just one month after Chen Shui-bian's wife was found to have transferred the US$1.9 million from a Singapore account to Goldman Sachs' London and Hong Kong operations. And it was about three months since Chen's first public admission that he and his family had some US$21 million deposited in Merrill Lynch Bank (Suisse) in Geneva and an arm of the Royal Bank of Scotland in Zurich.

Taken together, the three separate money laundering scandals suggested that Chen Shui-bian and his wife had unlawfully wired a total of some US$41 million into bank accounts in foreign countries during his presidency.

As noted earlier, the above figures did not include the two U.S. properties which had a combined value of US$2.1 million. The two

---

76 Wegelin was forced to shut its doors permanently in 2013 after pleading guilty to a U.S. indictment charging the bank with helping American citizens to dodge taxes through secret accounts.

Chapter 3
How the Chen Family Laundered Money across the Globe

properties were purchased with the proceeds of bribes paid to the Chens, according to U.S. and Taiwanese investigators. They were placed in forfeiture proceedings by the U.S. Department of Justice in 2012 for violating American anti-money laundering laws. (The U.S. property scandal will be related in greater detail later in this chapter.)

Regarding the NT$540 million deposited at Wegelin in the names of the Chens' son and daughter-in-law, a closer examination by the SID prosecutors found the money was originally part of the NT$740 million, stored in a huge vault at Taipei's Cathay United Bank.[77]

There was no evidence of when the Chen family began hiding funds in the Cathay United Bank vault. Nor was there any reliable data on the source or sources of that money. But it was clear that Chen, as a public servant for most of his life, could not possibly have accumulated a fortune of that size on salary alone.

Yet the confessions made by the former first couple to investigators did reveal some vital information concerning the above questions. Mrs. Chen revealed the Cathay United Bank vault was rented in the name of her sister-in-law Chen Chun-ying. At one point, she said, it contained cash over NT$1.1 billion or about US$34.38 million. All such funds were donated as "political contributions" by domestic financial holding companies and industrial enterprises. The confessions made by Chen Shui-bian himself at court hearings were

---

77 Liu Chun-koo, Mrs. Chen Shui-bian Urges Tu Li-ping not to Disclose the Origin of NT$540 Million Wired Abroad, United Daily News, December 19, 2008.

the same, according to newspaper reports.[78]

At the time the scandal was first exposed, according to testimony from prosecutors at court hearings, there was a total of NT$740 million in the bank vault. It was later moved to another location – the basement of a financier's private residence. From there, the bulk of the funds were secretly remitted outside of Taiwan.

It was in the second half of 2006, according to investigators, that Mrs. Chen Shui-bian came up with the idea of moving the NT$740 million away from the Cathay United Bank vault. She asked a director at Yuanta Financial Holdings, Tu Li-ping, a longtime friend of hers, to help find a new hiding place, stating that "several persons had learned about the money and its location."

Mrs. Chen had reason to be particularly careful not to allow the funds in the Cathay bank vault to be discovered as the president and his family members were facing an array of political and legal difficulties. First, Chen Shui-bian himself was fast becoming a lame-duck president, making him an easy target for his opponents. Even worse, both his family and his administration were assailed by mounting allegations of corruption.

Chen's son-in-law Chao Chien-ming had just been charged with suspected insider trading and the first lady was coming under daily attack for allegedly using her influence to obtain financial gains. Family troubles aside, two of Chen Shui-bian's top aides were implicated in financial scandals also at the time.

78 Wang Wen-ling, Chen Shui-bian Confesses the Amounts of Money Hidden at Cathay United Bank at One Time Ran Much Higher than NT$700 Million, United Daily News, December 19, 2008.

It was against such a background that Mrs. Chen found it necessary to move the money from the Cathay bank vault to a "safer" place. After learning of the first lady's concerns, Tu Li-ping, the Yuanta board director, advised her that a storage space was available in a vault in the basement of the private residence of the chief executive officer of Yuanta Financial Holdings -- Ms. Tu's boss.

Moving NT$740 Million in Cash to the Yuanta CEO's Home

Mrs. Chen, with the help of half a dozen people, moved the NT$740 million in cash, contained in up to eight suitcases, from the Cathay bank vault to the basement of the home of Ma Wei-chien, the Yuanta CEO. Those who helped move the funds included Mrs. Chen's son, her brother Wu Ching-mao and his wife, and the Yuanta director, Ms. Tu Li-ping.[79]

Ma Wei-chien, the Yuanta CEO, later told a court hearing that he had agreed to keep such a huge sum of money for former President Chen Shui-bian "purely out of sympathy." He explained: "The first lady's brother Wu Ching-mao came to my office one day and pleaded with me, saying that the Cathay bank vault money was set aside to provide for Chen's living expenses after his retirement."

However, according to court documents, Yuanta's help went beyond the storage of those funds. In 2004, the company had paid a

---

79 Ku Liang-chieh and Wang Chih-yu, Mrs. Chen Shui-bian Asks Wu Ching-mao et al to Help Move NT$740 Million from Cathay Bank to Ma Wei-chien's Residence, China Times, December 19, 2008.

NT$200 million (about US$6.5 million) bribe to the first lady in exchange for support from her husband's government for the company's bid to gain controlling ownership of a smaller financial company, Fuhua.

Ma Wei-chien only narrowly escaped judicial punishment for his actions. In December 2009 when the SID indicted Chen Shui-bian, his wife, and their son and daughter-in-law for money laundering and crimes involving corruption, the Yuanta's CEO was also indicted. His alleged crimes involved bribing the Chens and helping them conceal corrupt funds. Ma, however, was finally acquitted of the two charges by the Supreme Court, as were the many other defendants. He was acquitted because the court found that existing law lacked suitable provisions to punish businessmen for the kind of crimes they were charged with.

The NT$740 million did not stay in its new hiding place in the basement vault for long. Several months later in early 2007, Mrs. Chen Shui-bian, again through her friend Tu Li-Ping, told the Yuanta boss that she wished to move the basement funds into the "official banking system." Mrs. Chen gave two reasons for doing so, according to Ms. Tu's testimony. One, she feared the money could someday be traced to Ma Wei-chien's basement vault. Two, she wished to use the money to make investments overseas, according to Ms. Tu's court testimony.

Yuanta CEO Helps Move Money Offshore

To comply with Mrs. Chen's instructions, Ma Wei-chien worked out an overseas investment plan and personally presented it to the first lady

Chapter 3
How the Chen Family Laundered Money across the Globe

for her approval. As called for in the plan, Ma took NT$540 million
(US$17.2 million) out of the NT$740 million that the Chens had just
relocated into his basement vault for investment overseas.

To avoid detection by government authorities, Ma devised a
sophisticated plan for making the remittances intended for offshore
investment: First, he established a shell company, called Asian Piston
Investment Ltd. and registered it in the British Virgin Islands, on behalf
of the first lady. The officers and directors of the shell company
included Tu Li-ping, Ma, and his mother. Then, he moved funds from
his personal overseas accounts to Asian Piston. Finally, he recouped
the funds taken out from his personal overseas accounts by making
daily withdrawals from the cash that Mrs. Chen had stored in his
basement vault.[80]

Several months later in or around August 2007, Mrs. Chen again
instructed Ma to transfer a total of US$17.5 million from Asian Piston
into an account in the name of Avallo Ltd. at Wegelin Bank in
Switzerland.

In December of the same year, Avallo transferred US$17.5 million
from its account to an account owned by Bravo International Holdings,
an Island of Nevis company. Notably, the son of the former Taiwan
president had sole signature authority over the accounts of both Bravo
and Avallo.[81]

---

80 The information about how Ma Wei-chien helped Mrs. Chen Shui-bian
    wire the NT$540 million to Asian Piston and then to the Wegelin bank
    of Switzerland--a significant portion of which was later moved to the
    United States—was sourced from U.S. and Taiwan judicial papers.
81 Ibid.

With the NT$540 million sent overseas, the balance of funds, amounting to more than NT$170 million, was also pulled away from Ma's basement vault and deposited in a number of other domestic banks under dummy accounts. These fake bank accounts, however, failed to escape detection by investigators. They were seized by the SID soon after the money laundering scandal broke.

For the SID, the hardest part of pursuing this third case of money laundering by the Chen family was recovering the NT$540 million (about US$17.2 million) that had been transferred to the Wegelin bank via the shell company Asian Piston.

The SID first wrote to the Swiss Office of Attorney General asking it to freeze Chen Chih-chung's Wegelin bank accounts in December 2008, one month after Taiwan's investigators became aware of its existence. The Swiss attorney general agreed to the request and ordered Wegelin to freeze those deposits. However, Swiss authorities were slow to return the deposits to Taiwan, and some of the funds presumably remain in Switzerland to this day.

One difficulty the SID encountered in retrieving the Wegelin deposits was that the Chen family had refused to comply with its request to remit the funds to Taiwan. Such compliance was necessary as Wegelin would not allow its customers' funds to be withdrawn by an unauthorized third party.

This was a different situation than in the effort to retrieve the US$21 million at Merrill Lynch Bank (Suisse) and the Royal Bank of Scotland (Zurich). In those cases, the Chen family had agreed to remit the deposits in the hope that their cooperation with judicial authorities would win Chen Shui-bian's release from detention. The former president at the time had been in custody for several months since his arrest in November 2008. His family members were keen to win the court's permission to free him on bail, promising to return "all the funds" they had wired abroad.

Besides the willingness of the Chen family to cooperate, the attitude taken by Switzerland at the time was also helpful in the SID's effort to recover the amount of US$21 million. In that case, the Swiss government, in effect, took the initiative to unfreeze the related funds, allowing them to be returned to their homeland.

Why was that so? One, it was the Swiss Office of Attorney General that ordered the freeze of the Chen family's accounts at Merrill Lynch Bank (Suisse) and the Royal Bank of Scotland (Zurich). It gave the order because the deposits at the two banks were found by Swiss investigators to be illegitimate money, "originating from the criminal activities of Taiwan's former President Chen Shui-bian."

At the same time, prosecutorial investigations, indictments, and court convictions in Taiwan had all proved that the US$21 million indeed were payments that Chen Shui-bian and his wife took, including a Longtan land procurement deal, a corruption scandal involving the construction of the Nangang Exhibition Center, and the embezzlement of public funds.

These two factors -- the agreement of the Chen family to return their illegal funds and the willingness of the Swiss judicial authorities to release the money -- made it much easier for the SID to recover the US$21 million. Ultimately, it took about two years.

Chen Family Blocks Return of Wegelin Deposits

In the Wegelin bank deposit case, however, the Chen family refused to withdraw the deposits as the family insisted these funds were "clean" money stemming from "political donations" by supporters, not illegally acquired funds as charged by the SID. As mentioned earlier, Wegelin insisted on consent from the legitimately registered holders of those deposits.

Yet the Chen family's refusal to cooperate was not the only difficulty the SID had encountered in recovering the Wegelin deposits. Sharply differing opinions held by presiding judges at different courts in Taiwan on two underlying bribery cases and a separate money laundering charge against Chen Shui-bian and his wife further complicated the SID's efforts to retrieve the funds from the Wegelin bank.

From the start, the SID suspected the US$17.5 million (NT$540 million) that the younger Chens deposited at Wegelin were bribes paid to their parents by two Taiwan financial groups: Cathay and Yuanta. And these illegal funds were later moved to the Swiss bank to escape judicial prosecution. Therefore, Chen Shui-bian and his wife were indicted by the SID for alleged bribery and money laundering crimes, as cited above. However, owing to sharply different legal opinions, Taiwan's courts were slow to reach conclusive final verdicts on these cases. Without convictions, the SID was unable to prove the Chen family's Wegelin deposits were the proceeds of bribes and should be returned to Taiwan.

In December 2012, the Supreme Court finally made rulings on the two cases, convicting Chen Shui-bian and his wife of receiving NT$200 million (about US$6.4 million) from Yuanta in return for help in its acquisition of Fuhua Securities. But in the same verdict, the Supreme Court returned a separate case, in which the Chens were accused of taking NT$300 million (roughly US$9.5 million) from Cathay Financial Holdings in a similar bank merger scandal, to the Taiwan High Court for retrial on the grounds of failing to provide sufficient evidence.

With the proof of the Supreme Court's guilty conviction in connection with Yuanta, the SID in 2013 requested Switzerland return to Taiwan the US$6.4 million, a portion of the Chens' Wegelin deposits allegedly linked to the payments made by Yuanta.

In response, the Swiss Office of Attorney General in April 2014 agreed to return the requested amount to Taiwan.[82] But the younger Chens contested the Swiss move and appealed it to Switzerland's Federal Criminal Court. The appeal was turned down by the Swiss court in January 2015. The couple then took the case to the Supreme Court of Switzerland, where it was rejected again. The judgment by the Swiss Supreme Court was final. According to the SID, Taiwan received the funds released by Wegelin in connection with the Yuanta case, shortly after the Swiss Supreme Court ruled that the money should be returned.

With the portion of the money linked to Yuanta recovered, the question left for the SID was how to retrieve the remaining US$9.5

---

82 Chen Chih-hsien, Switzerland Returns US$6.74 million of Chen Shui-bian's Deposits to Taiwan, China Times, September 5, 2015.

million, suspected by investigators to be bribes paid by Cathay Financial Holdings and still frozen in the younger Chens' Wegelin bank accounts by Swiss authorities.

Retrieving the US$9.5 million became a question because of the uncertainty about how the court would rule on the related bribery case -- one in which Chen Shui-bian and his wife were charged with taking the said amount of funds from Cathay Financial Holdings. Allegedly, the Cathay Financial group gave the money, delivered in three installments between 2001 and 2004, to the Chens in exchange for the couple's support for its bid to merge with the former World Chinese United Bank, according to newspaper accounts quoting court sources.

The SID described the actions in this case as typical "negotiated bribery." But during trials at the Taipei District Court, a three-judge panel acquitted Chen Shui-bian and his wife Wu Shu-chen of such charges in both the Cathay and Yuanta bribery cases. The SID protested and appealed the rulings to the Taiwan High Court. After deliberation, a panel of three high court judges trying the multiple bribery cases reversed the district court's acquittals. They convicted Chen Shui-bian and his wife, sentencing them to 18 and 11 years in jail, respectively.

Not surprisingly, the defense appealed to the Supreme Court where more drama ensued. In December 2012, the highest court convicted Chen and his wife of corruption in the Yuanta case, sentencing the couple to lengthy jail terms: 10 years for Chen and eight years for his wife. However, the Supreme Court returned the bribery case involving alleged payments by Cathay Financial to the Taiwan High Court for retrial. The Cathay case has languished in the high court ever since.

Things took a further abrupt turn in January 2015 when Chen Shui-bian was released on medical parole. He was suffering from multiple illnesses, including "severe depression" and "brain degeneration." Eventually, there would be a total of five cases implicating Chen, including the Cathay case, where trials were suspended by Taiwan's district or high courts.

So the risk is that, if the Cathay case remains stalled at the high court -- which is most likely to be the case -- the SID would have no legal basis to prove to Swiss authorities that the remaining US$9.5 million from the accounts at the now defunct Wegelin bank are truly from ill-gotten gains and should therefore be returned to Taiwan.

Under these circumstances, Chen Shui-bian's son and daughter-in-law would not be able to withdraw the funds from Wegelin either. The reason is obvious: The failure of Taiwan's court to try the Cathay case because of the principal defendant's inability to attend hearings could not be construed as a ruling that the former president was innocent of the corruption charges and the family was entitled to the funds.

Bribes and Luxury Homes in the U.S.

In July 2010, the U.S. Department of Justice filed forfeiture complaints against two properties -- a condominium in New York and a house in Virginia, both owned by Chen family members. By that time, it was known that the first couple had huge amounts of money stashed away in Singapore and Switzerland, but it was not widely known that the family had hidden wealth in the United States.

Unlike the family's holdings in Singapore and Switzerland, which were kept in cash, the money wired to the U.S. eventually wound up in real estate. A property purchase in a foreign country by a former president shortly after leaving office might raise eyebrows but little more than that. The Chens, however, had two problems with their U.S. properties: The money for the purchases was from illegal payments and funds were funneled into the U.S. through complex, illegal means, violating universally enforced anti-money laundering laws and regulations.

The methods the Chen family used to transfer their questionable funds prompted two former U.S. officials who participated in investigating the case to make this comment: The actions taken by Chen Shui-bian and his son in purchasing the U.S. properties through an offshore shell company "can virtually serve as a textbook example of international money laundering."

According to the U.S. forfeiture complaints, the Chen family's two houses were bought for a total of US$2.1 million. As in the case of the family's Swiss bank deposits, the U.S. residences were registered in the names of Chen's son and daughter-in-law.

Unlike the investigation of the Chens' other overseas money laundering activities, the probe of their two U.S. properties was conducted almost entirely by the U.S. side – in this case, the Justice Department and Department of Homeland Security, with Taiwan playing only a supporting role, providing investigative assistance. The U.S. government spent at least about two years seeking to impound the two properties. In the process, it sent prosecutors and customs agents to Taiwan several times to obtain information and exchange views with the SID.

The civil forfeiture complaints, which were filed in U.S. district courts in New York and Virginia, were announced by Assistant Attorney General Lanny A. Breuer and Immigration and Customs Enforcement Director John Morton. "The forfeiture actions serve as a warning to those corrupt foreign officials who abuse their power for personal financial gains and then attempt to place those funds in the U.S. financial system," Morton said in a news release.

The U.S. judicial complaints stated that in 2005 and 2006 Taiwan's Yuanta Financial Holdings paid bribes totaling NT$200 million to the then-first lady to ensure that her husband's government would not oppose its bid to acquire Fuhua Securities.

The forfeiture complaints further noted that Mrs. Chen "orchestrated the movement of funds from Taiwan by using shell companies created in the British Virgin Islands and the Island of Nevis. These shell companies in turn held Swiss bank accounts controlled by her son Chen Chih-chung and his wife Huang Jui-ching."

The complaints also stated: "A portion of these bribe proceeds were then transferred from Switzerland to the United States and were used to purchase the Manhattan condominium and the Virginia house. The younger Chens wanted to purchase the properties while concealing their ownership in them."

The two properties were forfeited to the U.S. government in November 2012, one year after final seizure orders for the properties were made by the New York and Virginia district courts. The seizure actions were taken by the Kleptocracy Asset Recovery Initiative of the U.S. "The Kleptocracy Initiative was established to prevent foreign corrupt leaders from using the United States as a haven for their ill-gotten gains," said Assistant Attorney Lanny Breuer in the news release.

A few months earlier in August, the U.S. Department of Justice had entered into a settlement agreement with Avallo Ltd., the legal entity that purported to be the legal owner of both the Manhattan condominium and the Virginia house. Avallo agreed to forfeit its interests in the two properties in exchange for US$225,000 and US$67,321, respectively, from the net proceeds from the sale of the two properties.[83]

According to U.S. government sources which were reported by Taiwan media, the New York condominium was auctioned for US$1.5 million in April 2013, while the Virginia residence sold for about US$390,000 shortly thereafter.

The SID had previously asked the U.S. to share the sales proceeds with Taiwan.[84] In mid-2016, the U.S. government announced it would soon return US$1.5 million to Taiwan from the sale of the two properties. "We are committed to rooting out foreign official corruption preventing corrupt officials from enjoying their spoils in the United States. We appreciate the cooperation of Taiwan law enforcement in this matter," Assistant Attorney General Leslie R. Caldwell of the Justice Department's Criminal Division said in a statement.

In response to the U.S. announcement, the SID said that the "latest

---

83 In Taiwan, forfeiture of assets can only be carried out after court proceeding are completed, while U.S. civil law allows forfeiture in the absence of conviction.
84 Under U.S. law, parties that have provided assistance to locate assets obtained with illegal funds can ask to share the proceeds from the sale of such properties.

move exemplifies mutual legal assistance between the two countries based on a Taiwan-U.S. Mutual Legal Assistance Agreement."[85]

When approached by Taiwan reporters for comment on the seizure, Chen Shui-bian's son continued to deny wrongdoing by the family. The younger Chen blamed the U.S. government for being "unfamiliar with Taiwan's laws." He insisted the funds used to buy the real estate came from "political donations" to his father. "These are all legal funds," he maintained.

But his argument was no longer tenable. Taiwan's Supreme Court had already reached a final verdict on the Yuanta bribery case. The court convicted both his father and mother of taking an NT$200 million bribe from Yuan Financial Holdings and sentenced them to 10 years and eight years in prison, respectively.

The younger Chen also insisted that the family's purchases of properties in New York and Virginia broke no U.S. laws or regulations. But he ignored an important point contained in the forfeiture complaints. The Florida attorney, Stefan Seuss, who helped the Chen family buy the real estate using the name of a British Virgin Islands shell company, Avallo Ltd., admitted to U.S. investigators that he had established the Chen family's shell company to conceal the ownership of the properties. (Seuss had been charged with fraud in an unrelated case. To reduce his sentence and share in forfeiture proceeds, he admitted the purpose of his role in the Chen family purchases).

The Chen family also denied that the agreement with the U.S.

---

[85]   ROC Thanks the U.S. for Help over Chen Shui-bian's Alleged Bribery Case, China Post, July 9, 2016.

government was an admission of guilt. Instead, they insisted that it was based on a calculation of the value of the properties and the cost of further litigation. "It was simply the result of a settlement reached with the U.S., based on the principle of 'procedural economy', having nothing to do with the question of being guilty or not guilty," Chen said.

Chen's Lawyer: U.S. Trying to Curry Favor with Taiwan

Jonathan Harris, an American lawyer hired by the Chens to defend the family in the forfeiture case, said in an interview with the Wall Street Journal that the U.S. government statement "grossly mischaracterizes the situation," noting that the Chen family entered into a settlement forfeiting the properties without admitting any liability. "The whole case was just the U.S. government trying to curry favor with the government of Taiwan," Harris said. [86]

During court hearings, the Chen family's attorney argued that in the New York and Virginia district courts, where the forfeiture complaints were heard, the funds used to buy the two U.S. properties "are not traceable to unlawful conduct" in Taiwan. But that argument was rejected by the courts as untrue.

According to a Virginia district court paper, U.S. prosecutors and Homeland Security investigators simulated a cross-national border money laundering route -- believed to have been adopted by the Chen

---

86 Samuel Rubenfeld, U.S. Seizes Ex-Taiwan Leader's Manhattan Condo, Virginia House, Wall Street Journal, November 15, 2012.

family in moving their funds across the globe -- based on a related December 2009 indictment filed by the SID of Taiwan's Supreme Prosecutor's Office against the Chen family, as well as results of the U.S. judicial personnel's investigation. [87]

The movement of funds started from the vaults at Cathay United Bank in Taipei, where large amounts of "political contributions" to the family, including the NT$200 million (US$6.4 million) payment from Yuanta Financial Holdings, were stored.

After Taiwan's 2004 presidential election, Mrs. Chen wanted to relocate the money "because several persons had learned about the money and its location." With the consent of Yuanta chief executive officer Ma Wei-chien, several suitcases of cash, totaling more than NT$700 million, were moved, with the help of her son and close family friends, from the Cathay United Bank vault to the basement vault of Ma's private residence.

Shortly after the funds were relocated, Mrs. Chen hoped to move the cash into the formal banking system and make overseas investments. She directed Ma Wei-chien to send NT$540 million overseas for that purpose. To facilitate the investments, Ma established Asian Piston Investment Ltd. (Asian Piston), a British Virginia Islands company, on behalf of Mrs. Chen. Several months later, the first lady instructed Ma Wei-Chien to transfer US$10 million into an account in the name of Avallo at Wegelin & Co. Private Bankers in Switzerland.

In August 2007, Mrs. Chen, through Yuanta board director Tu Li-

---

87 Judge Norman K. Moon, Memorandum Opinion, Civil Action No. 3:10-0037 in the United States District Court for the Western District of Virginia--Charlottesville Division.

Ping, asked Ma Wei-chien to transfer the balance of the funds, about US$7.57 million, from Asian Piston to Avallo. On or about December 17, 2007, Avallo transferred US$17.5 million from its account to an account owned by Bravo International Holdings, an Island of Nevis company. Mrs. Chen's son had sole signature authority over the accounts of both Bravo and Avallo.

In May and June 2008, Bravo made two transfers totaling approximately US$2 million from its account to the trust account of Mitchell S. Polansky, Esq., an attorney for Seuss & Partners, LLC, in Miami, Florida. Chen Chih-Chung and his wife had retained Seuss & Partners in the spring of 2008 to assist in the acquisition of real estate in New York and Virginia.

"In summary," Judge Moon quoted the U.S. government's forfeiture complaints as saying, "...the funds used to purchase the defendant's properties can be traced from Polansky's trust account to Bravo and Avallo accounts controlled by Chen Chih-chung, to the Asian Piston account managed by Ma Wei-chien, and ultimately to cash payments made to Wu Shu-chen, in exchange for the government's goodwill and non-interference in the Yuanta acquisition," according to wire service and newspaper reports.

Years later in June 2016, two former U.S. officials personally involved in investigating the Chen family's illegal property case, were invited to tell the story behind the Chen family's illegal activities in a program entitled "How to Hide a Million Dollars in Plain Sight" aired

Chapter 3
How the Chen Family Laundered Money across the Globe

by the National Public Radio of the United States.[88]

The two officials were Brian McCormick of Homeland Security at the time of the investigation and Sharon Levin, chief of the money laundering and asset forfeiture unit at the U.S. Attorney's Office for the Southern District of New York, an arm of the Justice Department. McCormick said that following painstaking probes, investigators came to know the real owner of the Manhattan apartment was Chen Shui-bian's son Chen Chih-chung.

Initially, McCormick said he found that the apartment was purchased by Pegasus Virginia LLC, which was owned by West 28th Street LLC (WLLC), and that WLLC was, in turn, managed by another company registered in the British Virgin Islands. The major shareholder of the BVI firm was a trust fund registered in Saint Kitts and Nevis.

In a document issued by the trust fund, McCormick found Chen Chih-chung's signature, prompting him to travel to Taiwan several times to collect related evidence. "Through further investigation, it was uncovered that the funds used for the purchase were obtained through bribery," he said. "The funds were first remitted to Switzerland before they were finally transferred to the U.S. to honor the purchase."

In the same radio program, Ms. Levin used the following comments to describe the money laundering skills that the Chen family used to hide their ill-gotten funds: "The complexity of the case demonstrated a level of sophistication beyond 'textbook laundering'

---

88 National Public Radio, How to Hide a Million Dollars in Plain Sight, Former U.S. Officials Shed Light on Ex-Taiwan President's Money Laundering, May 27, 2016.

practices, as the funds were routed through so many sites including Taiwan, the U.S., the British Virgin Islands, Hong Kong, and Switzerland, while the U.S. government spent more than a year completing the judicial process and was finally authorized to seize and auction off the Manhattan apartment."

Lending Some Credence to an Early Rumor

The U.S. civil forfeiture complaints stated that Chen Shui-bian's properties in New York and Virginia were both bought in June 2008, less than one month after Chen Shui-bian stepped down from his presidency. But according to the International Consortium of Investigative Journalists, the purchases seemed to have been even more urgent. The ICIJ quoted U.S. authorities as stating that "on May 29, 2008 -- nine days after Chen had completed his second and final term as Taiwan's president -- money from the Miami account was used [by the Chen family] to buy a prime piece of a real estate in yet another destination [New York] in the money's global odyssey."[89]

The timing of the property purchases was significant in that it prompted many in Taiwan to recall a rumor circulating in the local media shortly after Chen's retirement. Media reports suggested that the former president might be seeking to flee to the United States to escape judicial prosecution.

At the time, Chen and his wife had both been placed under

---

89 Michael Hudson, Ionut Stanescu and Samuel Adler-Bell, International Consortium of Investigative Journalists, New York - Just Another Island Haven, July 3, 2014.

Chapter 3
How the Chen Family Laundered Money across the Globe

investigation by the SID. The rumor was sparked by Chen's hurry to file a passport application in July, less than two months after he transferred power to his successor. Chen quickly refuted the press reports as absurd. But why did he want to apply for a foreign travel document so soon after stepping down and at such a sensitive time?

He had just been banned by the SID -- with court approval -- from leaving Taiwan. His explanation, made through his secretary Chen Hsin-yi, was that he needed a passport to visit several foreign governments and private institutions in reply to their invitations, extended in the period before his retirement.

The media reports about Chen's interest in fleeing Taiwan in the months following his departure from office have never been independently confirmed. But the subsequent U.S. forfeiture documents and the ICIJ's revelations that the Chen family had owned a New York condominium and a Virginia residence and that these properties were purchased in a hurry--just days after Chen stepped down as president--lent some credence to the early speculation in the local media.

Chapter 4
Turning Divisive Issues into Political Assets

Playing the Ethnic Card

In the previous three chapters (1-3), my account of Chen Shui-bian's presidency and its legacy was focused on these major topics: How the former Taiwan leader fell from grace, the multiple corruption charges and convictions after he left office, and how the former first family laundered tens of millions of U.S. dollars and moved the funds out of Taiwan.

The following sections will be devoted to recounting some of the most controversial words and deeds of Chen Shui-bian from his eight years in office. In this section, chapter 4, the author will recount how Chen Shui-bian played the ethnic card, exploited the tragic 228 Incident of 1947, and manipulated the theme of Taiwan's future being confined to a narrow choice between independence and unification with the communist mainland. His exploitative behavior would always produce strong reactions from his critics and opponents who attacked him for cynically utilizing deeply divisive issues to score political points.

For starters, the issue of ethnicity in Taiwan refers primarily to the historic division between Taiwanese -- those whose ancestors came to the island centuries ago -- and mainlanders -- those who arrived in Taiwan in the late 1940s to escape the communists or were the offspring of those migrants. More than one million mainlanders fled to the island along with Chiang Kai-Shek's Nationalist government and his armed forces as Mao Zedong's communist armies swept to victory on the mainland in China's civil war.

Chen Shui-bian, who was born in 1951, did not create the island's ethnic, cultural, and linguistic differences, but he found them to be a handy weapon that could be used against his political opponents, many of them mainlanders.

By playing the ethnic card, he hoped to galvanize native Taiwanese -- the largest of Taiwan's four major ethnic groups -- to secure electoral gains. He would employ a divisive strategy to generate a widespread perception among voters that "Taiwanese vote for Taiwanese" and "mainlanders vote for mainlanders." The native-born Chen Shui-bian and his home-grown DPP would stand to benefit due to their greater numbers. [90]

Chen played the ethnic card in many different ways, depending on the circumstances. Sometimes, for example, he intentionally spoke the Hoklo dialect, or Taiwanese, in addressing the public instead of Mandarin, the official language of the country. While this was partly to communicate with his audience more effectively, it also served to highlight an ethnic as well as a linguistic divide, creating an "us" versus "them" mentality among his listeners.

During his campaign for reelection in 2004, for example, Chen faced strong competition from his challenger, mainland-born Lien Chan. His response was to speak of "Taiwanese versus mainlanders"

90 Yoshiyuki OGASAWARA, Lee Teng-hui Administration and Taiwanese Nationalism, presented at Australian National University, December 15, 1998.

when addressing campaign rallies and portraying himself as a "real" Taiwanese. Chen tried to capitalize on his native Taiwanese origin and his early reputation as a "son of Taiwan."

At the same time, Chen derided Lien Chan of the KMT and his running mate James Soong of the People First Party as "fake" Taiwanese. The insulting ethnic label for Lien and Soong had to do with their birthplaces. Both Lien and Soong were born in mainland China, and Chen alleged that Lien and Soong were "aliens, not native or real Taiwanese." [91] [92]

What Chen Shui-bian said about Lien and Soong was of course campaign language intended to alienate the Lien-Soong ticket from the native electorate. The truth is, according to many anthropologists, all of the four major ethnic groups in Taiwan, except the aboriginals or indigenous people, are Chinese from the mainland. The difference is that some came earlier and others came later. Only the indigenous people, who constitute less than 2% of the local population, can claim to be "native Taiwanese".

But there was another factor behind this election strategy of labeling opponents as outsiders from the Chinese mainland. If Chen Shui-bian succeeded in painting Lien and Soong as "fake" Taiwanese because they hailed from the Chinese mainland, they could be

---

91 Lien Chan was born in Xian, Shaanxi province, China, but was raised and educated in Taiwan. He spent all of his years teaching and serving in the ROC government before retiring.

92 James Soong was born in Xiangtan, Hunan province, China. He and his family fled to Taiwan in 1949 along with the Nationalist government. He received his education and worked in Taiwan before retiring from public service.

characterized as being "inherently pro-China." Lien and Soong, therefore, were more likely to "sell out Taiwan" in any future cross-strait negotiations, should they win the presidential election. People unnerved by this characterization would shun Lien and vote for Chen instead.

Time and again Chen played the ethnic card when he or his party faced strong competition from the KMT and needed a way to mobilize pro-independence supporters. Two years earlier in the 2002 election for mayor of the capital city of Taipei, Chen used the same tactics.

One such example was a campaign rally for the DPP's candidate Lee Ying-yuan, who was lagging far behind the KMT's incumbent Ma Ying-jeou in opinion polls. As chairman of the DPP as well as president, Chen was eager to help Lee Ying-yuan overtake Ma.

He told his audience that Ma Ying-jeou was an "outsider from Hong Kong" and not a "native" Taiwanese. In other words, Ma did not belong to Taiwanese society biologically and was not "one of us." By describing Ma Ying-jeou in this way, Chen intended to cast doubt among voters over the KMT candidate's avowed love for Taiwan.

Many analysts said Chen used this smear tactic to bring out the DPP's core voters by stoking their unease about Ma's loyalty to Taiwan and influencing swing voters in favor of his party's candidate Lee Ying-yuan.

Chen had a knack for creating catchy labels for his opponents and the "outsider from Hong Kong" was an effective one. Ma was indeed born in Hong Kong, but he stayed there for just two years before he was brought to Taiwan by his parents.

Chapter 4
Turning Divisive Issues into Political Assets

After calling attention to Ma's Hong Kong roots, Chen followed up with a provocative question for the assembled audience. "Do you want a Hong Kong Special Administrative Region leader to govern the city of Taipei?" he asked.

By connecting Ma to his birthplace in Hong Kong -- a British colony that became a special region of the People's Republic of China in 1997 -- Chen built a fraudulent link between the KMT candidate and the communist government in Beijing, hoping to undermine Ma's support. Unfortunately for Chen, the ethnic card didn't work this time. Ma Ying-jeou easily won reelection as Taipei's mayor.

A day after Taiwan's 2004 presidential election, the noted Singapore-based Straits Times carried an article analyzing the poll results and their impact.[93] Lawrence Chung, the author of the article, devoted much of his analysis to Chen Shui-bian's use of the ethnic card and its impact on Taiwan. "President Chen Shui-bian won a second term in this election, but he had to face a politically divided Taiwan attributable to his play of ethnic issues," Chung wrote. "By playing the ethnic card," Chung pointed out, "the DPP leader has split Taiwan into two ideologically different camps"

'A Divider, Not a Unifier'

Chung, a longtime journalist who previously covered Taiwan for Reuters as its Taipei bureau chief, noted, "President Chen Shui-bian

---

93 Lawrence Chung, President Chen Wins a Second Term, Straits Times, March 23, 2004.

once said that he, if elected, would help to build ethnic harmony in Taiwan, but the record shows he has divided Taiwanese society." Chung concluded his analysis of Chen's re-election with this observation: "Chen Shui-bian is a divider, not a unifier."

Below is another example of how Chen Shui-bian played the ethnic card. In Taiwan's December 2005 local elections, President Chen went so far as to assert that Taiwan would be "finished" if the opposition won the mayoral and county contests: "If the KMT and the People First Party win [the December 2005 elections], Taiwan will be finished. They will pass a Taiwan version of the anti-secession or surrender law. Taiwan will have to accept the principle of 'one China' and become a part of China. It will become a local government, a special administrative region, like Hong Kong and Macau."

But to his disappointment, the KMT won the 2005 mayoral and county elections with overwhelming support. Moreover, the victories did not turn Taiwan into an impotent local government under Beijing's authoritarian rule.

Chen's political maneuvering and the frequent use of the ethnic card were factors that contributed to the DPP's defeat in the 2008 presidential election. (Term limits prevented Chen from running again). As noted earlier, Chen highlighted differences between native Taiwanese or benshengren and mainlanders or waishengren in his reelection bid in 2004, and in the local and central elections that successively followed. During such public office contests, he was often forced to appeal to a more fundamentalist faction within the DPP to secure his support base. While that may have won over some deep-greens, or fundamentalists, it alienated not only mainlanders but also

178

many independent voters and even some within the green camp.
Ultimately, the strategy backfired.

Exploiting the Bloody 228 Tragedy

Chen had other ways of capitalizing on social divisions. During his two
terms in office, Chen Shui-bian regularly revisited the painful theme of
the "228 Incident," a brutal crushing of protests against corruption and
repression in 1947. The military crackdown killed thousands of people,
most of them native Taiwanese, and it was the KMT that led the
government and military at that time. But Chen's goal was to ensure
that the social wounds from that bloody incident remained raw and
ready to use at election time.

Chen's constant revisiting of the 228 Incident was also viewed as
an effort to build a direct link between the bloody suppression of 1947
and all mainlanders. During those early post-World War II years, the
KMT, the Nationalist government, the military, and the security forces
were the four most powerful institutions in Taiwan, dominating its
economic and political activities. These institutions were all headed by
people from the Chinese mainland at that time. For that reason, Chen
concluded that bringing back the topic of the 228 Incident could
logically create an impression among the public, particularly the native
Taiwanese population, that all mainlanders were responsible for the
bloody suppression.

In the decades since then, numerous research studies by public
and private institutions have been conducted on the 228 Incident
concerning how the tragic event unfolded, the implications for Taiwan,

and the results of the reconciliation efforts initiated nearly a half-century later amid the island's transformation from authoritarian rule to democracy.

The tragic incident had far-reaching effects on Taiwan's ethnic tensions, and it deserves to be discussed in greater detail here. After the discussion, an account will follow of how Chen Shui-bian exploited the event to serve his political interests during his years in office.

The incident arose on February 27, 1947, when agents of what was then known as the Taiwan Provincial Monopoly Bureau stopped a middle-aged woman suspected of selling black-market cigarettes. The agents of the bureau, which controlled all production and sales of tobacco products, tried to confiscate the suspected contraband. In an ensuing quarrel, one of the agents struck the woman on the head with his gun and knocked her to the ground. An angry crowd gathered and one of the bureau agents fired into the crowd killing one man.

What began as a quarrel over cigarette sales escalated into a violent anti-government protest that swiftly spread across Taiwan. Protesters occupied the monopoly bureau, tossing its inventories into the street and setting them on fire. A police station was overrun. A handful of protesters gained access to a radio station and broadcast news of the unrest. The mass protests were eventually brought under control only through the use of military force.

Troops were dispatched from the mainland to suppress the protests, and they were sent with the approval of Chiang Kai-shek, head of the Nationalist government and commander of the Armed Forces of the Republic of China. Chiang was in Nanjing directing his government's protracted struggle with Communist leader Mao Zedong

Chapter 4
Turning Divisive Issues into Political Assets

and his People's Liberation Army. Chiang reportedly agreed to dispatch the troops, the 21st Division of the Nationalist Army, only after he received a telegram from the governor of Taiwan, General Chen Yi, asking for military reinforcements. General Chen reported to Chiang that the ongoing violent protests in Taiwan had been staged and orchestrated by Chinese communists as well as local gang leaders, to overthrow the provincial administration.

The 1947 incident occurred against a complicated background. The protests and the subsequent military crackdown occurred barely one year and four months after Chiang's government formally took control of Taiwan following Japan's surrender at the end of World War II. The takeover brought an end to 50 years of Japanese occupation. However, the departure of Japanese authorities did not erase the mutual distrust between the island's new rulers, who had fought Japanese occupiers on the mainland, and the local population, who were often seen as collaborators. Tensions were running high between Taiwan's new government and residents due to policy missteps, such as a "de-Japanization" policy, as well as economic mismanagement and rampant corruption. Cultural, socio-economic, and linguistic differences between the native Taiwanese and the mainlander administration added to the volatile mix. (Note, more than one million people, mostly government employees and military personnel as well as their families, fled to Taiwan ahead of advancing communist armies as the Nationalist government collapsed on the mainland.)

There is no way to know exactly how many people perished in the nearly two weeks of civilian-military clashes and their aftermath. The estimates of deaths cited in all available studies on the tragedy vary considerably -- ranging from a low of 800 to as many as 30,000. An independent investigation, commissioned by former President Lee Teng-hui and his governing KMT in 1992 and completed two years later, put the death toll at between 18,000 and 28,000.

Yet even this independently determined death toll was brought into question by a subsequent development. The number of families of 228 Incident victims applying for government financial compensation was surprisingly smaller, fewer than 800 in total. The financial compensation, as part of a wide-ranging reconciliation program, was made available after the publication of an official 228 Incident investigation report.

If the smaller number of applications for financial compensation was any indication, then the estimates of the death toll running into many tens of thousands, as cited in some research studies, were probably far too high. Some historians and scholars said they believed the number of people killed in the incident was probably several thousand.

Shao Ming-huang, director of the KMT Party Archives, was one such historian. In an interview that he gave in mid-2005 to one of the authors of the book Taiwanese Identity in the 21st Century, Shao said: "I believe that only about 1,000 to 2,000 people died in the incident. But when people talk about 10,000 or even more victims, then this is merely an arbitrarily given number that cannot be supported by historical evidence. As a historian, one has to refer to reliable sources, and not dream up some ridiculous numbers."

But a pro-independence Taipei Times article Facing a Violent Past quoted some unidentified historians as estimating that "around 30,000 people were killed" in the incident.[94] Generally speaking, historians and politicians critical of the KMT tended to put the death toll from the 228 Incident at the high end of all estimates.

Long-Lasting Ethnic Rivalry

Whatever the true extent of the bloodletting, the 228 Incident had wide implications for Taiwan and its society. Chief among them was a deep social wound that formed a prolonged political rivalry. The rivalry emerged from the initial civilian clashes that began on February 28 between natives and mainlanders, the subsequent military crackdown, and the mass political purges launched in the aftermath. The founding of Chen Shui-bian's Democratic Progressive Party (DPP) -- Taiwan's first organized opposition -- in the mid-1980s was widely seen as an outgrowth of that rivalry.

The "outgrowth" theory was not without foundation. The DPP was founded essentially as a "native" Taiwanese party, and it remains so to this day. The vast majority of its leadership, members, and supporters have been native Taiwanese -- a social and political landscape that has now become known as the "pan-green" camp.

If the above observation is not convincing enough, it can be reinforced by some of the comments made by Chen Shui-bian. When he was at the helm of the party, Chen often liked to claim that the DPP was "the sole native party representing the Taiwanese people." The primary mission of the DPP was to challenge the KMT, he said. At the

---

94 Ko Shu-ling, Facing a Violent Past, Taipei Times, February 28, 2003.

same time, he always branded the KMT as an "alien" party, transplanted to Taiwan from the Chinese mainland.

That description, of course, was not true. The KMT had long since reinvented itself as a party of multiple ethnic groups. Its membership and support base had long expanded to include all of Taiwan's four major ethnic groups — indigenous people, Hoklos, Hakkas as well as the mainlanders.

228 Was a Taboo Subject under Martial Law

Despite its wide political, ethnic, and social impact, the 1947 incident was a taboo subject for many decades. It became open to public discussion only after 1987 when martial law was lifted, and a strengthened democracy gave greater protections to freedom of speech.

Once the curbs on public discussion were discarded, calls by opposition politicians and human rights activists for an investigation of the 228 Incident became stronger and stronger. The opposition urged the government to redress the wrongdoings inflicted on the victims and their families by previous authoritarian rulers, in what they called a necessary step toward transitional justice.

A turning point in this effort was reached in 1990 when then-President Lee Teng-hui ordered a full investigation of the 228 Incident. Lee Teng-hui had succeeded Chiang Ching-kuo (one of Chiang Kai-shek's sons) two years earlier, becoming Taiwan's first native-born president. Lee had sufficient political capital to enable him to tackle this contentious historical issue.

Chapter 4
Turning Divisive Issues into Political Assets

Under Lee's instructions, an independent panel of renowned scholars was commissioned by the government to study and compile a comprehensive report on the incident. Members of the panel were permitted to examine all related official archives, which previously had been strictly classified. The panel, headed by Lai Zehan of the prestigious think tank Academia Sinica, submitted its findings in the "228 Incident Research Report" in 1992.

The report was widely viewed as one of the most important achievements in contemporary research on the 228 Incident.[95][96] Based on that research paper, Lee Teng-hui and his KMT government soon introduced a series of administrative and legislative measures to redress injustices committed under the army crackdown, with the ultimate goal of achieving ethnic reconciliation.

Post-enactment tasks accomplished during the period from 1993 to 1996 included the construction of 228 memorials, Lee Teng-hui's formal apology as president, financial compensation to the 228 victims and their relatives, and the designation of February 28 as an official day of remembrance.

In the KMT government-commissioned research report, Lai Zehan and his fellow panelists also addressed the three most crucial issues in connection with the 228 Incident. First, they defined the 228 Incident as an "unfortunate tragedy," a departure from the KMT's past

---

95 Nicholas D. Kristof, Taipei Journal; The Horror of 228: Taiwan Rips Open the Past, The New York Times, published April 3, 1992.

96 Stefan Fleischauer, Perspectives on 228: The 28 February of 1947 Uprising in Contemporary Taiwan, Taiwanese Identity in the 21st Century.

official position. Previously, the KMT had endorsed Governor Chen Yi's initial version of events -- that it was a mass uprising orchestrated jointly by local gang leaders and the Chinese communists.

The panel's view also differed from the conclusion reached by the KMT's opponents, mainly DPP politicians and Taiwan independence advocates. A separate research effort led by noted historian Chang Yen-hsien blamed the uprising on the KMT-led Nationalist government's high-handed policies, which they said: "prompted the people to stand up and resist." [97]

As noted earlier, Lai Zehan's panel estimated the number of people killed in the incident and its aftermath at 18,000 to 28,000. This figure was close to the estimated range of 20,000 to 30,000 made previously by politicians and researchers critical of the KMT.

But as noted previously, even the more conservative estimate of deaths was much higher than the actual number of applications for financial compensation from families of 228 victims. The total number of applications was below 800 even after the application deadline had been repeatedly extended to allow more time for families of victims to present their cases for financial compensation.

Two likely factors may explain why there was such a large gap between the researchers' estimates of the death toll and the actual number of applications for financial compensation. One, the data available for studying the historical event was fragmented and incomplete, forcing researchers to make judgments based on what they

---

97 Chang Yen-hsien, former chairman of the Academia Historica and convener of the 228 Memorial Foundation's 228 Massacre Truth Research Task Force, authored the DPP-backed research report.

read or heard on the subject, paying little attention to the question of whether or not their sources were reliable. A more likely factor was that some original estimates of 228 victims might have been intentionally exaggerated because of political bias. There was a widely held view that many people sympathetic to the DPP or its independence cause -- be they scholars or ordinary citizens -- tended to exaggerate the number of 228 victims to add to the existing resentment against the KMT.

Chiang Kai-shek's Role in the 228 Incident

A third hotly debated issue concerned Chiang Kai-shek's role in the bloody incident of 1947. For many longtime KMT critics, Chiang Kai-shek, as the leader of the Republic of China at the time with authority over the KMT, the administration, and the military, should bear the main responsibility for the 228 Incident.

"Chiang, allowing himself to be misled by his General Chen Yi, the governor of Taiwan, took the 1947 uprising as an attempt to break from China. Because of that misjudgment, Chiang made the final decision to dispatch reinforcements from the mainland to Taiwan to suppress the protests militarily, resulting in large numbers of deaths of innocent people. Therefore, Chiang Kai-shek was the culprit behind the 228 massacres and should bear the main responsibility for it."

The above remarks were written by Chang Yen-hsien after a book entitled "Research Report on Responsibility for the 228 Massacre." Chang, a longtime advocate of Taiwan's independence, was a scholar renowned for his research into Taiwan's history, the 228 Incident in particular. This new research report, compiled and published with the blessing of the Chen Shui-bian administration (2000-2008), however, differed noticeably from the one commissioned by the KMT a decade earlier concerning Chiang's responsibility.

In the KMT-commissioned research report of 1992, Chiang Kai-shek was blamed only for failing to investigate the 228 Incident thoroughly and putting too much trust in Governor Chen Yi to accept his request for military reinforcements. That report, however, was quick to add that Chiang at the time was fighting a bitter civil war on the mainland, having little time to personally look into the uprising in Taiwan. According to Lai Zehan, who co-authored the 1992 report, Chiang later came to understand the truth, but the tragic mistake had already been made and could not be rectified.

Given Taiwan's deep political divide, the 228 Incident is likely to remain a controversial topic. But with the public and private efforts to address the wrongs and implement transitional justice in the early and mid-1990s, the controversy surrounding the tragic events of 1947 could reasonably be expected to become less acrimonious.

The transitional justice efforts made under Lee Teng-hui were generally viewed favorably. "Under the presidency of Lee Teng-hui, the KMT made determined efforts [in the 1990s] to meet the demands of the opposition; most prominently, the financial compensation of the victims, the construction of memorials, the opening of government files, an official apology for the incident and the designating of February 28 as a National Day of Remembrance."

The passage cited above was written by sinologist and political scientist Stefan Fleischauer in the work "Taiwanese Identity in the Twenty-first Century." He went on to say: "This (transitional justice) endeavor has been largely successful." Fleischauer authored a chapter in that study titled "The 28 February 1947 Uprising".

Professor Shih Cheng-feng of National Dong Hwa University stated that Taiwan, in pursuing transitional justice, emphasized seeking truth, paying compensation to the victims, and promoting reconciliation between mainlanders and native Taiwanese. Shih made the observation in an article titled "Taiwanese Identity and the Memories of 2-28: A Case for Political Reconciliation, "co-authored with Mumin Chen, associate professor of political science at National Chung Hsing University.

"Even though ethnic identities are still a divisive factor," Shih and Chen wrote in the study, "hostilities between ethnic groups in Taiwan have greatly declined, due mainly to recent decades of efforts made by both the government and the opposition to uncover the truth and redress past wrongdoings. Today it is unimaginable that a politician or party would openly advocate discriminative action against any group. Political parties of all stripes are careful to maintain equality among ethnic groups, an effort conducive to nurturing further reconciliation."

Yet all the achievements that Taiwan attained in transitional justice and ethnic reconciliation seemed to be lost on one of its most important political leaders: Chen Shui-bian. After defeating the KMT at the polls and coming to power in May 2000, Chen made the 228 Incident a constant theme in pursuit of his political agenda, even though this meant reopening old wounds and damaging hard-won ethnic reconciliation.

Cashing in on the 228 Tragedy

Below are several high-profile examples of how former President Chen Shui-bian exploited the 228 tragedy to make political gains. On February 28, 2004 -- weeks ahead of Taiwan's presidential election in which Chen was running for a second term, he and his ruling party mobilized one million supporters to join hands and form a 500-kilometer-long human chain around the island. In Taiwan, February 28 is a national holiday marking the tragic incident of 1947.

But Chen Shui-bian broke with tradition and organized the human chain to dramatize the observance ahead of the presidential election and thereby drum up support for himself. Chen and the co-organizers of the event described the mass gathering as "228, one million people hand in hand to defend Taiwan." The protest, they explained, was held to protest mainland China's deployment of large numbers of missiles along its southeast coast opposite Taiwan.

Many questioned the timing of the mass event as the mainland's missile threat to Taiwan was hardly new; the missiles had been in place for many years. Some analysts suggested the event was inspired by a similar protest held in the three Baltic states of Latvia, Lithuania, and Estonia in 1989. That protest saw more than two million people gather to call for independence from the former Soviet Union.

Chen may have seen the demonstration as a way to promote support for independence for this island. Chen hinted at that as he explained the significance of the day-long activity at a news conference. "We wanted to show the world our determination to identify with Taiwan and defend Taiwan."

Chapter 4
Turning Divisive Issues into Political Assets

In addition to promoting independence, Chen Shui-bian was also seen as once again attempting to deepen hostility toward Beijing. Mainland China claims sovereignty over Taiwan and has threatened to attack if the island declares independence.

Whatever the stated intention, Chen's key aim in bringing out one million people just weeks before the March 2004 presidential election was to energize voters who were angered by the mainland's missile threat and supportive of independence.

Chen also wanted to revive the memories of the KMT's atrocities of 1947 to embarrass the party and create hostility toward its presidential candidate Lien Chan. Opinion polls at this point showed the incumbent president falling significantly behind Lien Chan, his sole opponent in the 2004 election.

So for Chen Shui-bian, even more than five decades on, the 228 tragedy remained a convenient political tool for him to mobilize supporters either to antagonize Beijing or discredit the KMT. But using that historical incident to shame the KMT was hardly convincing in 2004.

The following observations, made by Craig A. Smith of the University of British Columbia, explain how Chen Shui-bian's attempt to use the 228 military suppression to discredit the KMT was less than convincing. "The KMT of today is not the KMT of 1947. The liberalization of Taiwan that spanned the 1980s and 1990s under presidents Chiang Ching-Kuo and Lee Teng-hui also resulted in great change for the party, which is no longer seen as an entity entirely controlled by mainlanders and in opposition to Taiwan's interests," he wrote. "Confrontation and competition with the Dangwai movement (an informal forerunner of the Democratic Progressive Party) and the DPP have led the KMT closer to the political center of Taiwan. Therefore, the simple association of the KMT with the 228 Incident no longer holds the persuasive strength it once did."[98]

Another example is given below of how Chen Shui-bian exploited the 228 tragedy for political gains. In early 2006, Chen was mired in a new round of severe tensions with Washington over his plan to abolish a symbolic but politically significant presidential council on unification with mainland China. Washington aside, Chen also faced vehement criticism from domestic opponents for unnecessarily provoking Beijing. At this time, the beleaguered president seemed to feel a need to do something to divert public attention away from his controversial policy. Once again, he turned to the 228 tragedy.

Speaking at a ceremony held on February 28 of that year to mark the 59th anniversary of the 1947 military crackdown on civilian protesters, Chen went out of his way to condemn the KMT for "distorting the truth of the bloody event."

"All over the years, the KMT has always tried to simplify, twist, or even falsify the facts about the 228 Incident. It was untrue to say the 1947 event was a social uprising caused by government corruption," Chen was quoted by the pro-independence Taipei Times as saying. He claimed: "The incident in nature was a systematic slaughter and organized suppression of the Taiwanese people. It was carried out by an authoritarian foreign regime to consolidate its power." He went on

---

98 Craig A. Smith, Taiwan's 228 Incident and the Politics of Placing Blame, University of British Columbia.

to say: "We can forgive this atrocity, but we must not forget it...We must find out the truth of the event, so justice can be served and lessons can be learned."

It's worth noting that Chen's accusations against the KMT of committing "systematic killings of the Taiwanese people" and "distorting the truth of the 228 incident" came more than a decade after the publication of the independent "228 Research Report" commissioned under the administration of President Lee Teng-hui. Nowhere in that report were there any accusations against the KMT that mirrored those made by Chen Shui-bian.

Moreover, Chen -- while accusing the KMT of distorting the facts about the 228 Incident -- made no mention at all of the various transitional justice measures implemented by the government led by the KMT's Lee Teng-hui. As noted earlier, those measures included offering an official apology for the tragedy and compensating the families of the 228 victims.

Below is a third example of how Chen Shui-bian used the 228 Incident to create social divisions and win votes. In 2007, Chen Shui-bian was in the 7th year of his eight-year presidency and the campaigns for the 2008 legislative and presidential elections were well under way. Chen himself was not on the ballot, but his party was. Opinion polls showed poor ratings for the DPP's presidential and legislative candidates, most of them lagging far behind their KMT opponents. This indicated that the DPP as a whole was facing serious challenges to its grip on power. Signs of the party's declining popularity with the people had already been reflected in the 2005 local elections, in which the DPP lost control of most cities and counties to the KMT.

The root cause of the DPP's fast-plunging popularity was Chen Shui-bian himself. He routinely manipulated policies and issues, resulting in constant gridlock in the lawmaking body. That had an impact on economic growth. He continued to vex Washington and anger Beijing with radical pro-independence remarks and policies, especially during his second term. His behavior alienated even the DPP's loyal supporters -- the deep greens.

Instead of seeking to bolster the DPP's popularity by improving his leadership style, Chen resumed his favorite tactic of playing the ethnic card. He called for efforts to find out the "real perpetrators" of the 1947 military crackdown and punish those responsible for the bloodletting.

Writing in his online newsletter in 2007 ahead of the 60th anniversary of the tragedy, Chen Shui-bian was at his bombastic best. "Temples around the country (should) ring bells and beat drums simultaneously on February 28 at 2:28 p.m. as a way to commemorate this big anniversary." He said, "We want to pray for the early realization of justice, peace, reconciliation, and forgiveness." Chen continued: "In addition to learning a lesson from the incident and protecting the country's hard-fought democratic achievements, the government must address the issue of transitional justice...Above all, we need to identify the past authoritarian rulers' responsibility for human rights violations."

Discussing the same theme, a day later at a forum held to mark the anniversary, the president went further in denouncing the late Nationalist Party (KMT) leader Chiang Kai-shek as the "true murderer" behind the 228 Incident. Chiang was to blame for dispatching the mainland troops to Taiwan and the heavy loss of life.

"The 228 Incident must not just be seen as a historical event," he said. "We have to examine the various criminal and legal issues involved. Those who are found guilty of committing crimes and violating human rights should be prosecuted and stand trial." He insisted that moves to block this campaign would be futile. "Any effort to address such transitional justice matters may certainly encounter resistance and obstruction from the opposition. But we firmly believe that fairness and justice will eventually prevail."

Chen seemed to think that his designation of Chiang Kai-shek as a "true murderer" behind the army suppression of the 228 protests was insufficient to energize his supporters. He followed up with a campaign to rid the island of the memory of Chiang Kai-shek. Before long his administration launched a drive to rename Taipei's Chiang Kai-shek Memorial Hall as the Taiwan Democracy Memorial Hall and remove statues of the former ROC president in the capital city and elsewhere around the island.

Chen and other DPP politicians argued that Taiwan should dismantle those monuments to Chiang Kai-shek for historical reasons, but many critics saw the DPP as cultivating feelings of injustice among voters to score electoral points.

But Chen Shui-bian's endless replay of the 228 tragedy did little to bolster his party's performance at the polls in 2008 as the DPP lost both the presidential and legislative elections to the KMT. Many analysts concluded the DPP's election defeats reflected voter dissatisfaction with the ruling party and, in particular, Chen Shui-bian's political machinations in the run-up to the votes in January and March of that year.

Manipulating the Unification vs. Independence Issue

In an editorial in August 2003, the English-language China Post had this to say about the upcoming presidential election: "Increasingly, President Chen Shui-bian appears to be steering the ongoing campaign for next March's presidential election into a vote on the advocacy of an independent Taiwan versus the support of one China."[99]

That comment was valid. Weeks earlier Chen Shui-bian, who was known to be seeking a second term but had yet to formally declare his candidacy, had made that campaign strategy clear to the public. During a meeting with the news media, Chen stated: "The upcoming presidential race will be a vote to choose between a politician who would pursue a pro-independence agenda and one who would be more willing to promote closer relations with Beijing. As a consequence, the March 20 election will have a major impact on Taiwan's political direction and its ties to the mainland."

Chen Shui-bian used three major pro-independence themes to mobilize voters in his reelection campaign. He espoused a theory of what he called "one country on each side of the Taiwan Strait," called for a new constitution to be passed by a referendum and backed a

---

99 Editorial, March Election May Have a Vital Impact on Beijing Ties, China Post, August 18, 2003.

defensive referendum on China's missile deployment. The defensive referendum was held alongside the 2004 presidential election.

In August 2002, Chen first declared his controversial "one country on each side of the Taiwan Strait" theory to define Taiwan's political relations with the mainland. In addressing a meeting of pro-independence supporters, Chen said: "With Taiwan and China on the two sides of the strait, each side is a country...This is the description of the status quo." Chen continued to promote this concept throughout his campaign.

Chen's theory put his challenger, Lien Chan of the KMT, in an awkward position on the issue of Taiwan's political status. On one hand, Lien wanted to dispute Chen's stance as an attempt to openly advance his long-held position that "Taiwan is an independent state." But if Lien did so, he would run the risk of being labeled by Chen as willing to accept Beijing's line that "Taiwan and the mainland both belong to China."

On the other hand, if Lien and the KMT ignored Chen's pro-independence view and, instead, engaged him on economic and other domestic issues, they might risk alienating the party's traditional supporters. Those supporters might blame Lien for being too weak in the defense of their core values and principles. (Note, the KMT and its supporters are traditionally opposed to independence for Taiwan and seek to improve relations with mainland China.)

Chen's formulation of "one country on each side of the strait" caused quite a stir, due largely to his adroit maneuvering on the issue. "He has subtly portrayed his concept of 'one country on each side of the strait' as a policy crucial to defending Taiwan's political legitimacy amid growing unification pressure from Beijing," opined the August 2003 editorial in Taipei's China Post.

Chen Shui-bian's manipulation of "unification versus independence" also included a vital element of smearing his opponents with red paint. In the lead-up to the March 20, 2004, presidential race, Chen frequently portrayed the KMT's Lien Chan and his running mate James Soong of the People First Party as politicians ready to compromise with Beijing to the extent they would accept reunification under a formula of "one county, two systems." He was referring to the model that Beijing applied to Hong Kong on its return to Chinese sovereignty in 1997 after 156 years of British rule. People in Taiwan are generally opposed to that model. They fear that accepting the "one country, two systems" formula could eventually lead to unification with the communist mainland, sacrificing the free lifestyle they now enjoy on this island.

Maneuvering on the Issue of Constitutional Reform

Constitutional reform was another key theme in Chen Shui-bian's reelection campaign. Before September 2003, he merely floated the idea of revising the existing ROC constitution. But after successfully organizing two large-scale campaign rallies which encouraged him to adopt a more resolute stance on the constitutional issue, he ratcheted up his rhetoric.

One of the rallies was held in the capital city of Taipei in September 2003. Its highlight was an appeal to change the national name from the Republic of China to Taiwan. The rally attracted an

Chapter 4
Turning Divisive Issues into Political Assets

estimated 150,000 people from all over the island. On the surface, the event was promoted by several groups advocating independence, including the Taiwan Solidarity Union---a more radical political party supported by former President Lee Teng-hui, who had become an outspoken advocate for independence after leaving office. (Lee was expelled by the KMT in 2001). In reality, Chen Shui-bian's party, the ruling DPP, played a key role in mobilizing participants and rendering logistical support for the rallies.

Emboldened by the huge support for pro-independence activities, Chen stepped up his campaign for a new constitution in the following weeks. At a subsequent gathering of pro-independence Presbyterians in early October, for example, Chen said "Taiwan must write a new constitution to make it possible for this island to shed its current 'abnormal' political status and become a 'normal' country'."[100]

In late October, Chen's ally Lee Teng-hui, and his Taiwan Solidarity Union held another "name rectification" demonstration in the southern city of Kaohsiung. That event attracted an even larger crowd of 200,000 people. The two rallies significantly boosted Chen Shui-bian's campaign momentum.

"The two big name-rectification demonstrations gave an impetus to the idea that the people of Taiwan were ready for such change...and made the people on this island realize that the upcoming presidential election was crucial for its future," said an unsigned article posted on

---

100 Editorial, Chen Clarifies His Agenda for a Taiwan Nation, China Post, October 8, 2003.

the pro-independence website Taiwan, Ilha Formosa, commenting on the significance of the Taipei and Kaohsiung demonstrations.[101]

With his campaign gaining momentum at home, Chen Shui-bian shifted gears and sought to publicize his new constitution concept abroad. Taking advantage of a transit stop in New York City in early November 2003, he told the international media there why it was necessary for Taiwan to write a new constitution.

Surprisingly, Chen's high-profile promotion of his new constitution plan in New York did not prompt any serious pushback from the host country. The lack of an immediate response was unexpected because Washington in the past few months had openly expressed disapproval of Chen's radical campaign, particularly his push for a new constitution and his characterization of Taiwan and the mainland as two countries on either side of the Taiwan Strait.

Chen Shui-bian skillfully pressed ahead with his new constitution drive. He employed his meeting with a group of international journalists in the city to announce his plan but realizing that his remarks might provoke protests from Washington and Beijing, he offered assurances that the plan would not breach the "no-independence" commitment he made at the start of his presidency in 2000. He concluded that his assurances would be able to alleviate concerns in Washington and other key political capitals that his reform program could result in a change in Taiwan's political status.

---

101 Year 2004 Referendum and Presidential Election, Taiwan, Ilha Formosa home page, March 17, 2004.

After returning from his successful New York stopover, Chen Shui-bian became more assertive in advancing his new constitution concept. A week later in mid-November 2003, Chen told a group of visiting U.S. academics, "The only way for Taiwan to fix the problem with its old constitution was to write a new one and have it decided by the people via a referendum."[102]

Chen told his visitors that the current ROC constitution, which was enacted in mainland China in the 1940s, "does not suit the needs of the 23 million people of Taiwan." Although this constitution had since undergone six amendments, he said, the "changes were fragmentary, and many problems remained unresolved."

He then added that if his new constitution "can be approved in a referendum in December 2006 as scheduled, it would be formally proclaimed on May 20, 2008 -- the inauguration day for the winner of that year's presidential election."

But just as Chen Shui-bian revealed his new constitution timetable to the American visitors in Taipei, the U.S. State Department released a report to the Senate that conveyed a clear warning about developments in Taiwan. In its report, the State Department concluded that "if Taiwan removes all mention of the ROC name from the existing constitution because of a revision or rewriting of the basic law, it runs the risk of inviting an armed attack from Beijing."

The State Department also issued a statement reiterating that "Washington remains concerned about Chen's constitution and

---

102 Chang Yun-ping, Chen Drafts Timetable on Constitution, Taipei Times, November 12, 2003.

referendum plans." It went out of its way to state that the welcome it gave to Chen during his stopover in New York by no means represented an agreement with his policy.

Yet Washington's clarification came 10 days after President Chen Shui-bian returned from his New York visit. That gave the incumbent time to tout his U.S. visit as a "major diplomatic breakthrough" and led to a surge in popularity in the opinion polls. [103]

The delayed response also left the impression that Washington was employing a two-faced policy toward the Taiwan leader. On the one hand, the U.S. wanted to restrain Chen from extreme positions that would endanger cross-strait stability, but at the same time, it hoped to make some friendly gestures toward the Taiwan president. By giving him a warm reception during his New York stay, Washington wanted to show the Taiwanese public that Chen Shui-bian still enjoyed the firm support of the U.S., despite his troubling political rhetoric. This was of great importance to Chen as he fought an uphill battle for a second term.

Introducing Taiwan's First Referendum

A third controversial theme on Chen Shui-bian's reelection campaign agenda was a call to hold an island-wide referendum, alongside the March 2004 presidential election.

Commentary, Chen's High-Profile Transit Hints at U.S. Policy Change, China Post, November 5, 2003.

Chapter 4
Turning Divisive Issues into Political Assets

In a democratic country, it is not unusual to use a national or local referendum to settle a deadlocked public policy that could not be resolved through normal legislative measures.

But in the case of Chen Shui-bian's push for a referendum while campaigning for reelection, it was a different matter. His call for Taiwan to hold an unprecedented referendum was seen as not just a bid to build momentum for an electoral victory. Many observers feared he might be seeking to use the referendum to set a legal precedent for a vote on self-determination for Taiwan in the future.

That was not a baseless concern. The goal of determining Taiwan's political future via a popular vote was enshrined in the charter of the pro-independence DPP. The party in October 1991, following a heated debate among its various factions, finally adopted a resolution that called for the establishment of a "Republic of Taiwan" through a plebiscite by the residents on this island.[104]

So when Chen first made known his plan in May 2003 to hold a referendum, it immediately aroused concerns in Beijing and Washington. Beijing attacked his proposed referendum as a serious challenge to China's sovereignty. Washington too expressed disapproval, saying that while deciding what would be voted on was Taiwan's internal affair, the U.S. would not want to see either side of the strait say or do anything that would endanger the security of the region.

---

104 Susan Hsu, DPP Divided on Whether to Drop Independence Clause, Taiwan Journal, December 16, 1994.

But Chen dismissed such concerns as interference in Taiwan's internal affairs. In a swipe at Washington, he told the people of Taiwan "We are not a state of any country." And he let loose a rhetorical arrow in Beijing's direction as well. "Taiwan is an independent state, not a subordinate province of any country," he said.[105] By aiming such stinging remarks at Beijing and Washington, according to some observers, Chen wanted to portray himself as a strong leader who dared to say "no" to the world's two largest powers.

But in private he instructed his government to move quickly to allay Washington's worries. The president reassured Taiwan's principal partner that he remained committed to his pledge not to push for a plebiscite on Taiwan's political future during his years in office. At the same time, he signaled to Beijing that maintaining peace and stability in the Taiwan Strait continued to be the core of his cross-strait policy.

Chen continued to employ a complicated mix of tactics. Just days after reassuring the United States that he would never push for a referendum on Taiwan's political status during his presidency, his party and administration moved to step up their push for an open-ended draft referendum law at a bipartisan legislative session.[106]

Lin Cho-shui and his fellow DPP caucus whips attending the session severely criticized the two opposition parties, the KMT and the PFP, for jointly sponsoring a counter-referendum act. The opposition version included provisions against holding any referendums aimed at

105 Editorial, President's Referendum Strategy Could Backfire, China Post, June 25, 2003.
106 Fiona Lu, Date Set for Review of Referendum Law, Taipei Times, November 14, 2003.

changing the constitution, sovereignty, or national name. "No referendum law," Lin hit back, "should set stipulations limiting people's rights to determine Taiwan's political future."

Traditionally, the KMT and the PFP were opposed to the enactment of any plebiscite because it would serve as a legal basis for holding referendums in the future. But then the two parties shifted their strategy. They actively pressed for a prompt passage of a referendum law at an extra legislative session scheduled for July 2003. They decided on the strategy shift to counter Chen Shui-bian's accusations they were an "anti-reform group."

But to everyone's surprise, the president responded to the new policy stance of the KMT-PFP alliance by reversing his position and putting aside the proposed plebiscite law. "A plebiscite law is not all that urgent," Chen told reporters. "We need to devote the extra legislative session to discussing economic and other more urgent bills."

The real reason behind Chen's about-turn was that he now had other considerations: Chen said he hoped to replace his proposed plebiscite law with an "administrative directive." Specifically, he wanted to use his administrative authority to conduct a series of non-binding "consultative" referendums. Such "consultative" referendums, he explained, would be used to "sound out public opinion" on some controversial public issues. He planned to hold a vote on issues such as applying for entry into the World Health Organization and halting a partially completed multi-billion-dollar nuclear power plant.

Many observers saw Chen Shui-bian's tactic of conducting "consultative" referendums with no binding powers as a wise calculation. Holding referendums of this kind would be less sensitive politically and avoid tensions with Washington and Beijing. At the same time, Chen could use these actions to build momentum for his presidential campaign. To his great disappointment, Chen Shui-bian failed to push through his "consultative" referendum plans due to strong resistance from the opposition parties. His reluctance to give priority to enacting a plebiscite law at an extra legislative meeting allowed the debate on the proposed legislation to be postponed until the autumn when lawmakers returned from their summer recess for a new session.

By that time the opposition KMT and its ally the PFP had decided to shift their position. Their new stance was to actively support the enactment of a referendum law, but they adopted a more flexible attitude toward what provisions should or should not be written in the legislation.

As scheduled, the Legislative Yuan resumed debate on competing bills from the ruling and opposition parties. Lawmakers from the governing DPP and the main opposition KMT at their first joint meeting agreed to an end-of-November 2003 deadline by which a plebiscite law would be enacted.

The bill introduced by the KMT and PFP alliance prohibited referendums on any sovereignty issues, such as changing the nation's name, flag, or anthem. The opposition parties disagreed with the DPP about its provision that the government was authorized to hold an independence referendum should Taiwan come under attack. Additionally, the KMT and the PFP strongly objected to a DPP proposal that the government should be allowed to initiate referendums. They insisted that only the people had that right.

In a bid to win over undecided voters in the final stages of the March 2004 presidential election, the KMT and the PFP took a more flexible position on what could be voted on in a referendum. This was characterized as an effort to protect the popular right to initiate referendums. But support for a more broadly defined plebiscite act on the part of the KMT and the PFP -- parties that normally supported closer cross-strait relations -- intensified concerns and anxiety in both Beijing and Washington.

Beijing issued a tough response to the latest developments in Taiwan's inter-party conflict over enacting a referendum law. Wang Zaixi, vice minister at the Taiwan Affairs Office of China's State Council, told China's state media, "If the Taiwan authorities collude with separatist forces to openly engage in pro-independence activities and challenge the one-China principle, the use of force may become unavoidable."

The U.S. also reacted swiftly. It warned China not to consider the use of military force against Taiwan. State Department spokesman Adam Ereli said, "The use of force to resolve cross-strait differences is unacceptable." Speaking at his regular daily press briefing, Ereli added, "We oppose any attempt by either side to unilaterally change the status quo in the Taiwan Strait."[107]

At the same time, Washington intensified communication with Taipei. It persuaded the KMT-PFP alliance, which held a majority of seats in the Legislative Yuan, into passing a less provocative

---

107 Charles Synder, U.S. Warns China not to Use Force against Taiwan, Taipei Times, November 21, 2003.

referendum law by rejecting a pro-independence clause and denying the administration the right to write a new constitution.

At the same time, the U.S. exerted greater pressure on Chen Shui-bian, forcing him to personally intervene in the ongoing legislative negotiations at the last minute. In response, Chen asked a fellow DPP lawmaker, Chai Trong-rong, to withdraw a hardline bill. If passed, the bill sponsored by Chai would have authorized changes regarding territorial sovereignty and the national name. Chen also was pressured into retreating on a crucial referendum article proposed by his administration and containing his call to write a new constitution.

In the end, the Legislative Yuan passed what many called a watered-down Referendum Act on November 27, 2003. The new legislation set no provision for writing a new constitution – one of Chen's initial objectives. The referendum law made it even harder for any attempt to change sovereignty symbols such as the national name and flag, by setting extremely high thresholds for passage.

Months of tensions with the U.S. and the mainland eased with Taipei's passage of a less provocative referendum law that excluded a series of pro-independence articles. But this turned out to be a very brief respite.

Three days later on November 30, Chen suddenly announced that he would call a "defensive" referendum to "safeguard Taiwan's sovereignty and security" by invoking a defense clause stipulated in the newly enacted plebiscite law. The proposed referendum, he said, would be conducted on March 20, 2004, in conjunction with the presidential election.

Chapter 4
Turning Divisive Issues into Political Assets

Indeed, there was a provision in the newly enacted plebiscite law that gave the president the power to launch a referendum on matters relating to national security, or when Taiwan faced an "imminent threat" to its sovereignty. But when Chen made his "defensive" referendum announcement, there were no obvious indications that Taiwan was under threat. In the period immediately before Chen announced his "defensive" referendum, Taiwan's defense minister had twice reassured the public that no "unusual troop movements had been monitored on the mainland's southeastern coast opposite this island."

Chen justified his call for the "defensive" referendum by citing the many hundreds of missiles positioned on the mainland for use against Taiwan. But the reality was that those missiles had been deployed there for years and could not be viewed as a new military development on the part of the mainland. Hence, the mainland's missiles were anything but an "imminent" threat to the security of Taiwan.

Beijing sharply criticized Chen Shui-bian's new plan to launch a "defensive" referendum as "part of an action plan to split Taiwan from the Chinese mainland."[108]

Meanwhile, the U.S. was also angered by Chen's "defensive" referendum plan, so angry that then-President George W. Bush delivered harsh public criticism of the Taiwan president on December 9 during a visit to Washington by mainland Chinese Premier Wen Jia-bao. "The comments and actions made by the leader of Taiwan indicate

---

108 Commentary, Beijing Feels Desperate After Failing to Block Referendum, China Post, February 11, 2004.

that he may be willing to make decisions to unilaterally change the status quo, which we oppose," Bush said.

A State Department spokesman, in a subsequent news conference, singled out Chen Shui-bian's "defensive" referendum for criticism, saying that designating a "particular date" for a referendum on a "particular subject" was a political action aiming at moving in a "particular direction." The spokesman added: "The referendum plan will not have the support of the United States."

Still, the vigorous opposition from the U.S. and mainland China failed to deter Chen Shui-bian from pressing ahead with his "defensive" referendum plan. But he did reword the text of the questions on the referendum to such an extent that it contained no language openly challenging the political status quo in cross-strait relations.

The following were the two questions put forth in Chen Shui-bian's "defensive" referendum in its final form. Question one: "If Communist China refuses to withdraw the missiles it has targeting Taiwan and renounce the use of force against us, would you agree that the government should acquire more advanced anti-missile weapons to strengthen Taiwan's self-defense capabilities?" Question two: "Would you agree that our government should engage in negotiations with China about the establishment of a peace and stability framework for cross-strait interactions to build mutual understanding and for the welfare of the people on both sides?"

The "defensive" referendum was conducted on March 20, 2004, alongside the presidential election. Voters almost unanimously agreed on the two questions, but both failed to pass due to insufficient turnout

Chapter 4
Turning Divisive Issues into Political Assets

as the number of votes fell short of the required minimum 50 percent of registered voters.

But Chen Shui-bian won the presidential election, acquiring a second term with a razor-thin margin of less than 30,000 votes. He received 50.1 percent of the total votes cast, while challenger Lien Chan took 49.9 percent. Many political analysts attributed Chen's win to his adroitness in manipulating the various political issues mentioned earlier. But there were other factors, including a mysterious election-eve shooting incident that left Chen with a minor bullet wound but probably won him a significant number of sympathy votes. Perhaps it was a combination of the two factors that allowed him to eke out a victory. (The election-eve shooting incident will be discussed further in later pages.)

How Chen Shui-bian interpreted the significance of his new mandate and the various challenges he encountered as he sought to advance his pro-independence agenda during his second four-year tenure will be narrated in the following chapter and beyond.

Chapter 5
Elected to a Second Term

Posing a Formidable Challenge for China and the U.S.

In March 2004, Chen Shui-bian won a second term as president, running on a pro-independence platform. He was reelected with a very narrow margin, but the victory allowed him to claim he had a new mandate to pursue his political goals over the next four years aggressively.

The reality was, however, that he faced serious opposition from the world's two superpowers, China, which claims sovereignty over Taiwan, and the United States, which has binding obligations to help defend this island, but only against unprovoked attacks.

In the election campaign, Chen passionately promoted three radical objectives: the concept of "one country on each side of the Taiwan Strait," his plan to enact a new constitution, and nationwide referendums on public policies.

Regarding the last point, an underlying plebiscite law had already been passed as a legal basis for conducting almost any referendums in the future -- thanks to Chen's hard promotion in the campaign. "With the establishment of such a legal basis, it meant that President Chen Shui-bian could conduct any referendums in the future, perhaps on the theme of independence," observed Robert L. Suettinger, former national intelligence officer for East Asia during the Clinton administration.[109]

As noted earlier, Chen Shui-bian defeated his KMT challenger Lien Chan in the 2004 presidential race by a very narrow margin of about 30,000 votes. But he garnered 50.1 percent of all votes -- versus Lien's 49.9% -- and could claim to have majority support. "My reelection demonstrated that most of the people of Taiwan agreed with my political beliefs," he told a huge crowd of supporters on election night.

In several post-election media interviews, he repeatedly stressed that he would make good on his campaign promises. He vowed to go forward with plans to write a new constitution for Taiwan within the next two years and stuck firmly to his "one country on each side of the Taiwan Strait" stance.

In a high-profile interview with the Washington Post one week after his reelection, Chen touted the significance of his victory, reasserting Taiwan's independent status and rejecting Beijing's "one China" principle as unacceptable. Below are excerpts from that interview:[110]

"The fundamental reason I won this presidential election is that there is a rising Taiwan identity, and it has been solidified. I think the Beijing authorities should take heed of this fact and accept the reality.

109 Robert L. Suettinger, Leadership Policy toward Taiwan and the United States in the Wake of Chen Shui-bian's Re-Election, China Leadership Monitor, Issue 10, Spring 2004, The Hoover Institution.
110 Philp P. Pan and David E. Hoffman, Taiwan's President Maintains Hard Line: Chen Rebukes China in Interview, Washington Post, March 30, 2004.

Chapter 5
Elected to a Second Term

I think we have reached an internal consensus that insists on Taiwan being an independent, sovereign country...

"For the 23 million people of Taiwan, whether our country is called Taiwan or the Republic of China, it does not change the fact that we are an independent, sovereign country. We are not a local government of another country. So, this is the status quo. We want to maintain this kind of status quo. We certainly don't want Taiwan's current status quo to be changed unilaterally...

"If the Chinese government insists on the 'one China' principle as a precondition for talks, Taiwan will answer that China must recognize this island as a separate country. Then, I believe the two sides will be forever deadlocked, major differences cannot be solved and it will be impossible for both sides to sit down and talk. So don't raise the 'one China' principle."

In the run-up to the March 20, 2004, election, Beijing kept its anger largely in check despite Chen's China-bashing and pro-independence remarks as it hoped to avoid galvanizing voter sympathy for the incumbent president. But Chen's reelection was a significant embarrassment to Beijing, which worried about the president's post-election vows to press ahead with his plan for a new constitution. That plan was widely seen as an attempt to pursue de jure independence.

After the election, Beijing realized it had to get tougher with Chen Shui-bian. In the two months leading up to his inauguration on May 20, PRC authorities kept sending stern messages to the Taiwan leader, warning him not to "underestimate the resolve and the ability of the Chinese government and its people to protect the territorial integrity of

China." They vowed that the PRC government would be willing to fulfill that mission at any cost.

In the meantime, Beijing stepped up pressure on Washington to constrain Chen Shui-bian from taking provocative actions. It believed that the best way to persuade Washington to do so was to convince the U.S. that China would not hesitate to use force should Chen move to change the status quo.

On March 21, the day after Chen won reelection, Chinese Foreign Minister Li Zhaoxing made a phone call to U.S. Secretary of State Colin Powell, urging the United States to "adhere to the one-China policy and do more to contribute to peace and stability across the Taiwan Strait and the development of cross-strait relations." Minister Li also asked Washington to observe the three China-U.S. joint communiques and oppose any moves by the Taiwan authorities to unilaterally change the island's status quo.[111]

Li Zhaoxing's March 21 phone conversation with Powell was made public three days later by PRC Foreign Ministry spokesman Kong Quan. The spokesman said in a news release that China "has noted the U.S. viewpoints on the current events in Taiwan. We must point out that the election in the Taiwan region is only a local election of China and no matter what outcome it produced, it cannot alter the fact that Taiwan is a part of China."

China's heightened concerns over Taiwan's post-election political situation and its avowed resolve to use military measures if necessary

111 Chinese FM Talks with Powell via Phone, website of the Consulate General of the People's Republic of China, Chicago, March 24, 2004.

Chapter 5
Elected to a Second Term

were also conveyed to U.S. Vice President Dick Cheney during his visit to Beijing in mid-April. Cheney was in the Chinese capital for talks regarding the war on terrorism, North Korea's nuclear weapons program as well as Taiwan.

The U.S. vice president met with Chinese President Hu Jintao and his predecessor Jiang Zemin. Jiang at the time was still chairman of China's powerful Central Military Commission. The two Chinese leaders told Cheney that China was prepared to take action militarily should Chen persist with his independence agenda. A war, the U.S. visitor was told, would be unavoidable unless Chen was forced to change course.

To underscore the seriousness of Beijing's concerns about the latest political developments in Taiwan, the PRC's Taiwan Affairs Office spokesman Zhang Mingqing issued a strongly worded statement on the day of Cheney's arrival, saying: "No person or force should underestimate the determination and capability of the Chinese government and its 1.3 billion people to safeguard national unity and sovereignty and territorial integrity at any price."

Beijing's top-level threats before and during Cheney's visit were taken seriously in Washington and Taipei. Barely a week later, Assistant Secretary of State for East Asian and Pacific Affairs James Kelly warned Taiwan that unilateral moves toward independence could prompt a Chinese military response "that could destroy much of what Taiwan has built and crush its hopes for the future." Kelly, who was testifying before a congressional hearing, continued: "It would be irresponsible of us and of Taiwan leaders to treat these statements as empty threats." He further reminded Taipei that the U.S. pledge to defend Taiwan "must not be perceived as a blank check."

Kelly's testimony is quoted, in part, below:[112] "The United States does not support independence for Taiwan or unilateral moves that would change the status quo as we define it. For Beijing, this means no use of force or threat to use force against Taiwan. For Taipei, it means exercising prudence in managing all aspects of cross-strait relations. For both sides, it means no statements or actions that would unilaterally alter Taiwan's status...

"The President's message on December 9 of last year (2003) during PRC Premier Wen Jiabao's visit reiterated the U.S. government's opposition to any unilateral moves by either China or Taiwan changing the status quo...The United States will fulfill its obligations to help Taiwan defend itself, as mandated in the Taiwan Relations Act. At the same time, we have very real concerns that our efforts at deterring Chinese coercion might fail if Beijing ever becomes convinced Taiwan is embarked on a course toward independence and permanent separation from China, and concludes that Taiwan must be stopped in these efforts...

"The United States strongly supports Taiwan's democracy...but we do not support its independence. A unilateral move toward independence will avail Taiwan of nothing it does not already enjoy in terms of democratic freedom, autonomy, prosperity, and security...

---

112 Testimony of Assistant Secretary of State for East Asian and Pacific Affairs James Kelly at hearing held by the House International Relations Committee on "The Taiwan Relations Act: The Next 25 Years," April 21, 2004.

Chapter 5
Elected to a Second Term

"While strongly opposing the use of force by the PRC, we must also acknowledge with a sober mind what the PRC leaders have repeatedly conveyed about China's capabilities and intentions...It would be irresponsible of us and of Taiwan's leaders to treat these statements as empty threats...We encourage the people of Taiwan to regard this threat equally seriously. We look to President Chen to exercise the kind of responsible, democratic, and restrained leadership that will be necessary to ensure a peaceful and prosperous future for Taiwan...

"As Taiwan proceeds with efforts to deepen democracy, we will speak clearly and bluntly if we feel as though those efforts carry the potential to adversely impact U.S. security interests or have the potential to undermine Taiwan's security. There are limitations concerning what the United States will support, as Taiwan considers possible changes to its constitution...

"Our position continues to be embodied in the so-called 'Six Assurances' offered to Taiwan by President Reagan. We will neither seek to mediate between the PRC and Taiwan nor will we exert pressure on Taiwan to come to the bargaining table. Of course, the United States is also committed to making available defensive arms and defensive services to Taiwan to help Taiwan meet its self-defense needs. We believe a secure and self-confident Taiwan is a Taiwan that is more capable of engaging in political interaction and dialogue with the PRC, and we expect Taiwan will not interpret our support as a blank check to resist such dialogue...

219

"War in the Strait would be a disaster for both sides and set them back decades. We continue to urge Beijing and Taipei to pursue dialogue as soon as possible through any available channels...

"The PRC has explicitly committed itself publicly and in exchange with the United States over the last 25 years to a fundamental policy to strive for a peaceful resolution of the Taiwan question. If the PRC meets its obligations, and its words are matched by a military posture that bolsters and supports peaceful approaches to Taiwan, it follows logically that Taiwan's defense requirements will change..."

PRC and the U.S. Join Hands to 'Co-Manage' Chen

Officially, Beijing rebuked Kelly's testimony as interference in China's internal affairs. But privately, the PRC and the U.S. appeared to have reached a tacit understanding about how to "co-manage" Chen and prevent him from pursuing formal independence for Taiwan during his presidency. According to media reports, Washington launched talks with Chen Shui-bian and his top aides immediately after his reelection. The U.S. wanted to obtain two key assurances from Chen before he began his second term on May 20, 2004. One was that Chen must not use his second inaugural address to declare Taiwan as an independent country. Two, he had to reaffirm his "five noes" commitment not to change the status quo, or Taiwan's political status.

Before discussing how Chen Shui-bian responded to the U.S. request for him to reaffirm his "five noes" commitment in his second

Chapter 5
Elected to a Second Term

inaugural speech, it is appropriate to examine those five pledges and the circumstances in which they were made.

Chen's 2000 commitment consisted of "four noes, one without." The "four noes" meant no declaration of independence, no change in the national title, no inclusion of the state-to-state theory in the constitution, and no referendum on the issue of independence versus unification. The meaning of the "one without" was, in essence, no abolition of the National Unification Council or the Guidelines for National Unification. As time went by, Chen Shui-bian's 2000 commitments came to be known as the "five noes."

Why was Chen Shui-bian requested to make these pledges? Why did these pledges matter to the PRC, the U.S., and Taiwan itself? To answer these questions, it is necessary to start with Chen's independence-leaning background and the core value of his party, the Democratic Progressive Party, as well as his position on Taiwan's relations with mainland China.

Chen Shui-bian has long been an advocate of independence for Taiwan. During his early years as an opposition legislator, he was a vocal opponent of Beijing's "one China" principle. He argued that the "one-China" principle referred to the People's Republic of China and that it had nothing to do with Taiwan.

Chen ran in the 2000 presidential election as the candidate of the DPP, a party that has never been shy about espousing its cause of building a Taiwan republic that is distinct from mainland China. In a full party congress in 1991, five years after its founding, the DPP openly enshrined a Taiwan independence clause in the party charter. As a strategy to win broader voter support, however, the DPP adopted

221

a relatively conciliatory resolution on Taiwan's future in 1999. Even so, the 1999 resolution still maintains that "Taiwan is a sovereign and independent country. Any change in the independent status quo must be decided by all the residents of Taiwan through a plebiscite."

As a candidate for president in the 2000 election, Chen moderated his pro-independence stance slightly by saying that "Taiwan is a de facto sovereignty and its name is the Republic of China according to the constitution." As for the question of the "one-China" principle, he said that "once in office, the issue could be put on the negotiating table." This suggested that Chen considered Beijing's "one-China" principle could be accepted only as a subject of discussion.

In the run-up to polling day, Chen moderated his political stance further, saying that if elected, he would not push for independence for Taiwan. "Taiwan would declare independence only if it faces invasion by China," he said.

But Beijing, which regards Taiwan as part of China, was unconvinced by Chen's campaign assurances. On the eve of the March 18, 2000, presidential election, Chinese Premier Zhu Rongji warned Taiwan's voters to "think twice before casting their ballots for the 'candidate of independence' lest they regret it afterward."

The U.S., Taiwan's longtime supporter, made a timely response to the Chinese premier's intimidating remarks, urging Beijing not to intervene in Taiwan's elections. Then U.S. Secretary of State Madeleine Albright told Beijing unequivocally that Washington could not accept its blatant intimidation of this island. She reiterated

Chapter 5
Elected to a Second Term

America's position that any differences across the Taiwan Strait needed to be resolved through peaceful means.

It was unknown how much of a calming influence Albright's remarks had on Taiwan's voters. On election day, the Taiwanese people voted for the DPP candidate Chen Shui-bian as their next president in defiance of Beijing's warnings.

Chen's victory raised hackles in Beijing. Commenting on the results of the election, a spokesman for Beijing's Taiwan Affairs Office said that Chen Shui-bian would have to "return to the 'one-China' principle before contacts can be resumed between the two sides."

By contrast, Chen's election was positively received in Washington. U.S. officials warmly welcomed the election result. The U.S. had reason to respond positively to Chen's election: He was the first politician from an opposition party to win the ROC presidency -- a milestone in Taiwan's democratic development.

But at the same time, U.S. officials worried that the independence-leaning Chen Shui-bian might lead Taiwan in his desired direction after taking power, breaking away from China. They feared that the scenario could provoke Beijing to use force. While the U.S. no longer had diplomatic relations with Taiwan, it maintained defense ties to the island. Under the Taiwan Relations Act, Washington has obligations to help Taiwan defend against "unprovoked" attacks.

All this meant that the U.S. had to be careful not to be dragged into a conflict with China over the issue of Taiwan's independence. The U.S. had good reason to be especially cautious about such a risk. Barely a year or so earlier, then-President Clinton had managed to prevent a new cross-strait crisis. Tensions had suddenly increased after outgoing President Lee Teng-hui angered Beijing with his characterization of Taiwan-mainland relations as a "special state-to-state relationship."

As Taiwan's president-elect, Chen Shui-bian faced two major challenges. One, the mandate he obtained in the 2000 election was a weak one, garnering only 39% of the vote. This meant Chen Shui-bian needed the support of the anti-independence KMT if he wanted to provide stable governance. The KMT, although having lost the presidency, still held two-thirds of the seats in the legislature and controlled most local governments.

The other major challenge confronting the new president was how to allay public concerns about Taiwan's security and stability under his administration. People were worried that the mainland could attack Taiwan if it was perceived as moving toward independence. Failing to effectively deal with such security concerns could trigger a wave of human and capital flight, something that Taiwan could ill afford.

It was against such a background that Chen Shui-bian made the "four noes and one without" commitment in his 2000 inaugural address as a series of pledges to reassure Washington and Beijing that he would never alter Taiwan's political status after assuming the presidency.

Chen's pledge to respect the "five noes" had been made known to both Washington and Beijing beforehand, according to media reports. Some newspapers even reported that Washington played a behind-the-scenes role in drafting his 2000 inaugural speech. These reports said that Raymond Burghardt, the director of the American Institute in Taiwan's Taipei office -- the de facto American embassy, "got in close contact with Chen Shui-bian and his top aides immediately after the election results came out." Through such direct and private communications, the U.S. wanted to make sure that the president-elect included all of the "five noes" in his inaugural speech without saying anything contradicting them. Those reports were strongly denied by AIT, but Chen's vice president Annette Lu repeatedly insisted that her boss's "five noes" commitment was made "under strong pressure from the United States." [113]

By pressuring Chen into making this commitment, the U.S. sought to play a balancing role between Taiwan and the mainland in the interests of maintaining peace and stability in the region by forestalling moves by either side of the strait to unilaterally change the political status quo.

More specifically, Washington hoped to use Chen's "five noes" to oblige him to preserve Taiwan's political status quo and not push for independence. At the same time, the U.S. wanted to see to it that the PRC would not use force against Taiwan or threaten to use force, so long as Chen Shui-bian kept his "five noes" pledges.

Under Chen Shui-bian, relations between Taiwan and the mainland turned from bad to worse. Cross-strait ties seemed to be relatively calm in the first two years of Chen's first term, as the president kept his pledges. But beneath the calm façade, relations were

---

113 AIT Head Denies Role in Drafting of Chen's Inaugural Speech, Central News Agency, May 13, 2000.

— The Fall of a President —

strained due to Chen's consistent refusal to accept Beijing's "one China" principle.

Bilateral ties deteriorated further in the final two years of Chen's first term. This was partly because of Chen's "one country on each side of the Taiwan Strait" formulation, first raised in August 2002. It also reflected his unrelenting push for a new constitution and a defensive referendum as he sought a second term.

Chen violated the first four of his "five noes" pledges during his first term by advocating the concept of Taiwan and the mainland being two separate countries, pressing for the enactment of a new constitution, and holding a "defensive" referendum. Left unbroken was the last pledge, or the "one without." But he reneged on that one in the middle of his second term by deciding to "cease the function of the National Unification Council and cease the application of the Guidelines."

Chen's behavior constantly strained Taiwan's relations with the U.S., which plunged to their lowest levels in decades. "During his first administration, Taiwan President Chen Shui-bian traversed the full spectrum of relations with the United States: from a trusted democratic friend and quasi-ally with increasingly convergent views, to highly distrusted and disliked leader, viewed by Washington as potentially destructive of some vital U.S. interests," observed Michael D. Swaine, a senior associate at Carnegie Endowment for International Peace.[114] The single most important factor in the dramatic downturn in Chen's

---

114 Michael D. Swaine, Taiwan's Management of Relations with the United States during the First Chen Shui-bian Administration, China Program, Carnegie Endowment for International Peace, May 5, 2005.

Chapter 5
Elected to a Second Term

Washington relations, Swaine said, was that he "placed narrower, short-term political calculations above fundamental, enduring strategic interests in addressing relations with the United States."

So Chen Shui-bian's reelection in March 2004 to a second term posed an especially difficult challenge for U.S. leaders. Why was that so? To begin with, Chen had been regarded by the George W. Bush administration as "a highly untrustworthy leader by the end of his first term in office," according to Swaine. Bush distrusted Chen because of his unrelenting manipulation of independence and cross-strait issues, provoking Beijing and putting regional peace and stability at risk. Chen had a record of showing little respect for his commitments made to the U.S. not to change Taiwan's political status.

Still, Washington had to face the reality that Chen Shui-bian was an incumbent president who won reelection on a pro-independence agenda and would lead Taiwan for the next four years. This meant that if the U.S. wanted to continue to play a balancing role in cross-strait relations or just to protect its strategic interests in the region, it would need to engage with Chen.

Policymakers in Washington recognized this uncomfortable reality. The challenge was how to rein in Chen Shui-bian and prevent him from pursuing formal independence for Taiwan. The best option was to get Chen to reaffirm his "five noes" commitment of 2000, when he began his second term as president on May 20, 2004.

But it was no easy task getting a reelected president to return to a set of pledges that he had repeatedly ignored in the past. At this point, Chen was armed with majority support from the voting public, and for him to reembrace those past promises might be viewed as breaching his new mandate.

Given the difficulties, the U.S. government adopted a carrot-and-stick approach in trying to persuade Chen Shui-bian to reaffirm his 2000 pledges of "five noes" in the two months leading up to his second inauguration.

The carrot was a fresh reassurance. Washington moved quickly to assure Chen Shui-bian anew that the United States would continue to support him and his administration, putting aside his pre-election political provocations that constantly stirred up tensions in the Taiwan Strait.

Below are two notable instances of how the Bush administration renewed its support for Chen Shui-bian following his reelection victory. First, the White House and the State Department sent a congratulatory message to Chen Shui-bian while the election results were still hotly contested by Lien Chan, Chen's opponent, over alleged voting fraud. At that point, one week after the election, a court-backed recount of the results had not been completed.

Chen's reelection was contested not just because the victory margin was so slim, but also because of a mysterious election-eve shooting incident that left him with a minor bullet wound to his abdomen. Many believed this won him enough sympathy votes to produce the winning margin – a mere 30,00 votes. Lien Chan refused to recognize the election results.

The other instance of the U.S. swiftly renewing its support for Chen Shui-bian was as follows: On March 31, barely 10 days after Chen declared victory, the U.S. Department of Defense announced that

Chapter 5
Elected to a Second Term

it had agreed to sell US$1.8 billion in long-range radar systems to Taiwan to enhance its ability to detect PRC missile launches.[115] The sale of the radar systems had been repeatedly postponed by the Bush administration to express its disapproval of Chen's provocative remarks and actions during the campaign. The KMT and its supporters questioned the timing of the U.S. government's announcement of the sale of the advanced weaponry systems to Taiwan.

At the same time, Washington continued to exert pressure on Chen Shui-bian. It warned that if Chen failed to reiterate his 2000 "five noes" commitment and exclude any reference to his "one country on each side of the strait" concept in his second inaugural speech, it would have grave consequences for Taiwan.

A stern warning was issued by Assistant Secretary of State for East Asian and Pacific Affairs James Kelly on April 21 in testimony before the House of Representatives Committee on International Relations. As mentioned earlier, Kelly stated bluntly that the United States "does not support independence for Taiwan or unilateral moves that would change the status quo as we define it."

The carrot-and-stick approach adopted by the Bush administration appeared to work. Following weeks of intense bilateral negotiations, Chen softened his stance. He agreed to exclude sovereignty issues from his upcoming inaugural address and include a statement about his willingness to work toward reconciliation with Beijing. He even went further by sending Presidential Office Secretary-

---

115 Bradley Graham, Pentagon Announces Plans to Sell Radars to Taiwan, Washington Post, April 1, 2004.

General Chiou I-jen and Mainland Affairs Council Chairwoman Tsai
Ing-wen to Washington in late April to communicate a draft outline of
his constitutional program and his new policy toward mainland China.

But U.S. officials insisted on seeing the final full text of Chen's
second-term inaugural speech in advance to ensure that what he was
going to say would be in line with what he had promised to the United
States. Washington's insistence reflected a profound lack of trust in
Chen.

By May 8, less than two weeks before his inauguration,
Washington was still unsure that its concerns would be fully addressed
by Chen in his speech. "The U.S. was still looking to seeing and
hearing the inaugural speech of President Chen," said then-Secretary
of State Colin Powell in a media interview that day.

Beijing, for its part, was even more anxious to learn what Chen
was going to say about his cross-strait policy for the next four years.
In what was seen as a last-minute attempt to influence Chen, the PRC
issued a seven-point statement to Taipei on May 17, just three days
before his inauguration.[116]

The statement, issued jointly by the PRC's top-level Central
Taiwan Affairs Group -- headed by President Hu Jintao himself -- and
the Taiwan Affairs Office, read in part: "At this juncture, cross-strait
relations are severely tested. To put a resolute check on the 'Taiwan
independence' activities aimed at splitting the island from China and

---

116 Curbing Taiwan Independence Most Urgent Task, the People's Daily,
May 17, 2004.

safeguarding peace and stability in the strait is the most pressing task facing the compatriots on both sides of the strait...

"We will never compromise on the one-China principle, never give up our efforts for peace negotiations, never falter in our sincere pursuit of peace and development on both sides of the strait with our Taiwan compatriots, never waver in our resolve to safeguard China's sovereignty and territorial integrity, and never put up with Taiwan independence...

"Only two roads are lying before the Taiwan leader: One is to rein in the horse before the cliff by suspending separatist activities and accepting the position that both sides of the Taiwan Strait belong to the same China. The other is to persist in the pursuit of independence to split Taiwan from China. The choice of this latter road is to play with fire and will, in the end, lead to self-destruction."

U.S. Praises Inaugural Speech

The strong pressures the U.S. and the PRC had exerted on Chen Shui-bian since his reelection in March 2004 yielded generally encouraging responses from the Taiwan leader, as seen in his second inaugural address.[117]

Most noticeably, he did not include any reference to his "one country on each side of the Taiwan Strait" framework in his new inaugural speech, to the relief of PRC and U.S. officials.

---

117 Presidential office of the Republic of China, President Chen's Inaugural Address: Paving the Way for a Sustainable Taiwan, May 20, 2004.

He also promised not to touch on sensitive sovereignty issues in carrying out his constitutional reform. He had this to say: "I am fully aware that consensus has yet to be reached on the issues relating to national sovereignty, territory, and the subject of unification/independence; therefore, let me explicitly propose that these particular issues be excluded from my constitutional re-engineering project."

From the above remarks, one can see Chen not only promised to avoid sovereignty issues, he also softened his reference to a new constitution, a focus of his campaign, referring to it as only "my constitutional re-engineering project." This made it sound like he no longer envisioned an entirely new constitution. Instead, he merely wanted to reform the existing one.

Chen went on to explain in his address the significance of his constitutional reform program: "The constitutional re-engineering project aims to enhance good governance and increase administrative efficiency, to ensure a solid foundation for democratic rule of law, and to foster long-term stability and prosperity of the nation...By the time I complete my presidency in 2008, I hope to hand the people of Taiwan and our country a new constitution -- one that is timely, relevant, and viable -- as my historic responsibility and my commitment to the people." [118]

"Procedurally," he continued, "we shall follow the rules as set out in the existing constitution and the amendments attached to it." The

---

118 President Chen's second inaugural speech was available in both Chinese and English. While he said "new constitution" in Chinese, the official English translation used "a new version of our constitution."

latter remarks represented another big concession. In the campaign, Chen had advocated passing a new constitution via an island-wide referendum, bypassing the opposition-dominated Legislative Yuan -- a lawmaking body that is legally authorized to approve any constitutional changes.

Besides the constitutional issue, Chen also stated that he would stick to his 2000 inaugural "four noes and one without" commitment. However, he did not specify what that meant. Instead, he said: "Today I would like to reaffirm the promises and the principles outlined in my inaugural speech in 2000. Those commitments have been honored -- they have not been changed over the past four years, nor will they change in the next four years."

Chen reportedly had reached an understanding with Washington beforehand about why he was unwilling to go further and spell out the "four noes and one without" pledges in his new inaugural speech. Chen's reluctance to specify these issues was due to strong opposition from hardline independence supporters. These hardliners, already angered by Chen's agreement to make concessions on the constitutional plan, had strongly urged him to express these themes in a deliberately vague manner to leave room for maneuvering in the years ahead.

On relations with the Chinese mainland, Chen said in the inaugural address: "If both sides are willing, based on goodwill, to create an environment engendered upon 'peaceful development and freedom of choice, then in the future, the Republic of China and the People's Republic of China -- or Taiwan and China -- can seek to establish relations in any form whatsoever. We would not exclude any possibility, so long as there is the consent of the 23 million people of Taiwan."

Chen's second inaugural address won him high praise from the U.S. government. Both the White House and the State Department welcomed the address as "responsible and constructive." Yet the positive U.S. response came as no surprise as the speech had been cleared by the Bush Administration at the last minute. Informed sources in both Washington and Taipei revealed that American officials went over the speech "literally word for word" to ensure that Washington's concerns were appropriately addressed.

The high-handed U.S. role in Chen's May 20, 2004, inaugural speech was later confirmed indirectly by C.J. Chen, then director of the Taipei Economic and Cultural Representative Office in Washington (Taipei's de facto embassy in the U.S. capital). C.J. Chen, who left his U.S. post one month after his boss began his second term, admitted at a farewell party that President Chen had faced immense pressure from the U.S. as he formulated his second inaugural speech. "I would be lying if I said there was no pressure from the U.S. government. The U.S. pressure was enormous."

Chen Shui-bian also won Washington's support for the peace overtures he made to Beijing in his address. U.S. officials hoped that Chen's proposals could help lay the foundation for the resumption of dialogue between Taipei and Beijing. "We hope that Chen's message -- especially on Taipei's willingness to engage across-the-board on cross-strait issues, not excluding any possible formula for creating an environment based on 'peaceful development and freedom of choice'-- will be greeted positively by the PRC and taken as a basis for dialogue, which can lead to the peaceful resolution of outstanding differences," said Deputy Assistant Secretary of State for East Asian and Pacific Affairs Randal Schriver.

The positive U.S. response to Chen's second inaugural speech reflected the Bush administration's appreciation of Chen's support for U.S. policy on cross-strait relations. For Chen Shui-bian, the significance was that he had won continued U.S. political and defense backing as a result of the political concessions he made in his speech.

However, the warming Taipei-Washington relations following Chen Shui-bian's second inauguration did not last long. The Taiwan president quickly returned to his favorite political themes, as he sought to build momentum for his party's candidates in the year-end legislative elections.

Beijing Suspicious of Chen's Intentions

The PRC's reaction to Chen Shui-bian's inaugural speech was not as positive as the response from the U.S., however. "The root of tensions in the Taiwan Strait has not been eliminated. The peril affecting peace and stability in the Asia-Pacific region still exists. Whether a war will erupt in the strait will depend on Chen's attitude." These comments, made by Taiwan Affairs Office spokesman Zhang Mingqing, were Beijing's first official reaction to Chen's 2004 inaugural speech. [119]

---

119 Chen's Speech Signals Split Attempt, People's Daily Online, May 25, 2004.

Beijing viewed Chen's concessions on excluding the themes of sovereignty, territory, and independence/unification from his constitutional reform program as being "vague." The vagueness, it said, was deliberately created to leave room for maneuvering over the next four years. Furthermore, Beijing was dissatisfied with the way Chen addressed China in his speech. "He still refused to recognize that Taiwan and the mainland both belong to one China," Zhang said.

Beijing's comments made it clear that it remained suspicious of Chen's political intentions. Zhang said at a news conference, "Admittedly, Chen Shui-bian did not repeat the term of 'one country on each side of the strait.' But his speech brimmed with the concept of 'Taiwan independence,' signaling an attempt to split the island from China."

The PRC's suspicion was not without reason. In strict terms, there were plenty of places in the speech that showed Chen having neither backed off from his drive for a new constitution nor softened his advocacy of an independent Taiwan.

For example, the reason Chen cited for his decision to leave out the sovereignty themes in his constitutional re-engineering project was his awareness that "consensus has yet to be reached" on such sensitive issues. This seemed to suggest that plans for a revision of national sovereignty and territory could be revived once his party won a strong majority in the legislature in future elections, or when Taiwan's public opinion shifted in favor of making such constitutional changes.

Chen, while making no direct reference to his controversial "one country on each side" line in his speech, time and again in the text used his double talk skills to present the concept of a separate Taiwan

Chapter 5
Elected to a Second Term

independent from China. The following three examples from the speech show how Chen adroitly portrayed Taiwan as independent from China:

One, "The Republic of China now exists in Taiwan, Penghu, Kinmen, and Matsu. This is a fact. Taiwan's existence as a member of the international community is also a fact." Two, "In the future, the Republic of China and the People's Republic of China -- or Taiwan and China -- can seek to establish relations in whatever form. We would not exclude any possibility so long as there is the consent of the 23 million people of Taiwan." And Three, "Let the Taiwan Republic of China work toward solidarity and harmony, fairness and justice, prosperity, and equality."

So it could be said that Chen Shui-bian, a shrewd and talented politician who won a reputation for employing clever but deceptive arguments to advance his ideas, took full advantage of his internationally televised second-term inaugural address to promote his assertion of Taiwan being an independent country.

Yet from President Chen's perspective, his willingness to drop his campaign plan to enact a new constitution that would create a legal basis for Taiwan to achieve de jure independence was in effect the hardest concession he could make. The PRC's insistence that he abandon the independence cause outright and embrace the one-China principle was simply unacceptable to him.

Taiwan leaders, unlike their PRC counterparts, draw their power directly from the people. When Chen claimed that his reelection was an indication that most of the people of Taiwan supported his position on China, this was generally true.

Also worthy of note, the PRC and the U.S. differed sharply in their reaction to Chen Shui-bian's "peace overtures." Soon after Chen began his second term, the Bush administration called on the mainland to respond positively to his peace proposals and re-open dialogue with him and his administration. But the mainland refused to do so because Chen Shui-bian failed to accept its "one China" principle.

One main reason for the difference was that the U.S. and the PRC have drastically different interests in their Taiwan policy. For the U.S., maintaining the status quo -- with Taiwan neither pursuing independence nor leaning toward the mainland -- was best for America's strategic interests in the region. Similarly, if Taiwan and the mainland could resume dialogue and promote free trade, it would be most welcome as it would suit the needs of American companies doing business across the Taiwan Strait.

As Chen had reaffirmed the "four noes and one without" commitment to not change Taiwan's political status and expressed his willingness to open talks with Beijing, it was natural for Washington to renew support for Chen and his policy, including his calls for the resumption of dialogue with the mainland.

Unlike Washington, the PRC's policy on Taiwan extends beyond opposition to independence for the island. It also insists on Taiwan leaders accepting the "one China" principle, recognizing that Taiwan and the mainland belong to China. So Chen's reaffirmation of his commitment to not alter the status quo did not go far enough to persuade Beijing to reopen talks with him.

Chapter 5
Elected to a Second Term

In contrast, the U.S., with its concerns having been addressed, moved swiftly to resume arms sales to Taiwan in line with its policy of helping the island defend itself and maintain the status quo.

The first such arms sale, as mentioned earlier, was two radar systems worth US$1.8 billion. Then in June, hardly two months after Chen Shui-bian's second inauguration, the Bush administration invited a Taiwan military procurement delegation to visit the U.S. and discuss issues of mutual concern.

During the delegation's stay, U.S. and Taiwan officials negotiated new sales of advanced weapons worth hundreds of millions of dollars. Senior U.S. officials also advised Taipei to invest more to enhance its defense capabilities.

In addition to arms sales, according to media reports, U.S. and Taiwan authorities also discussed steps to build a quasi-military alliance by increasing exchanges of military personnel visits and sending more U.S. officials and specialists to train troops and advise on war games.

Washington's arms sales to Taiwan and its efforts to strengthen military cooperation with the island prompted a series of strong protests from the PRC. Shortly after the Taiwan military procurement delegation concluded its U.S. visit, the Chinese embassy in Washington held a press conference to voice Beijing's anger at the recent American military activities with Taiwan. An embassy official said the Chinese government had demanded the U.S. government stop selling advanced weapons to Taiwan and cut military links.

Days earlier, Jiang Zemin, chairman of China's Central Military Commission, in a meeting with visiting U.S. National Security Advisor

Condoleezza Rice, warned that the Chinese government would not "sit idle" if foreign forces supported Taiwan's independence.[120]

"The U.S. side's recent series of actions, particularly its plans to sell arms to Taiwan, made Chinese people feel seriously concerned and dissatisfied," said Jiang. "If Taiwan authorities are stubbornly pushing for independence and if foreign forces are intent on supporting such separatist activity, we would not sit idle without doing anything," he warned.

According to the AFP news agency, Rice personally conveyed to Jiang the reaffirmation by President George W. Bush of the U.S.'s one-China policy and its "non-support" for independence or any actions by Taiwan to change the status quo. But Rice was also quoted as reiterating Washington's commitment to the Taiwan Relations Act, under which the United States pledged to defend the island against unprovoked attack.

Chen Shui-bian's relations with the U.S., severely damaged by his pre-election political rhetoric and actions, promptly improved, both politically and militarily, after he reaffirmed in his May 2004 inaugural speech the "four noes and one without" commitment not to push for independence.

In contrast, his relations with the PRC remained tense. Beijing maintained its pressure on Chen Shui-bian. The People's Liberation Army, for example, staged a new series of large-scale military exercises off the mainland's southeastern coast opposite Taiwan,

---

120 China Warns Rice It Won't 'Sit Idle' If U.S. Backs Taiwan Independence, Asia Pacific News, AFP, July 9, 2004.

Chapter 5
Elected to a Second Term

shortly after Chen began his second term. This was while Washington sought to boost arms sales to Taiwan and strengthen military cooperation.

Military intimidation aside, the mainland, at the government level, continued to refuse any resumption of talks with Chen Shui-bian and his government unless Taiwan accepted its "one China" principle.

President Chen Shui-bian did take the initiative to improve relations with the mainland, but his effort did not gain a positive response, due to the failure to address the underlying "one China" dispute.

As part of the initiative, the new administration extended an invitation to Wang Daohan, the longtime president of the mainland's Association for Relations Across the Taiwan Straits, to visit Taiwan, but the invitation was declined by the mainland side. A spokesperson for the Taiwan Affairs Office explained the decision by saying: "The premise for Wang Daohan's visit to Taiwan is that Taipei must accept the principle of one China. But the foundation for Wang to come to Taiwan and meet with his counterpart C.F. Koo does not exist under the present cross-strait atmosphere."

In early June, about two weeks after Chen started his second term, Taiwan also proposed opening negotiations on the issue of establishing direct air, sea transport, and postal services between the two sides.

But Beijing insisted that the issue of transport services between Taiwan and the mainland "must be defined as an internal affair of the Chinese people on both sides of the strait." This meant that any cross-strait flight or shipping services had to be treated as part of "China's domestic routes." Unsurprisingly, this Beijing position was unacceptable to Taiwan's pro-independence government.

Beijing repeatedly reminded all listeners of the statement it made on May 17, 2004, on the eve of Chen Shui-bian's inauguration. In that statement, the PRC also held out an inducement to Taiwan, in addition to the threat of force. In concrete terms, Beijing would like to "resume talks, end the state of longtime hostility, and set up a confidence-building mechanism, if Chen Shui-bian was willing to accept its one-China principle."

Commenting on existing cross-strait differences, Beijing's Taiwan Affairs Office spokesman Zhang Mingqing said: "The key issue facing cross-strait relations is whether Taiwan wants to accept the one-China principle or not. This principle is the cornerstone of preserving the peace and stability across the Taiwan Strait and developing bilateral relations."

But Chen Shui-bian stuck to his refusal to accept the one-China principle while shifting the rhetoric to suit the circumstances. Before his 2000 presidential election campaign, for example, he described the term "one China" as referring to the People's Republic of China, having nothing to do with Taiwan. After winning the 2000 election, Chen said in his first inaugural speech that he believed the "leaders on both sides possess enough wisdom and creativity to jointly deal with the question of a future 'one China'." But soon after taking office, he had this to say: "Accepting the concept of one China would be tantamount to eliminating the ROC on Taiwan."

In the middle of his first term, in August 2002, Chen Shui-bian's position on the "one China" issue shifted even further when he described Taiwan-mainland relations as "one country on each side of the strait."

Under pressure from Beijing and Washington, Chen did not repeat his "one country on each side" remarks in his second inaugural address, but he once again dodged the "one China" issue. Instead, he came up with a proposal to "build a peace and stability framework for cross-strait interactions." This was dubbed "the principle of peace."

He described his "principle of peace" as a "compromise" approach devised to replace the rival stances -- Beijing's "one China" principle and his theory of "one country on each side of the strait." He argued that his peace plan "is the best way for the two sides to break the political impasse and move their stalled relations forward."

As he explained in the post-election interview with the Washington Post in April 2004, the logic behind his argument was as follows: "...Because if the one-China principle is emphasized, then Taiwan will have other demands in response, for example, 'one country on each side of the strait' versus the 'one China principle'. Then I believe the two sides will be forever deadlocked, major differences cannot be solved and it will be impossible for both sides to sit down and talk. So don't raise the 'one China' principle. Don't raise one country on each side of the strait."

But Beijing, through the official Xinhua News Agency, criticized Chen Shui-bian as trying to use his peace principle to counter the mainland's "one China" principle. "It's a deceiving tactic, attempting to employ the name of peace to advance his independence cause."

So Chen Shui-bian's conciliatory 2004 inauguration remarks and his new formula for cross-strait interactions still failed to win Beijing's approval to resume dialogue. What is more, Chen's persistent refusal to accept the "one China" principle reinforced the PRC's suspicion that the Taiwan leader was still firmly committed to his independence cause.

As a result, Taiwan-mainland ties remained strained as Chen Shui-bian entered his second term. Tensions escalated as he launched new political campaigns over the remainder of his presidency.

Mainland relations aside, Chen's new campaigns also hurt his warming relations with Washington. The U.S. government was forced to get tough with the Taiwan leader again, seeking to rein him in lest his political actions provoke Beijing and endanger peace and stability in the Taiwan Strait.

In sum, President Chen Shui-bian's relations with Washington and Beijing slid to their lowest level during his second term. The following segment, Chapter 6, will explore the fraying ties and explain why this was the case.

Chapter 6
Tensions with Beijing Near Boiling Point

The Most Dangerous Flashpoint

The harsh rhetoric and tensions that characterized Chen Shui-bian's relations with Beijing during his first term as president (2000-2004) approached the boiling point in his second. The rising tensions prompted many political analysts and military experts to designate the Taiwan Strait as the most dangerous flashpoint in the Asia-Pacific region.

The dominant factor in the escalation of cross-strait tensions was that Chen Shui-bian, with the backing of a new mandate derived from his 2004 reelection, pushed his pro-independence agenda even more aggressively, further provoking Beijing.

The PRC government was so incensed that in early 2005, just one year after Chen's reelection, it adopted what it called an "Anti-Secession Law" that authorized the use of "non-peaceful" means against Taiwan if the island was perceived as moving toward formal independence.

Besides rising tensions with the PRC, Chen Shui-bian's relations with the U.S. during his second term were also severely strained by his ever-increasing aggressiveness in the pursuit of formal independence, violating his solemn commitment not to change Taiwan's political status.

The severity of the deterioration in Chen Shui-bian's U.S. and

PRC relations could be seen from the fact that he was branded a "troublemaker" by both U.S. President George W. Bush and the PRC leadership. [121] During the final two years of Chen Shui-bian's presidency, the Bush administration even refused to deal with him and his government, viewing him as untrustworthy.

This chapter will examine Chen's provocative rhetoric and actions, particularly in the final two years of his second term. These were viewed by Washington and Beijing as attempts to promote independence for Taiwan, breaching his "four noes and one without" pledges. He first made these pledges in his 2000 inaugural address and then reiterated them in 2004 to assure the PRC and the U.S. that he would not alter the cross-strait status quo.

Chen started his second term in May 2004. The priority he set for his new term was to campaign for DPP candidates in the year-end legislative elections. Chen hoped to ride the momentum of his fresh reelection and win an overwhelming majority in the Legislative Yuan. Control over the lawmaking body was critical to his bid to push through legislation that would promote his pro-independence program.

That being the case, Chen and his new administration quickly set in motion a pro-independence agenda in line with the DPP's campaign for the December 2004 legislative elections. Items on the agenda were mostly politically charged issues, such as calls for "name rectification" and textbook revision.

Initially, these and other political programs were promoted in a

---

121 China Calls Taiwan President a Troublemaker, VOA News, Last Updated October 31, 2009.

low-key manner to avoid a public backlash. However, as the December 11 legislative polls drew near, Chen turned more aggressive in stumping for his party's candidates. On such occasions, Chen always allowed electoral interests to outweigh the potentially damaging consequences that his radical campaign programs would have for cross-strait relations.

Generally speaking, Chen Shui-bian in the December 2004 legislative elections campaigned on the same pro-independence and anti-China platform as he did in his reelection bid, but with a more aggressive tone. Key political advocacies that Chen Shui-bian and his DPP colleagues advanced in the December 2004 legislative campaign included the following:

---Reasserting the "one country on each side of the strait" concept: In the months leading up to the December 11 poll, Chen Shui-bian more frequently than ever made statements asserting that Taiwan was a sovereign state, independent of China. In his October 10, 2004, National Day address, for example, Chen made these assertions: "Taiwan is a small country...The sovereignty of the Republic of China is vested in the 23 million people of Taiwan...Taiwan is the Republic of China and the Republic of China is Taiwan." "Taiwan is a sovereign, independent country." At other times when he ratcheted up his China-bashing rhetoric, people could also hear him claiming that "China is not only a foreign country but also an 'enemy' country'." [122]

At a campaign rally in early December of 2004, Chen told

---

[122] Office of the President of the Republic of China, President Chen's Address to the National Day Rally, October 10, 2004, http://www.gio.gov..tw.

supporters that gaining a majority in the legislature would enable him to "build Taiwan into a normal, complete, progressive, beautiful and great country."[123]

---Renewing his call to write a new constitution: At a rally a week or so ahead of the election, President Chen Shui-bian told crowds that he planned to write a new constitution and pass it following a popular referendum. The current constitution, he said, "is a China constitution." It had to be replaced with "a new one, written and endorsed by the Taiwanese people themselves."

---Stepping up a politically charged name-rectification drive: In a last-minute bid to energize pro-independence voters, Chen ramped up his push for replacing references to "China" with "Taiwan" in the names of all state-owned companies. Additionally, he also called for using the name "Taiwan" in the title of the government's representative offices in the more than 70 countries that had no formal diplomatic relations with Taipei.

Addressing a campaign rally three days ahead of polling day, Chen urged everyone "to say aloud that the country's name is 'Taiwan' as long as we believe in the name."[124] He added, "There is no need to worry about China's threats over Taiwan's bid to rectify its name."

The name-rectification drive was hardly new. It was part of a broader localization, or Taiwanization, movement long pushed by Taiwan independence activists. But Chen revitalized that drive after he

---

123 Jason Dean, Taiwan Election Is All about China, Asian Wall Street Journal, December 7, 2004.
124 Jewel Huang, Say Taiwan Aloud, Chen Urges People, China Times, December 9, 2004.

Chapter 6
Tensions with Beijing Near Boiling Point

came to power in 2000 and made major advances in the name-rectification movement in 2003. The Foreign Ministry in that year issued a new passport with the term "Taiwan" printed in English on its cover, right below the national title, the Republic of China.

Chen then went further to add a new dimension to the drive by claiming that the purpose of his name-changing effort was to "distinguish between Taiwan and China" and to "correct the perception among nations around the world that Taiwan is part of China."

Chen did strike a conciliatory note toward Beijing in his October 2004 address, amid his vehement "China-bashing" rhetoric. He proposed that Taiwan and the mainland use the "1992 meeting in Hong Kong as the basis" for resuming dialogue and consultation. He suggested the two sides should sit down and discuss ways to reduce cross-strait tensions and hostility. He proposed a range of topics, which included weaponry controls, a confidence-building mechanism, and a code of conduct for cross-strait relations, as well as bilateral transport links.

But Chen's olive branch was greeted by Beijing more as a publicity stunt aimed at his audience in Washington rather than genuine peace overtures. Beijing's skepticism was not without reason. Chen had from the start of the legislative campaign been promoting Taiwan as a separate country, independent of China, and as noted earlier, he had branded China as an "enemy country." Against this background, it was hard to imagine his offer of peace talks would be taken seriously.

Beijing did not respond to Chen's remarks until three days later. The mainland, through its Taiwan Affairs Office spokesman Zhang Mingqing, slammed Chen's proposals to reduce cross-strait tensions as deceptive and part of a veiled effort to gain independence.

"Chen Shui-bian claimed that he intended to ease tensions and confrontation across the Taiwan Strait, but he has obstinately stuck to his separatist stand of 'one country on each side' of the strait," Zhang said at a news conference in Beijing. "If Chen Shui-bian persists in his Taiwan independence activities," Zhang continued, "he will never bring peace and prosperity to the Taiwan compatriots but will only cause a catastrophe for them."

Unlike Beijing, the U.S. government responded positively to Chen's speech. State Department spokeswoman Darla Jordan said, "We welcome the constructive message conveyed in President Chen's speech, which we believe offers some creative ideas for reducing cross-strait tensions and resuming dialogue."

The different U.S. and Chinese reactions to Chen's peace talk overtures reflected two different sets of views on how to break the political standoff across the Taiwan Strait. The U.S., for its part, believed that the most important thing at this juncture was for the two political rivals to restart dialogue and settle their differences through negotiations. In Washington's view, the willingness of Chen to sit down and discuss ways to reduce tensions deserved to be encouraged.

But Beijing had a more fundamental concern. If the Chinese government agreed to reopen dialogue and hold negotiations with Chen at a time when he continued to assert that "Taiwan is an independent, sovereign state," it would be tantamount to accepting Chen's assertion of sovereignty. Beijing insisted that Chen had to first accept the principle of one China before any bilateral talks could be restarted.

Powell: Taiwan Does Not Enjoy Sovereignty as a Nation

While welcoming Chen's calls for dialogue with Beijing, the U.S. also openly expressed its disapproval of his latest string of provocative remarks and actions. Shortly after Chen Shui-bian reasserted his view that "Taiwan is a sovereign, independent country," for example, U.S. Secretary of State Colin Powell refuted the Taiwan leader's assertion, using the occasion of his visit to Beijing in late October. "There is only one China. Taiwan is not independent. It does not enjoy sovereignty as a nation, and that remains our policy, our firm policy." Powell made his comments both in talks with senior Beijing officials and subsequent media interviews. [125]

In the past, no senior administration official had been so direct in describing Taiwan's status. Previously, U.S. government officials were deliberately vague on the subject to maintain flexibility on cross-strait issues. Powell's unusual departure from this tradition, according to some Washington observers, reflected the Bush administration's extreme unhappiness with President Chen Shui-bian's continued pushing of the envelope on Taiwan's political status in cross-strait relations.

Besides the statehood claim, Chen's renewed effort to hold a referendum in 2006 to adopt a new constitution also raised concerns in Washington. State Department spokesman Richard Boucher demanded

---

125 Joseph Kahn, Powell Relates U.S. One-China Policy, Angering Taiwan, The New York Times, October 28, 2004.

that the Taipei leader clarify his latest remarks on the constitution and referendum.

Boucher said at a press conference that the U.S. was "opposed to any referendum that would change Taiwan's status or move toward independence." He called attention to the "five noes" pledges that Chen made in 2000 and reiterated in 2004. Under these pledges, Boucher pointed out, Chen would not declare independence, change the name of Taiwan's government, or add the two-state theory to the constitution, and not promote a referendum on independence or unification.

When asked by a journalist whether Chen's latest remarks about his plan to write a new constitution and approve it through a national referendum was a violation of those pledges, Boucher said the Taiwan leader's "pledges were very, very important, and they need to be respected."

On the issue of Chen's name-rectification drive, which was intensified on the eve of the December 2004 legislative elections, the State Department openly stated that the Bush administration did not support the effort. Spokesman Adam Ereli said, "These changes of terminology for government-controlled enterprises or economic and cultural offices abroad, in our view, would appear to unilaterally change Taiwan's status and, for that reason, we're not supportive of them."

At the end of the months-long campaign, Chen Shui-bian's DPP failed to secure a majority in the lawmaking body. The president's party gained only two additional seats, for a total of 89. Its ally, the Taiwan Solidarity Union, a more radical smaller party that advocated faster independence for Taiwan, lost one seat, cutting its total to 12. Together the pro-independence "pan-green" alliance held just 101 seats in the 225-member legislature.

The main opposition KMT gained 11 seats for a total of 79, making it the biggest winner in the legislative elections. The KMT, in sharp contrast to the pro-independence DPP, favored closer relations with the Chinese mainland. The more pro-Beijing People First Party had the worst showing, losing 12 seats, leaving it with only 34. The far-right New Party kept its only seat. Collectively, the KMT, the PFP, and the New Party, or the "pan-blue" coalition, had 114 seats, enough for them to maintain a majority in the crucial lawmaking body. Independents retained 10 seats.

The 2004 legislative election results were significant in two important ways. One, the failure of the DPP to win a majority meant that Chen Shui-bian and his administration would remain subject to the strict scrutiny of the opposition-controlled legislature. This would make it harder for Chen to deliver on his promise to draft a new constitution.

Two, the poor showing of Chen's party in the legislative elections reflected the rejection by voters of the president's radical pro-independence position. But few had foreseen the severity of the DPP's setback as many of the party's high-profile candidates failed to retain a seat in the legislature.

In a subsequent review of the election results, the DPP leadership admitted the party had been too aggressive in advancing its independence agenda during the campaign. The many radical political pitches they made scared away middle-class voters who had backed

Chen Shui-bian in his reelection in March. [126] Bowing to intense pressure, Chen Shui-bian resigned as DPP chairman days after the December 2004 legislative elections.

DPP Legislative Poll Defeat Eases Cross-Strait Tension

In terms of cross-strait relations, the failure of Chen Shui-bian's party to gain a legislative majority and the lukewarm support it received in the polls was good news. The outcome was seen restraining pro-independence steps over the remainder of Chen's presidency. This, in turn, would help de-escalate tensions with Beijing.

The easing of tension was quickly reflected in cross-strait relations. In the spring of 2005, a far-reaching détente occurred between Taiwan's main opposition KMT and the mainland's ruling Chinese Communist Party.

The fact that the mounting cross-strait military and political tensions in the run-up to Taiwan's December 2004 elections did not escalate into armed conflict was itself proof that the victory at the polls for the moderate "pan-blue" alliance was stabilizing relations across the Taiwan Strait.

It is not an overstatement to say the situation between Taiwan and the mainland was nearing the boiling point in 2004. Military tension in the strait continued to intensify following the reelection of Chen Shui-

---

126 Katherine Hille, Taiwan's President Promises to End Political Infighting, Financial Times, December 15, 2004.

bian in March of that year. Beijing, already worried by his campaign promises to write a new constitution and hold a defensive referendum alongside the presidential election, was blatantly threatening to use force against Taiwan.

The People's Liberation Army staged a series of joint land, sea, and air exercises in the summer of 2004 on Dongshan Island off the coast of Fujian province, just about 150 miles away from Taiwan's Penghu (Pescadores) Islands. Communist Party chief and PRC President Hu Jintao, in an address to a meeting of senior party and administration officials amid the joint military exercises, vowed to crush any attempt to separate Taiwan from China.

According to a July 11, 2004 report in the China Daily, the joint military exercises, featuring mock attacks on Taiwan targets from land, sea, and air, were conducted to send "a substantial warning to 'Taiwan independence' elements."[127]

At almost the same time, Taiwan held its own Han Kuang exercise to test the military's combat readiness and ability to defend against an attack from the People's Liberation Army. According to Taiwan's then-Defense Minister Lee Jye, there were signs that the PRC might use force to take this island at some point in the future if Chen Shui-bian's government continued to move in the direction of independence.

The United States, which has legal obligations to help defend Taiwan, was not standing by idly. The Pentagon held a crisis-simulation drill called Dragon's Thunder in early June 2004 in response to the growing tensions between Taiwan and the Chinese mainland.

---

127 Maneuvers Planned at Dongshan Island, China Daily, July 11, 2004.

In addition, the U.S. Navy conducted a massive exercise, known as Operation Summer Pulse 2004, in waters off China's southeast coast near Taiwan. According to a news release issued by the Department of Defense, Summer Pulse 04, involving the "near-simultaneous deployment of seven carrier strike groups," began in June 2004 and continued through August of the same year. [128]

The Defense Department said the joint operation was designed to allow the U.S. Navy to test and maintain "the ability to respond to crises around the globe, enhance regional security and relationships, and demonstrate a commitment to allies and coalition partners."

In an article on "Operation Summer Pulse 04," John J. Xenakis of Generational Dynamics, a U.S. website analyzing current events, gave the following summary: "This unprecedented display of naval force by American forces near China, planned for later this month [July], mirrors a large display of force by China in the Strait of Taiwan. The precipitating factors include moves towards independence by Taiwan's president, and American plans to review its 'one China' policy." [129]

The Los Angeles Times also ran a report on Summer Pulse 04 with the title "China, U.S. Each Hold Major War Exercises."[130] Writer John M. Glionna, quoting military analysts, said in the report that the war games suggested that rising hostilities across the 100-mile-wide Taiwan Strait appeared to have reached a critical juncture.

128Seven Carrier Strike Groups Underway for Exercise Summer Pulse 04, special release from the U.S. Department of Defense, June 3, 2004.

129John J. Xenakis, Operation Summer Pulse 04, Generational Dynamics, July 6, 2004.

130 John M. Glionna, 'China, U.S. Each Hold War Exercises, Los Angeles Times, July 20, 2004.

Chapter 6
Tensions with Beijing Near Boiling Point

The report quoted Andrew Tan, a security expert at the Singapore-based Institute of Defense and Strategic Studies, as saying that the danger level had been rising while the world's attention was focused elsewhere. "Beneath our notice, as the world watched North Korea, the conventional conflict between China and Taiwan could now be well on the way to breaking out into something more serious," said Tan.

"The largest naval exercise the United States has ever held is meant to send a direct signal to the Chinese. It's gunboat diplomacy and its point is to warn China not to step over the mark when it comes to Taiwan," he said.

Andrew Yang, an analyst at the Chinese Council of Advanced Policy Studies, an independent think tank in Taipei that is focused on military issues, was also interviewed in the same Los Angeles Times article. Yang said the Chinese military exercises had been planned and were not staged in response to the American buildup. "But the message to Washington is nonetheless clear: China is ready to back up its political position here," he said.

"They want to show the American Congress that China means business, that it's not a paper tiger and its pledge to retake Taiwan is not an empty threat. China also wants to explore the U.S. bottom line: Are the Americans ready to confront China militarily for the sake of Taiwan?"

Taiwan and the U.S., as two longtime defense partners, also stepped up military cooperation at the time to jointly counter a simulated invasion by the PRC. According to unconfirmed media reports, Taiwan was invited to send navy ships to take part in Summer Pulse 04, to familiarize its leaders with coordination of joint operations.

In another development, Taiwan's Han Kuang exercises in 2004 reportedly, for the first time, adopted a U.S.-provided multiple theater-level simulation system, one that enabled the Taiwan military to link up with the American Pacific headquarters in Hawaii in time of war.

As the People's Liberation Army staged intimidating military exercises, Beijing was pushing ahead with its effort to enact a law that would authorize the use of force against Taiwan, if the island was seen as breaking away from mainland China. The mainland authorities had in the past undertaken studies of various legislative proposals related to Taiwan, including a unification bill. However, a proposal to enact a law against Taiwan's independence movement gained momentum in late 2003 and early 2004, fueled by Chen Shui-bian's campaign promise that he, if reelected, would write a new constitution.

Chen moderated his constitutional position after the start of his second term, but the mainland's process of enacting an anti-independence law had already gathered pace in the months leading up to Taiwan's December 2004 legislative elections. During that period, Chen renewed his pro-independence and anti-China rhetoric in his attempt to win a legislative majority.

Although Chen ultimately failed to gain control of the lawmaking body and thereby speed up his drive for formal independence, the process of creating a legal framework to justify military action against Taiwan was by then well underway. As one political analyst described it, "the train had already left the station," and there was no way to apply the brakes.

The "Anti-Secession Law," as approved by the National People's Congress in March 2005, was negatively received in Taiwan. While

Beijing claimed that the purpose of the new law was to preserve the status quo, Taipei responded angrily, arguing that the legislation amounted to giving the People's Liberation Army a "blank check" to attack Taiwan.

The law consists of 10 articles, and it was Article 8 that provoked the most concern and controversy in Taiwan. The article states that mainland China shall use 'non-peaceful' means under these conditions: 1) if 'Taiwan independence' forces, under whatever name and method, accomplish the fact of Taiwan's separation from China, 2) or if a major event occurs which would lead to Taiwan's separation from China, 3) or if all possibility of peaceful unification is lost. [131]

Taiwan's Politics Take a Dramatic Turn

In Taiwan, events took a dramatic turn following the December 2004 legislative elections. In late February 2005, President Chen Shui-bian reached an unlikely agreement with James Soong, chairman of the People First Party (PFP), the smaller of the two main opposition parties. Chen and Soong agreed that their two parties, the DPP and the PFP, would work together to form a legislative majority "in the interest of law-enacting efficiency," breaking a longstanding gridlock in the lawmaking body.

Chen's willingness to enter into cooperation with a party long known for supporting close mainland relations was seen as a shift

---

131 Top Legislature Passes Anti-Secession Law, China Daily, March 14, 2005.

toward the political center after his radical pro-independence appeals were rejected by voters. In a joint declaration, Chen reaffirmed the "no-change-to-the-status-quo" pledges he made in 2000 and reiterated in 2004. Chen and Soong also stressed the "primacy of the ROC constitution and sovereignty."

Although the Chen-Soong legislative alliance lasted for only a very short time, it did reflect a realization on the part of Chen Shui-bian that he needed to moderate his extreme political stance and reach some common ground with the opposition, if he were to govern efficiently in the remaining three years of his presidency.

Taiwan's December 2004 legislative election results provided a much-needed check on President Chen's political ambitions. This development, together with the leader's post-election reaffirmation of his pledges not to change the status quo, was not lost on Beijing's leadership. Communist Party chief and President Hu Jintao, in a speech on Taiwan in early March, said, "We have noticed the latest developments in Taiwan's politics, which we think were positive and helpful in restraining the separatist activities of the island's independence forces."

In the same March speech, Hu also declared that the tensions in the Taiwan Strait were showing "some signs of easing." This was the first time Beijing had positively assessed the cross-strait situation. Mainland leaders in the past two years or so had repeatedly warned Taiwan that bilateral relations faced the unrelenting danger of war, in an attempt to maintain pressure on Chen Shui-bian.

Another new development in the wake of the decisive 2004 legislative elections was a sea change in cross-strait relations marked

Chapter 6
Tensions with Beijing Near Boiling Point

by a visit to Beijing by Lien Chan, the chairman of Taiwan's largest opposition party, the KMT. No other political leader before him had ever set foot on the Chinese mainland since the 1940s when a bitter civil war generated a deep political divide between the two sides.

Lien Chan traveled to Beijing in late April and early May of 2005 in his capacity as chairman of the KMT. Lien's mainland visit truly was an ice-breaker, precisely what he had hoped for before leaving Taipei. The visit paved the way for Taiwan and its longtime political adversary on the mainland to bury the hatchet and move toward political reconciliation.

During his eight-day mainland tour, Lien met with Hu Jintao and other top Chinese leaders. They held discussions on cross-strait relations and reached a range of resolutions that made it possible for the governments of the two sides to subsequently open talks and liberalize economic exchanges. This in turn led to a boom in cross-strait trade, investment, transport services, and travel in the decade that followed.

Had the December 2004 elections not delivered a legislative majority to the mainland-friendly KMT, it would have been impossible for Lien Chan to visit Beijing without being accused of treason by Chen. Traditionally, Taiwan had banned government officials and politicians from traveling to the communist-controlled mainland. Although such prohibitions had been greatly relaxed over the past decade with the strengthening of Taiwan's democracy, opposition leaders still refrained from going to the mainland for fear of being "painted red" by Chen and his DPP party. Once a politician was accused of having links to Beijing, his or her loyalty to Taiwan would be questioned, and that could undermine public confidence in that person.

Now with the pro-mainland KMT gaining a huge victory over the DPP in the legislative polls, Lien as the party's chairman had a clear mandate to visit Beijing and discuss how to improve bilateral relations. During the campaign, the KMT had promised to improve ties with Beijing as an alternative approach to the DPP's anti-China stance, which had led to a political impasse across the strait.

Besides the KMT's legislative election victory, Lien's groundbreaking trip to Beijing was also helped by a growing public desire, particularly from the business community, to reduce tensions with the mainland and expand bilateral exchanges. More and more people had come to realize the danger of continuing to provoke Beijing by pushing for formal independence. They were especially concerned that the United States would not come to Taiwan's aid in the event of a mainland attack that was provoked by Taiwan. Washington officials had repeatedly reminded Taiwan of that potential scenario.

It was in this context that Lien Chan decided to visit Beijing, no longer worrying that his bold embrace of the Chinese mainland could cause him and his party to lose voter support.

Shortly after Lien's return from Beijing, PFP chairman James Soong also made a visit to the Chinese capital. Soong's visit attracted particular public attention because he reportedly brought to Hu Jintao a personal message from President Chen Shui-bian, who was said to have expressed a desire to repair bilateral relations. But Soong returned home empty-handed. Sources familiar with the PFP chairman's Beijing talks cited Chen's unwillingness to compromise with the mainland authorities over the "one China" dispute.

While both Lien and Soong were warmly received by Hu Jintao, the two Taiwan visitors carried different weight with their host, because of the big differences in the power they wielded back home. The KMT was the largest opposition party and enjoyed far stronger support at the grassroots level. Thus for Beijing, an improvement in relations with the KMT would be more helpful in achieving its Taiwan policy objectives.

One thing worth special mention was that the significance of the Lien-Hu Beijing meeting went beyond a hard-achieved thaw in relations between Taiwan and the mainland. The fact that the two leaders of the Kuomintang and the Chinese Communist Party agreed to sit down and communicate with each other also had enormous symbolic significance for their respective parties. Their meetings represented a rapprochement between the two longtime foes. In the late 1940s, the Kuomintang-led ROC government under Chiang Kai-shek and Mao Zedong's Chinese Communist Party fought a bitter civil war, with Chiang's government retreating to Taiwan in 1949. Taiwan has since governed itself separately. Until the 2005 meeting between Lien and Hu, the KMT and the CCP had remained hostile toward each other, refusing to open formal dialogue.

Lien-Hu Joint Press Communique

At the end of their historic meetings, Lien Chan and Hu Jintao issued a joint communique pledging to work together to end six decades of hostilities between Taiwan and the mainland. Below are excerpts from the communique of April 29, 2005:[132] [133]

"Over the past 56 years, the two sides of the strait have followed different paths and developed different social systems and ways of life...

"More than 10 years ago, based on goodwill and on seeking common ground while reserving differences, the two sides launched consultations, dialogue, and nongovernmental exchanges, filling cross-strait ties with hopes of peace and vitality in cooperation...

"In recent years, however, the basis for cross-strait mutual trust has repeatedly been damaged and the situation in cross-strait ties has undergone sustained deterioration...

"Cross-strait ties are now at a crucial point in historical development; the two sides should not fall into a vicious circle of confrontation but instead enter a virtuous circle of cooperation, seek together opportunities for peaceful and steady development of cross-strait ties, trust and help each other, and create a new situation of peaceful win-win, to bring about brilliant and splendid prospects for the Chinese nation."

The two parties in the communique agreed on the following: "It is the common proposition of the two parties to uphold the 'Consensus of 1992,' oppose 'Taiwan independence,' pursue stability in the Taiwan Strait, promote the development of cross-strait ties, and safeguard the interests of compatriots on both sides of the strait."

Based on the "1992 consensus," the CCP and the KMT urged the

---

132 News release, CPC, KMT for Formal End of Cross-Strait Hostility, China Daily (Xinhua), April 29, 2005.
133 Text of KMT-Beijing Agreement, News.BBC.Co.UK, April 29, 2005.

following specific tasks:

1. Promote the resumption of cross-strait negotiations as soon as possible and pursue the happiness of the people on both sides.
2. Promote an end to the state of hostilities and reach a peace accord.
3. Promote all-round cross-strait economic exchanges and establish a cross-strait economic cooperation mechanism.
4. Promote consultations on issues of participation in international activities, which concern the Taipei public.
5. Establish a platform for periodic party-to-party contact.

However, the five-point Lien-Hu agreement, while having brought about a detente between the KMT and the Chinese Communist Party as well as an easing of tension across the Taiwan Strait, did not produce a quick thaw in relations at the government-to-government level. This was so because Beijing refused to accept the independence-leaning Chen administration. At the same time, Chen Shui-bian and his administration felt marginalized by the warming KMT-CCP relations and, therefore, found no incentives to relax restrictions on exchanges with the mainland.

An across-the-board expansion in exchanges between Taiwan and the mainland began only after the KMT recaptured the presidency three years later in 2008. Ma Ying-jeou, president and KMT leader, inherited the spirit of the Lien-Hu agreement and, more fundamentally, he fully supported the "1992 Consensus" -- a tacit agreement that obliges both sides to accept the principle of "one China" but allows them to interpret what that means. As a result, Taiwan under the Ma government quickly resumed negotiations with the mainland. During Ma's eight-year presidency, the two sides signed dozens of trade and economic agreements, including an end to a six-decade ban on direct flights across the strait as well as an easing of restrictions on investment, travel, and tourism.

So it could be seen that Chen Shui-bian failed to improve and expand economic relations with the mainland mainly because he refused to recognize the "92 Consensus," making it impossible for him to break the "one China" impasse. As a result, Beijing rejected any dialogue with Chen's administration. In return, Chen retaliated by refusing to liberalize exchanges with the mainland.

But Chen's persistence in maintaining the various suffocating restrictions on cross-strait trade and investment exchanges hurt Taiwan's economy more than the mainland's by depriving local companies of golden opportunities to expand operations and sales in a vast and fast-growing Chinese market.

Prohibiting companies from implementing projects on the mainland also damaged the local economy in another important way. While Korean and other foreign companies could freely relocate their operations to the Chinese mainland to take advantage of lower labor and land costs, Taiwanese firms were shackled by restrictive government rules that kept them in their home market. That resulted in weakened competitiveness due to higher production costs. Similarly damaging were bans on direct flights and shipping across the strait. Under such bans, cargo and passenger traffic had had to be routed through third locations, such as Hong Kong, adding costs for companies doing business with the Chinese mainland.

Yet Chen paid a heavy price for his persistent refusal to liberalize trade and investment relations with the mainland, which were crucial to reviving the Taiwan economy. A sluggish economy, together with a series of alleged corruption scandals involving Chen's aides and party stalwarts, were the two primary factors contributing to the DPP's devastating losses in the mayoral and county magistrate elections in December 2005. This was the second electoral defeat for the party in a year since the December 2004 legislative elections.

In the 2005 local elections, the DPP retained only six out of Taiwan's 23 cities and counties, down from the 10 it controlled previously. The main opposition KMT came out as the largest winner, expanding its total to 14. The remaining three seats were shared by the KMT's two allies: the People First Party and the New Party.

The local election results were widely seen as a referendum on President Chen Shui-bian and his administration. In the campaign, the opposition had focused its criticisms on the allegations of corruption against the Chen administration and the persistent failure to revitalize the economy.

The DPP's huge losses in the 2005 local government elections were hardly a surprise. On the eve of the elections, the multinational financial institution, Merrill Lynch, had concluded that a setback in the polls for the DPP would be positive news for investors. In a report prepared for its investor clients, Merrill Lynch analysts had predicted that such a blow would prompt Chen Shui-bian to launch major policy reforms and become more conciliatory toward Beijing by significantly liberalizing restrictions on cross-strait exchanges. Many other analysts made similar assessments.

These analyses, however, were only partially accurate. The DPP indeed sustained huge losses in the 2005 local government elections, but President Chen, the party leader, failed to respond with policy reforms. On the contrary, Chen became even more vocal in promoting independence and antagonizing Beijing. He continued to act in a manner that concerned Washington and angered Beijing.

Chen's provocative remarks and actions were thought by many as intended to consolidate his "deep green" base at the expense of attaining broader electoral support. Consider the following: President Chen no longer had the same charismatic ability to energize voters. The party, under his watch, had already lost two consecutive elections since his own March 2004 victory that gave him a second term. In the latest local election campaign, he was even seen by many in his party as a liability. Many DPP candidates kept their distance from him, making it clear they did not want him attending their campaign rallies.

After the December 2005 polls, moreover, Chen's already low approval ratings plunged further to between 12.6% and 21%, while his disapproval ratings rose from 62% to 70.2%. A president with such low popularity amounted to having been deserted by the vast majority of the people. He no longer possessed the authority and influence to gather popular support for himself or his party. Chen himself was surely aware of that.

So Chen's renewed China-bashing rhetoric and stepped-up promotion of independence after the DPP's latest electoral defeat was more likely aimed at rallying his hardline independence supporters. He wanted to use this kind of rhetoric to motivate hardliners to back him and improve his political standing. By so doing, he certainly still held out hopes of creating an independent Taiwan identity as a major legacy of his presidency.

President Chen Shui-bian kicked off 2006 with a wide-ranging New Year message, focusing on two political issues: "Taiwan consciousness" and "Taiwan's sovereignty." In the message, he pointed out that Taiwan's continued democratization "has enabled a 'Taiwanese consciousness' to gradually take root on this land and thrive in the hearts of our people." [134]

The president continued, The emergence of 'Taiwan consciousness' and a wave of democratization has galvanized the aspiration of the Taiwan people to be masters of their land; all ethnic groups are coming to realize that issues concerning national identity are an inescapable reality that must be confronted and addressed.

"Yet it is grievously saddening that political circumstances forbid us from saying out loud the name of our country -- this is indeed a heartbreaking and humiliating predicament," he deplored.

He then reminded his audience in Beijing, "The sovereignty of Taiwan is vested in its 23 million people and is not subject to the jurisdiction of the People's Republic of China. Only the 23 million people of Taiwan have the right to decide Taiwan's future."

Chen also accused Beijing of seeking to "annex" Taiwan. "China employs a carrot-and-stick strategy concerning Taiwan. It has continuously deployed guided missiles, used a 'three-war' strategy (media, legal, and psychological warfare), and established specific timetables and goals for preparing for war against this island nation.

---

134 Main Points of President Chen Shui-bian's New Year's Day Message, Mainland Affairs Council of Executive Yuan, Republic of China (Taiwan), January 18, 2006.

These actions indicate that China's ambition to annex Taiwan remains unchanged."

Chen's 2006 New Year remarks on "Taiwan consciousness" and sovereignty came in the wake of his October 10, 2005, National Day address. In the National Day speech, Chen insisted that Taiwan's "long-term political stability and democratic sustainability required comprehensive reviews and revisions of the ROC constitution." He then announced that his envisioned constitutional changes would involve a "bottom-up, outside-in" process. By that, he meant that "any relevant amendment proposals will be initiated by civil groups before political parties are involved."

Chen Shui-bian's January 1, 2006, and October 10, 2005 addresses provoked no serious reactions from either Beijing or Washington. For Beijing, it was not seriously upset by Chen's latest remarks, presumably because of the following reasons:

First, in the view of Beijing, Chen simply could not possibly muster the substantial legislative support needed to pass any independence-oriented constitutional changes after failing to win a majority in the lawmaking body in the December 2004 elections. Furthermore, Taiwan's newly revised law sets very high thresholds for any constitutional amendments. It requires a three-fourths affirmative vote in the legislature and final approval by half of all eligible voters in a national referendum. The difficult legal hurdles needed to be overcome, if Chen wanted to press ahead with his plan to rewrite the constitution.

Second, cross-strait relations were now warming rapidly following Lien Chan's 2005 groundbreaking mainland trip, underscored by a growing boom in cross-strait trade and economic exchanges. This being the case, Beijing surely did not want to rock the boat by making a strong response to renewed political provocations by Chen Shui-bian. A strong response could create a backlash that could set back hard-won improvements in bilateral ties.

Third, Beijing now felt more optimistic that Taiwan's people would be more likely to use their votes to constrain Chen Shui-bian's extremist tendencies. This had already been reflected in the 2004 legislative and 2005 local elections when voters abandoned DPP candidates in favor of the KMT, which supported closer economic ties with the mainland.

As for Washington, it too did not make any comment about Chen's October 10, 2005 announcement that he would adopt a "bottom-up, outside-in" approach in revising the constitution. This was even though the new approach ran the risk of violating his inaugural pledges to abide by the existing constitutional procedure in amending the basic law. President George W. Bush, however, did address the issue of cross-strait relations one month later in November, on the eve of his visit to Beijing.

The U.S. president expressed his concern that "one party or the other might do something to unilaterally change the status quo." Bush was briefing journalists on what he would say in Beijing, about U.S. policy on cross-strait relations. "I'll confirm our 'one China,' three-communique policy, that not only says that we do not support independence but as well, we will adhere to the Taiwan Relations Act. I think that's important for the Chinese leadership and the people of Taiwan to hear."

The preview Bush gave to the press of what he was going to say in Beijing in his meeting with Chinese leaders only reflected the longstanding, neutral position Washington has held on cross-strait relations. It could hardly be interpreted as an expression of U.S. displeasure with Chen's October 10 remarks.

But Chen's reiteration of his plan to revise the constitution, in his wide-ranging 2006 New Year message, did draw a prompt response from the United States. This was the second time that Chen had called for amending the ROC constitution since he first raised the "bottom-up, outside-in" approach in the address made in October. That approach, in short, was intended to encourage the participation of grass-roots groups as well as political parties in his constitutional reform initiative.

In his latest talk on constitutional reform, Chen gave some more disquieting details, promising that he would deliver a new constitution, called "Taiwan's New Constitution," before he left office in May 2008. Such a constitution, he said, would be "timely, relevant, and viable."

Washington responded swiftly this time because his stepped-up effort to write a new constitution with a "bottom-up, outside-in" approach raised security concerns for the United States. A new constitution, drafted with the input of views from diverse political and social groups, could incorporate contents violating the pledge that Chen had made in his second inaugural speech. As noted earlier, Chen's speech included the promise that "issues concerning sovereignty, territory and unification/independence would be excluded" from his constitutional reengineering project. A violation of this politically sensitive pledge could provoke Beijing into attacking Taiwan, invoking its newly enacted "Anti-Secession Law." This, in

Chapter 6
Tensions with Beijing Near Boiling Point

turn, could drag the United States into military conflict.

The U.S. was worried by Chen's latest push for a constitutional overhaul. But interestingly, the Bush administration reacted rather mildly. The State Department issued a statement expressing Washington's "expectation" that President Chen would keep his promises and take no steps in the constitutional amendment process that could be interpreted as crossing Beijing's "red lines" on independence, leading to confrontation across the strait.

In the past, the U.S. had reacted strongly to any of Chen's remarks thought to be challenging the cross-strait status quo. But the way the State Department responded this time to Chen's "new constitution" talk appeared to be more restrained, only advising him not to cross Beijing's "red lines" to avert a provoked attack.

Chen administration officials made no secret of their happiness that Washington had not lodged something like a protest with Taipei. A spokesman said that although the U.S. government had expressed its concerns about Chen's New Year speech, it did not "protest" and its attitude was "moderate and neutral."

If that observation was accurate, the U.S. might indeed have made a subtle shift in its attitude toward President Chen, becoming more sympathetic to him and turning more tolerant of his provocative remarks. This subtle shift appeared to be related to Beijing's passage of the "Anti-Secession Law" in March 2005 and political events in Taiwan. These events included the opposition-led efforts to improve relations with the mainland, which in turn brought about a rapidly spreading China fervor on the island.

The U.S., according to some observers, was concerned that such

273

developments could weaken Chen's position as an elected leader, undermining Taiwan's democratic system. This concern was well-founded. After Lien Chan's Beijing visit, Chen to some extent was marginalized in addressing cross-strait relations. Beijing still refused to open dialogue with him. Instead, it reached out to Taiwan's opposition parties and business groups directly over cross-strait economic exchanges and related issues.

In addition to the concern that Beijing's new strategy of bypassing Chen and his government could weaken Taiwan's democratic system, Washington also seemed to feel uneasy about the potential impact of Taiwan's mounting enthusiasm for China, characterized by companies relocating their investment and operations to the mainland en masse. Such a wave of relocations could make Taiwan overly dependent on mainland China. That would quickly lead to a shift in the balance of power across the strait, in Beijing's favor.

Washington's renewed backing for President Chen was demonstrated in President George W. Bush's speech in Kyoto, Japan, in November 2005, on his way to Beijing. In the speech, Bush again urged mainland China to open dialogue with Chen and his government. "The United States will continue to stress the need for dialogue between China and Taiwan that leads to a peaceful resolution of their differences," Bush said.[135]

Speaking on "freedom and democracy," Bush praised Taiwan's economic and democratic achievements. "Taiwan is another society

---

135 News release, Bush Hails Taiwan, the White House Office of the Press Secretary, November 16, 2005.

that has moved from repression to democracy as it liberalized its economy...Economic liberalization in Taiwan helped fuel its desire for individual political freedom -- because men and women who are allowed to control their wealth will eventually insist on controlling their own lives and their futures...By embracing freedom at all levels, Taiwan has delivered prosperity to its people and created a free and democratic Chinese society."

Bush then went on to say: "As China reforms its economy, its leaders are finding that once the door to freedom is opened even a crack, it cannot be closed. As the people of China grow in prosperity, their demands for political freedom will grow as well...I have pointed out that the people of China want more freedom to express themselves, to worship without state control, and to print Bibles and other sacred texts without fear of punishment. The efforts of ... China's people to improve their society should be welcomed as part of China's development."

Bush appeared to be holding up Taiwan as a model for mainland China, although senior White House officials traveling with the president quickly denied that was the intent. Nevertheless, Beijing took offense. Chinese Foreign Minister Li Zhaoxing said: "Taiwan is a part of China, an inseparable part of China, and China does not brook any outside interference in its internal affairs."

In contrast, Taipei was greatly encouraged by Bush's praise for the island as a model of democratic reform. Some senior Chen administration officials even took Bush's pro-Taiwan democracy remarks as fresh proof that Taipei-Washington relations "are bound" together by their "shared values."

Also significant was Bush's use of his Asian travel -- including stops in Japan, South Korea, China, and Mongolia -- to publicly praise Taiwan. This marked a striking improvement in bilateral relations after years of tensions stirred up by President Chen's repeated remarks that suggested an effort to change the island's political status quo.

Two years earlier in December 2003, Bush had rebuked President Chen in the presence of visiting Chinese Premier Wen Jiabao, stating that "the comments and actions made by the leader of Taiwan indicate that he may be willing to make decisions unilaterally to change the status quo, which we oppose." The scolding was prompted by provocative statements by Chen in his campaign for a second term in the March 2004 presidential election.

According to Taipei's chief representative in Washington David Tawei Lee, Bush's comments about Taiwan on the Kyoto stopover represented "the restoration of trust and confidence to some extent between our leaders and also better communication between our two governments."

But Chen managed to upend the revival of trust soon after, with a new series of potentially destabilizing political assertions and actions. Not all of those things were new, but they all were set to be promoted with renewed vigor in the final years of Chen's presidency.

As noted earlier, Chen opened 2006 with a New Year message focusing on sovereignty and a new constitution. That message had already raised concerns in Washington, prompting the State Department to warn him not to "cross Beijing's red lines."

However, Chen did not take the U.S. warning seriously. Weeks later he unnerved Washington again. In a speech given at a Lunar New

Year party on January 29, 2006, in his hometown Tainan in southern Taiwan, Chen outlined three tasks for the year: "Abolishing the National Unification Council and Guidelines, drafting a new constitution by the end of the year and seeking to enter the United Nations under the name 'Taiwan'."[136].

Abolishing Unification Guidelines

The decision to abolish the National Unification Council (NUC) and the National Unification Guidelines (NUG) came as a complete surprise to the Bush administration, prompting it to move swiftly to stop Chen from putting his provocative plan into action and head off a potential crisis in the Taiwan Strait.

In the Lunar New Year speech, Chen first questioned the legitimacy of the NUC and the NUG. He sarcastically likened the NUC to "a moribund store whose sign has disappeared and shelves are empty of goods." But despite this fact, he continued, the "NUC still seeks a unified China. But just what Chinese unification are we after?" he asked.

Turning to the NUG, the unification guidelines, Chen said they were similarly problematic. "They even accept the 'one China' principle, contradicting the opinion of the public." He added, "Now is an appropriate time to seriously consider abolishing the National Unification Council and the National Unification Guidelines to reflect

---

136 Ko Shu-ling, Scrap Unification Guidelines, Chen Says, Taipei Times, January 30, 2006.

the current state of Taiwanese consciousness."

The NUC was created in 1990, as a governmental body, under an executive order by then-President Lee Teng-hui of the KMT. The following year the NUC adopted a set of guidelines for national unification. In essence, the unification guidelines upheld a "one China" concept, namely Taiwan and the mainland both belong to China. In addition, the guidelines set "a goal to pursue a unified China that is governed by a democratic and free system with equitable distribution of wealth."

One main reason cited by Chen for abolishing the NUC and the NUG was that the two entities were outdated and "an absurd product of an absurd era" that failed to reflect the view of the majority of Taiwan's people. Even before Chen announced his decision to abolish the NUC and the NUG, he had technically frozen the council and the guidelines after he came to power six years earlier by refusing to convene any meeting to discuss unification policy.

Despite the fact the NUC and NUG were no longer functional, they were considered to have symbolic significance. They symbolized Taiwan's continued embrace of the concept of "one China" and its commitment to eventual cross-strait unification. This was why Chen had to commit to not abolishing the National Unification Council and the Guidelines in both his 2000 and 2004 inaugural speeches.

The above commitment was among the well-known "five noes" pledges that Chen Shui-bian made to reassure Taiwan's defense ally, the U.S., and its adversary, the PRC, that he would not alter the island's political status quo during his term in office.

Washington was shocked to learn that Chen had decided to

abrogate the NUC and the NUG, worrying that the president was taking actions to pursue formal independence for Taiwan, which could provoke Beijing and endanger cross-strait peace and stability, threatening to damage America's interests.

The State Department issued a statement reaffirming Washington's basic cross-strait policy: "The United States does not support Taiwan independence and opposes unilateral changes to the status quo by either Taiwan or Beijing. We support dialogue in the interest of achieving a peaceful resolution of cross-strait differences in a manner that is acceptable to the people on both sides of the Taiwan Strait."

At the same time, the White House privately dispatched a special delegation, consisting of Dennis Wilder, an Asia specialist on the National Security Council staff, and Clifford Hart, who handled Taiwan affairs at the State Department, to Taipei in mid-February that year to try to persuade President Chen Shui-bian not to abolish the NUC and the NUG.[137]

Chen rejected the appeals of the U.S. delegation, and the two American diplomats left Taipei empty-handed. Chen remained adamant about his plan to scrap the unification council and the guidelines, defying persistent pressure from the U.S. and the mainland.

A State Department spokesman, in reply to a question by the Taipei-based Central News Agency following Wilder and Hart's return to Washington, said the United States was "strenuously" conveying this

---

137 Tim Culpan and Edward Cody, Taiwan Scraps Council on Unity with China, Washington Post, February 28, 2006.

message to Taipei: "We do not support Taiwan independence and oppose steps by either side that raise tensions or alter the status quo as we define it."

At almost the same time, Beijing warned that the "Taiwan leader's actions of promoting the abolishing of the island's 'National Unification Council' and 'National Unification Guideline' were a dangerous sign of escalation of separatists' activities and posed a serious threat to cross-strait relations." Chen Yunlin, director of the Taiwan Affairs Office of the State Council, said further, "We'll keep a close watch on their activities and prepare to deal with any possible complicated situation at any time."

On February 22, 2006, days after Wilder and Hart left Taipei, Chen repeated to visiting U.S. congressman Rob Simmons his dismissal of the NUC and NUG as "absurd products of an absurd era" and asserted that they needed to be abolished. On the same day, the Central Standing Committee of the president's political party voted to endorse the plan to eliminate the council and the guidelines.

Things took a subtle turn in the following week, however. On February 27 when President Chen announced his final decision on the fate of the NUC and NUG, he did not say he was abolishing the two entities, as he had vowed to do. Instead, he declared that the National Unification Council would "cease to function" and that the National Unification Guidelines would "cease to apply."

The language change, as it was later known, was a compromise reached with the U.S. following weeks of intense negotiations behind the scenes.[138] The terms "cease to function" and "cease to apply" satisfied the U.S. because it avoided the word "abolish." Not abolishing the NUC and NUG, as mentioned earlier, was one of the five inaugural pledges that Chen made to the United States not to alter Taiwan's political status. Having him keep these pledges was of great importance to maintaining peace and stability in the Taiwan Strait.

Both the White House and the State Department responded favorably to President Chen's announcement, all expressing support for the way he dealt with the National Unification Council and Guidelines. Both were convinced that Chen's action did not amount to a unilateral change in the status quo.

"We welcome President Chen's reaffirmation of his administration's commitment to cross-strait peace and stability, and Taiwan's commitment to the pledges that President Chen made in his inaugural address to not unilaterally alter the status quo in the Taiwan Strait," White House spokesman Scott McClellan told reporters. Chen's latest decision "did not abolish the National Unification Council and the Guidelines," McClellan stressed.

Adam Ereli, a State Department spokesman, said at a daily press briefing: "On the question of the National Unification Council, it's our understanding that President Chen did not abolish it, and he affirmed Taiwan's commitment to the status quo. We attach great importance to that commitment, and we'll be following his follow-through carefully."

For President Chen, the wording "cease to function" and "cease to

---

138 Edward Cody and Anthony Faiola, Chen Plans to Debate on Taiwan Charter, Washington Post, March 14, 2006.

apply" was acceptable because it enabled him to get U.S. support to "deactivate" the NUC and NUG, though only nominally. The NUC and NUG had already been dormant since he came to power in 2000. A question arises here. What did Chen get in return for finally bowing to U.S. pressure by not insisting on using the word "abolish?" One senior U.S. official when asked that question replied emphatically there was "no quid pro quo" entailed in the compromise made on the issue of the NUC and NUG.

The nearly one-month-old diplomatic row with Washington by now would have drawn to a close, if it were not for an attempt by the Chen administration to spin the just-reached compromise as a diplomatic coup for the president. Senior Taipei officials were quoted by local news media as saying that there was no difference between "abolishing" the National Unification Council and having it "cease to function."

Taipei Urged to Explicitly Reaffirm Its Feb. 27 Announcement

The media reports angered the Bush administration, with the State Department immediately issuing a press statement urging Taipei to explicitly reaffirm its February 27 announcement regarding the cessation of the NUC. The statement: "We have seen reports that senior Taiwan officials have said, concerning the National Unification Council, that there is no distinction between 'abolish' and 'ceasing activity' and that the effect of Taiwan's action earlier this week was to abolish the Council...

Chapter 6
Tensions with Beijing Near Boiling Point

"We have been informed, however, that the reports misquoted Taiwan officials. We expect the Taiwan authorities to publicly correct the record and unambiguously affirm that the February 27 announcement did not abolish the National Unification Council, did not change the status quo, and that the assurances remain in effect."

In reply to a press question about the dispute, Adam Ereli, deputy spokesman for the State Department, said, "Our understanding from the authorities in Taiwan was that the action Taiwan took on February 27 was deliberately designed not to change the status quo, as Chen Shui-bian made clear in his 7-point statement. Abrogating an assurance would be changing the status quo, and that would be contrary to that understanding. We believe the maintenance of Taiwan assurances is critical to the preservation of the status quo. Our firm policy is that there should be no unilateral change in the status quo, as we have said many times." [139]

Taipei's response to the State Department's demand for explicit clarification was a flat denial that any of its officials had ever made those controversial comments. The Ministry of Foreign Affairs, through its representative office in Washington, went further to explain to the Bush administration that the "concerned officials were misquoted and the media reports were inaccurate." At almost the same time, Chen's Foreign Minister James Huang, testifying before a

---

139 The seven points were contained in President Chen Shui-bian's February 27, 2006 announcement. Point 2 stated his government had no intention of changing the status quo and Point 3 stressed that ceasing the function of the National Unification Guidelines did not involve changing the status quo. Further information is available at www.president.gov.tw/.

legislative hearing, reaffirmed that the unification council had "ceased to operate" and its policy guidelines "ceased to apply," adding that these terms "were in no way equivalent to an abolition of the entities."

Still, Taipei never explicitly responded to Washington's call to "unambiguously" clarify the NUC's status following its February 27 announcement. All the responses or relevant comments it had made were either vague or elusive. On March 21, 2006, when Chen Shui-bian received the new U.S. representative, AIT Director Stephen Young, he pledged, "There will be no change in the commitments that I have made to the U.S. government, to President George Bush." But he did not use the meeting with Young to unequivocally declare that his February 27 announcement did not abolish the NUC and did not change the status quo.

Then at a June 9, 2006 meeting with visiting AIT Chairman Raymond Burghardt at his presidential office, Chen gave another reassurance that the "four noes" pledges he made to the U.S. in both his 2000 and 2004 inaugural addresses remained unchanged. "They have not changed over the past six years and will not change during the next two," he said.

At first glance, Chen reaffirmed his inaugural commitments once again and manifested a determination to abide by them. But a closer look at his latest reaffirmation would show that he quietly left out a fifth and final of his well-known "five noes" pledges: not "abolishing the National Unification Council and Guidelines."

Chen defended his action on the NUC, contending that it was a move aimed merely at deepening Taiwan's democracy and respecting the freedom of its 23 million people to "choose their destiny." It was not intended to change the status quo, he said.

In the process, Chen also blamed Beijing for his NUC decision. He explained that when he first made his "five noes" pledges in 2000, he did so on the assumption that Beijing would not use force, or threaten to use force, against Taiwan. But the PRC's increasing missile deployment opposite this island over the years and its 2005 adoption of its "Anti-Secession Law" already had violated the "no use of force" condition. So it was the mainland side that continued to change the status quo in the Taiwan Strait, President Chen argued.

Aside from defending his position and blaming Beijing, Chen remained reluctant to clearly state that his February 27 announcement did not change the status quo, as demanded by Washington. He was viewed as being deliberately vague on the issue to leave room for maneuvering. But this policy risked further undermining his credibility in Washington and Beijing.

Alan Romberg, director of East Asian Studies at the Henry L. Stimson Center and an expert in the triangular relationship linking Washington, Beijing, and Taipei, offered his observations on the row with the US over President Chen's move to abolish the NUC and NUG.

Romberg said some people in Taiwan were too carried away with what they considered a "victory" -- referring to President Chen Shui-bian's agreement to cease the function of the NUC -- and this "risked damaging an understanding" between Washington and Taipei on the matter. The U.S. expert made his comments, during an interview with the Taipei-based Central News Agency's Washington correspondent, at the height of the controversy over whether the term "cease to function" amounted to the word "abolishing." The interview was carried out by the English-language newspaper, the Taipei Times.[140]

"When the U.S. negotiated the language used in President Chen's seven-point statement, it felt that whatever the nuances of the Chinese-language version, the ambiguity of the English permitted the interpretation that the NUC and the Guidelines had not been abolished...

"Since then, however, some people in Taipei have trumpeted their 'victory' too loudly, even to the point of seeming to equate 'cease to function' with 'abolish' ...the impression among many in Washington is that there has been a breach of faith and that Taipei's claim of maintaining the status quo' rings hollow."

Romberg continued, "The statement by a U.S. official requesting Taiwan to 'unambiguously affirm' it 'did not abolish' the NUC has revealed an 'underlying level of U.S. frustration' in its dealings with Taiwan over the NUC episode. Any further statements from Taipei on this or other cross-strait issues will be very closely scrutinized...The U.S., like China, has been concerned about what 'next steps Chen will take."

Separately, according to a Washington Post interview with Chen Shui-bian in mid-March, two weeks after he announced his final decision on the NUC and NUG, the president stated that "he originally wanted to say the council had been 'abolished,' but was dissuaded by the United States on grounds that he had promised in 2000 not to eliminate it." That promise, explained Edward Cody and Anthony

---

140 U.S. Academic Warns about Washington Frustration over NUC, Taipei Times, March 5, 2006.

Faiola, the two Post reporters who conducted the interview, was one of several -- including a pledge not to substantially revamp the constitution -- made by Chen to pacify concerns in the United States and China that he could create trouble with his passionate quest for Taiwan independence.

The word change -- from "abolish" to "cease to function" -- was negotiated over several weeks between Taiwan and U.S. officials, the Washington Post reported, quoting Chen's Mainland Affairs Council Director Joseph Wu. "In the end, Chen's statement also included an affirmation that he was 'not changing the status quo' and would 'follow legal procedures in any constitutional revision'." As a result, the Bush administration reacted "mildly" [to Chen's February 27 action on the NUC and NUG], according to the report.

Mainland China, which had repeatedly warned Chen Shui-bian against abolishing Taiwan's National Unification Council since the president first floated the idea of considering doing away with the body a month earlier, reacted angrily. Chinese President Hu Jintao condemned Chen's final decision to "cease the function of the unification council and application of the unification guidelines," calling it "a grave provocation" and "a dangerous step on the road toward Taiwan independence."

Hu, in remarks published by the official Xinhua News Agency, said the move threatened stability in the Taiwan Strait and the region. "We will continue to strive for the prospect of peaceful reunification, but never tolerate the secession of Taiwan from the motherland," he warned.

The Taiwan Affairs Office said in a statement, "Although Chen did not use the term 'abolish' and changed the term to 'cease function,' this is merely a word game. He is tricking the Taiwanese people and international opinion." The statement went on to say, "Everyone knows what Chen Shui-bian schemes for is 'Taiwan independence.' He claims that his decision does not 'involve changing the status quo.' But it is crystal clear that his real purpose is to step up his Taiwan independence activities through ceasing the function of the National Unification Council and ceasing the application of the Guidelines." [141]

China also displayed its dissatisfaction with Washington's perceived failure to effectively rein in President Chen over the NUC issue. Chinese Foreign Ministry spokesperson Liu Jianchao, at a specially held press conference, said, "We urge the U.S. to fully realize the gravity and danger of Chen Shui-bian's splitting activities and strictly abide by its commitment to China on the Taiwan issue. Washington should take concrete actions to oppose Chen's splitting activities and make concerted efforts with China to maintain a sound China-U.S. relationship as well as peace and stability across the strait."

In response, U.S. State Department spokesman Adam Ereli said, "We will continue to hold President Chen by his commitments not to take unilateral moves." At the same time, Ereli appealed for calm and urged both sides [of the Taiwan Strait] to resume stalled talks on closer relations.

So what was the final status of the NUC after a prolonged period of contention between Taipei, Washington, and Beijing? Was the NUC

---

141 PRC Foreign Ministry Spokesperson Liu Jianchao's Press Conference on February 28, 2006.

still in existence, after Washington repeatedly urged Chen Shui-bian to "unambiguously" clarify that his February 27, 2006 announcement to "cease the operation" of the body did not mean "abolishing" it? Or was the NUC still counted by President Chen as his "fifth no" commitment -- a pledge not to scrap the National Unification Council?

The above questions were answered by President Chen himself during an interview with the Financial Times' Taipei correspondent Kathrin Hille in early November 2006, nine months after he ordered the cessation of the NUC. Hille asked Chen the following question: "When you first took office, you pledged the "Five Noes". Later, the fifth no seems to have gone missing. Most recently, you tend to prefer the pledge of not changing the status quo. So does the fact that you no longer explicitly repeat your Five Noes pledge reflect some change in your commitments?"

Chen's answer to this question was: "As far as the Five Noes are concerned--the fifth No is already gone after the termination of the National Unification Council and Guidelines. Because originally there was the special staff at the Presidential Office for the NUC, the staff is now gone. The NUC's operations ceased a long time ago, and there's not even a budget anymore. So the fifth No is gone. Now there's only Four Noes left."

Chapter 7
Endorsing a 'Second Republic' Constitution

Entering 2007 with a Slew of Political Actions

Chen Shui-bian headed into his final year and a half in office with a slew of political initiatives. They included calls for constitutional reform, a renewed push for "name rectification," and a campaign to hold a referendum on whether the island should join the United Nations under the name of Taiwan. None of these programs were new, but they were all pursued with intensified vigor.

These were extremely controversial, and many observers wondered aloud why Chen Shui-bian devoted so much time to this passionate quest just as his presidential authority was waning. Some speculated that Chen was reluctant to be seen as a lame-duck president, while others opined that he wanted to ensure that Taiwan's politics continued to revolve around his pro-independence agenda.

While this may have been true, there was a more fundamental reason: Chen hoped to use his remaining time in office to consolidate a "Taiwanese consciousness" and carve out a "sovereign Taiwan identity" separate from China -- in case his goal of pursuing de jure independence proved to be unattainable.

By now, the president was known to have set a timetable for accomplishing his ambitious constitutional reform goal: To propose a draft new constitution and enact it via an island-wide referendum in 2006. The new constitution, if approved by the voters, would then be proclaimed by him before he stepped down on May 20, 2008.

Yet Chen Shui-bian did not specify what form his new constitution would take until late 2006 when he openly voiced his support for enacting a "second republic" constitution for Taiwan.

Chen first brought up the idea of a "second republic" on October 15, 2006, before a crowd of supporters gathered to celebrate the 80th birthday of his former presidential advisor Koo Kwang-ming.[142] Koo, a longtime advocate of independence for Taiwan, had previously raised the concept of a "second republic," calling for Taiwan to "freeze" the existing ROC constitution and enact a new one to be used as a legal basis for the so-called "second republic."

President Chen, in his remarks at the birthday party that day, did not give any details about the "second republic" idea itself. He merely called for supporters and members of the general public to "spend time thinking about whether a 'second republic' was a good idea or if it was suitable for Taiwan."

His "second republic" remarks, however, prompted an immediate reaction from the U.S. The following day, the State Department made its dim view of the idea abundantly clear. "The U.S. does not support Taiwan's independence. We oppose unilateral changes to the status quo by either side [of the Taiwan Strait]," it said.

Yet Chen Shui-bian was undeterred by the U.S. warning. About two weeks later during an interview with the Financial Times, Chen went further, elaborating on the concept of a "second republic"

---

142 Hsu Yung-ming, 'Second Republic' a Second Chance, Taipei Times, October 20, 2006.

constitution and adding his views in his role as the president of the ROC and the chairman of the ruling DPP. The interview was published in the November 2, 2006 edition of the Financial Times.[143]

Chen was asked by the British newspaper's Taipei correspondent Kathrin Hille the following question: "We observe that you have started to discuss some of the possible contents of a new constitution, including the definition of the 'existing national boundaries' and the concept of a 'second republic' constitution. Will you get even deeper involved in the discussion of the constitutional contents? Will you start giving some answers and reveal your views on these issues?"

Discussing Ways to Address National Territory

The following are excerpts from President Chen's lengthy reply to the Financial Times: "The DPP's party platform that was passed on October 7, 1990 mentions: Our country's de-facto sovereignty does not extend to mainland China and Outer Mongolia. The future constitutional system and domestic as well as foreign policies should be based on this factual territorial scope. So no matter if factual sovereignty or factual territory, we have already said in very clear terms that these do not include mainland China and Outer Mongolia...

"But according to the existing constitution, the country's territory is defined with reference to 'the existing national boundaries.' But what are the existing national boundaries?... Does it really include mainland

---

143 Taiwan Set for 'New Clash with Beijing', Financial Times, November 1, 2006.

China and Outer Mongolia? Mainland China is currently the territory of the People's Republic of China, and Outer Mongolia is another country named the Republic of Mongolia. Further, do the 'existing national boundaries' include Taiwan? This is also very controversial…

"So then somebody has proposed the concept of the 'second republic'. Actually, the second republic means that the current constitution would be frozen, and a new Taiwan constitution would be written. Freezing the ROC constitution also means keeping some kind of a link to the current constitution and not cutting it off completely…

"This is a very interesting idea. It deserves observation, and everyone can discuss it. That is why some people say that the second republic constitution's preamble should define the territorial scope that this constitution applies to, whether it includes mainland China or Mongolia, or whether it is limited to the existing territorial and sovereignty scope of Taiwan, [and its outlying islands] …

"Also, the General Provisions of the existing constitution, including article 4 with its 'existing national boundaries', are not to be touched, but will address the issue in the second republic Taiwan constitution where it talks about its application scope. Would that work and be acceptable to everyone? I think that's a very interesting thought."

The comments Chen made in the Financial Times interview and on the earlier occasion of Koo Kwang-ming's birthday party suggested that the president at the time not only encouraged public consideration of the "second republic" constitution concept but even offered his views on how such a new constitution should be written. The first and foremost thing, in his view, was that the constitution had to be based on the DPP's party platform. That platform claims "our country's de facto sovereignty does not extend to mainland China." This meant that Taiwan and the Chinese mainland should be defined in the new constitution as two separate countries.

Additionally, he believed a "second republic" or "Taiwan constitution" would not need to make changes to the current ROC constitution, which would be frozen at the same time as the new one went into effect. Freezing the existing constitution, Chen maintained, could allow him to address the territory of Taiwan in the "second republic" constitution without touching the relevant sections of the old basic law, thus avoiding a change to the status quo. Chen was referring to his repeated pledges to the U.S. and the international community not to change Taiwan's political status.

'Second Republic' Constitution Worries Beijing

Chen Shui-bian's open advocacy of enacting a "second republic" constitution for Taiwan also rang alarm bells in Beijing. The Chinese authorities were so disturbed by the Taiwan leader's new political action that a senior Beijing official paid a personal visit to then-U.S. Ambassador to China Clark T. Randt, Jr. to express Beijing's concerns. The visit by Chen Yunlin, the director of the Taiwan Affairs Office (TAO), came just over one week after the Financial Times' publication of an interview with President Chen about his views on the "second republic" concept.

During the meeting, according to a U.S. diplomatic cable, the TAO director first informed Ambassador Randt that "China remains concerned about Chen Shui-bian's attempt to pursue de jure independence for Taiwan through constitutional reform." The Beijing official warned that Chen's constitutional reform was moving along a dangerous path. He hoped the United States "will pay close attention to Taiwan's latest developments, not sending any wrong signals to Chen Shui-bian or causing him to misunderstand the position of the U.S."

The message delivered at the meeting, described by Ambassador Randt in his cable, was tagged as secret, but a copy was obtained by Wikileaks and posted on its website.[144] According to the U.S. embassy cable, the mainland learned that Taiwan's political and activist groups had drafted at least four different versions of a new constitution. No details were given in the cable as to where such information was obtained.

The TAO compiled the key points of each of the four constitutional drafts in a document, which was personally handed to Ambassador Randt by Chen Yunlin at the meeting. But Chen Yunlin told the U.S. ambassador that he wanted to discuss in more detail the fourth one, the so-called "second republic" constitution. He stated that Chen Shui-bian appointed a group of pro-independence scholars to draft a "second republic" constitution, modeled on the French Second Republic Constitution.

"This draft," according to the TAO director, "rejects the notion that Taiwan is a part of China and that it was returned to China in 1945

---

144 Wikileaks, Chen Yunlin Raises Taiwan Constitution Concerns with Ambassador, U.S. Embassy, cable -06Beijing23736, November 13, 2006.

Chapter 7
Endorsing a 'Second Republic' Constitution

[by Japan]. It instead advances a separatist 'two-state theory' or advocacy of "one country on each side of the strait.' The draft also distorts the U.N. Charter in a bid to change the cross-strait status quo."

After describing the draft "second republic" constitution, the TAO director then concluded that "this version denies Taiwan is an indivisible part of China, denies that there is only one China in the world, and denies the historical fact that Taiwan has never existed as a separate country." All in all, Director Chen added, Chen Shui-bian and his supporters were attempting to deceive the international community into supporting their "second republic" constitution.

The following are brief descriptions, as provided by Chen Yunlin, of the other three drafts. They also were part of the U.S. embassy cable, along with the fourth draft -- the "second republic" constitution:

---"The first draft blatantly advocates the establishment of a Republic of Taiwan. It defines the territory of Taiwan, plus Penghu, Kinmen, and Matsu, as the area of national jurisdiction. This is essentially a constitution for an independent Taiwan."

---"The second draft declares that Taiwan is a democratic republic called the Republic of China. It incorporates a 'two-state' theory. The draft constitution stipulates that any change in the political relationship between the PRC and ROC must have the consent of the people of Taiwan through a referendum."

---"The third draft constitution contains the following provisions: One, abolishing the current constitutional concept of one country and two regions [a reference to Taiwan and the mainland], and doing away with the call for national unification as the ultimate goal. Two, dropping all references [in the current constitution] to the Chinese mainland. Three, redefining the domain of the traditional territory of China. And four, lowering the threshold for holding a national referendum. This draft, while called an amendment to the constitution, virtually amounts to the creation of a new one."

In the same U.S. embassy cable, the TAO director also was quoted as stating one other item of concern to China: Beijing leaders worried that the Bush administration could be misled by some U.S. opinion leaders, who believed that Chen Shui-bian would ultimately be forced to back off from his provocative political agenda. They cited the many corruption allegations against him that tended to undermine his image, authority, and influence.

But the TAO official contended that the opposite was more likely to be true. "Facts have proven that Chen Shui-bian has no credibility," said the TAO director. In the diplomatic cable, he also reportedly made the following charges against Chen Shui-bian: "The Taiwan leader cared nothing about the interests of others, including the United States. He was a 'political hooligan'."

According to the cable, the Beijing official also urged the U.S. to maintain close communication with China on developments in Taiwan over the remainder of Chen Shui-bian's term because "many things could happen" during that sensitive period. "While the Chinese government is already making preparations for the worst-case scenario," he continued, "we hope the United States will not provide any opportunities for that 'troublemaker' Chen Shui-bian to avail of."

In response, the cable said, Ambassador Randt told TAO Director Chen that President Bush "has been very clear that the United States opposes unilateral changes to the cross-Strait status quo by either side."

Additionally, the ambassador in his conversation with the senior Beijing official repeatedly stressed the point that "maintaining open channels of bilateral communication is in the interest of all sides."

As things turned out, the beleaguered President Chen Shui-bian did not back away from his political agenda to concentrate his time and energy on defending himself, as some U.S. opinion leaders predicted. Instead, he doubled down on his efforts to further his independence drive.

Even as the controversies sparked by his support of a "second republic" constitution lingered on, President Chen Shui-bian incensed Washington and Beijing again, this time with a fresh series of provocative remarks and actions starting from the beginning of 2007.

In his New Year's address that year, the president provocatively proclaimed that "Taiwan is a part of the world, not of China." He was speaking about Taiwan's relations with the mainland. "Taiwan's national territory measures 36,000 square kilometers and its sovereignty belongs to the entire 23 million people [of the island]," he claimed.

In the speech, Chen also commented on Taiwan's political future. He asserted that only the Taiwanese people have the final say in the country's future. "Setting unification with China as the only choice for the country's future not only deprives the Taiwanese people of their right to self-determination but also violates the fundamental principle of democratic sovereignty," he pointed out.

Then in late January of that same year, Chen went further to call for the people of Taiwan to "act now" on drawing up a new constitution. He maintained that without a new constitution, Taiwan could not be a "normal, complete and progressive new democracy."

His call for writing a new constitution prompted immediate criticism from Washington. John Negroponte, President George W. Bush's nominee for deputy Secretary of State, cautioned that President Chen Shui-bian's call for a new constitution for Taiwan might be "at cross purposes" with the "one-China policy" of the United States.[145]

Negroponte was testifying during his Senate Foreign Relations Committee confirmation hearing. When asked about his opinion of President Chen Shui-bian's recent push for a new constitution, Negroponte cited Washington's adherence to a "one-China policy" and the three U.S.-China communiques it signed with Beijing after Nixon resumed contacts with China in 1972. "We believe that it would be unwise to do anything that might be at cross purposes with those three [documents]," he said.

Even before Negroponte made his remarks in late January, the Bush administration had been anxiously communicating with Taipei through both public and private channels, relaying its concerns about Chen's support for a "second republic" constitution, and, more recently, his New Year statements advancing Taiwan's statehood.

Most notably, the State Department issued a solemn statement urging Chen to stick to his "four noes" commitments. "President Chen's fulfillment of his commitments will be a test of leadership, dependability, and statesmanship, as well as his ability to protect Taiwan's interests, his relationships with others and to maintain peace

---

145 AP and AFP dispatches from Washington, Negroponte Wary about New Constitution for Taiwan, China Post, February 1, 2007.

and stability in the strait," the statement said.

'Four Wants and One Without'

In open defiance of the State Department's advice, President Chen on March 4, 2007, issued a declaration of "Four Wants and One Without" in a predominantly pro-independence speech. The declaration came one month after he called for a stepped-up campaign to write a new constitution and two months after he publicly challenged Beijing's "one-China" policy in his New Year message.

Chen's "Four Wants and One Without" speech was delivered to the Washington-based, independence-advocating Formosan Association for Public Affairs (FAPA) on its 25th anniversary. The "four wants and one without" read as follows: "Taiwan wants independence, wants name rectification, wants a new constitution, and wants development. And Taiwan faces no such division as leftist or rightist policy lines. It confronts only the question of whether to reunite with the Chinese mainland or become independent."[146]

Chen Shui-bian drew his inspiration, though sarcastically, from his famous "Four Noes and One Without" pledges which he first made in his 2000 inaugural address. In it, Chen pledged that "as long as Beijing had no intention of using military force against Taiwan during my time in office, I would not declare independence, not change Taiwan's name, not add the state-to-state theory to the constitution, not promote a referendum on the issue of independence versus unification,

---

146 President Declares Four Wants, Central News Agency, March 4, 2007.

and there would not be the question of whether to abolish the National Unification Guidelines and the National Unification Council." These pledges soon became better known as Chen's "Five Noes" commitments.

Chen administration officials insisted that the president's latest remarks did not contradict his 2000 inaugural commitments. But even so, as Alan Romberg of the Stimson Center observed, "advocacy of these new positions is a violation of his pledges to maintain the status quo and promote peace and stability. It is at direct odds with America's national interests."

In addition to his latest declaration, Chen also made the following assertions in the same March 2007 speech: "Taiwan is a sovereign state independent of China, seeking independence is the common goal of the people of Taiwan ...Taiwan is the best name to be used in the country's bid to join the United Nations and other international organizations...To become a normal and complete state, Taiwan must have a new constitution that suits its needs."

Chen's "four wants and one without" remarks raised worries, particularly for local investors. They feared that his radical independence remarks could escalate tensions with the U.S., Taiwan's most important defense supporter, and the Chinese mainland, the island's largest export market. The investor fears sent Taiwan's stock and currency markets sliding to their lowest levels in years.

Beijing unsurprisingly was infuriated by Chen Shui-bian's provocations. PRC Foreign Minister Li Zhaoxing condemned the Taiwan leader at a press conference, saying "Whoever wants to split Taiwan from the mainland will become a criminal for the ages."

Chapter 7
Endorsing a 'Second Republic' Constitution

Nonetheless, the Chinese government refrained from any further response beyond the angry rhetoric.

In a similar vein, Washington's reply to President Chen's provocative remarks was less harsh than on earlier occasions. State Department spokesman Sean McCormack responded in this way: "The U.S. does not support independence for Taiwan...President Bush has repeatedly underscored his opposition to unilateral changes to the status quo by either Taipei or Beijing...Any rhetoric that would raise doubts about Chen's inaugural commitments and assurances is unhelpful."

Why did Washington and Beijing react in such a restrained manner despite Chen's defiant tone in pushing his pro-independence policies? Two notable views were expressed on that question.

One was from the widely read "Black and White" column of Taiwan's mass circulation Chinese-language United Daily News. The column observed a day after the publication of Chen's "four wants and one without" remarks: "Chen Shui-bian tossed off the 'four wants and one without' assertions, but both Washington and Beijing have seen through the fact that he looks tough in appearance but is cowardly at heart. Even though Washington reprimanded him harshly and Beijing issued a statement rebuking him, these were nothing more than routine practices. The Taiwan financial markets were the innocent victims, reacting with steep declines, as investors feared that Chen's inflammatory statements could intensify tensions with Beijing and Washington, hurting Taiwan's economy."

Another view was offered by Alan Romberg of the East Asia Program of the Henry L. Stimson Center. He told the Central News

Agency: "Chen's assertions are not an 'action plan,' and one should not over-read the practical significance of his remarks. It is no more realistic now than before to expect he can bring about the changes he calls for, nor is it clear whether he actively plans to seek most of these measures in the remaining more than one year of his term."[147]

In March 2007, Chen Shui-bian's call to enact a new constitution for a "second republic" elicited a concrete response. With the blessing of the president, the pro-DPP Taiwan Thinktank announced the completion of a draft "second republic" constitution that month.[148] This came five months after the president openly encouraged the public to study whether a second republic was suitable for Taiwan.

The think tank's draft was authored by a group of university professors, most of them supporting an independent Taiwan. They included Chen Ming-tong, a professor at National Taiwan University who was appointed soon after by President Chen to head his cabinet-level Mainland Affairs Council, responsible for making mainland policy and regulating cross-strait exchanges.

The draft "Second Republic" constitution claimed that Taiwan and China were two separate countries and that the Taiwanese people should have the final say in their country's future. The proposed new constitution, in its preamble, noted that the Republic of China (ROC) was founded in 1911 and relocated to Taiwan in 1949 after the establishment of the [communist-led] People's Republic of China

---

147 Jorge Liu and Lilian Wu, Chen Shui-bian's 'Four Wants, One Is Not' Statement, Central News Agency, March 6, 2007.
148 Ko Shu-ling, Group Pushes New Constitution, Taipei Times, March 18, 2007.

Chapter 7
Endorsing a 'Second Republic' Constitution

(PRC).

The proposed basic law stipulated that the jurisdiction of the ROC covers Taiwan, Penghu, Kinmen, Matsu, and other offshore islets. Any change to the political relationship between the ROC and PRC must be decided through negotiations between the two sides, based on equality and peace, pending approval by the people of Taiwan.

"Until China and Taiwan agree on their relationship through a democratic process," the draft constitution asserted, "the existing constitution should cease to apply and a 'second republic' constitution should be enacted."

Professor Chen Ming-tong who headed the drafting of the "second republic" constitution, stated: "If China wishes to assimilate Taiwan, it should convince the Taiwanese in a civilized way, rather than using military intimidation or military oppression."

According to the chief of the drafting project, there were as many as 15 different versions of how the current ROC constitution should be reformed. They were proposed by various political and activist groups in Taiwan, in response to President Chen's earlier call for "bottom-up, outside-in" mass participation in his constitutional reengineering project. The Taiwan Thinktank-sponsored 'Second Republic' constitution draft was, in Chen Ming-tong's words, "just an alternative proposal."

It was about a year or so since the spring of 2006 when Chen first declared: "We should adopt an open attitude regarding the sensitive issues of whether to change the national moniker, national territory or national flag" in reforming the ROC constitution.[149]

During this period, the mainland had been closely monitoring events in Taiwan. So when Taiwan Thinktank formally published its draft "second republic" constitution in March 2007, there was an instant storm of protests in mainland China, from the government to state media and from think tank experts to university scholars.

Yang Yi, spokesman for the Taiwan Affairs Office of the State Council, criticized the draft "second republic" constitution as a "direct response to Chen Shui-bian's conspiracy to realize de jure independence for Taiwan through what he called constitutional reform."

In a statement released through the state-run Xinhua News Agency, the spokesman said the draft constitution "overtly writes in the secessionist assertion of 'one country on each side [of the strait],'" denying the fact that both the mainland and Taiwan belong to one China.

"We are closely monitoring the situation," the spokesman said, adding: "We will never allow the Taiwan secessionist forces to separate Taiwan from China in any name or by any means."

Yu Keli, director of the Institute of Taiwan Studies at the Chinese Academy of Social Sciences, offered a similar warning: "It will seriously harm cross-strait relations should the draft constitution be adopted by the Democratic Progressive Party [administration] and submitted to the Legislative Yuan for deliberation." That would be the

---

149 Edward Cody, Interview with Taiwan's Leader, Washington Post, March 13, 2006.

Chapter 7
Endorsing a 'Second Republic' Constitution

case, Yu went on to say, because "it amounts to taking a concrete step toward seeking de jure Taiwan independence."

In an interview with Xinhua, Yu also noted that the Taiwan Thinktank-sponsored draft "calls the second republic constitution a constitution of Taiwan, and advocates determining cross-strait political relations through a public referendum." He described the proposed constitution as a "Taiwan independence scheme that aims to change the status quo that both the mainland and Taiwan belong to one China."

Yu warned that the "activities of advancing de jure Taiwan independence will not only directly impair the interests of Taiwan compatriots, but also seriously threaten peace and stability across the Taiwan Strait and even the whole Asia-Pacific region."

The proposed "second republic" constitution also drew sharp criticism from Huang Jiashu, another leading mainland scholar who taught at China's Renmin University. He told the Xinhua News Agency that this draft constitution "is more deceptive compared with previous versions straightforwardly advocating Taiwan independence."

Professor Huang was referring to the constitution's passages proclaiming that "the state's jurisdiction is only confined to Taiwan, Penghu, Kinmen, Matsu, and affiliated islands" and that "its territorial air space, territorial waters and adjoining waters conforming with the stipulations of international law."

In a way, Huang said, the draft of the "second republic" constitution was an attempt by its authors and backers to "reduplicate the trick" by Chen Shui-bian. Chen had managed to freeze the National Unification Council and Guidelines in early 2006 with the acceptance of the U.S., even though that move violated the final pledge under the promises of the "five noes." This fifth pledge was that there would be no abolition of the National Unification Council and National Unification Guidelines.

The mainland's criticism of the draft "second republic" constitution soon faded away, however. That was because it had become increasingly apparent that Chen Shui-bian wouldn't be able to accomplish any constitutional changes during his remaining time in office. By mid-May 2007, Chen had only one year left in office, but the president and his party still had not yet agreed upon a final version from the dozen or so draft constitutions that would need to be submitted to the legislature for deliberation.

But even if he had been able to reach a decision, he would have had no chance of getting it approved, first by the legislature and then through a public referendum. This was because both the legislature and the Referendum Act set extremely high thresholds for sovereignty-related constitutional changes. In addition, the ruling DPP at this time was still unable to attain a majority in the Legislative Yuan which would be needed to approve a new constitution.

As recently as May 9, 2007, Chen Shui-bian himself, during an interview with Channel News Asia, acknowledged that his ambition to enact a new constitution might be an unattainable goal. He acknowledged describing to the Singapore-based news channel the difficulty of enacting sensitive constitutional amendments. "It is a complicated difficult process," he said.

"We must still follow existing constitutional procedures -- a high threshold of a three-quarters majority of a quorum of at least three-fourths of the total number of legislators must vote in favor of it. Then at least half of eligible voters must vote for it in a referendum for such an act of constitutional engineering to be completed. This is an extremely challenging process. It is a mission impossible."

In the same interview, Chen also suggested he was pinning his hopes on people power to accomplish his constitutional reform task. "...But we believe that, by and by, a consensus will be reached among the people. By then, we will be able to claim success when all political parties are compelled to bow to the power of the people."

But the reality was that by this time President Chen himself was dealing with a low approval rating, around 20%. A president with such limited appeal could hardly be expected to command the authority and influence to drum up huge popular support for a highly controversial bill, such as Chen's constitutional reform proposal. So his attempt to resort to people's power to enact a "second republic" constitution or sovereignty changes, was nothing less than self-deception.

Ratcheting Up a Name Rectification Campaign

In the opening months of 2007, Taiwan's news media gave extensive coverage to Chen Shui-bian's "second republic" constitution and his "four wants and one without" declaration, but another highly contentious policy was largely overlooked. That was the intensified campaign to promote name rectification across Taiwan -- part of a broader de-sinicization movement, which was aimed at reducing Chinese cultural influence.

On February 8, 2007, President Chen Shui-bian formally announced the renaming of three long-established state-owned public-service companies. Chinese Petroleum Corporation became CPC Corporation Taiwan; China Shipbuilding Corporation became CSBC Taiwan; and Chunghwa (Chinese) Post Company was renamed Taiwan Post Company.

In a separate but concerted action carried out around the same time, the national name ROC disappeared from the country's postage stamps, long a key element of stamp design. In its place was the name Taiwan in both English and Chinese.

As a result of an earlier renaming effort rolled out under the Chen Shui-bian administration, the national moniker ROC appeared in government documents with the name "Taiwan" added in parenthesis, making it part of the country's official title. Similar additions were also made to signs with the names of governmental institutions.

Four of the five rectified names cited above involved replacing the term "China" or "Chinese" with the word "Taiwan." In the fifth case, the moniker ROC was not replaced, but was accompanied by the word "Taiwan."

So why were these changes necessary? The ostensible reason was to remove the confusion surrounding the use of the name "China," but in fact, the moves were made for ideological reasons.

When the name changes were first rolled out, Chen Shui-bian and Premier Su Tseng-chang offered these explanations. When asked by Channel News Asia to comment on the name change campaign, Chen said: "Taiwan must have name rectification. We have not altered the national title, but the name 'Republic of China' cannot be changed, nor can it be used internationally. Therefore, we must use a name that is familiar to everyone, the name of our mother, 'Taiwan.' 'Taiwan' is also

Chapter 7
Endorsing a 'Second Republic' Constitution

the most beautiful and powerful name, and we hope to use it when stepping out to participate in global organizations and international activities. We hope to use the name 'Taiwan' to apply for accession to the World Health Organization and the United Nations. This does not violate my 'four noes' pledges, as we have not changed the national title, but merely wish to use the name 'Taiwan' in the international arena."[150]

Su Tseng-chang, Chen's premier, told the press that the reason for removing the references to "China" and "Chinese" from the titles of government corporations and replacing them with the word "Taiwan" was to avoid confusion between Taiwan and China in the international community. "It was as simple as that," he said. "So long as it is a good thing for the companies and the country, we will keep doing it."

But things were not that simple. A closer look will reveal there were deep-rooted ideological reasons behind the campaign to rectify names. The name rectification campaign was part of a wider Taiwanese localization movement.

The localization movement was increasingly becoming a widespread de-sinicization program under the Chen administration. The Chen administration moved to roll back government policy and practices imposed by the former KMT government in the late 1940s to promote Chinese culture in Taiwan. The ultimate goal of the de-sinicization program was to establish a separate Taiwan identity, independent of China. [151] Major measures taken over the years included revising school textbooks, lifting the ban on the use of

150 Channel News Asia Interview with President Chen Shui-bian, Mainland Affairs Council, May 9, 2007.
151 The Name-Change Fever, China Post, February 11, 2007.

Taiwanese in schools and broadcasting, as well as rectifying names.

The latter measure of rectifying names was targeted at government agencies, state corporations, and public establishments that bore titles containing the words "China" or "Chinese." Generally speaking, the vast majority of the corporations and agencies so named were established on the Chinese mainland and withdrawn to Taiwan during the post-World War II years, along with the KMT government led by Chiang Kai-shek. Others were set up in Taiwan during those early days.

President Chen had vowed to complete the rectification of the names of all related government agencies and state-owned corporations to "Taiwan" in the remaining years of his second term. This would be a major achievement of his presidency. This effort would also include rectifying the titles of Taiwan's overseas diplomatic and representative missions.[152]

Chen, however, did not go further and set a timetable for "rectifying" the nation's official title. Seeking to change the national moniker to Taiwan from the Republic of China was a central part, or the ultimate aim of the overall name rectification campaign, as espoused by President Chen, his party, and other pro-independence activists and groups.

Chen's reluctance to set a timetable or a formal plan for achieving the goal of changing the national title reflected his awareness that it would be political suicide should he take concrete steps in this direction.

---

152 Huang Tai-lin, Chen Pledges to Change Names, Taipei Times, December 4, 2004.

Chapter 7
Endorsing a 'Second Republic' Constitution

When Chen began his first term in 2000, as noted earlier, he promised not to change the national moniker -- one of his high-profile "five noes" pledges that he had made to the international community to preserve Taiwan's political status. He reaffirmed these commitments in 2004 at the start of his second term. This being the case, if he rashly broke the pledge to avoid changing the ROC moniker, it would certainly alienate Washington and infuriate Beijing. Replacing the ROC national title with the name Taiwan would amount to a declaration of independence and this could provoke military intervention by Beijing.

Setting a timetable for changing the national name ROC to Taiwan could also prove suicidal for Chen and his party in another way. It could drive away voters, because the overwhelming majority of the people of Taiwan, as opinion polls consistently showed over the years, preferred the status quo.

Aware of the repercussions that a change of the national title could have for Taiwan's security and his party's electoral well-being, Chen usually avoided being personally involved in major name rectification activities during his presidency, be they sponsored by his party or their allies or other pro-independence groups.

He was noticeably absent, for example, from a high-profile September 2003 mass demonstration that saw tens of thousands of independence supporters and activists taking to the streets of the capital city of Taipei to call for the country's official name to be changed to Taiwan from the Republic of China.

The mass demonstration was led by Chen Shui-bian's predecessor, former president Lee Teng-hui, and organized by an alliance of some 70 pro-independence groups. Many demonstrators participating in the activity voiced their opinions on why Taiwan needed to change its official title.

"Taiwan has never run mainland China," 45-year-old participant Chen Feng-ming told Reuters. "Why should we insist on calling our country the Republic of China?"[153]

Another demonstrator, unnamed in the Reuters interview, insisted that the name the Republic of China "is a legacy from the era when the Nationalist Party ruled mainland China." That was before the Nationalists were defeated by the Chinese communists and retreated to Taiwan in 1949.

Lee Teng-hui, who led Taiwan from 1988 to 2000, recounted his personal experience as president: "As I worked to advance the cause of freedom and democracy in Taiwan during my 12 years as president, I met with many difficulties and obstacles that brought me to the conclusion that Taiwan is not a 'normal country'..."[154].

"Whether in the area of domestic governance or foreign diplomacy, I came to realize that all the difficulties Taiwan encountered are linked to its impractical official name, 'Republic of China.' To resolve the problems, Taiwan must begin by correcting its name, making the nation and its official name consistent with reality."

Chen Shui-bian, like Lee Teng-hui, believed that Taiwan, although having become a democratic country with independent sovereignty, was not what they called a "normal country." They actively pushed for "corrective measures," such as name rectification

153 Alice Hung, Thousands March in Taiwan to Demand Name Change, Reuters, September 7, 2003.
154 Ditto.

and constitutional reform, to be taken to turn Taiwan into a "normal country."

Urging Adoption of a 'Normal Country' Resolution

Unlike Lee, however, Chen held an even more assertive view about Taiwan's political status and its future. In a speech given in September 2007 before the World Taiwanese Congress, he said, "The evolution of history shows quite clearly that Taiwan is already a nation with independent sovereignty, but Taiwan is still not a normal democratic country. We, therefore, need to continuously and aggressively seek name rectification, constitutional reform, and apply for United Nations membership using the name of Taiwan...and to build a normal and great democratic country." This was the reason why he repeatedly called for the adoption of a "normal country resolution" to promote the normalization of Taiwan's statehood, he said.

But surprisingly when the members of the ruling DPP responded to his call by proposing two "normal country resolution" drafts, one hardline and one relatively moderate, Chen Shui-bian chose to endorse neither one. Moreover, when the two proposed resolutions were put to a vote at a DPP national congress at the end of September 2007, Chen decided to abstain, watching the voting from the sidelines. But Chen's absence cost him the opportunity of a crucial pre-vote debate to weigh in with his position and views.

At the end of the debate, delegates to the DPP national congress voted down the hardline version -- the one presumably preferred by Chen Shui-bian. The rejected draft "normal country" resolution, proposed by then DPP chairman Yu Shyi-kun and endorsed by dozens of other independence fundamentalists, would have called for the country's official name to be changed to Taiwan from the Republic of China outright.[155]

In the end, the moderate version was overwhelmingly approved by the DPP national congress. The new DPP document reaffirmed the party's commitments to "push for Taiwan's name rectification and write a new constitution." In comments made afterward, central party authorities said the newly adopted "normal country" resolution "will serve as a road map for the DPP administration in its efforts to fortify a Taiwan-centric consciousness and create a Taiwan identity."

In a news analysis titled "DPP Congress Approves Resolution to Turn Taiwan into Normal Country," Dennis Engbarth, a reporter for the pro-independence Taiwan News, made the following two salient observations: One, the resolution while calling for "name rectification" for Taiwan, did not go further and call directly for changing the "national moniker" to Taiwan. Two, the resolution set no timetable for accomplishing the task of changing the national title. [156]

The "normal country" resolution adopted by the September 2007 DPP national congress fell far short of the expectations of the many hardliner independence supporters, including President Chen Shui-bian himself. Chen had, just a few weeks earlier, stressed the importance of adopting a tough document as an official DPP policy to

155 Sofia Wu, DPP Congress Pledges to Make Taiwan a 'Normal Country and Happy Homeland', Central News Agency, October 1, 2007.
156 Dennis Engbarth, DPP Congress Approves Resolution to Turn Taiwan into 'Normal Country,' Taiwan News, October 1, 2007.

oblige its leaders to "aggressively push for name rectification and constitutional reform."

The failure of the DPP Congress to adopt a more aggressive resolution reflected, in part, Chen's fading influence. With less than eight months left in office, Chen at the time had already become a lame-duck president, unable to influence party delegates and allies to approve the programs he desired. His decision not to attend the debate ahead of the Congress indicated he had come to realize his diminished status. He might have concluded that even if he chose to participate in the discussion, he would have been unable to change the minds of delegates to the Congress and influence their votes no matter what he said or did.

Electoral interests played a key role in the reluctance of the DPP Congress to pass a tougher "normal country" resolution. According to the same Central News Agency report, many congress delegates chose to pass the moderate version out of concern that approving the hardline proposal might scare away middle-of-the-road voters, who preferred maintaining Taiwan's political status quo.

The DPP national congress took place at a time when the whole party and its candidates were focused on campaigning for voter support ahead of two crucial public-office contests -- one for legislative seats on January 12, 2008, and one for the presidency on March 22.

Frank Hsieh, the DPP's standard bearer in the presidential contest, had earlier questioned the wisdom of aggressively promoting the party's pro-independence agenda at such a sensitive time. Hsieh explained that he supported the campaigns for name-change, constitutional revision, and so on, but it was not wise to set exact deadlines for achieving these goals in the middle of two important elections.[157]

So perhaps presidential candidate Frank Hsieh's reservations about the timing of adopting a stronger normal country resolution explain why DPP president Chen Shui-bian decided to keep a low profile during the DPP Congress debate on the resolution issue, in contrast to his hawkish position in the past.

From the DPP's debate on the "normal country resolution," many analysts pointed to the hypocrisy of Chen Shui-bian and many of his fellow party politicians who often played two-faced political games, saying different things to different people. When addressing influential pro-independence groups, Chen always insisted that Taiwan "must rectify its official title" and that a "normal country resolution" needed to be adopted to aggressively build Taiwan into a normal country.

But then when he came under pressure from party candidates who were concerned that extremely radical political actions could scare away centrist voters, he did an about-turn by refraining from actively joining the party's fundamentalists in pushing for a tougher "normal country resolution."

Similarly, presidential candidate Frank Hsieh's comments on the "normal country" resolution issue were also a form of two-faced politics. On the one hand, Hsieh said he "supported the goals of name change and constitutional revision." These words were intended to pacify the party's hardline politicians and supporters. But at the same

---

157 Alan D. Romberg, Applying to the U.N. "in the name of 'Taiwan,'" China Leadership Monitor, No. 22.

time, he pointed out that in the "middle of the presidential and legislative elections, it was not the right time to set an exact timetable for accomplishing these tasks." By adding these remarks, Hsieh wanted to suggest to moderate voters that he was against pushing the party's political goals provocatively.

Strictly speaking, the "normal country" resolution in its final form and adopted by the DPP, was merely a set of political slogans rather than an action plan, after its national congress delegates refused to outline in the document a demand for a national title change and a timetable for accomplishing it.

But ironically, the DPP after the September 2007 national congress unabashedly issued a declaration with an ambitious, but vague promise of "leading Taiwan to go down its road under its name." But even so, the DPP set a precondition for carrying out that promise: The party had to be kept in power. The DPP promise, as stated in the same Central News Agency article, said: "Taiwan would be able to break out of old shackles and go down its road under its name so long as the DPP can continue its grip on the presidency and win more than half of legislative seats in next year's elections." So the DPP declaration amounted to nothing more than an election gambit.

That said, Chen Shui-bian, and his administration, indeed had made some impressive progress on the wide-ranging name rectification campaign during his eight-year presidency from 2000 to 2008.

One of his most high-profile acts in the name-rectification campaign took place in 2003 when the Ministry of Foreign Affairs began adding the word "Taiwan" in English to the cover of a new version of ROC passports. As noted earlier, authorities claimed the addition was aimed at helping foreign customs officials and airlines distinguish Taiwan citizens from mainland Chinese.

Other politically sensitive name changes were the renaming of Chiang Kai-shek International Airport to "Taiwan" Taoyuan International Airport in 2006 and changing the name of Chiang Kai-shek Memorial Hall in the capital city of Taipei to National "Taiwan" Democracy Memorial Hall in 2007.

There was also a series of landmark name changes involving major state-run companies including airlines and companies in the shipbuilding, petroleum, telecommunications, and steel sectors. These changes came after February 8, 2007, when President Chen launched a new wave of name rectification. This latest action resumed tensions with Washington and angered mainland China.

The Bush administration's response to Taipei's renewed "name rectification" campaign was swift and unequivocal. On the following day, February 9, State Department spokesman Sean McCormack expressed Washington's concern at a daily news briefing, saying, "We do not support administrative steps by the Taiwan authorities that would appear to change Taiwan's status unilaterally or move toward independence. The U.S. does not, for instance, support changes in terminology for entities administered by the Taiwan authorities."

McCormack also read out a formal statement: "President Chen's fulfillment of his commitments will be a test of his leadership, dependability, and statesmanship, as well as his ability to protect Taiwan's interests, its relations with others, and to maintain peace and stability in the strait."

However, Washington's concerns and warnings did not appear to

Chapter 7
Endorsing a 'Second Republic' Constitution

restrain Chen and his administration. At a meeting with senior administration and party officials the day after Washington voiced its disapproval, President Chen instructed that the name change plan be implemented as scheduled, but in a low-key manner.

The president also revealed to the attending officials that he intended to push for changes to the names of Taiwan's foreign embassies and representative offices around the world during his remaining 15 months in office.

In a show of solidarity with President Chen, the administration and the DPP were unanimous in rebuking the U.S. government for objecting to Taiwan's name-change plan. "This is Taiwan's internal affair and foreign countries should not interfere. Taiwan will carry on with its established name change policy," said a statement issued in the name of both the DPP and the administration.

Taipei's open defiance, however, did not prompt any further reaction by the U.S., at least not in public. The U.S. government, for example, did not make any request that Chen annul the alterations already done to several state-owned companies under his February 8 order. These alterations had been judged by Washington to be "steps that would appear to change Taiwan's status unilaterally or move toward independence."

The failure of Washington to ensure that its opposition to the name rectification issue was taken seriously seemed to suggest that the U.S. government was losing influence on a late-term Taipei leader. Or you could say that Chen at this point might have felt he no longer needed to worry about any political repercussions.

Chen's defiance toward the U.S. was a sharp departure from his interaction with the Bush administration in handling a similar event three years earlier. In late 2004, the Chen administration launched a name rectification drive in the hope of using this to rally support among pro-independence voters ahead of the year-end legislative and local government elections.

But after the U.S. expressed strong opposition to Taipei's provocative actions at the time, Chen and his government moved quickly to halt all name-changing activities. As a result, Taipei's tensions with the Bush administration soon eased.

In Beijing's view, however, Washington was to blame for the Taipei leader's open defiance of U.S. opposition to his renewed name-change campaign. China's Ambassador to the U.S. Zhou Wenzhong, in comments released through the state-run Xinhua News Agency, criticized the Bush administration for responding "too mildly" to Chen's latest round of political provocations.

Ambassador Zhou's criticism, however, needed to be discounted. Beijing, refusing to open dialogue with Taipei, had long relied on the United States, Taiwan's defense ally, to exert pressure on Chen Shui-bian over cross-strait issues. The U.S., as a third party, inevitably had its own stance and considerations in addressing its relations with Taiwan.

In Beijing, authorities took Taiwan's latest moves to change the names of its state-owned companies and revise its high school history textbooks as stepped-up bids to cut cultural links with China and promote independence.

Regarding Taiwan's history textbook revisions, they said the "Nanjing Massacre is a painful chapter of history that all sons and

Chapter 7
Endorsing a 'Second Republic' Constitution

daughters of China should remember…Taiwan's high school history textbooks should impart an objective and true face of history to the next generation on the island."

Li Weiyi, a spokesman of Beijing's Taiwan Affairs Office, blasted the Chen administration saying: "Chen Shui-bian's increased efforts to cut historical and cultural links with China are part of an overall plot to create a favorable social climate for achieving the goal of de jure independence for Taiwan. We will continue to closely monitor the developments there, not allowing Taiwanese separatist forces to realize their political schemes."

Provocative as they were, Chen Shui-bian's latest name-changing activities did not escalate tensions to dangerous levels with either Beijing or Washington. Professor Yang Kai-Huang of Taipei's Ming Chuan University offered the following explanation: "In essence, what all involved were mainly Taiwan's domestic politics. While Washington and Beijing both were concerned about Chen's political actions, they also avoided overreaction for fear that it might work to Chen's advantage by stoking sympathy and voter support for his ruling party."

The following segment, Chapter 8, will discuss former President Chen Shui-bian's bid to join the World Health Organization (WHO) as Taiwan, and the various controversies it provoked.

Chapter 8
Applying to Join the WHO as 'Taiwan'

Writing to the World Body Secretariat Personally

Of the various policies that Chen Shui-bian pursued as his presidency drew to a close, the most controversial were the drive to join the World Health Organization and the United Nations, along with a plan to hold a referendum on whether to join the U.N. using the name "Taiwan." These prompted strong responses from mainland China and the United States.

The U.N. referendum, for example, was assailed by the Bush administration as a move "designed to change Taiwan's status quo unilaterally." This would constitute a breach of a prior commitment by President Chen, it added.

Mainland China, already angered by Chen's past provocations, was even more incensed. "The situation across the Taiwan Straits has entered a perilous period," warned PRC President Hu Jintao at a meeting with U.S. President George W. Bush. Hu delivered the alert on the sidelines of the September 2007 APEC summit meeting in Sydney, Australia.[158]

Within Taiwan, Chen Shui-bian's applications for admission to the WHO and the U.N., along with the U.N.-related referendum

---

158 Hu Tells Bush: It's Time to 'Get Tough' on Taiwan, china.com, September 7, 2007.

became hot-button issues -- so hot that they dominated the campaigns for the coming legislative and presidential elections. The former contests were scheduled for January 2008, while the presidential race followed two months later in March.

Given the controversy surrounding the applications to join the WHO and the U.N. as well as the plan to hold a U.N.-linked referendum, greater discussion of these complicated issues is warranted. This chapter and the succeeding two will focus on these three issues.

On April 9, 2007, Chen Shui-bian personally wrote a letter to the Geneva-based WHO Secretariat in his capacity as the president of the Republic of China (Taiwan). In the letter, he called for the U.N. public health body to consider his application for Taiwan to join the organization. The application was made using the name "Taiwan."

This was not the first time Taipei had applied to join the WHO. However, all previous applications had been turned down because of strong opposition from mainland China, which cited its claim of sovereignty over Taiwan. As a result, it insisted that this island was ineligible for admission to the WHO or any other international organizations that required statehood for membership. To overcome Beijing's opposition, Taipei had in the past tried to use some less politically sensitive names, such as Chinese Taipei, in its application, but to no avail.

In the April 2007 application, President Chen broke with tradition and used the name Taiwan on its application to join the WHO. Yet his strategy made things even more complicated. The fundamental problem involved was that Taiwan is not widely recognized as a sovereign country. Governments around the world mostly accept Beijing's position that "Taiwan is a part of China."

So using the name Taiwan to apply for entry into the WHO, which requires statehood for membership, was not workable either. Beijing saw Chen Shui-bian's WHO application plan as an open challenge to its "One China" policy.

In the past, Chen Shui-bian had made no secret of his political intentions. He wanted to use the name Taiwan to join international organizations as a way to project this island as "a sovereign, independent state, separate from China."

That said, it would be unfair to only criticize Chen Shui-bian for his political calculations without at the same time pointing to Beijing's longstanding suppression of Taiwan in the international community. To some extent, Chen's decision to use the name Taiwan to apply for admission to the WHO also represented a pent-up backlash against Beijing.

That's why his renewed effort to join the WHO enjoyed a great deal of domestic support. According to survey data quoted by the Ministry of Foreign Affairs at the time, more than 90 percent of the island's people believed that Taiwan should be admitted into the WHO. Popular support aside, the Legislative Yuan voted overwhelmingly to back Chen's 2007 WHO bid in a motion that garnered strong bipartisan support, something rarely seen in the polarized law-making body.

Theoretically speaking, the World Health Organization, as a specialized U.N. agency concerned with public health, should set advancing public health in every corner of the world as its first and foremost consideration in handling any membership applications, putting politics aside.

But this did not seem to be the case, at least not in its handling of Taiwan's applications over the years. The WHO rejected Taiwan's participation request year after year. In doing so, the world body always cited its adherence to the "principle of 'one China.'" This meant the WHO accepted Beijing's position that "Taiwan is part of China," and Taiwan was not eligible for membership.

Before Chen's presidency, "pragmatic diplomacy" had evolved under Chen's predecessor Lee Teng-hui (1988 to 2000) to overcome Beijing's political interference. Under this strategy, the administration of President Lee kept its application policy flexible as far as the name and status of its membership were concerned.

This flexible policy sometimes worked well, as it met less vigorous opposition from Beijing while winning greater international support. As a result, Taiwan was able to become a member of the Asia Pacific Economic Cooperation (APEC) forum under the name of Chinese Taipei and join the World Trade Organization (WTO) as an economy (the "Customs Territory of Taiwan, Penghu, Kinmen, and Matsu"), for example.

Facing Greater Isolation

However, this flexible approach became almost completely unworkable after the pro-independence Chen Shui-bian came to power in May 2000, as Beijing intensified its efforts to block Taiwan's bid to join international organizations.

In the early years of his presidency, Chen had focused mainly on efforts to participate in the politically less sensitive WHO, essentially following the pragmatic policy of his predecessor in that effort. But his efforts yielded little success.

It was out of a deep sense of despair, combined with an increasingly strong desire to promote an independent Taiwan identity, that Chen was driven to change his strategy by using the name Taiwan on the application for admission. On April 9, 2007, he wrote to the WHO Secretariat for admission to the global health organization using the name Taiwan in his application.

On May 11, 2007, one month after Chen Shui-bian filed his application letter, he held an international press conference to tout his renewed WHO bid. This came about a week before the World Health Assembly (WHA), the decision-making body of the WHO, convened its annual meeting in Geneva.[159]

The president, speaking from Taipei via a video link, recounted his frustration at the WHO's repeated refusal to admit Taiwan over the years. He then explained why he had decided to apply for membership using the name Taiwan.

Chen told journalists stationed in Taipei and Geneva that for nearly a decade, Taiwan had explored various "avenues" for entry into the WHO but to no avail due to persistent opposition from mainland China.

Since 2002, he said, "We had even expressed a willingness to be admitted as a 'health entity.'" By being willing to accept such an

---

159 President Chen's Video Press Conference, News release, Office of the President of the Republic of China (Taiwan), May 11, 2007.

arrangement, he explained, "We hoped to resolve the dispute of statehood and thus facilitate our participation as an observer in the WHA." However, he said, this endeavor also failed, once again because of China's opposition.

"But the WHO's continued exclusion of Taiwan," Chen pointed out, "has created a gap in the global disease prevention system, placing the island's 23 million people in particular danger in the event of an epidemic attack or when a natural disaster strikes."

Chen was not exaggerating. According to local and foreign experts, Taiwan's exclusion from the WHO hurts this island in two important ways: First, when an epidemic breaks out in other countries, the WHO does not share information about the disease with Taiwan because it is excluded from the world body's Global Disease Outbreak Alert and Response Network. This exclusion added to Taiwan's difficulty in prevention and vaccine research efforts.

Second, when an epidemic strikes Taiwan, assistance from the WHO is not available because the island is not a member of that agency. If the WHO decided to render assistance, help was slow in coming, as a result of Beijing's interference.

Chen cited the outbreak of the SARS (severe acute respiratory syndrome) epidemic in Taiwan in 2003 as proof of how the WHO's refusal to admit Taiwan could endanger the safety of its people through the failure to provide timely assistance.

SARS and Taiwan's Exclusion from the WHO

"In the early stages of the SARS attack the WHO had refused to dispatch medical experts to Taiwan to provide much-needed assistance under pressure from mainland China," Chen recalled. "When the WHO's help finally arrived after a delay of six weeks, the disease had already taken dozens of lives on this island."

The SARS epidemic spread to Taiwan in early 2003 from southern China. In total, 73 people lost their lives in Taiwan in the hard-fought battle against the highly contagious disease. That made Taiwan one of the areas hit hardest by the deadly virus – following mainland China and Hong Kong.

In a book entitled China's Rise, Taiwan's Dilemmas and International Peace, co-author Dennis V. Hickey devoted a separate chapter to discussing the WHO's exclusion of Taiwan and its harmful consequences for this island. In the chapter -- The High Cost of Excluding Taiwan from the WHO -- Hickey gave a more detailed account of the setbacks Taiwan suffered in seeking assistance from the world health institution, as it scrambled to treat and contain the SARS disease. The following passages are taken from that chapter.[160]

"In March 2003, the SARS epidemic that had been festering in China since November 2002 finally reached Taiwan. Taiwan health officials reported the outbreak to the WHO. Initially, no one from the WHO responded, and no assistance was offered...

---

160 China's Rise, Taiwan's Dilemmas and International Peace, Tayler & Francis eBooks, online publication date: March 2006.

"Several days later, however, Taiwan authorities received word that the organization could not provide any direct assistance to the island because it was a "province" of China. After a delay of almost two months, the WHO finally sent officials to Taiwan to investigate the island's deteriorating situation...

"As with the 1999 earthquake [that hit central Taiwan]," Beijing had blocked all efforts by Taipei to secure help from the WHO. To be sure, the lack of assistance from the WHO was not the only factor that contributed to the 2003 medical emergency in Taiwan. However, most Taiwanese medical authorities concur that it made a bad situation worse. As one high-ranking health official lamented, "this help did not come quickly enough."

Hickey, in discussing how the WHO's refusal to admit Taiwan hurt this island, also cited two earlier cases in which Taiwan was victimized by its exclusion from the World Health Organization: The 1998 attack of a virulent strain of enterovirus disease type-71 spread from Malaysia and the 1999 devastating earthquake that rocked central Taiwan.

Regarding the first case, Hickey wrote: "In 1998, this exclusion [from the Global Outbreak Alert and Response Network of the WHO] contributed to the deaths of more than 80 Taiwan children when an outbreak of a virulent strain of enterovirus type-71 spread from Malaysia to Taiwan. After this disease struck the island, international assistance was slow to come. As Taiwan's Director General of Health explained, 'We were virtually left alone to fight it and felt isolated.' When help finally did arrive from the United States, it was 'not timely' for the children who had died."

Regarding the second case, Hickey wrote: "On September 11, 1999, central Taiwan was rocked by a massive earthquake measuring 7.6 on the Richter scale. Thousands perished in the disaster. Valuable time was lost as the WHO attempted to figure out "unofficial' and 'indirect" ways to offer assistance to Taiwan. Not upsetting Beijing took precedence over providing a quick response to a humanitarian crisis. As the WHO dithered, the death count rose."

Friendly Countries Call for 'Meaningful Participation' by Taiwan

Taiwan's non-WHO membership-induced dilemma highlighted in the 2003 SARS epidemic this time evoked sympathy from many friendly countries, including the U.S., Japan, and some European states. They began to explore the possibility of Taiwan being granted "meaningful participation" in WHO-related activities and meetings before it "obtains observer status in the WHA."

However, such exploratory discussions somehow led to the signing in May 2005 of a secret memorandum of understanding (MOU) between the WHO Secretariat and Beijing without the participation of Taiwan itself. With the MOU in place, a set of implementation rules were issued two months later in July, detailing ways of contact and interaction between Taiwan and the WHO.

The key contents of the implementation rules soon leaked out, becoming known to Taipei, and sparking concerns and protests there. Under the MOU and its implementation rules, Taiwan's participation in related WHO activities was subject to approval not only by the WHO

Secretariat but also by China's Ministry of Health. Taipei protested the secret documents for undermining Taiwan's vital interests.

In his May 11, 2007, international press conference, President Chen Shui-bian also touched on the MOU in question. He complained of the many unreasonable arrangements in the MOU: "...According to the intelligence we have recently collected, the MOU that China and the WHO Secretariat signed in 2005 states that, whenever Taiwan's medical or public health professionals want to join technical meetings or activities hosted by the WHO, they must send their applications to the agency five weeks in advance. Upon receipt, the WHO is then to forward the applications to China's Ministry of Health for approval."

Chen continued, The MOU also stipulates that representatives from Taiwan can only participate in designated WHO meetings or activities in a private capacity and that no Taiwan officials senior to the director-general level are permitted to attend. What's more, the memorandum calls for all conference documents from Taiwan representatives to be referred to as from "China, Taiwan."

Here Chen blamed Beijing for the politically biased arrangements for Taiwan's contact with the WHO. He said, "The leaked WHO document shows how China has managed to denigrate and suppress Taiwan in every possible way, using its growing political leverage. So Beijing's intervention has left our endeavors to pursue 'meaningful participation' in the WHO entirely meaningless."

The MOU and the stringent rules that it sets for interaction between Taiwan and the WHO were also discussed in a number of other studies. According to Björn Alexander Lindemann, who included Taipei's WHO bid as a case study in his book on cross-strait relations and Taiwan's participation in international organizations, the MOU implementation rules stipulate three broad types of interactions with Taiwan.[161]

Three Broad Types of WHO Interactions with Taiwan

These interactions are: Inviting Taiwan medical and public health experts to take part in technical activities organized by the WHO Secretariat; **Dispatching** staff members or experts to Taiwan to investigate the medical or epidemiological situation and providing technical assistance to the island's medical and public health services; and organizing the response of the WHO Secretariat, should an acute public health emergency occur in Taiwan.

In addition, according to Lindemann, the MOU implementation rules provided detailed instructions on how the above-cited interactions were to be carried out.

Also standing out was a so-called "Focal Point," which was created as a central unit operating under the WHO headquarters, as called for in the MOU. This unit was charged with the task of screening interaction requests initiated by either Taiwan or the WHO. All such requests, if considered justified, would have to be sent to the Permanent Mission of China in Geneva, from there they then were to be forwarded to the Chinese Ministry of Health in Beijing for final approval.

That Taiwan's interaction with the WHO had to gain prior

---

161 Bjorn Alexander Lindemann, Cross-Strait Relations and International Organizations, Springer DE, www.springer-vs. de

approval from mainland China is of course unthinkable. So it was little wonder that Chen Shui-bian considered the MOU document, devised mainly by the WHO Secretariat and mainland China, as just one more example of "how Beijing has managed to denigrate and suppress Taiwan in every possible way."

Sigrid Winkler of the Brookings Institution was also critical of the MOU, saying that the document's provision to allow Beijing to decide Taiwan's interaction with the WHO was tantamount to putting the Taipei government in a subordinate position. Moreover, she said, the complex multi-level screening procedures effectively created administrative obstacles for Taiwan's participation in WHO activities. Below are Winkler's comments contained in her essay entitled Taiwan's U.N. Dilemma: [162] "Taiwan neither had a part in the negotiations of the MOU nor was it ever informed about the exact contents of this document that determines its status in the WHO. An implementation document outlining the specific rules was leaked though. The bottom line of the implementation document was that any interaction between Taiwan and the WHO, other than in a case of acute emergency, was subject not only to approval by the WHO Secretariat but also by the Chinse Ministry of Health in Beijing...

"Apart from leaving it to China to decide whenever Taiwan could enter into contact with the WHO -- a stipulation that effectively put Taiwan's government into a place of de facto subordination to Beijing, the MOU also entailed long and cumbersome procedures which created

---

162Sigrid Winkler, Taiwan's U.N. Dilemma: To be or not to be, Brookings, June 2012.

administrative obstacles for Taiwan's participation in WHO technical meetings and other interactions with the organization. The MOU has been guiding the relations between Taiwan and the WHO ever since."

Strangely, the United States, Taipei's strong ally which had led a bid to negotiate "meaningful participation" for Taiwan in the WHO, supported and even praised the controversial MOU. According to a series of four AIT (American Institute in Taiwan) cables dated between late 2004 and mid-2005 and disclosed by WikiLeaks years later, Washington was supportive of the MOU, while it was being negotiated, even perceiving it a "step forward" in facilitating interaction between Taiwan and the WHO.[163]

In the negotiation process, the U.S. even discouraged protests from the Chen Shui-bian administration over the terminology "Taiwan, China" used in the MOU and over the requirement for the WHO to notify China's representation in Geneva before interacting with Taiwan.

A Quid Pro Quo Arrangement

Examined from these leaked cables, the secret MOU appeared to be part of a quid pro quo arrangement worked out in 2005 in Geneva to win Beijing's concessions in exchange for Taiwan's access to the WHO's International Health Regulations (IHR). The purpose and scope of the IHR are to prevent, protect against, control, and provide a public health response to the international spread of disease. The

---

163 Shih Hsiu-chuan, Cables Show U.S. Role in WHO-China MOU, Taipei Times, September 12, 2011.

decades-old global health regulations are also called IHR 2005 because they were revised by WHO members at the annual meeting of the World Health Assembly in May of that year.

One cable, dated May 13, 2005, showed the MOU was an integral part of a four-part package that had been worked out after considerable effort by U.S. negotiators "to enable Taiwan to participate in the IHR framework for infectious disease control."

From the May 13 cable, the then-DPP administration was aware of what was being discussed in the IHR revision negotiations. In this cable, AIT Deputy Director David Keegan told Victor Chin, director-general of the Department of North American Affairs of the Foreign Ministry, that U.S. negotiators worked on the negotiations "in full consultation with their Taiwan counterparts [in Geneva.]"

The same cable also showed that Taiwan "cannot accept the use of the terms 'Taiwan, China" in the MOU. Besides, Taipei argued that it "is unreasonable for the WHO to notify the PRC representative office in Geneva before interacting with Taiwan under the IHR."

In a much earlier cable, dated October 24, 2004, Taiwan had tried, with the help of Nicaragua, to add language to Article 65 of the IHR to extend the coverage of the legally binding health rules to any "territory exercising competence over its external health relations" and request U.S. assistance in getting it accepted.

However, Taipei later softened its opposition, as shown in a March 2, 2005 cable. In it, then-AIT director Douglas Paal was quoted by John Chen, director-general of the Foreign Ministry's Department of International Organizations, as saying: "The U.S. was grateful that Taiwan and its diplomatic allies had not again raised the proposal to amend Article 65 of the IHR."

Paal went further to explain to John Chen that "The PRC had indicated it would withdraw its concessions if there were further mention of Article 65." According to Paal, Beijing had concurred that "there would be direct discussions between WHO and Taipei's CDC (Centers for Disease Control) on the condition that there was no publicity" and that "WHO teams could go to Taiwan in the event of any public health emergency of international concern ... subject only to WHO notification of the Chinese mission in Geneva."

Apparently because of such "concessions," the U.S. "wanted Taiwan to accept the nomenclature and urged it not to make the text of the MOU public." In a later cable dated May 16, 2005, David Keegan said "Taiwan must not allow its sensitivity over nomenclature to prevent this step forward in its WHO access and this improvement in its international stature."

In response to the U.S. concerns, then-Vice Foreign Minister Michael Kau called the AIT deputy director and told him that Taiwan's Geneva delegation had not yet obtained a copy of the memorandum of understanding, but it intended to respect the confidentiality of the MOU and its language. Still, the vice minister was also quoted as saying, "We hate the use of the terms 'Taiwan, China.'"

Keegan, in his meeting with Victor Chin, director-general of the Foreign Ministry's Department of North American Affairs, according to the May 13, 2005 cable, pointed out that "the MOU language would not be a public document, and that it would be hardly surprising if a U.N. organization or a U.N. member used U.N. terminology to refer to Taiwan, however much Taiwan might disagree with that terminology."

At the May 11, 2007 press conference, the president was repeatedly asked why he wanted to use the potentially confrontational name "Taiwan" in its application, particularly while it was trying to build global support.

Chen told a reporter from the Taipei-based Central News Agency. "Over the past decade, Taiwan has adopted a very low-profile approach in its WHO accession bid, including applying for membership in the WHA as a 'health entity,' but to no avail. The U.S. and some other friendly countries then tried to help by seeking to grant us 'meaningful participation' in WHO technical meetings. Disappointedly, such an effort only led to the conclusion in 2005 of a secret MOU between the WHO Secretariat and China. This MOU virtually downgrades our status to 'Taiwan, China,' with Beijing having the final say on our participation in WHO meetings and events."

"Because of all such frustrations," Chen continued, "we now decide to forthrightly apply for WHO membership under the name 'Taiwan.' According to the WHA's rules of procedures, if we apply for WHO membership, the WHO Secretariat must abide by the procedures and invite the applicant, Taiwan, to become an observer in the WHA."

But Chen did not say why his new approach of using the name "Taiwan" in its application for entry into the WHO would provide a better chance of success. Taipei's diplomatic isolation worldwide had truly deepened since he came to power. One main reason, as many analysts observed, was his increasing aggressiveness in promoting Taiwan as an independent identity, prompting Beijing to retaliate by tightening its squeeze on the island's international space.

In reply to a reporter from Radio France, Chen explained, "Our use of the name 'Taiwan' does not involve any change in our national title and does not go against the 'four noes' commitments [I made]. Thus, there is no need for the international community to get worked up about it, or to demean it." But he quickly added, "This is the name we find most satisfactory, and we hope that it can catch everyone's attention and everyone's support."

Chen was even more direct in responding to a similar question from the Financial Times. "Taiwan is a sovereign state, and its sovereignty is in the hands of its 23 million people, not of China and its 1.3 billion people. Taiwan and China are two independent countries, with neither subject to the other's jurisdiction," he said. "Therefore, we have the right to participate in international organizations. We hope our application will be taken seriously and discussed and debated by the WHO according to its standard procedures for membership applications."

Responding to a reporter from Taiwan's China Times, the president gave what seemed to be a more likely reason for the new WHO tactic. "Seeking to take part in various international organizations, including the WHO and the United Nations with the name 'Taiwan' has been an important diplomatic goal of the pro-independence DPP, the current ruling party. And these goals were enshrined in the party's '1999 Resolution on Taiwan's Future.' In fact, at this moment we're preparing to launch a U.N. bid also under the name Taiwan."

Chen and his party's extraordinary passion for using the name Taiwan to join world organizations had a compelling reason behind it: The DPP has since its founding in 1986 set the creation of a "Republic of Taiwan" as its highest, ultimate political aim.

So in a sense, Chen saw this as fulfilling an obligation to advance their independence cause. But this aggressive pursuit tended to alienate even Taipei's longtime friends.

At the same press conference, a journalist from NHK of Japan posed this question: "Three years ago, the Japanese government started to support Taiwan's participation in the WHA as an observer. The ruling party in Japan recently stated, however, that if Taiwan applies for WHO membership under the name Taiwan, the Japanese government might not be able to support it. So I would like to ask you, Mr. President: Are you worried that this move might make it difficult for countries such as Japan, which have supported you in the past, to continue doing so?"

Chen's reply to the NHK reporter's question is excerpted below: "It is my understanding that the Japanese government's policy of supporting Taiwan becoming a WHA observer and its meaningful participation in the WHO has in no way changed. Japan has always assured us of its willingness to continue providing such support...

"We call on the Japanese government and the international community to heed the health rights of the people of Taiwan. We hope that the Japanese government will continue to remain true to its principles and give us the greatest possible encouragement. And even if it cannot support our accession to the WHO under the name Taiwan, we sincerely hope it will not oppose it."

Chapter 8
Applying to Join the WHO as 'Taiwan'

Chen's High-Profile WHO Bid Rejected

President Chen Shui-bian's high-profile WHO application in 2007 was rejected outright. This surprised no one, given the extent of Taiwan's diplomatic isolation and Beijing's fast-rising political clout on the world stage. This hard reality explained why the impassioned appeal President Chen Shui-bian made for international support on the eve of the WHA vote failed to get more countries to support Taiwan.

But what was unexpected was that Taiwan's membership application failed to be discussed and debated at the full session of the World Health Assembly of the WHO. A general committee at a prior procedures meeting on May 14, 2007, voted 148-17 against placing Taiwan's application on the agenda of the assembly's annual session.

Twelve of Taiwan's diplomatic allies, including Paraguay and The Gambia, had proposed to submit the island's application to the full session of the WHA for discussion.[164] During a two-hour, closed-door meeting of the general committee, health ministers from the above-mentioned two countries pointed out that Taiwan's exclusion from the WHO violated the body's constitution, which calls for the "highest attainment of health for all people."

But China and its ally Cuba strongly objected to the proposal, saying that "Taiwan is part of China, and China has always looked after Taiwanese people's rights."

Japan and the United States, both of which had previously voiced

---

164 Mo Yan-chih, WHA Roadblock Kills Taiwan Bid, Taipei Times, May 15, 2007.

support for granting Taiwan observer status at the WHA, had kept silent this time during the debate at the committee meeting.

WHO Director-General Margaret Chan defended the health organization's refusal to address Taiwan's application, arguing that "Taiwan is not a sovereign state and thus is not eligible to apply for membership."

On April 15, 2007, a day after Taiwan's application was voted down by the general committee of the WHA, PRC Foreign Ministry spokesman Qin Gang made the following comments at a press conference in Beijing:

"The WHO is a specialized United Nations agency, whose membership is only open to sovereign states. Taiwan is simply not qualified to join or apply for membership in the WHO. In recent years, the Taiwanese authorities have time and again put forward Taiwan-related proposals at the World Health Assembly conference, but all such proposals have been thwarted. Whatever means the Taiwanese authorities take, they will not succeed in their schemes to use health issues to serve "Taiwan independence" secessionist activities."

President Chen called for the WHO to treat Taiwan's application as it did the application of East Germany which was seated alongside West Germany. But China's permanent representative to the U.N. Sha Zukang pushed back on this two-state formula, saying East Germany was recognized at the time by most countries of the world. "We [China and Taiwan], on the other hand, are still fighting over the 'one-China' policy…The situation is different."

While refusing to vote in favor of Taiwan's membership application, the U.S., Canada, and Germany (on behalf of the EU) later called on the WHA to support Taiwan's participation in its related technical meetings.

At a roundtable discussion afterward, the U.S. Health and Human Services Secretary Mike Leavitt reiterated the U.S. position of supporting Taiwan's "meaningful participation" in the WHO, rather than full membership.

"We do not support Taiwan's participation for membership," he said. "However, there is a virtue in having Taiwanese technical experts included in the discussions."

The 2007 defeat of Taiwan's application for membership in the WHO came as widely anticipated. Major world powers, such as the U.S., Japan, Canada, and European states, all had made clear their position on the issue in advance. They would not support Taiwan's admission either as a member or an observer. Rather, they would be willing to back Taiwan's "meaningful participation" in WHO-associated technical meetings. That was why none of those powers attending the WHA meeting voted in favor of placing Taiwan's membership application on its agenda.

Judging from the WHO's handling of Taiwan's membership application this time, the concept of supporting "meaningful participation" for this island appears to have become a majority consensus and an established policy among member countries, based on the 2005 secret Memorandum of Understanding reached between the WHO Secretariat and China.

Yet for Taiwan, such a policy was unreasonable as it amounted to authorizing Beijing to dictate what kind of WHO meetings and activities this island could or could not attend. It could be said that the galling situation was the result of mainland China using Taipei's public health concerns to impose its "one China" policy on this island. Taiwan, meanwhile, sacrificed political interests only to gain limited participation in the WHO's technical meetings.

That said, Taiwan had no options. According to the WHO charter, only countries that are members of the United Nations may become members of the WHO. Others can be admitted as members only when their applications have been approved by a majority of the World Health Assembly. Taiwan was not a U.N. member and could not muster even a simple majority of supporters in the WHO. The number of countries recognizing Taiwan stood at no more than two dozen.

Chen's insistence on using the name Taiwan rather than the more politically neutral title "Chinese Taipei" in its application for WHO admission only complicated the effort and precipitated Taiwan's humiliating defeat. Chen and his strategists had surely anticipated the difficulty of applying for admission to the WHO and the certainty of defeat. But as a senior administration official admitted later, "We cared more about the process of the application than the end."

That point was made clear by Chen Shui-bian himself in a media interview given on the eve of the WHO vote on Taiwan's bid. Chen was asked by a Reuters reporter what he would do "If Taiwan's application is once again denied next week." His reply was such: "If we do not succeed this year, we will try again next year. We will keep trying. We hope that the international community will eventually pay more attention to our case and sympathize with us."

There appeared to be an unstated reason behind the repeated use of an unsuccessful strategy for acquiring WHO membership. Chen and his party saw this as a tool for generating publicity for Taiwan's separate identity. This in turn, they believed, would help achieve their ultimate political goal of creating an independent Taiwan.

Taking the WHO Case to the Washington Post

Days before the World Health Assembly convened its annual meeting on May 14, 2007, Chen also wrote a letter to the Washington Post to vent his anger at the WHO and its Secretariat in particular.[165] The letter to the Washington Post came at almost the same time as he called the international press conference in Taipei to voice his complaints against the WHO over its handling of Taiwan's application.

In the letter, Chen first drew attention to the 2005 secret memorandum signed by the WHO and China. "It is improper and unprecedented for an international humanitarian organization to enter into a secret pact with one of its member states, especially an authoritarian one. More importantly, the memorandum has been used to obstruct Taiwan's participation in WHO activities...The WHO Secretariat has effectively jeopardized the health of the people in Taiwan..."

In that letter, Chen also blasted the Secretariat for overstepping its authority in handling Taiwan's application. "On April 11, 2007, I sent a letter to the WHO formally requesting our nation's application for membership under the name Taiwan. The secretariat responded on

---

165 Chen Shui-bian, The Shunning of a State, Washington Post, May 11, 2007.

April 25, claiming that Taiwan is not a sovereign state and therefore not eligible for WHO membership. This is legally and morally deplorable."

He refuted the Secretariat view, noting that "Article 3 of the Constitution of the World Health Organization stipulates membership in the organization shall be open to all states, while Article 6 provides that states such as Taiwan that are not members of the United Nations may apply to become members and shall be admitted as members when their applications have been approved by a simple majority vote of the World Health Assembly."

Chen then pointed out that the WHA Rules of Procedures stipulate that "Applications made by a State for admission shall be addressed to the Director-General and then shall be transmitted immediately" to WHO members…

"The authority to determine whether Taiwan is eligible for admission to the WHO belongs to its members, many of which have diplomatic relations with Taiwan and cannot be co-opted by any individual or administrative office," Chen said.

Regarding Taiwan's political status, Chen argued in the same letter: "Taiwan, formally known as the Republic of China, is indisputably a sovereign state, satisfying all of the criteria cited in Article 1 of the Montevideo Convention on the Duties and Obligations of States.[166] It has a permanent population, a defined territory, a functional government, and the capacity to conduct relations with other

166 The Montevideo Convention on the Rights and Duties of States is a treaty signed at Montevideo, Uruguay, on December 26, 1933 during the Seventh International Conference of American States.

states. It also has its own internationally traded currency and issues its own passport, honored by virtually all other nations...

"Another broadly affirmed criterion for recognizing the legitimacy of a state is the principle, enunciated in the U.N. Universal Declaration of Human Rights that the sovereignty a state exercises should be based on the will of the people. A truly 'sovereign' state, in other words, is free and democratic. We find no better words to describe Taiwan...

"Ultimately," Chen concluded, "the question of Taiwan's participation in the WHO is a moral one. The systematic shunning of Taiwan is unconscionable not only because it compromises the health of our 23 million people but also because it denies the world the benefit of our abundant public health and technical resources. Taiwan's public and private sectors have donated more than US$450 million in medical and humanitarian aid to more than 90 countries over the past 10 years."

The U.S. Becomes Target of Criticism

After slamming the WHO for rejecting his 2007 membership application, Chen Shui-bian shifted his criticism towards the United States. The venue was also a video news conference held at Washington's famed National Press Club on May 29, 2007, with Chen speaking from his Presidential Office in Taipei.[167]

The president told his mainly American audience that he just

---

167 Ko Shu-ling, Chen Speaks to Media, Politicians, Taipei Times, May 30, 2007,

could not understand why the U.S. had been opposed to many of his crucial policy initiatives. They included Chen's holding of referendums, "cessation" of the National Unification Council and National Unification Guidelines, and, more recently, his drive to apply for admission to the WHO and the U.N. under the name Taiwan.

Chen's pent-up anger at the U.S. was sparked by the Bush administration's persistent opposition to his bid for WHO membership. Before filing the application to the WHO in April 2007, Chen had his Foreign Minister James Huang sound out the U.S. attitude toward his plan, but he failed to gain a positive response.

Chen then sent a lobbying mission to the U.S. capital to try to persuade policymakers there, but they refused to receive his delegation, which was headed by a senior member of his National Security Council, Joanne J.L. Chang.

Even more embarrassing for Chen, the Bush administration's Health and Human Services Secretary Mike Leavitt openly voiced objections to Taiwan's application at a press conference held in Geneva on May 13, 2007. This could not come at a worse time, as the WHO -- headquartered in Geneva -- was to convene its annual assembly the following day, where Taiwan's application would be addressed.

And as if the open expression of its opposing stance had not done enough to hurt Taipei, the U.S. took one step further, voting against considering membership for Taiwan, along with most other WHO member nations, on May 14 when the island's application was put to the vote.

From Chen's standpoint, he indeed had reason to be angry with Washington for its refusal to back a loyal ally like Taiwan on a vote of great significance for him and his administration. But he failed to recognize that the U.S. had its own policy interests to defend. For many years the American government has maintained that it, while willing to help Taiwan broaden its international space, would not support Taiwan's participation in any world body that requires statehood for membership. Otherwise, as some U.S. officials explained, it would run counter to America's longstanding "one China" policy.

In the speech to the National Press Club in Washington, the president complained that U.S. policy often baffled him: "Washington had always wanted me to talk more about human rights, less about sovereignty." But "just what constitutes sovereignty and what are human rights?" he asked.

He described to his audience in Washington that "Taiwan's campaigns to join the U.N. and the WHO and its policy to abolish the National Unification Council all are human rights issues. They involve human health and political rights. One cannot say that Taiwan can only choose eventual unification with the Chinese mainland and must not pursue independence." As such, Chen asked, "Why should the U.S. deprive the 23 million Taiwan people of their basic rights?"

In the speech, Chen also challenged Washington's view that Taiwan lacks statehood, a deficiency that has accounted for continued U.S. refusal to support Taiwan's application to join the WHO and other international organizations that require statehood for membership.

This Washington policy, he pointed out, was running the risk of violating America's own law, the Taiwan Relations Act (TRA). He said that some in the U.S. held the view that "Taiwan is not a country," but they failed to note some relevant TRA provisions.

Chen drew attention to Article 4 of the TRA which prescribes that "domestic U.S. laws that refer to foreign countries or governments shall apply to Taiwan." "Judging by the Article 4 provision, the TRA apparently treats Taiwan as a sovereign country," he argued.

In addition, he continued, "Section D of the same article provides that nothing in the TRA may be construed as a basis for the U.S. to endorse the exclusion or expulsion of Taiwan from the World Health Organization or any other international institutions."

In the National Press Club speech, entitled "Democratic Taiwan: Challenges and Perspectives," President Chen also made accusations against his archrival Beijing. He charged that the Chinese government continued to use the claim that Taiwan is part of China to undermine the island's international standing.

He cited a more recent case, in which the World Organization for Animal Health voted to downgrade Taiwan's membership to a non-sovereign status under strong pressure from Beijing. "China is trying to denigrate and isolate us in every way they can."

He also used the teleconference, attended by U.S. politicians, public opinion leaders as well as a pool of international journalists, to refute Beijing's claim of sovereignty over Taiwan. "Taiwan is a sovereign independent country. Taiwan is Taiwan, China is China. Taiwan and China are two countries on either side of the Taiwan Strait," he argued.

Chen called on the international community, particularly the U.S., Japan, and the EU member states, to pay serious attention to Beijing's suppression of Taiwan and its growing threat to regional stability. "The world must not turn a blind eye to China's irrational behavior just because of its growing might. History has repeatedly told us that appeasement always breeds aggression," he warned.

Chen's speech to Washington's National Press Club via videoconference was arranged by the club. Chen was invited to address the conference as the guest speaker under a regular club program called "Morning Newsmaker Breakfast."

However, Peter Hickman, chairman of the speaker's committee at the club, said it was Washington's Taipei Economic and Cultural Representative Office (TECRO) that initiated the videoconference idea and asked the "press club to hold it." TECRO, Hickman revealed, also offered to pay for breakfast for all participants coming to listen to Chen's speech.

When approached by a Taipei reporter, TECRO Deputy Representative Stanly Gao, who helped arrange the event, gave the following explanation: "They (members of the club speaker's committee) believe that President Chen is definitely a newsmaker. And we believe this is a wonderful opportunity for Chen to personally address [Taiwan] issues before an American audience, or even an international audience as one may call, taking advantage of modern IT and telecommunications technologies."

Chen's Speech Greeted with Mixed Reaction

Chen's speech and his answers to questions from the news media got a mixed reception. A senior U.S. State Department official, when approached by Taiwan's reporters, complained that Chen used modern teleconference technologies to circumvent U.S. regulations banning senior Taipei officials, including the president, from visiting the capital city of Washington.

The official, who declined to be named because of the sensitivity of the matter, was also angry with President Chen for using the press conference to promote Taiwan as a separate state. He said, "Our views on this issue are well known. We do not support Taiwan's independence. The U.S. has a 'one China' policy based on the three U.S.-China communiqués and the Taiwan Relations Act."

Washington correspondent Vincent Chang of the Taipei-based United Daily News, who was covering the meeting, criticized President Chen for failing to grasp the spirit of the Taiwan Relations Act. The journalist was referring to Chen's argument that the Bush administration violated TRA provisions by citing a lack of statehood as the reason to oppose Taiwan's application for WHO membership.

Chang's comments were collected and cabled back to Washington by the American Institute in Taiwan -- the de facto U.S. Embassy in Taipei. The following extract is from the AIT cable, dated May 30, 2007. [168]

"Applicability does not mean recognition; Chen Shui-bian misinterpreted the Taiwan Relations Act...Having had nearly 30 years of pragmatic experience, the TRA has been widely recognized as a law of wisdom in dealing with cross-strait issues. It has been cited by the U.S. government as the cornerstone of U.S. policy in addressing cross-strait and Taiwan-U.S. relations. The spirit of 'strategic ambiguity' as

---

168 WikiLeaks, Media Reaction, American Institute in Taiwan, May 30, 2007.

shown in the TRA has offered U.S. policy implementers ample leeway and flexibility when they were engaged in discussions and faced the substantive challenges of cross-strait issues."

Chas Freeman Jr., a former senior American diplomat, was asked by the Associated Press about the news conference where Chen spoke via satellite without being impeded by travel restrictions imposed by the U.S. on Taiwan officials. Freeman replied that he considered the arrangement sort of "enormous ingenuity displayed by Taiwan's representatives in scoring points in some game that, frankly, most Americans neither care about nor are aware is even going on."

Therese Shaheen, a former managing director and chairwoman of the American Institute in Taiwan, was quoted by Taipei's pro-independence Liberty Times as saying she fully agreed with Chen that "appeasement would lead to aggression."

Shaheen, who was once listed by Taiwan's opposition parties as an "unwelcome figure" for her perceived involvement in the island's election politics, heaped praise on Chen, describing his performance at the video conference as "an excellent job of communication."

Still, she concurred with several other U.S. attendees, including Randall Schriver, a former Deputy Assistant Secretary of State at the time (and later Assistant Secretary of Defense), who offered this view: "The speech Chen delivered at Washington's National Press Club is unlikely to prompt any change in U.S. policy on Taiwan."

The following section, Chapter 9, will be dedicated to recounting ex-President Chen Shui-bian's application to join the U.

Chapter 9
A Bid to Join the United Nations

On July 19, 2007, President Chen Shui-bian sent an electronic application to then-U.N. Secretary-General Ban Ki-moon seeking permission for the island to join the world organization under the name "Taiwan" -- undeterred by the World Health Organization's rejection of a similar request two months earlier.

Chen Shui-bian's U.N. admission bid came shortly after he angered Washington and Beijing with the announcement of a related plan to hold a provocative referendum asking voters whether they supported joining the United Nations under the name Taiwan.

The president disclosed the referendum plan at a meeting in Taipei with Edwin Feulner of the Heritage Foundation, the Washington-based think tank. Chen told his U.S. guest that the referendum would be held alongside Taiwan's presidential election in March of the following year.

But his referendum announcement immediately aroused a new wave of tensions not only with mainland China but also with the U.S. On the following day, the U.S. State Department issued a blunt statement laying out U.S. objections to Chen's proposed U.N. referendum.[169]

The statement read: "The U.S. opposes any initiative that appears designed to change Taiwan's status unilaterally. This would include a referendum on whether to apply to the U.N. under the name

---

169 State Department, Daily Press Briefing, June 19, 2007

Taiwan. While such a referendum would have no practical impact on Taiwan's U.N. status, it would increase tensions in the Taiwan Strait. Maintenance of peace and stability across the Taiwan Strait is of vital interest to the people of Taiwan and serves U.S. security interests as well."

"Moreover," the statement continued, "such a move would appear to run counter to President Chen's repeated commitments to President Bush and the international community. We urge President Chen to exercise leadership by abandoning the proposed referendum."

The response from Beijing was also swift. It condemned Chen's U.N. referendum plan as a dangerous move toward independence. Yang Yi, a spokesman for China's State Council, said: "The referendum promoted by Taiwan leader Chen Shui-bian about whether to join the U.N. under the name Taiwan was a dangerous step toward de jure independence. It will have a strong impact on cross-strait relations." He went on to say, "The mainland side has made all necessary preparations to deter any separatist activity."

The U.N. referendum became a source of constant tension in U.S.-Taiwan-PRC relations during the remaining months of Chen's second and final term. Actions and reactions escalated in intensity.

Media Attention Shifts Back to U.N. Entry Application

The March referendum was still relatively far off, but the application to join the U.N. might be raised at the annual session of the U.N. General Assembly in September. So the focus of local media attention shifted back to Chen Shui-bian's U.N. drive.

As with the effort to join the WHO, Chen Shui-bian's application to join the United Nations also met strong resistance from the U.S. and mainland China. Beijing, through the official Xinhua News Agency, issued a statement condemning the U.N. bid as a "scheme to split China." In the statement, Foreign Ministry spokesman Liu Jianchao said, "We resolutely oppose the membership application and will keep a close watch on the development of the issue."

The U.S., for its part, saw Chen Shui-bian's U.N. campaign as an "attempt to change the longstanding status quo that has governed relations among the U.S., Taiwan, and the Chinese mainland" over the years since Washington switched diplomatic recognition from Taipei to Beijing in 1979.

From a historical perspective, Taiwan's campaign to join the U.N. was part of a long-running struggle for international recognition. It reflected Beijing's unrelenting suppression dating back to 1971 -- a watershed in the history of cross-strait politics. Before 1971, the Republic of China had been China's sole legitimate representative in both the U.N. General Assembly and the permanent five-member Security Council.

Rivalry across the Taiwan Strait stemmed from the Chinese Civil War and the retreat to Taiwan by Chiang Kai-shek's government after its defeat on the mainland by Mao Zedong's communist forces in 1949. In that same year, Mao and his Communist Party founded the People's Republic of China, or the PRC, in Beijing,

In January 1950, barely three months after its founding, the PRC government cabled then-U.N. Secretary-General Trygve Halvdan Lie, demanding Taiwan's expulsion from the U.N. The PRC followed that protest with an annual challenge to the legitimacy of Taiwan's representation at the U.N. General Assembly.

In the more than two decades following its retreat to Taiwan, the ROC government in Taipei had been able to effectively defend its U.N. seat with the support of the United States and other powerful diplomatic allies in the international organization.

However, with its consolidation of power on the mainland and its growing success in gaining diplomatic recognition from countries around the world, the PRC finally ousted the ROC government from the world body in 1971. This largely ended more than two decades of struggle between Beijing and Taipei for U.N. membership as the legitimate representative of China.

On October 25, 1971, the 26th session of the U.N. General Assembly passed its historic Resolution 2758 recognizing the People's Republic of China as "the sole legitimate representative of China to the United Nations." Rather than suffering the humiliation of expulsion from the U.N., the ROC delegation, under the instructions of then-President Chiang Kai-shek, walked out of the world body before the General Assembly finished its final round of voting on the representation issue.

The loss of representation at the U.N. had a domino effect on the ROC's membership in other inter-government organizations. By the mid-1980s, Taiwan had lost representation in almost all of the U.N.-affiliated organizations, including the WHO, as well as the World Bank and the International Monetary Fund.

During the first two decades after the loss of its U.N. seat, Taiwan addressed the U.N. representation issue and participation in other international organizations with Chiang Kai-shek's guiding principle: "There will never be room for the legitimate [ROC] government and the rebel [PRC] bloc to coexist."

Lee Teng-hui's 'Pragmatic Policy'

However, Taiwan gradually began to pursue a "pragmatic policy" on foreign relations after Lee Teng-hui took over as president in the late 1980s. "Pragmatic" meant being flexible. Under Lee's guidance, Taiwan no longer claimed to represent all of China. It would even be willing to join international organizations under names other than its official title, the Republic of China.

In 1993, Lee Teng-hui launched a campaign to "return to the U.N." "Consequently," wrote American academic Dennis Hickey in a 2008 study, "a group of Taiwan's diplomatic allies began submitting proposals to the U.N. requesting that it find a way to allow Taipei's participation in the organization. At the time, it appeared that the ROC went out of its way to use a variety of names and strategies to garner support for U.N. participation without antagonizing the PRC or ruffling the feathers of the international community."[170]

The argument for Taiwan's admission to the U.N., as cited in the study cited above, was that "Resolution 2758 has solved the issue of China's representation in the United Nations but left the issue of

---

170 Dennis V. Hickey, Frictions between Friends: U.S. Policy and Taiwan's United Nations Campaign, The Tamkang Journal of International Affairs, Volume 11, Number 4, April 2008.

Taiwan's representation unresolved in a practical sense. The ROC government continues to hold control over Taiwan and other islets. While the PRC claims sovereignty over all of China and claims that Taiwan is part of China, it does not exercise sovereignty over Taiwan, and has never done so."

Lee Teng-hui's willingness to be more flexible concerning the use of the name used in applying to join inter-governmental organizations still failed. But his "return to the U.N." campaign, overall, neither caused serious confrontations with the PRC nor severely upset the United States, Taiwan's defense partner.

However, in 2007 there was a turn of events as President Chen Shui-bian jettisoned his predecessor's low-profile approach. The following are excerpts from ex-President Chen's July 19, 2007, application letter addressed to U.N. Secretary-General Ban Ki-moon:

"Participating in the United Nations is both a fundamental right and a long desire of the people of Taiwan…Excluding Taiwan from the international organization goes against its principles of universality and justice. As the President of Taiwan, I must express and fulfill the wishes of the people. I hereby formally submit Taiwan's application for membership and request that it be placed before the Security Council and the General Assembly for consideration." He signed his name and official title at the end of the letter: Chen Shui-bian, president of Taiwan.[171]

The application letter, however, was returned by the U.N.

---

171 President Chen Shui-bian's Letter to U.N. Secretary-General Ban Ki-moon Delivered on July 19, office of the President, July 20, 2007.

Secretariat just four days after it was submitted by the Chen administration. The world body cited its adherence to a "one China" policy and its recognition of the government in Beijing as the sole representative of China.

In a brief statement posted on the Chinese-language website of the United Nations, the U.N. Office of Legal Affairs explained that Taiwan's application was rejected under U.N. Resolution 2758 passed in 1971. That ended the recognition of the ROC government in Taipei as the representative of China and recognized Beijing as China's sole lawful representative to the world body.

Resolution 2758 Fails to Address Taiwan's Representation

In response, Taipei publicly deplored the decision of the U.N. Secretariat. "We regret that the U.N. Secretariat stalled Taiwan's application," said Foreign Ministry spokesman David Wang. "The 1971 2758 resolution should be reviewed, as it fails to address the question of the right of representation and participation by the Taiwanese people."

If the U.N. Secretariat's invoking of the "one China" policy upset the Chen administration, the remarks made by Ban Ki-moon to the press afterward angered Taipei even more. The secretary-general remarked that his office's decision to return Taiwan's application was based on the U.N. General Assembly's 1971 resolution that states that "the People's Republic of China represents the whole of China, and that Taiwan is part of China."

Besides stating that "Taiwan is part of China," Ban Ki-moon, as quoted by Taiwan's Central News Agency, added, "The decision until now about the wishes of the people of Taiwan to join the United Nations has been decided on that basis."[172]

Taipei accused the U.N. secretary-general of "over-interpreting" Resolution 2758. It argued that "the 1971 resolution merely transferred the U.N. seat from the ROC to the PRC, but it did not address the issue of Taiwan's representation in the U.N. Nor did it say that Taiwan is part of the PRC."

It should be noted that Washington also protested Ban Ki-moon's interpretation of U.N. Resolution 2758. U.S. officials repudiated the secretary-general's assertion even though the United States did not support Taiwan's membership in the U.N. and did not think Taiwan to be an independent, sovereign state.

Months earlier, the U.S. government had already been alerted by a newly issued U.N. Secretariat document that was viewed by many as the U.N. re-defining Taiwan's sovereignty in a way favoring the PRC.

According to John J. Tkacik, Jr., a senior research fellow at the Heritage Foundation, U.N. Secretary-General Ban Ki-moon issued a letter asserting that under the terms of U.N. General Assembly Resolution 2758 "the United Nations considers Taiwan for all purposes to be an integral part of the People's Republic of China." The letter of March 28, 2007, was made without consulting the United States or any

172 Dennis V. Hickey, Frictions between Friends: U.S. Policy and Taiwan's United Nations Campaign, The Tamkang Journal of International Affairs, Volume 11, Number 4, April 2008.

364

other Security Council members, except presumably China.[173]

Even though the letter was unpublicized and low-key, Tkacik said, it was a tremendous coup for Beijing. "It had finally persuaded the United Nations to take sides with China and against the United States and Taiwan on the matter."

He said U.S. concerns over the "misinterpretation" of U.N. Resolution 2758 presumably were twofold: First, this could provide a legal basis for Beijing and other countries to treat Taiwan as part of the PRC. Should that be the case, it would be a grave distortion of Taiwan-mainland relations in both legal and practical terms, posing a potential threat to peace and stability in the Taiwan Strait. U.S. officials, in refuting Ban Ki-moon's remarks, pointed out that the 1971 U.N. resolution did not in fact "establish that Taiwan is a province of the PRC." And there is "no mention in the resolution of China's claim of sovereignty over Taiwan."

Secondly, the U.N. Secretariat's newly issued statement that the organization considers "Taiwan for all purposes to be an integral part of the PRC" also contradicted the longstanding U.S. position over the sovereignty dispute between Taiwan and mainland China.

Tkacik noted the widely known fact that the U.S. used the word "acknowledges," rather than "accepts," in its response to the Chinese government's position that Taiwan is a part of China when Washington switched diplomatic recognition to Beijing from Taipei in the late 1970s. On the policy level, he said, the U.S. has been following a

---

173 John J. Tkacik, Jr. Taiwan's 'Unsettled' International Status: Preserving U.S. Options in the Pacific, the Heritage Foundation, June 19, 2008.

strategy of ambiguity in addressing sovereignty issues across the Taiwan Strait over the years.

Nowhere, Tkacik observed, is this strategy of ambiguity more manifest than in the many public comments made by current and past U.S. government officials concerning Taiwan's status. Among the most standard such remarks are: "The U.S. neither accepts nor rejects the claim that Taiwan is a part of China. The U.S. has long urged that Taiwan's status be resolved peacefully to the satisfaction of the people on both sides of the Taiwan Strait. Beyond that, we do not define Taiwan in political terms."

America's Bipartisan 'One China' Policy

Meanwhile, according to Asian affairs specialists Shirley Kan and Wayne Morrison, the United States has over the years crafted a bipartisan policy on the political relationship between Taiwan and the Chinese mainland. In a 2013 U.S. congressional research report, authors Kan and Morrison described that policy as follows: "The United States has its own 'one China' policy (vs. the PRC's 'one China' principle) and position on Taiwan's status. Not recognizing the PRC's claim over Taiwan nor recognizing Taiwan as a sovereign state, U.S. policy has considered Taiwan's status as unsettled."[174]

From John Tkacik's observations and the study by Shirley Kan and Wayne Morrison, the following two conclusions could be drawn

174 Shirley A. Kan and Wayne M. Morrison, U.S.-Taiwan Relationship: Overview of Policy Issues, Congressional Research Service, January 4, 2013.

as to how the United States has been addressing Taiwan's political status.

One, the U.S. "neither accepts nor rejects the claim that Taiwan is a part of China." Two, "U.S. policy has considered Taiwan's status as unsettled." In short, the U.S. has maintained a strategy of ambiguity in addressing sovereignty issues across the Taiwan Strait over the years.

Maintaining such an ambiguous strategy makes sense at the tactical level. However, arguing that "Taiwan's political status is unsettled" is not quite accurate. It mainly reflects the perspective of the United States. People sympathetic to the cause of Taiwan's independence also promoted the "status unsettled" theory. This theory, however, contradicts historical facts, cross-Taiwan Strait relations, and broad international norms.

Taiwan came under Qing (Manchu) dynasty rule in the late 17th century. The island was ceded to Japan after the Qing's defeat in the First Sino-Japanese War in 1895 but was returned to Chinese rule after Japan's surrender ending World War Two.

In terms of cross-strait relations, Taiwan and the mainland both claim the two sides of the strait as part of their respective territory. On the Taiwan side, the above territory concept is enshrined in its (ROC) constitution.

Examined from international norms or geopolitics, the vast majority of the more than 190 member states of the United Nations recognize China and concur with its position that "there is only one China in the world and that Taiwan is a part of China."

The U.S. accused the U.N. Secretariat of overstating the 2785 Resolution apparently because it conflicted with its strategy of ambiguity. The Secretariat's statement that "Taiwan is part of China" also worried Washington in another way, according to cross-strait specialist Sigrid Winkler. This "new U.N. view," Winkler observed, "could be taken as the basis for the argument that China should be allowed to decide on matters concerning Taiwan in international organizations -- which thus far had been avoided."[175]

"Therefore," Winkler said, "although Taiwan's U.N. bid was frustrating even to its major international partner, the United States, Washington protested Secretary-General Ban's statement, arguing that while this assertion is consistent with the Chinese position, it is not universally held by U.N. member states, including the United States."

According to several Taiwan news organizations, including the China Times and the Taipei Times, the United States in late July 2007 wrote a nine-point letter to the U.N. protesting Ban Ki-moon's controversial March 2007 letter regarding Taiwan and his subsequent remarks on why his office returned the island's entry application.[176]

Tkacik of the Heritage Foundation, in his article, provided more detailed information about the matter. He said the U.S. presented a nine-point demarche in the form of a "non-paper" to the U.N. Under-Secretary-General for Political Affairs. In it, Washington both restated the U.S. stance -- that it takes no position on the question of Taiwan's sovereignty -- and specifically rejected U.N. statements that the organization considers "Taiwan for all purposes to be an integral part

175 Sigrid Winkler, Taiwan's U.N. Dilemma: To Be or not To Be, Brookings, June 2012
176 Shih Hsiu-chuan, China Drops Plans for Vote on Taiwan, Taipei Times, September 6, 2007.

of the PRC."

A 9-Point U.S. Paper Rejects U.N. Secretariat Stance on Taiwan Status

The following nine points, entitled U.S. Non-Paper on the Status of Taiwan, are taken from Tkacik's article, Taiwan's Unsettled International Status: Preserving U.S. Options in the Pacific:

1. The United States reiterates its One China policy which is based on the three U.S.–China Communiqués and the Taiwan Relations Act, to the effect that the United States acknowledges China's view that Taiwan is a part of China. We take no position on the status of Taiwan. We neither accept nor reject the claim that Taiwan is a part of China.

2. The United States has long urged that Taiwan's status be resolved peacefully to the satisfaction of people on both sides of the Taiwan Strait. Beyond that, we do not define Taiwan in political terms.

3. The United States noted that the PRC has become more active in international organizations and has called on the U.N. Secretariat and member states to accept its claim of sovereignty over Taiwan. In some cases, as a condition for the PRC's participation in international organizations, Beijing has insisted the organization and its member states use nomenclature for Taiwan that suggests endorsement of China's sovereignty over the island.

4. The United States is concerned that some U.N. organizations have recently asserted that U.N. precedent required that Taiwan be treated as a part of the PRC and be referred to by names in keeping with such status.

5. The United States has become aware that the U.N. has promulgated documents asserting that the United Nations considers "Taiwan for all purposes to be an integral part of the PRC." While this assertion is consistent with the Chinese position, it is not universally held by U.N. member states, including the United States.

6. The United States noted that the U.N. General Assembly resolution 2758 adopted on 25 October 1971 does not establish that Taiwan is a province of the PRC. The resolution merely recognized the representation of the government of the PRC as the only lawful representation of China to the U.N. and expelled the representative of Chiang Kai-shek from the seats they occupied at the U.N. and all related organizations. There is no mention in Resolution 2758 of China's claim of sovereignty over Taiwan.

7. While the United States does not support Taiwan's membership in organizations such as the U.N., for which statehood is a prerequisite, we do support meaningful participation by Taiwan's experts as appropriate in such organizations. We support membership as appropriate in organizations for which such statehood is not required.

8. The United States urged the U.N. Secretariat to review its policy on the status of Taiwan and to avoid taking sides in a

sensitive matter on which U.N. members have agreed to disagree for over 35 years.

9. If the U.N. Secretariat insists on describing Taiwan as a part of the PRC, or on using nomenclature for Taiwan that implies such status, the United States will be obliged to disassociate itself on a national basis from such position.

Separately, according to an October 5, 2015, modified Wikipedia page on China and the United Nations, several Western governments, with the U.S. in the lead, protested in 2007 to the U.N. (and the U.N. Office of Legal Affairs) to force the world body and its secretary-general to stop using the reference "Taiwan is a part of China."

For its part, according to the same China Times report, Beijing in the early summer of the same year tried to push a unanimous U.N. vote to accept its "claim that Taiwan is part of the PRC." The proposed U.N. vote was widely seen as a measure to counter Taiwan's ongoing bid to join the U.N. under the name "Taiwan." However, the Chinese effort met with strong objections from the United States and others, forcing Beijing to drop the plan at the last minute.

In Taipei, when asked by reporters for comment on the China Times report, President Chen confirmed the news, saying that Washington had advised his government of Beijing's attempt and the U.S. opposition to the move.

Taipei's Foreign Ministry spokesman David Wang, in reply to press questions about the matter, commented that Beijing would certainly be unable to achieve its desired results even if it had succeeded in putting its proposal to a vote on the floor of the U.N.

General Assembly.

That would have been the case because "not every U.N. member would accept China's position," Wang said, adding that countries while negotiating the establishment of diplomatic relations with China, had used different tactics in responding to Beijing's insistence on the acceptance of its "one China" policy. "Some used the terms 'take note of' China's claim over Taiwan, others responded by saying they 'respect' China's claim, while still others made no mention of the 'one China' issue at all."

The United States is a striking example of those countries that avoided stating "acceptance" of Beijing's position on the issue when they established diplomatic relations with the PRC. The U.S. instead used the phrase "acknowledge Beijing's view," and the word "acknowledge," according to U.S. officials and political analysts, does not equate to "accept" or "agree." So by saying that the U.S. "acknowledges" Beijing's "one China" principle, Washington was telling the mainland authorities that it has its own view on Taiwan's political status.

This U.S. position has been widely seen as a strategy of deliberate ambiguity about the sovereignty of Taiwan. This strategy is a crucial element in U.S. policy on relations with both Taiwan and the mainland. It also provides leverage for the U.S. to address differences between the two longtime political rivals.

According to Shirley Kan of the Congressional Research Service, U.S. policy has considered Taiwan's status as unsettled, and this is why, when Beijing sought to push a U.N. vote on its claim to Taiwan in the summer of 2007 as a means to counter Chen Shui-bian's U.N.

Chapter 9
A Bid to Join the United Nations

membership application, Washington moved quickly to pressure the Chinese government into dropping that plan.

The U.S. Warns U.N. Secretariat to Avoid Toeing Beijing Line

In addition to blocking Beijing from introducing a proposal for the U.N. to unanimously accept its claim of sovereignty over Taiwan, the U.S. at the same time issued a serious warning against the world body toeing the Beijing line on the question of Taiwan's sovereignty.

The warning was contained in the final two points of the same "non-paper," which Washington lodged with the U.N. Secretariat to protest its misinterpretation of Resolution 2758 concerning Taiwan's sovereignty.

To show how seriously Washington took the U.N. Secretariat's willingness to "toe the Beijing line in handling matters concerning Taiwan," it appears appropriate to quote again the relevant two points—points 8 and 9 -- from the full text of the nine-point "non-paper" the U.S. submitted to the U.N.

"Point 8, The United States urged the U.N. Secretariat to review its policy on the status of Taiwan and to avoid taking sides in a sensitive matter on which U.N. members have agreed to disagree for over 35 years. Point 9, If the U.N. Secretariat insists on describing Taiwan as a part of the PRC, or on using nomenclature for Taiwan that implies such status, the United States will be obliged to disassociate itself on a national basis from that position."

Turning to President Chen Shui-bian's 2007 U.N. bid, Chen wrote a second letter to Ban Ki-moon, just about two weeks after his first message applying for admission to the U.N. But the U.N. secretary-general also rejected the second letter because "Taiwan is part of the PRC" and ineligible for membership.

Besides the letter to Ban Ki-moon, Chen also wrote a letter to the U.N. Security Council's rotating president, who, ironically, happened to be China's permanent representative to the U.N., Wang Guangya. As with the previous letter, Chen signed the second one "Chen Shui-bian, President, Taiwan."[177]

In the second letter to Ban Ki-moon, Chen refuted the secretary-general's interpretation of U.N. Resolution 2758 and pointed out that "my country, Taiwan, is an independent sovereign nation and that our people, per the U.N. Charter, have the right to participate in the United Nations."

Chen quoted the United Nations' own rules, arguing that "only the Security Council and the General Assembly have the authority to review and decide on U.N. membership applications. The U.N. Secretariat does not have the power to decide on such matters. I hope you will reconsider your decision."

Yet Chen's new letter protesting Ban Ki-moon's rejection of his earlier application was again turned back. A U.N. Secretariat spokesperson, Marie Okabe, in a terse statement, said the U.N.'s position on Taiwan's participation in the world body had remained

---

177 President Chen Shui-bian's Letters to U.N. Secretary General Ban Ki-moon and U.N. Security Council Rotating President Wang Guangya on July 31, 2007, Office of the President of the Republic of China (Taiwan).

unchanged.

In the letter to Wang Guangya, Chen's message was the same as his note to Ban Ki-moon, apart from these paragraphs: "It is regrettable that Taiwan's application for U.N. membership, which I submitted on behalf of Taiwan's 23 million people and in my capacity as President, was rejected by the U.N. Secretariat on July 23, 2007…I hereby direct my request to Your Excellency in your capacity as president of the Security Council that Taiwan's application for U.N. membership be duly processed following the relevant rules of procedure of the United Nations."

Speaking to reporters, Wang Guangya scornfully said that he returned Chen's letter the same day he received it. The Chinese permanent representative to the U.N., through the Xinhua news agency, called Chen's latest U.N. membership bid "a very serious separatist act seeking independence for Taiwan."

Wang was quoted as asserting that U.N. Charter articles stipulate only a sovereign state can apply for U.N. membership. Taiwan, as an "inseparable part of China, is ineligible to join the United Nations in any name or in any way."

Allies Urge General Assembly to Debate Taiwan's Entry Request

Taipei's 2007 U.N. bid did not end with the U.N. Secretariat's repeated rejections of its application letters. In mid-August, 15 of Taipei's 24 diplomatic allies jointly submitted to the U.N. a proposal urging that the Security Council process Taiwan's membership application according to Provisions 59 and 60 of the Provisional Rules of Procedure of the Security Council and Article 4 of the U.N. Charter.[178] Taipei's diplomatic allies requested that their proposal be placed as a supplementary item on the provisional agenda of the 62nd session of the General Assembly, opening in the following September.

All of the sponsors of the proposal were smaller states. They included the Solomon Islands, Nauru, The Gambia, Malawi, Palau, Swaziland, Tuvalu, Sao Tome and Principe, the Marshall Islands, Saint Kitts and Nevis, St. Vincent and the Grenadines, Honduras, Burkina Faso, Kiribati, and Belize.

But the sheer fact that those states are United Nations members enabled them to help get Taiwan's application accepted and processed by the U.N. General Committee, which is responsible for arranging the General Assembly's agenda. Without the help of these diplomatic allies, Taiwan's renewed entry bid would have again faced the same summary rejection by the U.N. secretary-general as with Chen's two application letters weeks earlier.

On September 19, Taiwan's request to join the U.N. was brought up at the General Committee to decide if the request should be put on the agenda of the General Assembly's new session that began that day. The Marshall Islands, speaking for Taiwan, had asked for the application to be considered at the new session.[179]

---

178 Taipei Thanks Allies for Submitting Proposal to Support Taiwan's Bid for U.N. Entry, Ministry of Foreign Affairs of Republic of China (Taiwan) August 15, 2007.
179 Taiwan Rejected in High-Profile Bid to Join U.N., Reuters, September 19, 2007

Chapter 9
A Bid to Join the United Nations

Countries sponsoring Taiwan's application demanded a full debate on the issue, but the PRC and its supporters argued for a limited debate of only two speakers each for "pro" and "con." This was put to a vote and the "two-plus-two" formula was adopted 24-3, with the United States voting with the PRC.[180]

At the end of such a limited debate, the General Committee decided against placing Taiwan's application on the General Assembly agenda after hearing strong opposition from Beijing, which claims the island as part of its territory.[181]

Joining China in opposing Taiwan's application was Egypt, while two of the island's diplomatic allies -- the Solomon Islands and St. Vincent and the Grenadines -- spoke in favor.

Despite the General Committee's refusal to put the application on the assembly agenda, Taiwan's allies at an Assembly meeting on September 21 initiated a floor debate on the wisdom of the committee's recommendation not to consider the Taiwan item.

The aim of initiating this particular floor debate, as explained by Taipei officials, was to draw greater attention to Taiwan's campaign for participation in the United Nations. The September 21 debate lasted for more than four hours, during which some 126 countries spoke against Taiwan and 14 spoke in favor.

On the following day, a report on the legal news website JURIST

---

180 Alan D. Romberg, Applying to the U.N. "in the Name of Taiwan,'" Romberg, China Leadership Monitor, No. 22, Hoover Institution, Stanford University, October 5, 2007.

181 Despite Defeat, Taiwan Vows to Continue Pursuit of U.N. Membership, Associated Press, September 20, 2007.

said the U.N. General Assembly had agreed by consensus to accept a committee recommendation that Taiwan's latest bid for U.N. membership be rejected.[182]

The United States, Taiwan's biggest political supporter, did not speak at the floor debate. But it did issue a news release through the U.S. mission to the U.N. reiterating Washington's opposition to Taiwan's U.N. entry effort and characterizing it as unproductive.

The news release read: "The United States supports Taiwan's meaningful participation in international organizations whenever appropriate. Such involvement is in the interest of the 23 million people of Taiwan and the international community, and we urge all U.N. members to set aside preconditions and work creatively toward this goal. Consistent with our long-standing one-China policy, the United States does not support Taiwan's membership in international organizations where statehood is a requirement, so it cannot support measures designed to advance that goal. We believe that efforts to urge U.N. membership for Taiwan will detract from our goal of advancing Taiwan's involvement in international society."[183]

The U.N. rejection of Taiwan's latest application to join the world body was hailed in Beijing, which had raised strong objections to the bid and described the decision as a reaffirmation of its claim of sovereignty over Taiwan. "It proves again that no one could change the fact that Taiwan is an inalienable part of China," Beijing's Foreign Ministry spokesman Jiang Yu said in a statement on the ministry's

182 Jeannie Shaw, U.N. General Assembly Rejects Taiwan Membership Bid, JURIST;org, September 22, 2007
183 The United States Mission to the United Nations, September 21, 2007.

website. "Any attempt that defies the 'one-China' principle and aims at splitting China is doomed to failure."

With mainland China holding a veto in the Security Council and having overwhelming support in the General Assembly, the defeat of Taiwan's U.N. bid was a widely anticipated result. But Taipei's Foreign Ministry spokesman David Wang said, "We will continue down this road and keep up our efforts. We must champion the people's right to U.N. representation."

Taipei Pleased to See U.N. Bid Debated 'Extensively'

President Chen Shui-bian himself even expressed pleasure that for the first time, the issue of Taiwan's representation had been discussed so "extensively" at the General Assembly that he said marked an "unprecedented" level of attention from the international community.

In an interview in December 2007 with Associated Press reporter Peter David Enav, Chen said that "even though my application letters to U.N. Secretary-General Ban Ki-moon were, unfortunately, rejected, with the help of our allies, 140 out of the 192 U.N. member states registered to take part in the discussion on the issue of Taiwan's participation during the 62nd session of the U.N. General Assembly. The discussion lasted for 4 hours and 15 minutes. Indeed, the question of Taiwan's participation in the U.N. this year received unprecedented attention and space for debate." [184]

---

184 Associated Press Interview with President Chen Shui-bian, Office of the President, Taiwan (R.O.C.), December 10, 2007

He went on to say, "We estimate that there were at least four to five times more international media reports and comments regarding Taiwan's U.N. participation this year than there were last year, reflecting growth of support for Taiwan's U.N. membership within the international community. Therefore, even though we have yet to gain U.N. membership, we have taken a promising first step."

But President Chen ducked a key question put to him in the same AP interview. He was asked how he would justify a campaign that had caused considerable damage to Taiwan's most crucial U.S. relations while offering no chance of success in the face of China's veto power in the Security Council.

The question raised by Enav, one that others might have been pondering as well, was as follows: "I'm wondering if I could follow up now by talking a little bit about the campaign to enter the United Nations. President Chen has invested a huge amount of political resources in pursuit of this goal, even though, because of China's veto power, there is no chance that Taiwan can enter the United Nations. And at the same time, the cost of this effort in terms of Taiwan's relations with the United States, its most important diplomatic partner, has been very, very substantial. I wonder, given the fact that it's very difficult, if not impossible, to overcome the Chinese veto, and the cost to relations with the United States seems to be so high, how can President Chen justify this effort."

Chen devoted most of his lengthy reply to reasserting Taiwan's status as an independent sovereign country and promoting an ongoing campaign for a referendum on whether to join the United Nations under the name of Taiwan. After that, he followed by replying: "The key to

Chapter 9
A Bid to Join the United Nations

Taiwan's success in its U.N. bid lies not in the international community or external factors but in internal factors -- whether we are united and have the same goal at heart. The common goal of all our people should be to join the U.N. under the name Taiwan. This is more important than any external factor. As long as we are united in expressing our aspiration and have enough internal strength, we will succeed."

Other than the above remarks, Chen said nothing that could justify the essential point that his U.N. entry campaign carried significant costs.

But if the U.N. bid had no chance of success, why did President Chen persist in making an application using the name Taiwan and risking repeated setbacks -- first an immediate return of his application letters by U.N. Secretary-General Ban Ki-moon and then a blunt rejection by the U.N. General Assembly?

Some analysts, including Alan D. Romberg of the Stimson Center, said that Chen's goal all along had been to fail spectacularly at the U.N. so he could use the rejection as a rallying point for his pet plan for a referendum and to boost DPP candidates in the legislative and presidential elections in early 2008.

The view from Beijing was somewhat different. PRC officials and state media speculated that Chen Shui-bian's U.N. bid was promoted also as an effort to shift attention from his governing failure and mounting corruption allegations against him and his family.

"He hoped that his provocation of the mainland would cause a crisis across the Taiwan Strait, which in turn would divert the island's people's attention from corruption cases involving both his administration and his family, and from the great mess his inability as a leader had created," the mainland's official China Daily newspaper commented, speaking of Chen's push to join the United Nations.

Beijing's view on Taiwan affairs usually needs to be read with caution. But its speculation that President Chen was trying to use his U.N. bid to distract public attention during a time of personal and political difficulties did have some truth to it.

Some Taiwan and foreign analysts, however, also suggested that Chen Shui-bian and his government's unrelenting push to join the U.N. in the name of Taiwan was part of an overall effort to solidify a long-term agenda of greater independence for Taiwan by stirring up anti-China sentiment on this island.

Chapter 10
Pushing for a Referendum on Joining the U.N.

Chen's Most Damaging Political Action

In late 2007 and early 2008, as President Chen Shui-bian neared the end of his second and final term in office, he intensified his campaign to promote a referendum on applying to join the U.N. under the name "Taiwan." His aggressive promotion of the provocative referendum infuriated both Beijing and Washington, sending relations with the two countries to their lowest levels since 2000 when he assumed his first term.

Chen Shui-bian first announced his plan to hold the U.N.-related referendum in June 2007. At the time, he also declared that the vote would be conducted alongside the March 2008 presidential election.

As mentioned in the previous chapter, the U.N. referendum plan met with strong opposition from Washington and Beijing from the very start. U.S. officials saw the proposal as a move toward achieving de jure independence for Taiwan, a development that would change the political status quo of this island.

Beijing, for its part, warned that the referendum would "have a grave impact on cross-strait relations and seriously endanger peace and stability across the strait and in the Asia-Pacific region."

The mainland's Xinhua News Agency quoted an unnamed official of the Taiwan Affairs Office as saying: "Be it the move to join the U.N. or the plan to hold a referendum on applying for U.N. membership, they all are intended to alter the status that Taiwan and the mainland both belong to China, with the ultimate goal of achieving independence for the island."

Some state-funded think tank analysts even threatened that, by advancing the U.N. referendum, Chen Shui-bian had already crossed Beijing's red line. The Chinese government, they said, could be forced to respond militarily, invoking its newly enacted "anti-secession" law.

Here it appears appropriate to give a brief explanation. As noted in the previous chapter, when Chen announced the U.N. referendum in mid-2007, he also filed an application to join the U.N. ahead of the General Assembly's annual session in September. That application, which failed to gain full discussion at the U.N.'s agenda-organizing General Committee, also provoked anger in Washington and Beijing. But the U.S. and China in particular took President Chen Shui-bian's U.N. referendum initiative this time much more seriously than their opposition to his parallel campaign to apply for admission to the U.N. Why was that the case?

Below are the main reasons cited by analysts and relevant authorities. First, any application for U.N. membership is a matter of power, as well as vote counts. The PRC, as one of the five founding, permanent members of the Security Council, enjoys veto power. This meant that Beijing could easily veto Taiwan's application whenever such a showdown occurred.

Veto power aside, the PRC has diplomatic relations with the vast majority of the more than 190 U.N. members. Taiwan, on the other hand, could only muster the support of some two dozen allies that were members of the world body.

Chapter 10
Pushing for a Referendum on Joining the U.N.

All this suggested that any U.N. membership bid by Taiwan would be certain to fail in the face of PRC opposition. Chen's 2007 application for entry into the U.N. was easily blocked by the world body's General Committee and the Rules of Procedure Committee. It also was unable to get support for a place on the agenda of the General Assembly for a full debate. And that was why Beijing had all along contained its anger at Chen Shui-bian's U.N. membership application.

But Chen Shui-bian's plan to hold a referendum on whether to join the U.N. under the name Taiwan solely involved the island's domestic electoral politics -- something that was beyond Beijing's control. Chen Shui-bian could exert a great deal of influence on the referendum outcome. If Chen could successfully mobilize voters, for example, he would be able to get the referendum passed. A simple yes vote would have far-reaching implications for Taiwan and cross-strait relations.

For instance, a yes vote could symbolize Taiwan's desire for independent sovereignty and international recognition. Chen himself had repeatedly asserted that a yes vote on the referendum on applying to join the U.N. under the name Taiwan would have binding power on his government [and the succeeding one]. Chen made the assertion in an interview with the German news weekly Der Spiegel in September 2007.[185]

---

185 Interview with Taiwan President Chen Shui-bian: China Is Trying to Push Us up against the Wall, Der Spiegel, September 26, 2007.

'A Referendum on Independence in Disguise'

In Beijing, according to leading American expert on U.S.-Taiwan relations Alan Romberg, Chen Shui-bian's proposed U.N. referendum was widely seen as a "substitute for a declaration of independence," or a "referendum on independence in disguise."

Romberg, who had recently returned to the U.S. from a trip to China, made the above remarks in an interview with Charles Snyder, the Washington correspondent of the Taipei Times. During his July 2007 visit to the mainland, Romberg met with some senior Chinese officials and scholars on the subject. He noted the officials viewed Chen's planned referendum as far more provocative than his many previous political actions.

In their view, Romberg said, the referendum on whether this island should apply for admission to the U.N. using the name Taiwan could have "substantive" effects on the independence movement. First, if a majority of the island's voters were in favor of using the name Taiwan to join the U.N. -- an organization that required statehood for membership, it would logically be interpreted by Chen and the DPP as an indication that most people preferred to use the moniker Taiwan as their national title.

Even if the referendum failed to gain the support of more than half of the electorate, Beijing officials worried it would still have the effect of setting a precedent for Taiwan to hold referendums in the future to decide vital public policies. This might include whether they wanted to unite with the Chinese mainland or split from it.

Chen Yunlin, director of the Taiwan Affairs Office (TAO), sharply

Chapter 10
Pushing for a Referendum on Joining the U.N.

condemned Chen Shui-bian's U.N. referendum. "It is an undeniable fact that the ultimate aim of Chen and the DPP, in pushing the U.N.-entry referendum, is to establish a Taiwan Republic. But that is something China absolutely cannot accept." Chen Yunlin of the TAO made these remarks in late July of 2007 during a meeting with mainland-based Taiwan business leaders.

According to an unidentified Taiwan businessman who attended the background briefing, Chen Yunlin warned: "Our original assessment was that if the DPP succeeded in retaining governing power in 2008 and continued with a pro-independence agenda, Taiwan and the mainland could face a showdown around 2010. But now if Taiwan insisted on the U.N.-entry referendum, the time for the confrontation could possibly be brought forward."

Chen Shui-bian's U.N. referendum campaign remained a major concern for Beijing as time went by. In early September, PRC President Hu Jintao used his meeting with U.S. President George W. Bush at the APEC annual gathering in Sydney to personally express such concerns. Hu told Bush that the "coming two years would be a dangerous period" for the Taiwan Strait and the Asian-Pacific region.

Angry as they were, PRC leaders had kept their reaction to Chen's U.N. referendum drive under control. Comments and criticisms generally were limited to reiterating Beijing's basic policy and warning him not to undertake "dangerous ventures."

The exercise of restraint that saved an escalation of tensions across the strait marked a practical policy adjustment on the part of the mainland. Aware of their past mistakes, mainland leaders avoided excessively harsh reactions in handling the contentious U.N.

referendum issue. They feared that an overreaction would alienate people in Taiwan and boost public support for Chen's party ahead of the legislative and presidential elections in early 2008.

Overreaction, such as overtly threatening to use force, could also lead to a tough response from Washington. In the past, the U.S. had frequently pushed back forcefully when the PRC intimidated Taiwan with saber-rattling.

The following is a striking example of this. On the eve of Chen Shui-bian's second inauguration on May 20, 2004, Beijing published a series of strongly-worded statements. In one of those statements, the PRC said it would "crush" Taiwan or "drown" it in a "sea of fire," should this island seek independence. During his reelection campaign, Chen Shui-bian had repeatedly promised to write a new constitution and adopt it through an island-wide referendum.

In a statement issued on May 17, Beijing sent the reelected Chen Shui-bian these warnings: "The Taiwan authorities have before them two roads: One is to rein in the horse before the cliffs by suspending separatist activities and accept the principle of one China. The other is to keep pursuing independence to split Taiwan from China. The choice of this latter road will in the end lead to self-destruction by playing with fire."

Beijing's intimidating remarks immediately drew a tough response from the Bush administration.[186] "We certainly would reject portions of the statement by China that threaten the use of force to

---

186 White House Sharply Denounces China's Harsh Warning to Taiwan, China Post, with quotes from international news agencies, May 21, 2004

resolve differences between Beijing and Taipei," White House spokesman Scott McClellan told reporters two days after Beijing's comments.

"Threats to 'crush' Taiwan, or drown it in a 'sea of fire,' have no place in civilized international discourse, and Beijing merely hurts its own case by using them in such comments," said McClellan.

"They are especially unhelpful at this delicate time. And they necessitate that we firmly restate our intention to fulfill our obligations under the Taiwan Relations Act," he said. The TRA commits Washington to ensure the island has the ability to defend itself.

Aside from the previously cited considerations, the mainland authorities also worried that overreacting to Chen Shui-bian's U.N. referendum campaign could undermine U.S. cooperation in reining in the Taiwan leader. Increasingly, Beijing relied on Washington to restrain Chen Shui-bian's political provocations in his final months in office, including his push to hold the U.N. referendum.

The Shortest Route to Taipei Is Through Washington

"Beijing now realizes the shortest route to Taipei is through Washington. They are telling the U.S., 'It was you who spoiled this child, you should spank him,'" said former ROC Ambassador to the Republic of South Africa Loh I-cheng, commenting on the PRC's turning to the U.S. for stepped-up efforts to rein in Chen Shui-bian.[187]

---

187 Kathleen Kingsbury, Taiwan's War of Words with the U.S., TIME, September 17, 2007.

— The Fall of a President —

Under this "go-through-Washington" policy, Beijing repeatedly conveyed its concerns about Taiwan's U.N. referendum through bilateral high-level contacts and on other occasions. Such expressions were often accompanied by a thinly veiled threat that if the U.S. could not stop the planned referendum, the PRC might be forced to take action on its own.

As noted previously, some mainland commentators had stated that if the U.N. referendum gained public approval, it would be seen as a major "incidence of Taiwan independence," likely to prompt the PRC to respond with force under its anti-secession law.

On May 30, 2007, PRC State Councilor Tang Jiaxuan used a meeting in Beijing with George Schwab, president of the National Committee on American Foreign Policy, a Washington-based association, to urge the U.S. to constrain Chen Shui-bian. (Note, by this time President Chen had already been pushing ahead with his U.N. referendum idea.)

Tang, a former foreign minister who still had a role in guiding Beijing's diplomacy, pointed out that "opposing and containing Taiwan independence and protecting the peace and stability in the Taiwan Strait suit the shared strategic interests of China and the United States."[188]

Tang asked Washington to "support China's efforts to improve and develop cross-Strait relations and adopt substantive and effective measures to halt Chen Shui-bian's various Taiwan independence provocations and dangerous ventures."

---

188 China Presses U.S. to Rein in Taiwan's Chen, Reuters, May 29, 2007.

Chapter 10
Pushing for a Referendum on Joining the U.N.

Aside from using the meeting with George Schwab to convey its objections to Chen's U.N. referendum, Beijing also expressed concerns through the "U.S.-China Senior Dialogue" at its June 2007 meeting in Washington.

The two-day meeting was co-chaired by U.S. Deputy Secretary of State John Negroponte and PRC Deputy Foreign Minister Dai Bingguo. Negroponte and Dai attended the meeting as chief delegates from their respective countries. Well ahead of the annual event, designed to address global as well as bilateral issues, Beijing had informed Washington of what it intended to bring forward for discussion with the U.S. side.

Beijing brought up only one topic up at the meeting: a request for the U.S. to use its influence with Chen Shui-bian to halt his U.N. referendum bid. Beijing wanted to ensure that Washington fully understood that Chen's vote was aimed at splitting Taiwan from China and that, if passed, it would have serious implications for peace and stability in the Taiwan Strait and the whole Asian and Pacific region.

The list of topics raised by the U.S. side ran long, including the denuclearization of the Korean peninsula, curbing Iran's pursuit of nuclear weapons capability, the humanitarian crisis in Darfur, Sudan, and peace and security in Northeast Asia.

As the U.S. had many more peace and security concerns, most of them requiring PRC cooperation, the Bush administration had good reason to seriously consider the Chinese side's unease over Chen Shui-bian's U.N. referendum and do its best to help block the vote.

Indeed, Deputy Secretary of State Negroponte did not let his Chinese counterpart down. According to the China Times' Washington correspondent Liu Ping, a U.S. source familiar with the two-day discussion revealed that no sooner had the delegates of the two countries sat down for talks than Dai Bingguo turned to the referendum issue.

In a news analysis, the correspondent said Negroponte was quick to hand the Chinese vice foreign minister a document bearing President Bush's personal signature and enunciating a U.S. condemnation of Chen's provocative referendum.

After reviewing the document, Dai was satisfied that Washington had indeed been making clear its opposition to Chen Shui-bian's U.N. referendum. With the concerns of the Chinese side addressed, the bilateral meeting then quickly proceeded to discuss U.S. priorities.

The document that Negroponte handed to Dai at the Washington meeting was a copy of a strongly-worded statement issued by the State Department two days earlier in response to Chen Shui-bian's surprise announcement of June 18 on the referendum. In that statement, Chen said he had decided to hold a referendum on whether to apply to the United Nations under the name "Taiwan," alongside the presidential election scheduled for the following March.

The note handed to the Chinese side at the Senior Dialogue meeting was meant to formally advise Beijing that the Bush administration had already lodged objections to Chen Shui-bian's U.N. referendum plan and urged him to drop it.

In sum, the Bush administration used the Washington round of the U.S.-PRC Senior Dialogue to reassure Beijing that the U.S. government would oppose Chen Shui-bian's proposed U.N. referendum and continue efforts to persuade him to abandon the plan.

Chapter 10
Pushing for a Referendum on Joining the U.N.

The U.S. wanted to adopt a hardline position against Taiwan's U.N. referendum out of two practical considerations. First, Washington had to oppose and stop the vote in exchange for Beijing's support and cooperation in its efforts to address global issues of vital importance to the interests of the United States. China's support was crucial, given its rapidly growing economic and political clout around the globe.

Another consideration was that should the U.S. take a hands-off policy and allow Chen to push the referendum through, Beijing could be tempted to respond with force. Under that scenario, the U.S. could be dragged into a war with the PRC, something that Washington clearly wanted to avoid.

Chen Turns More Defiant in the Final Months of His Presidency

Following the U.S.-PRC meeting in Washington, the Bush administration had assumed the main role in blocking Taiwan's provocative U.N. referendum. But the challenge was that Chen, as a president leaving office in less than a year and facing no reelection pressure, was becoming increasingly more defiant.

Chen's aggressive stance forced the Bush administration to be more critical in its opposition to the referendum. As a result, tensions between Taipei and Washington continued to escalate until Chen left office on May 20, 2008.

As mentioned previously, the State Department issued a statement voicing strong opposition to the referendum plan, a day after President Chen announced his decision. Below is the full text of that statement from June 19, 2007:[189]

"The United States opposes any initiative that appears designed to change Taiwan's status unilaterally. This includes a referendum on whether to apply to the United Nations under the name Taiwan. While such a referendum would have no practical impact on Taiwan's U.N. status, it would increase tensions in the Taiwan Strait. Maintenance of peace and stability across the Taiwan Strait is of vital interest to the people of Taiwan and serves U.S. security interests as well. Moreover, such a move would appear to run counter to President Chen's repeated commitments to President Bush and the international community. We urge President Chen to exercise leadership by rejecting such a proposed referendum."

But Chen ignored the warning and forged ahead with his U.N. referendum plan, dismissing U.S. objections as part of a policy of appeasing China. He alleged that the U.S. had been leaning toward China over cross-strait relations. Chen defended the proposed referendum as "an important element in practicing democracy and thus should not be restricted just because China opposed it."

Two days later, the ruling DPP came forward to support President Chen in his referendum drive, dismissing the U.S. statement. The DPP countered it "would ignore U.S. and Chinese objections and continue to push the U.N. referendum on whether to join the United Nations

---

189 Shirley A. Kan, China/Taiwan: Evolution of the 'One China' Policy-- Key Statements from Washington, Beijing and Taipei, CRS Report, June 3, 2011.

under the name Taiwan."[190]

By this time, the DPP had already collected more than 90,000 signatures in support of the U.N. referendum. Under the Plebiscite Law, it needed a total of nearly one million signatures, or 5 percent of total eligible voters, to cross the threshold for the party to formally launch the referendum.[191]

On the following day, June 22, President Chen followed up with a fresh rejection of the U.S. State Department's call for Taipei to drop the U.N. referendum plan. "The referendum on whether to apply to the U.N. under the name Taiwan will be held along with the March 2008 presidential election as scheduled," Chen reiterated at an "informal" meeting with reporters covering the Presidential Office.[192]

Chen maintained that, under the U.N.'s universality principle on membership, "Taiwan has every right to join the U.N." And applying for U.N. membership under the name Taiwan, he argued, "neither conflicts with Taiwan's pledges to the international community nor the commitments he made to the U.S. government and President George W. Bush." Chen also contended that holding the U.N. referendum "conforms to the mainstream view of the people of Taiwan."

So he continued to press ahead with his U.N. referendum plan. In an interview with the Washington Post on July 8, the president, speaking of the vote, asserted that "the path we have embarked on is

190 Kathrin Hille, Taipei to Snub U.S. and China on U.N. Plan, The Financial Times, June 21, 2007.
191 Shih Shih-Chun, Jimmy Chuang, Committee Says Yes to U.N. Referendum, Taipei Times, July 13, 2007.
192 Chronology, Mainland Affairs Council, Republic of China (Taiwan), June 22, 2007.

the right one, and we shall continue to follow it." He added that neither China nor the U.S. "have the right to block the referendum."[193]

In the interview, the newspaper's Taipei correspondent Edward Cody asked the president a wide range of questions. The one concerning the U.N. referendum was this: "Do you think, then, that the United States's objection to the referendum is the result of misunderstanding or their putting other interests that you don't share ahead of those you do share? In other words, why would the United States object, I mean, to the referendum we're talking about?"

Excerpts of Chen's answer to this question are given below: "I think it is because of China, and because the introduction of a referendum would not be in China's interests. The referendum represents the consolidation and deepening of Taiwan's democracy, and is in line with the development of Taiwan-centric consciousness...

"The decision to hold a referendum on applying for U.N. membership involves three major aspects, and we would like to know which one Washington's objection concerns. Is it about the matter of holding the referendum itself? Or about joining the U.N.? Or about using the name Taiwan? What reason is there to oppose any of these?

"At the same time, we value the concerns of and views expressed by the U.S. government and wish to continue our discussions with the U.S. If there are any misunderstandings, they should be cleared up so that our views do not become distorted by others. In this way, we hope to maintain the mutual trust between the U.S. and Taiwan and continue

---

193 Edward Cody, Interview with Chen Shui-bian, President of Taiwan, the Washington Post, July 8, 2007

our long-term friendships."

By the mid-summer of 2007, the U.S. opposition expressed in public statements and quiet diplomacy had done little to dampen Chen's enthusiasm for the U.N. referendum. Some analysts tried to explain Chen's actions, which carried significant risk with little prospect of success, as being aimed at bolstering Chen's personal legacy rather than achieving an immediate policy benefit.

"For Chen, who is coming to the end of his final term as president, it's an issue of legacy," said Loh Chih-cheng, a political science professor at Soochow University in Taipei (and later a member of the Legislative Yuan). "He's pushing to make his name in history."[194]

In an article dated September 17, 2007, Time magazine described the U.N. referendum as "less a declaration of independence than a political ploy by Chen to bolster his legacy, as well as voter turnout in next March for his DPP party."[195]

In the same article, Time quoted Chao Chien-min, a political science professor at Taiwan's National Chengchi University, as saying: "The ruling party doesn't have much to campaign about. The only thing they can do is promote the cause of independence or portray the opposition as Beijing's collaborator." Chao recalled that a similar strategy played a key role in Chen Shui-bian's reelection in the 2004 presidential race. In the 2004 campaign, Chen initiated a "defensive" referendum, the first of its kind in Taiwan, which many said greatly bolstered voter turnout.

---

194 Austin Ramzy, Taiwan's President Calls for Vote, Time, July 11, 2007
195 Kathleen Kingsbury, Taiwan's War of Words with the U.S., Time, September 17, 2007

After quiet diplomacy and public criticism failed to get Chen Shui-bian to back off from the referendum, the Bush Administration stepped up pressure on him and his government by taking a series of punitive measures.

U.S. Holds up Sale of 66 F-16C/D Jets to Taiwan

One such measure was to put off the sale to Taiwan of 66 advanced F-16C/D fighter jets -- a new batch of warplanes urgently needed by this island to beef up its air defense capability. According to Global Security, an influential source for military and security news, the Bush administration in mid-2007 had become so concerned over President Chen's call for an extremely provocative referendum that it decided to postpone its decision to sell 66 F-16C/D aircraft to Taiwan.[196]

In an interview with The New York Times in October 2007, President Chen admitted the F-16 C/D procurement program was being held up by the Bush administration. He told the newspaper "...As for the F-16C/D fighters, we can understand why although we have the budget ready, the U.S. government has yet to issue a letter of offer and acceptance, and that it seems likely that we will have to wait until the new administration comes into power and the next U.S. president takes office before the deal can be approved."

Meanwhile, in a campaign speech given before the Taiwan-based Association for the Promotion of National Security weeks ahead of the March 2008 presidential election, opposition KMT candidate Ma Ying-

---

196 John Pike, F-16 Fighting Falcon, www.globalsecurity.org, 2007

jeou blamed Chen Shui-bian for Washington's decision to suspend the sale of the F-16C/D warplanes.

Ma said, "It is imperative [for Taiwan] to replenish air power by supplementing or replacing existing hardware with newer and more advanced aircraft. But President Chen Shui-bian's unrelenting promotion of the 'Join the U.N. under the Name Taiwan Referendum' has been preventing us from doing so."

"Last year, we submitted several letters of intent to the United States on the purchase of the F-16C/Ds," he said. "We asked about the price and the possibility of purchase, but all of these letters were rejected. This is what happens when a president puts their party interests first, even at the expense of national security."

In the end, Ma Ying-jeou won the March 2008 presidential election. Soon after he took office on May 20, the Ministry of National Defense expressed a desire to revive the F-16 procurement program. What Taiwan intended to buy then was a set of weapons systems. They included the F-16C/D fighters, as well as long-range early warning ultrahigh frequency phased array radars, and the construction of the Regional Operations Control Center. All of these were essential components of Taiwan's air defense.

However, according to the Global Security report, the Bush administration in its final years would not accept any formal request from Taiwan for the F-16C/Ds. Part of the reason for its refusal to accept Taiwan's request was explained by the head of the U.S. Pacific Command, Admiral Timothy Keating, in a July 2008 speech delivered before the Washington-based think tank Heritage Foundation.

"U.S. policymakers saw no pressing need to sell advanced arms, such as the F-16 fighter, to Taiwan. U.S. decision-makers have reconciled Taiwan's current military posture, China's current military posture and strategy that indicate there is no pressing, compelling need for at this moment arms sales to Taiwan of the systems that we're talking about."

The Hawaii-based U.S. Pacific commander then added, "I'm more comfortable today ... than I was 15 months ago…that my belief is well founded that it is very, very, very unlikely that there will be conflict across the [Taiwan] strait."

On October 3, 2008, the U.S. Defense Department notified Congress that it had approved the sale of a US$6.46 billion package of weapons to Taiwan. The package included 330 advanced capability Patriot (PAC-3) missiles worth up to US$3.1 billion, 30 Apache attack helicopters valued at US$2.5 billion, along with 32 Harpoon sub-launched missiles, 182 Javelin guided missiles, and four E-2T system upgrades.

However, the approved weaponry supply list did not include the 66 F-16C/D fighters that Taiwan had sought. Still, newly inaugurated President Ma Ying-jeou lauded the sale, saying that the U.S. decision not only "marked the end of turmoil and confusion of arms purchase in Taiwan in the past eight years, but also symbolized the beginning of a new era of mutual trust between the two countries."

The new arms sale, however, drew a strong protest from China, which reacted by suspending military-to-military exchanges and nonproliferation talks with the United States. Months later in March 2009, five PRC ships surrounded and harassed a U.S. surveillance ship which the Pentagon said operated in international waters.

Chapter 10
Pushing for a Referendum on Joining the U.N.

Reportedly, the Bush administration had told Taiwan that it was not denying it any of the weapons approved in 2001 but was leaving the decision to the next administration under U.S. President Barack Obama. In April of that year, President George W. Bush, despite protests from China, approved the sale to Taiwan of a weapons package worth a staggering US$12 billion for four Kidd-class destroyers and assistance in buying eight diesel submarines from third countries. Yet this package was consistently held up by debate in Taiwan's legislature.

However, the Obama administration continued to refuse the sale of the 66 F-16 C/D fighters, despite repeated requests from Taipei. The main reason was the objections from the PRC. "The Obama administration refused to accept Taiwan's request for the F-16C/Ds because it worried that such a sale would anger Beijing," KMT Legislative Speaker Wang Jin-pyng stated in March 2009.

Instead, the Obama administration offered Taiwan a US$4.2 billion upgrade of its aging F-16 A/B fighter fleet. The State Department told Congress in September 2011 that upgrading the F-16 A/B fighter planes "will be able to meet Taiwan's defense needs at the present stage."

As of mid-2015 -- eight years after the Bush administration first decided to defer Taiwan's 66 F-16C/D procurement program to pressure Chen Shui-bian into dropping his provocative U.N. referendum -- the U.S. still seemed to be unwilling to sell these fighter jets to this island.

An indication of the U.S. reluctance to revive the long-stalled F-16C/D deal can be seen in a May 27, 2015, Defense News report, entitled "Taiwan Pushes for New Weapons on All Fronts," which quoted its Taipei defense sources as saying that "Taiwan's arms procurement system is motivated by eight conflicting factors."[197]

The conflicting factors cited included the following: "There is the equipment they do not want but the U.S. wants to sell to them, such as the Kidd-class destroyers. We did not want it. It was a white elephant. It could not even fit into our harbor... And there are things they can afford, but the U.S. refuses to sell, such as F-16C/D fighter aircraft."

U.S. Places Strict Limits on Chen's Transit

Beyond freezing the sale of 66 advanced F-16C/D fighter jets to Taiwan as discussed above, the Bush administration in mid-summer 2007 also imposed strict restrictions on President Chen's transits through the U.S. as further punishment for his insistence on pushing his provocative U.N. referendum.

Washington refused to allow him to set foot in any of the contiguous U.S. states during his transit to and from Central America. Chen planned a nine-day visit to Taiwan's three Central American partners of that era -- Honduras, El Salvador, and Nicaragua -- from August 21 to 29 2007. (Today, of those three states only Honduras retains diplomatic relations with Taiwan). Chen planned stopovers in the U.S. on the way to the region and return.

Instead, President Chen was only permitted to transit through the remote U.S. state of Alaska. Moreover, he was allowed to stay at the

---

197 Wendell Minnick, Taiwan Pushes for New Weapons on All Fronts, Defense News, May 27, 2105

Chapter 10
Pushing for a Referendum on Joining the U.N.

Anchorage International Airport just long enough for refueling. An overnight stay was ruled out.

The strict stopover restrictions represented a drastic downgrade in U.S. treatment of his transit stops. In the past, Washington had almost always given him a warm and dignified reception each time he made a stopover in the U.S.

Chen saw this kind of "open arms" welcome as a symbol of his success in cementing relations with Taiwan's most important political and defense ally. During his eight years as president, he sought out stopovers in the U.S., seizing the opportunity of every foreign trip, whether to Central or South America or the Caribbean. But all those pleasant U.S. transits had become things of the past, as his relations with Washington had gone sour.

Yet the humiliating restrictions imposed on Chen's travel plans by the U.S. government only antagonized him further and hardened his resolve to hold the U.N. referendum alongside Taiwan's presidential election the following March.

Upon arrival in Anchorage, Chen refused to get off his presidential plane in protest over Washington's strict transit arrangements.[198]

Although Chen did not disembark from his special plane, he did receive in his cabin the honorary chairman of the American Institute in Taiwan (AIT), William Brown, who made his way to Alaska to greet him in a gesture of diplomatic courtesy.

---

198 Dennis Engbarth, Undignified Transit Punishes Taiwan, Chen Says, Taiwan News, August 22, 2007.

However, the president received the senior U.S. diplomat without wearing a jacket or tie as customarily required. Moreover, when he met Brown, he wore a "U.N. for Taiwan" sticker on his shirt. Other ranking officials and legislators accompanying him on the Central American trip also wore similar stickers.

The message Chen and his presidential delegation intended to convey through such a collective protest was clear: "We are determined to go ahead with the referendum on whether to apply to the United Nations in the name of Taiwan, no matter what the U.S. says or does."

During the meeting, Chen complained to William Brown that he found his Alaska stopover treatment "inconvenient, uncomfortable, unsatisfactory, and [he felt] disrespected." "The ill-treatment," Chen argued, "was not a punishment against him personally but a sanction against the entire 23 million people of Taiwan."

Chen also told Brown that his planned referendum was a manifestation of direct democracy and that Taiwan's people could not accept having a line drawn that limited democracy -- a reference to Washington's warning that holding a referendum on the U.N. bid would be crossing a red line.

Despite a tight schedule, Chen always found time during his visit to each of the three Central American countries to speak out against the U.S. and the PRC for seeking to block his proposed referendum, in addition to continuing to tout the value of the referendum vote.

Yet what he argued on the nine-day, three-country visit mostly were views and assertions that he had covered time and again back home. He wanted to restate them while traveling abroad in an attempt to win international sympathy and support for him and his referendum.

Chapter 10
Pushing for a Referendum on Joining the U.N.

But what Chen may not have anticipated at the time was that his inflammatory remarks on the referendum were bound to provoke a strong backlash in Beijing and Washington. Below are excerpts from Chen's statements:

"Taiwan's ongoing efforts to deepen its democracy, which include the plan to conduct a referendum on whether to apply to the U.N. under the name Taiwan, should not be subject to any red lines or suppression. Conducting referendums is the exercise of direct democracy and democracy is a universal value that must not be compromised. While Taiwan is entitled to achieving full democracy, other countries keep changing the rules and then blaming us for violating them. Taiwan must not refrain from carrying out democratic reforms just because of opposition from the U.S. and the PRC. We should press ahead with the referendum plan, regardless of whether others support or oppose it. A democracy in which its people cannot hold referendums is not a true democracy...

"A country's sovereignty comes from the people. The Taiwanese people have the right to participate in international organizations based on the principles of democracy and human rights. Nobody should say no to it or threaten us. Holding referendums is a basic human right guaranteed by the Constitution. As president, I see it as my responsibility to ensure that the practice of this constitutionally protected right takes root in Taiwan during my tenure. I hope my efforts will make things easier for the next president and government. They will come to realize they need not fear others, be it the U.S. or China...

"Democracy is the most important asset for Taiwan and a referendum is the best weapon or the most effective 'theater missile defense' against the totalitarianism of the Chinese Communist Party. China has pushed Taiwan against the wall: Taiwan cannot use its official name, the Republic of China, in the international community. Yet the other names imposed by China, such as 'Chinese Taipei' or 'Taiwan, China,' have aroused resentment among the people of Taiwan. Under such circumstances, it is most natural for us to take part in international activities under the name Taiwan…

"Conducting the referendum on whether to join the U.N. under the name Taiwan is also meant to prevent this island from becoming a part of China. In other words, the U.N. referendum is to maintain the status quo. This policy conforms to the interests of the U.S. because the U.S., too, does not want Taiwan to become a part of China and is against changing its status. So Washington has no reason to oppose us holding the referendum…

"Whether or not Taiwan should conduct a referendum is not something that Washington or Beijing should and can decide. This is a decision that must be made by the Taiwanese people themselves. Taiwan's fate and future should be decided by its people through democratic procedure. That is, a referendum should be used to determine the future of Taiwan and its relations with China…

"It's impossible for me to use my position as president to call off a referendum that by this time has already been endorsed by both the ruling party and the main opposition KMT and that was supported by as many as 71% of the people. Canceling the planned referendum would amount to frustrating the democratic rights of Taiwan's people to express their views and guide government policies."

Judging from the above excerpts, Chen was attempting to portray his referendum as a democratic tool of great importance for Taiwan in realizing full democracy and advancing basic human rights. His effort was intended to promote widely accepted universal values, and as such should not be opposed by the United States, a leading champion of democracy and human rights in the world.

Besides linking the referendum with democracy and human rights, Chen also pitched the vote as a "defensive weapon" crucial to deterring any invasion by China and safeguarding Taiwan's status quo. So the U.S. and other democratic powers should show sympathy and support for the referendum, instead of joining the PRC in opposing it.

However shrewdly Chen packaged his U.N. referendum, the U.S. remained unconvinced. His sharp attacks on the U.S. made during his Central American visit infuriated the Bush administration, already upset by his insistence on promoting the referendum itself.

Negroponte Calls the U.N. Referendum a 'Mistake'

The U.S. responded quickly with a succession of harsh criticisms by senior administration officials, marking an escalation of U.S. opposition to Chen's U.N. referendum plans. It's worth noting again that just two months earlier the State Department had already issued a strong statement on the referendum issue. "The United States opposes any initiative that appears designed to change Taiwan's status quo unilaterally," it said. "This would include a referendum on whether to apply to the United Nations in the name Taiwan."

Heading the opposition to Chen's referendum was the State Department's No. 2 man, Deputy Secretary John Negroponte, who called the proposed vote a "mistake." "We oppose the notion of that kind of a referendum because we see that as a step toward a declaration of independence for Taiwan and toward the alteration of the status quo," Negroponte said.[199]

Negroponte's remarks were the harshest from a senior U.S. official since Chen first expressed his intention in mid-2007 to hold the U.N. referendum. Negroponte delivered the scathing remarks in an interview with the Hong Kong-based Phoenix Star TV. Reportedly, the deputy secretary of state had reached an agreement beforehand with the TV station that the interview would be only about Taiwan and the referendum. The questions had been discussed before the interview.

Also, the interview was carefully arranged to be aired on August 28, just one day before Chen was to return home through Anchorage from his Central American trip. This would allow time for AIT Chairman Raymond Burghardt, who was to fly to the Alaskan city to greet Chen as a diplomatic courtesy, to convey Negroponte's comments to him in person.

In the interview, Negroponte reiterated U.S. friendship and the American defense commitment to Taiwan. "But when it comes to the issue of the referendum as to whether or not Taiwan should join the United Nations in the name of Taiwan, we do have great concerns," he said. The senior U.S. diplomat suggested that holding such a referendum would be seen as a violation of the "four noes" stated in Chen's 2000 inaugural speech and repeated at his second inauguration

---

199 Agencies: Push for United Nations Entry a 'Mistake': Negroponte, China Post, August 29, 2007

Chapter 10
Pushing for a Referendum on Joining the U.N.

four years later.

"I would recall that in the past President Chen has made commitments to the American president, to the international community, and the people of Taiwan not to take any kind of steps that would represent a unilateral alteration of the status quo, such as a change in the national name of Taiwan."

Asked whether it concerned him that Taiwan's democratic development was "sliding out of U.S. hands," Negroponte said: "We feel that this is a time for the authorities in Taiwan to behave responsibly, to behave in a way that would advance the interests of Taiwan while, at the same time, not disturbing the situation across the Taiwan Strait. I think there's a way of doing that, of pursuing their democracy, pursuing their vibrant economy, benefiting from the friendship, the strong friendship of a country such as the United States and we are certainly committed to continuing that," he said. "But we believe that it has to be done seriously and responsibly," he said.

Negroponte was also questioned by Phoenix TV about whether the U.S. would downgrade its economic or military cooperation with Taiwan if the referendum went ahead. "I wouldn't want to get into that kind of a hypothetical discussion at this particular time. But what I would like to emphasize is that we believe it's important to avoid any kind of provocative steps on the part of Taiwan," he replied.

On the question of whether the U.S. would still be willing to earnestly defend Taiwan in the event of a cross-strait conflict that was considered to be provoked by Taiwan, Negroponte again thought it to be a hypothetical question. "Such a situation is very difficult to address before a specific situation might arise. You're correct in saying we're very committed to the defense of Taiwan under the Taiwan Relations Act. We wish the people and authorities on both sides of the Taiwan Strait to pursue their objectives through peaceful means. And it's this kind of spirit that we're encouraging the authorities of Taiwan to adopt as they address this question of a referendum, which we consider to be a mistake."

Chen Rebuts U.S. Criticism Point-by-Point

Chen responded to Negroponte's critical statements with a firm rebuttal during the meeting with AIT chairman Burghardt in Anchorage on his return. As he did on his outbound trip to Central America, Chen again declined to disembark from his plane while it was being refueled. The meeting with the AIT chairman was held in his cabin, which lasted for nearly two hours with Chen doing most of the talking.

Chen told Burghardt he disagreed with Negroponte's suggestion that his proposed referendum was a step toward independence. Major contents of Chen's conversation with the AIT chief were provided to reporters by Presidential Office Spokesman Lee Nan-yang during a subsequent press briefing.

"Taiwan is already an independent state. This is the fact and the status quo. There is no need for us to declare independence. Therefore, the charge that the referendum was intended to alter Taiwan's status was not true. Rather, the initiative was an effort meant to maintain and safeguard the status," President Chen was quoted by the spokesman as saying.

Chen also refuted Negroponte's allegation that his referendum on applying for U.N. membership under the name Taiwan was an attempt to alter the national name. "It was just untrue because the title we were planning to use in the U.N. membership bid was neither 'Taiwan state' nor 'Taiwan republic.' It should also be noted that in the past we've used many different names in joining world organizations. For example, we used the title 'Chinese Taipei' in both the International Olympic Committee and the Asian-Pacific Economic Forum. And the moniker we used in the World Trade Organization was 'Separate Customs Territory of Taiwan, Penghu, and Kinmen and Matsu.' So our decision now to use the name Taiwan to join the U.N., or to hold a referendum on whether to apply to the U.N. in the name Taiwan must not be criticized for attempting to change the national title either."

Chen also urged the U.S. to pay serious attention to several identity issues in Taiwan. One was about how to define the status of Taiwan's relations with the Chinese mainland. Chen quoted a recent but unidentified poll as saying that 74 percent of local citizens considered Taiwan an independent sovereign country. And those who agreed that Taiwan is part of China accounted for merely 11 percent.

The other question Chen raised concerned the issue of the national territory. Chen said that about 85 percent of the people believed the nation's territory covered only the areas of Taiwan, Penghu, Kinmen, and Matsu. True or false, Chen's alleged popular perception of the nation's territory conflicted with what the ROC constitution defines as the scope of the national territory.

A third point, Chen raised, was that 69 percent of the local people thought of themselves as Taiwanese, not Chinese. "The U.S. should not fail to note that this identity affiliation is Taiwan's mainstream political view and that it must not be ignored and suppressed," Chen said.

In the meeting with Burghardt, Chen also lambasted the U.S. for what he described as yielding to pressure from China at the expense of Taiwan. "Taiwan's democracy has long had the backing and the encouragement of the U.S. But now the American government wants us to practice only limited democracy by not allowing our people to use a referendum to express their wishes. Unfortunately, the U.S. does not want us to conduct the referendum just because China is opposed to the vote," he complained. "I must say that while Taiwan is fighting to defend democratic values, the U.S. is now more willing to protect its own interests."

Chen's harsh rebuke, however, did not discourage the U.S. from opposing his referendum. The Bush administration continued to exert pressure on him over the issue. Barely three days after Chen refuted Deputy Secretary of State Negroponte's critical comments made in the interview with Phoenix TV, Dennis Wilder, senior director for East Asian Affairs of the National Security Council, came out to speak against President Chen's plan.[200]

Wilder said it was "perplexing" to Washington as to why Taiwan thought it would be useful to hold a referendum on the U.N. issue, "given the fact that Taiwan is not going to be able to join the U.N. under the current circumstances and that it only adds a degree of tension to cross-strait relations that we deem unnecessary."

The White House official went on to say, "Membership in the

200 Dennis Wilder, Press Briefing on the President's Trip to Australia, the White House Office of the Press Secretary, August 30, 2007

Chapter 10
Pushing for a Referendum on Joining the U.N.

United Nations requires statehood. Taiwan, or the Republic of China, is not at this point a state in the international community. The position of the U.S. government is that the ROC, or the Republic of China, is an issue undecided, and it has been left undecided, as you know, for many, many years."

Wilder made the above remarks during a special White House briefing on President George W. Bush's upcoming talks with Chinese President Hu Jintao in Australia. Bush and Hu were set to attend the Asia-Pacific Economic Cooperation forum summit scheduled for September 6 to 7 in Sydney.

As Wilder had made clear at a briefing beforehand, Taiwan was the first topic of conversation between Bush and Hu when they met on the sidelines of the APEC summit. But neither of the two leaders brought up the referendum issue at their joint press conference held after their bilateral meeting.

Instead, they let their aides convey to the media the contents of their bilateral talks regarding the issue of Taiwan. According to Beijing's Foreign Ministry spokesman Liu Jianchao, Hu told Bush that Chen's proposed referendum could destabilize the region and urged him to issue more serious warnings to the Taiwan authorities. "President Hu Jintao stressed that this year and next year is going to be a highly sensitive and possibly dangerous period of the situation in the Taiwan Strait," Liu told reporters afterward.

For the U.S. side, Deputy National Security Adviser James Jeffrey briefed reporters about Bush's views.[201] "The president reiterated his position on Taiwan, reassuring Hu that his position had not changed," Jeffrey said. In his conversation with Hu, Jeffrey said Bush referred specifically to the comments made by U.S. Deputy Secretary of State John Negroponte a week earlier in his interview with Phoenix TV. (As noted earlier, Negroponte described the referendum as a step toward a declaration of independence and a mistake, warning that it could change the status quo across the Taiwan Strait.)

"So for the moment, we're going to stay with our position and continue to exert our good influence on the Taiwanese to see if we can change their position." Bush was also quoted as telling Hu: "We are concerned very much about this step that Taiwan has undertaken. We also don't want to see this blown up too big. We don't want to see anyone provoked by the actions of the Taiwanese." This was a subtle warning to China not to overreact to Chen's referendum drive.

Chen Vows to Push Ahead with Referendum

President Chen, following his return to Taipei from Central America, became more outspoken in promoting his referendum and independence. His attacks on the U.S. grew even fiercer. Such strong emotions believably reflected his anger at the humiliating treatment he had received during his transit stops in Anchorage, and the heightened U.S. criticisms leveled against him by John Negroponte and Dennis

---

201 Charles Snyder and Jessie Ho, Bush Warns on Referendum Being 'Blown up too Big,' Taipei Times, September 7, 2007.

Chapter 10
Pushing for a Referendum on Joining the U.N.

Wilder.

On September 6, speaking via satellite to a Washington think tank, the American Enterprise Institute, Chen Shui-bian vowed to push ahead with his referendum, and at the same time called for high-level, "substantive dialogue" between Taiwan and the United States to "prevent misunderstandings."[202]

He said that both sides needed to sit down and discuss issues, such as the referendum. "It was wrong that the U.S. had publicly denounced Taiwan and hurt the feelings of the Taiwanese." Chen said: "Taiwan may have played the role of a good boy for too long that Washington took Taipei for granted and ignored its interests."

Chen also pointed out that some U.S. officials, who saw his U.N. membership bid as a dangerous provocation of Beijing, were mistaken in treating the referendum as his political gambit. "This is not my agenda. This is the agenda of the majority of the 23 million here in Taiwan." He said that he "has been under tremendous pressure to push for the nation's bid to join the United Nations under the name of Taiwan, and to hold a referendum on the issue."

On Beijing's opposition to Taiwan's proposed U.N. referendum, President Chen said: "It is China that is the enemy of Taiwan in opposing our bid to join the United Nations. While the United States too is opposed to the U.N. referendum, it is by no means our enemy...

"Taiwan is not part of the People's Republic of China. Taiwan is an independent, sovereign country. So the PRC has no right and is

---

202 Paul Eckert, Taiwan's Chen Staunchly Defends U.N. Referendum Plan, Reuters, September 6, 2007.

unable to represent the 23 million people of Taiwan in the United Nations."[203]

Chen's latest outburst of pro-independence and anti-China remarks came a day after Chinese President Hu Jintao alerted President George W. Bush, on the sidelines of an Asia Pacific summit in Sydney, that "the coming years will be a period of danger for the Taiwan situation...And we must give stronger warnings to the Taiwan authorities."

On September 7 when addressing a group of independence supporters attending the World Taiwanese Congress, Chen offered up even more radical rhetoric. He told the congress, which convened its annual meeting in Taipei, that there is one country on each side of the Taiwan Strait, and "we must not mistake the enemy country as our motherland. Only Taiwan is our country and motherland."

He continued, "In the process of Taiwan's democratization from its first direct presidential election in the mid-1990s to the scrapping of the National Unification Guidelines in 2006, a new and independent nation was born. This new nation is Taiwan. It occupies an area of 36,000 square kilometers with a population of 23 million people."

He went on to say, "I believe that when the people reach a high degree of consensus on an independent Taiwan, it will be the time for us to declare independence. Pursuing independence is the right road to take. We must not be afraid or move back from this objective even if this might mean facing aggression by China."

---

203 Post staff and CNA, China, not United States, Is Our Enemy: Chen, China Post, September 8, 2007

Chapter 10
Pushing for a Referendum on Joining the U.N.

Appealing Directly to Taiwan's Voters

Chen's increasingly radical politics raised new uneasiness in Washington, prompting a frustrated U.S. government to change tactics to directly appeal to Taiwan's voting public over the referendum issue.

The "appeal-to-the-voter approach" was palpable in a major speech given on September 11 by Deputy Assistant Secretary of State for East Asian and Pacific Affairs Thomas Christensen, an expert on cross-strait relations. The speech was unusually direct and thorough, detailing why the U.S. had been so strongly opposed to President Chen's U.N. referendum plan.

At one point in the speech, the senior State Department official said, "…Fortunately, if the referendum goes forward unchanged, we anticipate that Taiwan's perceptive, intelligent citizens will see through the rhetoric and make a sound judgment that the referendum does not serve their interests because it will be fundamentally harmful to Taiwan's external relations."

The speech, entitled "A Strong and Moderate Taiwan," was delivered at the Defense Industry Conference, an annual event organized by the U.S.-Taiwan Business Council to discuss Taiwan's security and defense needs. In the speech to the gathering in the U.S. state of Maryland, Christensen revealed U.S. frustrations in dealing with the Taiwan leader, advised a moderate approach toward Beijing, and defined U.S. obligations to Taiwan. [204]

---

204 Thomas Christensen, Speech to U.S.-Taiwan Business Council Defense Industry Conference, September 11, 2007

Christensen stressed that he was speaking on behalf of the Bush administration to the conference participants – among them senior politicians, military officers, and business executives from both Taiwan and the U.S. He asked his audience to consider his comments in that light. The following excerpts are the gist of that address:

"We have expressed special concern about the Chen administration's support for a proposed referendum on U.N. membership in the name of Taiwan. The U.S. is not opposed to referenda. Taiwan is as entitled to hold referenda as any other democracy. But the topic and content of any particular referendum must be considered. Given that everyone knows the bulk of Taiwan's citizens would like to see Taipei apply to the United Nations and given that such a referendum would have no prospect of improving the likelihood of success in such an application, everybody would know that support for such a referendum would only be useful in domestic political posturing in Taiwan…

"What worries us, very specifically, is the issue of name change. The draft referendum raises the question of what Taiwan should be called in the international community. Moreover, it does so in what could be interpreted by many to be a legally binding popular vote. The simple reality is that in the world of cross-strait relations, political symbolism matters, and disagreements over it could be the source of major tensions or even conflict…

"It is the apparent pursuit of name change in the referendum, therefore, that makes the initiative appear to us to be a step intended to change the status quo. Arguments that the referendum, even if passed, would not amount to a pursuit of the name change, frankly, strike us as purely legalistic. After all, if the specific nomenclature does not matter, why include it in the referendum in the first place?...

"At a fundamental level, such legalistic arguments from supporters of the referendum make it seem that they do not take seriously Taiwan's commitments to the United States and the international community, are willing to ignore the security interests of Taiwan's most steadfast friend, and are ready to put at some risk the security interests of the Taiwan people for short-term political gains. Our bottom line is that the potential downsides of such an initiative for Taiwan and U.S. interests are potentially large, and, as with any U.N. referendum, the benefits for Taiwan's international status are non-existent, so we must oppose such an initiative strongly."

Christensen also provided direct U.S. responses to President Chen's questions and accusations. Regarding the question of U.S. interference, he said "I would like to face head-on the accusation that the U.S. position on the referendum constitutes interference in Taiwan's democracy. On behalf of the U.S. government, I reject this accusation categorically...

"Given the decades of America's commitment to Taiwan's security and support for its democratization, the idea just does not stand up to scrutiny. After all, it is not just Taiwan's peace and stability that Taipei's actions may threaten. As friends, we feel we must warn that the content of this particular referendum is ill-conceived and potentially quite harmful. Bad public policy initiatives are made no better for being wrapped in the flag of 'democracy.' Fortunately, if the referendum goes forward unchanged, we anticipate that Taiwan's perceptive, intelligent citizens will see through the rhetoric and make a sound judgment that the referendum does not serve their interests because it will be fundamentally harmful to Taiwan's external relations."

Turning to the people of Taiwan: "I would like to emphasize that we do not like having to express publicly our disagreement with the Chen administration on this or any other policy. Taiwan is a longstanding U.S. friend, and we do not like there to be gaps between us on important issues. I can assure you that we would not have done so had we not exhausted every private opportunity through consistent, unmistakable, and authoritative messages over an extended period. The problem here is not misunderstanding or lack of communication. It is that we believe this initiative is not good for Taiwan or us and that we have found ourselves with no alternative but to express our views directly to the Taiwanese people."

Regarding Chen's accusation of U.S. coordination with Beijing over Taiwan, Christensen responded: "There is no foundation to the assertion that the United States coordinates its Taiwan policy with Beijing. It just does not happen. Do Chinese views influence U.S. thinking? Of course. We would be reckless, as would Taipei if we did not consider them. But I can assure you that no U.S. official at any level spends any amount of time coordinating our policies toward Taiwan with Beijing.

"By the same token, while we have a close, friendly relationship with Taipei, we also do not let Taipei define our positions. For well-established reasons, the U.S. has declared its opposition to unilateral changes to the status quo on either side of the Taiwan Strait...

"Some Taiwan leaders in recent years have asserted that Taiwan independence is the status quo that should be defended. On that point, let me be clear: While U.S. opposition to Chinese coercion of Taiwan is beyond question, we do not recognize Taiwan as an independent state, and we do not accept the argument that provocative assertions of Taiwan independence are in any way conducive to maintenance of the status quo or peace and stability across the Taiwan Strait. For the reasons I have given above, we rank such assertions along with the referendum on joining the U.N. under the name Taiwan as needless provocations that are patently not in the best interests of the Taiwanese people or the United States."

On the U.S. commitment to Taiwan, he said: "U.S. support for Taiwan is enshrined in U.S. domestic law -- the Taiwan Relations Act. In short, strategic, moral, and legal requirements compel a continuous U.S. interest in Taiwan and its security. The same arguments, in turn, give us a legitimate voice on issues touching on Taiwan's security...

"Everything I say here is based on recognition of the growing PRC military threat to Taiwan posed by the fast-paced military build-up opposite Taiwan and by Beijing's refusal to rule out the use of force against Taiwan. The U.S. has demonstrated its rejection of any coercion of Taiwan through both its defensive arms sales to Taipei and maintenance of our unilateral capability to respond to such coercion if our president were so to choose."

Taiwan Advised to Combine Strength with Moderation

The deputy assistant secretary of state also advised Taiwan to combine strength with moderation. "The U.S. believes that a strong and moderate Taiwan is essential to the immediate and long-term security needs of the people of Taiwan. Anything less than strength and moderation leaves Taiwan vulnerable, endangers regional peace and potentially threatens U.S. interests," he said. "A strong Taiwan is, very simply, one that maintains the military capacity to withstand coercion for an extended period. To the extent that Beijing knows it cannot subdue Taiwan swiftly -- before the international community would be able to react -- deterrence is reinforced…

"I would now like to turn to the other indispensable dimension of Taiwan's security -- a moderate, sophisticated, effective political approach toward cross-strait relations. Without moderation, Taiwan's security will be compromised, no matter how much money Taipei spends on defense and no matter how wisely those defense dollars have been allocated…

"In terms of security, the proposition is reasonably simple: As long as Taiwan maintains a credible defensive capability, the chief threats to its welfare are political actions by Taipei itself that could trigger Beijing's use of force…It is for this reason that Taiwan's security is inextricably linked to the avoidance of needlessly provocative behavior. This does not mean that Taipei should or can be passive in the face of PRC pressure. However, it means that responsible leadership in Taipei has to anticipate potential Chinese red lines and reactions and avoid unnecessary and unproductive provocations...

"The frustrating truth is that needlessly provocative actions by Taipei strengthen Beijing's hand in limiting Taiwan's space and scare away potential friends who might help Taiwan. This is again an area where we have to acknowledge a tough truth. Whether we like it or not, most countries in the world accept Beijing's characterization of Taiwan, and, when energized, the PRC can call in overwhelming support to marginalize Taipei... Taipei needs to push back intelligently and in a sophisticated manner that plays to its strengths. Frontal assaults on Beijing's sensitivities are bound to fail and, at the end of the day, leave Taipei further behind. The referendum on the U.N. under the name Taiwan is just such a frontal assault with no hope of changing Taiwan's actual status on the international stage while increasing cross-strait tensions and alienating potential supporters of Taiwan's increased international support."

Beyond criticizing Chen's referendum plan as seriously provocative and suggesting that he was moving in an "unwise direction," Christensen also offered an important piece of advice for Taiwan in the future. "We look to Taiwan to adopt strategies toward cross-strait relations that combine strength -- both military and economic -- with moderation. When we see policies that diverge from these goals, we owe it to ourselves and to the Taiwanese people to speak out."

The final decision by the U.S. government to take the referendum issue to Taiwan's voters appeared to indicate that Washington had come to realize that there would be no way for it to stop Chen from moving ahead with his proposed vote.

Indeed, Washington at this point had no option but to appeal to the voting public of Taiwan. In the past it had taken a string of punitive measures against Chen but to no avail. The measures included the rejection of Chen's request to transit through any politically symbolic U.S. cities, the suspension of a scheduled high-level security dialogue with his administration, and the postponement of a crucial arms project selling 66 more advanced F-16s to Taiwan.

The difficulties and frustrations the U.S. faced in seeking to get Chen Shui-bian to abandon the U.N. referendum were further expressed by Secretary of State Condoleezza Rice in Beijing in early March of 2008, weeks before Taiwan held the U.N. referendum.

"Taiwan is a democratic entity," she said after a meeting with PRC Foreign Minister Yang Jiechi in which the referendum was a key issue of discussion. "Its leaders will decide for themselves." During the meeting, the secretary of state also repeated the U.S. opposition to the referendum, calling the plan provocative and a "bad idea." Still, Yang and other PRC leaders suggested that the U.S. had not done enough to get the referendum called off.[205]

In Taiwan, President Chen continued to press ahead with his referendum plan, ignoring the advice from Thomas Christensen on not unnecessarily provoking mainland China.

On September 15, Chen and his party held a mass rally in the southern Taiwan city of Kaohsiung to drum up support for the U.N. referendum. The event attracted some 100,000 participants. Chen told

---

205 Edward Cody, U.S., China Resigned to Taiwan Vote, the Washington Post, September March 6, 2008.

his listeners that "Taiwan has been suppressed and treated as an invisible nation. The people of Taiwan deserve every right to demand appropriate representation in the United Nations. "

Then in remarks on National Day on October 10, Chen reiterated his resolve to hold the referendum on applying for U.N. membership using the name Taiwan. Beyond that subject, he did not address issues concerning the wider society of Taiwan, as customarily called for on such an occasion.

As Chen delivered a pro-referendum speech, the façade of the Presidential Building was covered with a banner bearing giant Chinese characters, which read in English: "Taiwan for U.N." A huge billboard declared "U.N. for Taiwan/Peace Forever. " At National Day gatherings of the past, the front of the building would have been adorned with an upbeat but politically neutral banner featuring the slogan "Celebrating the Republic of China National Day."

The president was asked by reporters why the celebratory decorations on the front of the Presidential Building this year were different from those of the past. He gave this reply: "We wanted to use such new decorations as we celebrate this year's National Day to highlight the importance of the U.N. entry referendum, in hopes of garnering stronger support for the popular vote."

Chen's more recent referendum activities were not lost on the American Institute in Taiwan, the de facto U.S. embassy in Taipei. Weeks later on November 8, AIT Director Stephen Young, using what he called his semi-annual meeting with the press, took the initiative to raise the referendum issue in his opening remarks. "There is no question that we have hit a rough patch recently over this government's

U.N. referendum."

The AIT director pointed out, "We have no objection to the use of referenda in Taiwan, but as in all democracies, just because you can do something doesn't mean you should," a reference to President Chen's repeated accusation that the U.S.'s opposition to Taiwan's U.N. referendum was tantamount to interfering with its practice of democracy.

Director Young continued, "That is why we have felt it our obligation, as a close partner with Taiwan, respectfully to express our opposition to the referendum on applying to the U.N. under the name of Taiwan. We believe this referendum poses a threat to cross-strait stability and appears inconsistent, at the very least, with the spirit of President Chen's public commitments."

Here, Young echoed Deputy Assistant Secretary of State Christensen's idea of turning to Taiwan's voters: "We call upon Taiwan's politicians and voters to adopt a careful and moderate approach to cross-strait relations, and to avoid risky acts that cannot help Taiwan's actual international status."

Following Director Young's opening remarks, Jane Rickards of the Washington Post asked the following questions. "You mentioned during this press conference that several other high-ranking U.S. officials have warned against Taiwan going through with this referendum, entering the U.N. under the name Taiwan. What are you trying to achieve with all these warnings? It appears that President Chen Shui-bian is not listening and is going to go through with the plans to hold it. Would you take any action against Taiwan if these warnings were not heeded and, if not, what are you trying to achieve with these warnings? Are you trying to reach out to Taiwan's voters?"

Young replied "...I do think that there is a price to be paid in mutual trust when we talk past one another about an important issue like this and that is for Taiwan's political system to consider...I would stop short of saying that there was some sort of specific consequence, some sort of action or punishment, or something that is being envisioned here. It is simply that we would like the Taiwan voters, as you discussed, to understand the reasons why the United States thinks this is not the most felicitous of steps to take when the goal should be maintaining cross-strait stability."

U.S. Seeks to Ensure Peaceful Transfer of Power

With the March 22, 2008, presidential election and the U.N. referendum less than six months away, the U.S. was putting greater emphasis on the question of how to ensure that President Chen Shui-bian peacefully transferred power at the end of his term. At the same time, it continued to exert pressure on the Taiwan leader to drop the referendum plan.

Amid Washington's new unease about Taiwan's political stability before and after the election, AIT Chairman Raymond Burghardt flew to Taipei on December 8 to meet with President Chen and the two presidential candidates, Frank Hsieh of the ruling DPP and Ma Ying-jeou of the opposition KMT. His visit came exactly one month after AIT Taipei Office Director Stephen Young publicly expressed U.S. opposition to the referendum.

"All that Taiwan's U.N. referendum would do is cause trouble, and it will 'box in' Taiwan's next president," Burghardt said at a press conference where he disclosed some key points of his meetings with Chen and other Taiwan political leaders.[206][207]

Burghardt told reporters that Chen's drive to join the U.N. under the name Taiwan was "a clever way of going against the pledge to not change the name, not change the moniker." The AIT chairman was referring to Chen's insistence that his "referendum plan has nothing to do with changing the island's status quo or breaking the no-independence pledge." Chen had made the above assurance, commonly known as the "five noes," first in his 2000 inaugural speech and routinely thereafter whenever he faced accusations that he was straying from core policy. "President Chen insists that it doesn't do that, but it does appear to be a way to do it through the back door," Burghardt asserted.

He also pointed to Chen's more recent statements that the U.N. referendum would represent a vote against unification and for sovereignty. "It's not explicitly an independence vote, not in terms of the precise language of it. But saying that it's a vote against unification goes beyond the precise language of the referendum itself."

Burghardt pointed out that he and other U.S. officials understood the argument from Taiwan that it wanted its voice to be heard through the referendum and that it sought to highlight the Taiwan identity issue.

But since the planned referendum involved the issue of stability

---

206 Lawrence Chung, U.S. Official Raps Chen's 'Mischief' on Referendum, South China Morning Post, December 12, 2007
207 Taiwan's U.N. Referendum Causes Trouble: AIT Chairman, CNA, December 11, 2007.

in the Taiwan Strait, the issue of American commitments and lives, Burghardt said it required "prudent and careful action." He maintained that since it was obvious Taiwan stood no chance of joining the United Nations even if the referendum passed next March, the vote would merely "cause trouble."

In addition, he stated that the referendum would also restrain the next president, either Frank Hsieh or Ma Ying-jeou, in dealing with the mainland, making it hard for the new president to develop better relations with Beijing.

"The next president deserves to be his own man. He will have a chance to cope with new ideas of how to deal with cross-strait relations. He should not be boxed in by statements that people make now or actions they take now," Burghardt said.

This U.S. concern was not without reason. An affirmative vote would have a profound impact on Taiwan's post-election politics and its relations with the mainland. "A referendum represents the highest direct public opinion. If the U.N. referendum fails to pass, surely it will not be binding for the new president; but if it passes, the new president will have to carry it through. Or else he will violate the spirit of democracy."[208]

The above-quoted comments came from the pro-independence Chinese-language Liberty Times in its "Talking Freely" column. While these comments were made to refute as undemocratic Burghardt's statement that President Chen's planned referendum would unfairly

---

208 Pronouncements of Lord Burghardt, Liberty Times, December 13, 2007

hinder his successor in addressing cross-strait relations, they did help explain why the AIT chairman was worried that the proposed vote could "box in" the new president.

If a majority of this island's 23 million people mandated the use of the name Taiwan to apply for entry into the United Nations, which requires statehood for membership, this would also represent a popular rejection of Beijing's longstanding claim of sovereignty over Taiwan. This would pose a direct challenge to the "one China" position of the mainland authorities. In the worst-case scenario, it could invite military retaliation by Beijing.

On a more realistic level, a majority approval of the U.N. referendum would be a legally binding vote. The new president would have to adopt a policy of applying for U.N. membership under the name "Taiwan" every year. Even though there would be no chance of success, the campaign itself might be provocative enough to infuriate Beijing, as it underscored Taiwan's desire to be accepted by the international community as an independent country separate from China.

What if Taiwan didn't implement this policy to avoid escalating tensions with Beijing? Under Taiwan's democratic system, such inaction due to fear of offending Beijing would be political suicide for any new leader of Taiwan.

At a press conference ahead of his departure from Taiwan, Burghardt also implied that he had brought up the issue of Taiwan's post-election "power transfer" during his discussions with President Chen. "The U.S. does value President Chen's reassurance of keeping his promises and handing over power peacefully no matter who won

Chapter 10
Pushing for a Referendum on Joining the U.N.

the presidential election," he said.

Taiwan's leadership power transfer in the wake of the presidential election became a matter of concern for Washington because of a recent string of inflammatory remarks by Chen Shui-bian.[209] Those remarks caused fears of extreme acts during his remaining time in office.

One of his remarks -- that he considered the possibility of imposing martial law -- caused particular uneasiness. The unease was reinforced by a follow-up comment by Defense Minister Lee Tien-yu. The minister said he would obey a martial law order from the president even if the use of emergency powers failed to win legislative approval. The opposition KMT, in particular, feared that President Chen could use his emergency powers, once imposed, to postpone the legislative elections in January and the March presidential vote.

The fear that Chen could put off the two elections was not purely a matter of speculation. President Chen had frightened voters in a campaign speech that "A KMT-led coalition win of the presidency would not be a transfer of power to another political party, but a transfer of sovereignty." Chen's statements were taken to mean that he could refuse to transfer his power to the new president on the pretext of Taiwan facing an imminent invasion from China, for example.[210]

In Burghardt's meetings with Frank Hsieh of the DPP and Ma Ying-jeou of the KMT, the AIT chairman reportedly obtained a particular commitment from the two presidential candidates. That was, no matter which of them won the election, they would respond

209 Editorial, Why Dirty Tricks Persist, China Times, December 18, 2007.
210 'Black and White' Column, Hidden Intentions Exposed, United Daily News, December 13, 2007.

prudently to the results of the referendum if it was passed.

The pro-independence Liberty Times said in an analysis, "It is a widely known fact that the United States is opposed to the U.N. referendum, but it is also a fact that Taiwan has already launched procedures to hold such a referendum. So the real intent behind the U.S.'s recent strong statements on the issue is to ensure that Ma Ying-jeou or Frank Hsieh will not use the referendum results to further push for writing Taiwan independence into the constitution, or change Taiwan's national title in 2008. In other words, the U.S. can't wait to seek a commitment from Taiwan's new president."[211]

Meanwhile, the China Times, in an article examining Burghardt's talks with the two presidential candidates, had this to say: "What is most important is that the AIT chairman has smoothly secured commitments from both Ma and Hsieh that they will not seek to interpret or elaborate on the results of the referendum' in the wake of the March presidential election."[212]

From Burghardt's remarks at the press conference and media reports on his Taipei visit in December of 2007, one could conclude that Washington's current Taiwan policy focused on the following three tasks:

One, the U.S. had resigned itself to President Chen's insistence on holding the referendum, despite many months of warnings against the vote. But Washington would keep criticizing the referendum as

211 Nadia Tsao, The United States Is Eager to Seek a Commitment from Taiwan's New President, Liberty Times, December 12, 2007
212 Chiang Hui-chen, The United States Has Set the Tone for Taiwan Ahead of Time, the China Times, December 12, 2007

"provocative" and "unnecessarily threatening stability in the Taiwan Strait." By doing so, the U.S. hoped that the island's crisis-weary voters would send the referendum down to defeat.

Two, the Bush administration had begun to treat Chen Shui-bian, whose public approval ratings consistently lingered at around 20 percent, as a caretaker president. Efforts were being made to ensure that Chen would peacefully transfer his presidential powers after Taiwan's new leader was decided on in the March 2008 election.

Washington's third task was to consider measures to deal with the aftermath if the referendum passed. This would include pre-election meetings with the two presidential candidates Ma Ying-jeou and Frank Hsieh, and post-election negotiations with the president-elect. Such efforts had already been launched as the AIT chairman visited Ma and Hsieh and held talks with them during his latest Taipei trip.

By the start of 2008, it had been more than half a year since President Chen Shui-bian formally announced his plan to conduct the U.N. referendum. In the process, the PRC and the U.S. had never for a moment relented in their opposition to the plan. But the president remained unshaken in his determination to carry out the referendum, alongside the March 2008 presidential election. However, most of Taiwan's voters did not seem to agree with him, as shown in public opinion polls.

Ruling Party Suffers Huge Setback at the Polls

In the January 2008 legislative elections, voters delivered a devastating blow to President Chen Shui-bian's DPP, while rewarding the main opposition KMT with a landslide victory.

The results of the election showed the KMT winning 81 seats of the 113-member Legislative Yuan and the DPP retaining only 27 seats. The remaining five seats went to smaller parties and non-affiliated candidates. The overwhelming majority won by the KMT would allow the party to dominate lawmaking in the legislature during the next four years.

The ruling party's humiliating defeat was a fatal blow to a president who already was suffering low public approval ratings and was mired in a string of corruption scandals implicating him, his wife, and his son-in-law. Chen immediately resigned as chairman of the DPP to take responsibility for the electoral setback, saying: "I feel deeply apologetic and ashamed."

The legislative election results were widely seen as a repudiation of President Chen Shui-bian's radical pro-independence policies, especially the highly controversial U.N. referendum initiative, neglecting the economy and other issues of great importance to people's daily lives.

What's also worthy of note was that the January legislative ballot included two other referendums, unrelated to the one on U.N. membership. One was initiated by the ruling party and the other by the opposition. Both failed to reach the required minimum 50 percent turnout of total eligible voters.

The failure of these two referendums, held in conjunction with the legislative elections, augured badly for the fate of the U.N. referendum slated for March in two vital ways. One, the low turnout suggested a lack of popular appetite for referendums. Two, it demonstrated that

Chapter 10
Pushing for a Referendum on Joining the U.N.

Chen's ability to energize voters had diminished. This meant that he might be unable to build momentum for his pet U.N. referendum plan ahead of the March vote, just two months away.

Washington and Beijing, however, did not let up in their opposition to Chen Shui-bian's U.N. referendum. However, the Chinese and U.S. governments changed their strategy, placing greater emphasis on how to prevent the U.N. referendum from being passed by Taiwan's voters, after finding it was unlikely to persuade President Chen to call off the vote.

On February 1, 2008, Taiwan's Central Election Commission formally announced its backing for holding the U.N. referendum initiated by Chen and his party and an alternative referendum by the main opposition KMT. The two competing referendums, the commission declared, would be held on March 22, 2008, the same day as the presidential election. The following are the DPP and KMT referendums in their final version:

The text of the DPP's U.N. referendum read: "In 1971, the People's Republic of China replaced the Republic of China as a member in the United Nations, thus making Taiwan an international orphan. To strongly express the will of the people of Taiwan and to elevate its international status and participation, do you agree with the government to use the name 'Taiwan' to join the United Nations?"

Meanwhile, the KMT-sponsored referendum asked: "Do you agree that our nation should apply to 'return' to the United Nations and join other international organizations based on pragmatic, flexible strategies concerning the use of its name? That is, do you approve of applying to 'return' to the United Nations and to join other international organizations under the 'Republic of China' or 'Taiwan' or other names that are conducive to success, while at the same time preserving our nation's dignity?"

Beijing, like Washington, did not ease its opposition to the Chen- and DPP-backed U.N. referendum because of the governing party's devastating losses in the just-concluded January legislative elections. Shortly after Taiwan's Central Election Commission published the text of the two U.N. referendums, the mainland authorities issued a new warning to Taiwan that it was courting danger and might have to pay a heavy price.

The Chinese Communist Party's Taiwan Work Office and its government counterpart -- the State Council's Taiwan Affairs Office – said in a joint statement that the U.N. referendum was a "ballot on Taiwan independence in a disguised form." The statement warned, "Should this scheme be realized, it would seriously impact relations across the Taiwan Strait, harm the fundamental interests of compatriots on both sides of the strait, and imperil peace and stability in the Asia-Pacific region."

Beijing was referring to the referendum supported by President Chen and the DPP. What was also noticeable was that nowhere in the statement did Beijing express criticism of the KMT-sponsored U.N. referendum.

Why was the KMT spared? From the very beginning, the KMT had made clear its position about why it wanted to follow the example of the DPP in launching a U.N. referendum of its own. There were three major reasons, as gleaned from the remarks and comments that senior KMT officials and legislators had made on various occasions after the party introduced its own U.N. referendum in mid-2007.

First, the KMT needed to come up with an alternative version to compete with the ruling party on the U.N. referendum issue. While Chen and his party's insistence on using the name "Taiwan" to join the United Nations was politically motivated, it was an undeniable fact that the public desire in Taiwan to participate in international organizations had always been strong.

"This being the case, no opposition party or leaders could afford to ignore this public desire without provoking a backlash from the voters. So the KMT had to produce an alternative, or less provocative, program to counter Chen and his party's initiative to use the name Taiwan to join the United Nations." The above remarks were made by KMT Legislator Lo Shih-hsiong to AIT officials in an interview conducted in September 2007.[213]

The interview was held as President Chen was under mounting U.S. pressure to withdraw the referendum plan. Ahead of elections, AIT would traditionally survey ruling and opposition party politicians and other prominent figures for their views on key issues, particularly those involving the interests of the United States.

"If the KMT failed to positively respond to such popular wishes," Legislator Lo added, "it would run the risk of being defeated by the DPP in the coming legislative and presidential elections." The KMT legislator was elected from the southern Taiwan city of Kaohsiung, one of the strongholds of support for Taiwan's independence.

---

213 An AIT cable published by WikiLeaks on its website: A Southern Perspective on the U.N. Referendum Issue, AIT Taipei Office, September 10, 2007

Stressing the importance to the KMT of jumping on the U.N. referendum bandwagon, the same legislator said that the election prospects of the party's presidential candidate Ma Ying-jeou were enhanced by his willingness to introduce a KMT alternative. "No 'old-school' KMT politician would be willing to risk their political fortunes by initiating or advocating a citizen referendum," said the legislator.

The second reason why the KMT's referendum did not prompt as much criticism from the U.S. and the PRC was that it was different from the DPP's on one key point. The KMT, while also seeking to participate in the U.N., did not insist on doing so under the name Taiwan.

"The pan-blue camp (the KMT and allied political groups) and the pan-green bloc (the DPP and its supporters) share the same goal of helping Taiwan re-enter the U.N. But we should use a name that would not be viewed as an attempt to separate Taiwan from China, breaking the trust of Taiwan's friends," said Ma Ying-jeou in late June of 2007, when his party formally unveiled its plan to hold a referendum on U.N. participation.[214]

Ma went on to say that Taiwan had joined the WTO (World Trade Organization) under the name "The Separate Customs Territory of Taiwan, Penghu, Kinmen, and Matsu" and APEC as Chinese Taipei. In light of these past examples, he said, "The government should be more flexible on the use of the name in participating in international organizations."

---

214 Mo Yan-chih and Ko Shu-ling, KMT to Hold Referendum on U.N. Bid, Taipei Times, June 29, 2007

Chapter 10
Pushing for a Referendum on Joining the U.N.

And third, the KMT-sponsored U.N. referendum in a certain sense was just "a means, not an end." In other words, the KMT alternative was aimed at diluting the support for the DPP's referendum, in the hope that in the end, neither referendum would be able to gain enough votes for passage. If this tactic succeeded, senior KMT politicians said, Taiwan could avoid inviting a potential threat to its security.

The KMT's intention of diluting voter support for the DPP-initiated referendum was revealed by Wu Po-hsiung, party chairman, during a meeting with AIT Director Stephen Young on July 27, one month after the competing referendum was unveiled.

According to an AIT cable, the key points of Chairman Wu's conversation with Young were as follows: "KMT leaders fully understood that the DPP was using its U.N. referendum to promote 'Taiwan identity' and to draw green voters to the polls. In response, we believe the best strategy is to dilute support for the DPP referendum by offering voters a KMT alternative. Voters will support the DPP or KMT version, but not both, thus increasing the likelihood that neither one will pass. The KMT does not want any of the proposed referenda, including our own, to pass. But what we care most is that the KMT could not let the DPP referendum go unchallenged."[215]

At the end of the meeting, Director Young told Chairman Wu that "the U.S. supports Taiwan's democracy but wished to avoid actions that could damage U.S.-PRC-Taiwan relations." Chairman Wu then replied that the KMT "continues to view the U.S. as Taiwan's most important

---

215 KMT Chairman Wu Po-hsiung calls on AIT Taipei Director Stephen Young, KMT Referendum a Means, Not an End, AIT cable dated August 1, 2007

political, economic and military ally, and urged Washington to view the KMT referendum as consonant with U.S. efforts to keep Taiwan's democratic process from touching on sensitive sovereignty-related matters."

U.N. Referendum as Tool to Attract Voters

In a survey undertaken in mid-September of 2007, AIT/Kaohsiung officials also interviewed DPP politicians, including Legislator Guan Bi-ling, who was elected from the southern port city. According to the same AIT cable posted on the internet by WikiLeaks, Legislator Guan admitted to her interviewers that the U.N. referendum was a controversial issue. But she quickly added, "It can also attract and solidify voters. Focusing on Taiwan identity issues is a standard operating procedure for the DPP during elections." She went on to argue that "The DPP has numbers to prove that throwing out this kind of 'provocative' topic during an important election always gains votes for the party."

What the DPP legislator said indeed was true. But those were things of the past. Legislator Guan failed to foresee a range of new challenges facing President Chen and the DPP. They included shifting public opinion, increasingly harsh U.S. criticism of Taiwan, more precisely the Chen administration, and party presidential candidate Frank Hsieh's lukewarm support for their own U.N. referendum. These challenges combined to make the DPP's past strategy of using "provocative issues" to boost voter support no longer workable for the party in the 2008 legislative and presidential elections.

Chapter 10
Pushing for a Referendum on Joining the U.N.

The first challenge was that, increasingly, the DPP-initiated U.N referendum was viewed by the public, including many centrist voters, as a "fake proposal." In their view, it was nothing more than an election ploy. The reason for this public perception was that it was widely known that most people in Taiwan wanted participation in international organizations, including the United Nations.

This being the case, why was it necessary for the DPP government to call a vote to ask them whether to join the U.N. using the name Taiwan? And even if the referendum passed, it would not do anything to boost Taiwan's chance of success, as the overwhelming majority of the more than 190 U.N. members agreed with Beijing's "one China" position and the PRC had veto power in the U.N. Security Council.

Wu Chao-yu, KMT chairman in Tainan City, was quoted by AIT officials in the same September interview survey as saying: "The referendum issue is all about politics...and politics only. President Chen, potentially facing post-election indictment on charges of corruption in office, will do anything and say anything to keep his party in the presidential seat. If the DPP loses, Chen knows he will do prison time."

Professor Hsin Tsui-ling, a political scientist at National Sun Yat-sen University, was also suspicious of the DPP's motives. According to the AIT cable, the professor felt that the DPP "is using the referendum issue simply to shift the focus of public attention from a weak economy to ideological issues to boost the party's chances of winning the presidency in the March 2008 election."

Public dissatisfaction with Chen Shui-bian's political manipulation finally grew into an island-wide campaign in late 2007 to boycott referendums. The first casualties of the campaign organized by civil society groups were the two referendums unrelated to the U.N. but seen as part of a partisan political fight. Both were rejected by voters in the January legislative elections.

The boycott movement gathered strength with the approach of the March 22 presidential election. Ten days before the polling day, opposition KMT Chairman Wu Po-hsiung urged supporters to vote for the KMT referendum and boycott the DPP version.[216]

A second challenge that DPP Legislator Guan Bi-ling failed to foresee was the potential effect of Washington's new approach of appealing directly to Taiwan's voters.

As discussed in earlier pages, senior U.S. officials had in succession criticized President Chen's U.N. referendum since its launch in June 2007, and called on Taiwan's voters to be cautious about the severe implications of a "yes" vote.

Recent criticisms were made by AIT Taipei Director Stephen Young in November, and his boss AIT Chairman Burghardt in December at their respective press conferences in Taipei.

Some of their remarks made on the two occasions were particularly blunt, as noted earlier. Burghardt, at his meeting with Taiwan's media, said that "it was obvious Taiwan stood no chance of joining the United Nations even if the referendum passed next March, (but) what the vote would do was cause trouble.'"

Young told Taiwan reporters, "We believe this referendum poses

216 David G. Brown, Taiwan Voters Set a New Course, Comparative Connections, April 2008

Chapter 10
Pushing for a Referendum on Joining the U.N.

a threat to cross-strait stability. So we call upon Taiwan's politicians and voters to adopt a careful and moderate approach to cross-strait relations, and to avoid risky acts that cannot help Taiwan's actual international status."

Burghardt and Young's remarks, made in Taipei, as well as comments from other senior U.S. officials in Washington, ultimately achieved the desired effect of raising public awareness of the grave consequences that President Chen's U.N. referendum could have for Taiwan. Such awareness, in turn, made people think twice before voting for the DPP's U.N. referendum. That ultimately rendered ineffective the DPP's traditional policy of using radical political advocacies to boost voter support.

A third major challenge that DPP Legislator Guan Bi-ling failed to anticipate was the likelihood that the U.N. referendum would pose a conflict of interest for the party's presidential candidate Frank Hsieh. Hsieh, as a longtime advocate of Taiwan's independence and the standard-bearer of the DPP, had the responsibility of actively promoting the referendum on the campaign trail.

However, Hsieh needed to adopt a moderate political stance to broaden his support and attract middle-of-the-road voters. From the very beginning of the campaign, he had been lagging behind KMT presidential candidate Ma Ying-jeou.

Faced with this dilemma, Hsieh initially tried to tread a path that would allow him to neither disappoint his party's core supporters nor lose centrist voters. This, of course, was not an easy task.

Hsieh then sought to overcome his predicament by negotiating a less provocative, bipartisan referendum with the KMT and its presidential candidate Ma. But his suggestion was rejected after he failed to meet two demands raised by the opposition. One was that the DPP first withdrew its potentially disastrous U.N. referendum. Two, the ruling party would have to de-link any bipartisan referendum from the presidential election.

In the end, Hsieh was neither able to wholeheartedly tout the party's referendum on the campaign trail nor cast himself as a moderate DPP politician to win over independent voters.

Hsieh's inability to overcome this dilemma hampered his effort to elicit public support for his candidacy and his party's U.N. referendum. This was yet another factor that the DPP's Guan Bi-ling failed to anticipate in her conclusion that "provocative topics" always worked well for the party in important elections.

On March 22, 2008, Taiwan's voters made their final decisions at the ballot box. They blocked both the DPP-initiated U.N. referendum and the KMT alternative by giving their bills insufficient support to pass the legal thresholds. After the final results came in, the Central Election Commission declared the two referendums invalid due to low turnout. Taiwan's Plebiscite Law requires that for a referendum to become valid, it must cross two thresholds. First, more than 50 percent of total eligible voters need to cast a ballot, and second, of those who vote on the referendum, more than half must do so affirmatively.

For the KMT, the results were not a disappointment. Ten days before the vote, the KMT had made it clear that while voters were encouraged to reject the DPP-sponsored referendum, the party could accept a failure of its referendum.

But for the DPP, the U.N. referendum results were a major setback.

Chapter 10
Pushing for a Referendum on Joining the U.N.

The ruling party had persistently pushed its referendum up until election day in defiance of vehement opposition from the PRC and the United States. President Chen and the DPP had held high hopes for the referendum's passage.

The logic behind this was simple. A yes vote would have represented a majority of the people supporting using the name Taiwan to apply for U.N. membership. Moreover, it would have enabled President Chen and the DPP to treat it as a mandate to legitimately promote an independent Taiwan identity, separate from China.

The results of the presidential election were even more devastating for the DPP. Voters dumped the party's presidential candidate Frank Hsieh and gave KMT Ma Ying-jeou an overwhelming victory. Ma won 58 percent of the total votes cast, while Hsieh received 42 percent.

The KMT's landslide victory in the presidential vote came close on the heels of a sweeping success by the party in the January legislative elections and followed the KMT's convincing win in the 2005 local elections.

Political analysts and commentators saw the DPP's consecutive electoral defeats from local to central government levels as demonstrating widespread popular discontent with President Chen Shui-bian and his party. People in growing numbers had come to see Chen and the government he led as incompetent, impractical, and corrupt.

The DPP's heavy losses in the local, legislative, and presidential elections also appeared to reflect a shifting of public attitudes toward Taiwan's independence movement. According to political research, the movement for Taiwan's independence underwent a drastic upsurge in 2000, accompanied by independence advocate Chen Shui-bian's ascent to power in that year. The movement grew with Chen's reelection in 2004.

Yet this ideological high tide soon moved out during Chen's second term amid a string of election defeats for his party. Nowhere was it more evident than in the party's failure to retain the presidency in the 2008 election against a moderate politician.

Even more significant was that Ma Ying-jeou and his KMT had focused their campaign on improving relations with the Chinese mainland while Chen Shui-bian and the DPP intentionally antagonized Beijing as payback for Beijing's imposition of its "one-China" policy on Taiwan.

Chapter 11
Chen Shui-bian's Legacy as President

Deepening Democracy

During his final years in office, Chen Shui-bian often liked to expound on his views of his accomplishments during his eight years as president, and this was especially true when his audience was the international media. He often said that "deepening Taiwan's democracy" and "raising a Taiwan-centric consciousness" were the two achievements he was most proud of.

A third area that the former president was less inclined to mention was his highly controversial mainland, or cross-strait, policy. Throughout his eight-year presidency, he maintained tight controls on travel exchanges as well as trade and investment. Many critics said had he adopted a liberal policy on such economic and civil exchanges, it would have contributed considerably to Taiwan's economic well-being and the improvement of bilateral relations.

This concluding chapter assesses each of the three crucial areas mentioned above in greater detail. In the view of this author, those controversial policies are the most important legacy of Chen Shui-bian's presidency from 2000 to 2008.

In November 2006, Chen Shui-bian gave an interview to the Financial Times. The British newspaper's Taipei correspondent Kathrin Hille asked the president: "How do you define your role in history? What are your contributions and achievements for Taiwan?"[217]

According to an interview transcript, President Chen's answers were as follows: "Having been able to let a…party [referring to the KMT] which ruled in Taiwan for more than 50 years become the opposition party, complete the change of ruling party…"

"I don't dare say that's my biggest contribution toward Taiwan, but at least we have left our trace on Taiwan's road from authoritarianism to democracy. In the process of Taiwan's democratization, we have never wronged the people. So completing the first change of ruling party in history, (making) Taiwan a democratic country, at least this is something we can proudly present to the Taiwan people."

This is generally true. Chen Shui-bian and his Democratic Progressive Party made significant contributions to Taiwan's democratic reforms. However, Chen's democratic legacy also had a downside, and that will be examined in detail later on.

First, the discussion focuses on the positive aspects. In the presidential election of 2000, Chen Shui-bian was the standard bearer for the DPP -- an opposition party that was only some 14 years old at the time. Yet he defeated his rival Lien Chan of the KMT, which had governed Taiwan without interruption following the island's reversion from Japanese rule at the end of World War Two.

Chen won the 2000 election by only a narrow margin, but his victory carried two important democratic meanings. One, his triumph

---

217 Kathrin Hille, Interview transcript: Chen Shui-bian, Financial Times, November 2, 2006.

resulted in the termination of the KMT's more than half-century of authoritarian rule in Taiwan. It was Chen Shui-bian, an advocate of freedom and democracy, who inspired the people to vote out the long-entrenched KMT, breaking the party's monopoly on political power.

Two, as Chen's 2000 election victory legitimately replaced the KMT as the ruling party, the change ushered in a competitive two-party democratic system for Taiwan.

The Role the DPP Plays in Taiwan's Democratization

But it would be unjust, or at least incomplete, to discuss Chen Shui-bian's contribution to Taiwan's democratization without mentioning the role played by his party in this vital area, alongside two former KMT leaders and presidents, Chiang Ching-kuo and Lee Teng-hui.

The contributions of the DPP were fundamental to Taiwan's democracy. The party's push for political and democratic reform can be traced back to the mid-1970s when opponents of the KMT-ruled government launched a movement to press for greater political participation.

At that time, the formation of alternative political parties was forbidden. Hence, many opposition politicians were forced to run for public office as independents. These independents were classified in the media as the Tangwai, literally meaning they were politicians outside the ruling party -- the KMT. Many leaders and organizers of the Tangwai movement, as it was known, later worked together to form the DPP in the mid-1980s.

These Tangwai politicians used their limited number of seats in the Legislative Yuan to offer an alternative to the KMT. Outside the lawmaking body, they frequently organized large-scale pro-democracy rallies around Taiwan. The various pro-democracy activities carried out by the Tangwai politicians gradually brought forth an ever-expanding opposition force.

Increasing pressure from these political opponents prompted then-President Chiang Ching-kuo to speed up political reform. The most significant change undertaken by Chiang was the lifting of martial law in mid-1987. Martial law was imposed by Chiang Ching-kuo's father, President Chiang Kai-shek, in the late 1940s during the "Period of Mobilization for the Suppression of Communist Rebellion." The law, among other things, banned the formation of political parties and new investments in newspapers. By lifting martial law, the younger Chiang effectively removed two stifling barriers to Taiwan's democratic development.

After Chiang Ching-kuo died in 1988, his hand-picked vice president, Lee Teng-hui, took over as president and chairman of the KMT. During his 12-year presidency, Lee Teng-hui implemented two vital reforms. One was to fully open the Legislative Yuan to the electoral process so that all seats were filled through the popular vote. This was made possible by retiring all the elderly members selected from the Chinese mainland in the 1940s.

The other vital reform was to change the presidential election system to direct election. Previously, the ROC president was elected indirectly by national assemblymen with constituencies mainly on the mainland. With the adoption of the reform, the ROC president was elected by the people of Taiwan.

Chapter 11
Chen Shui-bian's Legacy as President

Lee Teng-hui himself was directly elected in 1996 for a four-year term. So despite the less-than-democratic system that installed Lee as president in his first two terms of office, the final four years of Lee's presidency could hardly be described as authoritarian rule.

By acknowledging the democratic achievements of Chiang Ching-kuo and Lee Teng-hui, this author is not seeking to diminish the contribution of Chen Shui-bian to the construction of Taiwan's democracy. Ending the lengthy rule of the KMT through the ballot box and consolidating Taiwan's two-party political system was instrumental in the transition to true democracy.

However, democracy is not just about elections and winning political power. It requires public officeholders to abide by the law and resist the temptations of corruption -- the basic qualities needed to ensure effective and efficient governance.

When held to this standard, it can be said that Chen Shui-bian did more harm than good to Taiwan's democracy during his presidency. Two salient examples are given below to show how Chen's presidency harmed Taiwan's democracy:

Using 'Deepening Democracy' to Pursue Independence

Chen Shui-bian frequently used the pretext of "deepening democracy" to advance his pro-independence agenda, especially during his second term. In late 2007 and early 2008 -- less than a year before his term of office expired -- Chen Shui-bian stepped up his efforts to promote a U.N.-related referendum. Voters were asked whether they supported the government's use of the name Taiwan to apply for admission to the United Nations.

The U.N. referendum met with strong opposition from mainland China and the United States. But Chen Shui-bian countered with the argument that his U.N. referendum was a key component of democracy and that holding referenda to let people express their views on public issues was an important way to 'deepen democracy.'"

Yet U.S. officials refuted his argument. Deputy Assistant Secretary of State for East Asian and Pacific Affairs Thomas Christensen, for example, described Chen's planned referendum as a "bad public policy initiative" that was "wrapped in the flag of democracy."

Christensen said, "DPP leaders undertook the U.N. referendum, including using the name of Taiwan because they believed it would help them in the 2008 elections."

Richard C. Bush III of the Brookings Institution shared that view and was similarly blunt in his criticism of Chen Shui-bian's "deepening democracy" argument. "The U.N. referendum was pushed to boost the DPP's election prospects and advance its political causes," he said.[218]

In addition to using the pretext of "deepening democracy" to promote political aims, Chen Shui-bian also damaged Taiwan's democracy by using his presidential influence to take bribes while in office.

He was found guilty in four corruption cases. They included

---

218 Richard C. Bush, U.S.-Taiwan Relations: What's the Problem? Brookings, December 3, 2007

taking bribes in a land procurement deal, receiving payment for an appointment to office, accepting bribes from a financial firm, and offenses related to money laundering.

All these four corruption cases also involved his wife Wu Shu-chen. But Mrs. Chen was also convicted of taking bribes in yet another case linked to the construction of an exhibition hall. Although the fifth case did not involve the president, it was focused on charges that his wife used her status as first lady to obtain bribes.

For these corruption offenses, both the president and the first lady were sentenced to 20 years in jail—the maximum prison time allowed in their situation.

By using political influence to take bribes from businessmen and private companies, Chen Shui-bian undermined the integrity not only of his presidential office but also of other democratic institutions. The erosion of government integrity made government agencies less transparent and less capable of preventing corruption. Chen's presidency weakened Taiwan's democracy, instead of deepening it, as he often claimed.

Raising Taiwan-Centric Consciousness

During an interview with the Washington Post in mid-2007, less than a year before he left office, Chen Shui-bian cited the rise in Taiwan-centric consciousness as the other key achievement of his presidency beyond the strengthening of democracy.

The interview was with the newspaper's Taipei correspondent, Edward Cody. Two of the questions -- and the president's answers --

are provided below:

"Q: I understand that the people have the right to decide. But do you think that this feeling of Taiwanese national identity is all finished already and that the people have decided in their minds what they want or not?"

"A: Taiwan is a democratic and pluralist society, and it would therefore be impossible for everyone to hold the same view on everything…Nonetheless, thanks to our hard work in the past seven years, we have seen Taiwan-centric consciousness present itself as a mainstream value in our society…

"The rise of Taiwan-centric consciousness is reflected in the growth and decline in the number of people who see themselves, respectively, as Taiwanese and not Chinese, and as Chinese and not Taiwanese. In 2000, when I first became president of this country, opinion polls showed that 36 percent of people in Taiwan considered themselves to be Taiwanese. By last November, this figure had risen to 60 percent, and, in the first half of this year, it had increased further to 68 percent."

"Q: Would you, looking back now in the final year of your presidency, with only nine months or so left in your second term, would you say this is your legacy? Is this what you want people to think of as what you brought about as president of Taiwan?"

"A: Of course, enabling Taiwan-centric consciousness to rise, grow strong, and become a mainstream value in society is one of the achievements during my eight years as president, (something) of which I am proud…

"The weightiest, most serious problem we face, however, is

national identity. I think that with the upsurge of Taiwan-centric consciousness, and it's becoming a mainstream value held by the majority of people in society, we can gradually build up the power of a united society. Only thereby can we become a normal country, because Taiwan-centric consciousness has the power to resolve divergent senses of national identity."

In reply to another question in the same Washington Post interview, Chen stated: "But now we have Taiwan-centric consciousness to counter the one-China principle of Beijing. Having Taiwan-centric consciousness means identifying with Taiwan and recognizing that this sovereign state of Taiwan and the PRC are independent of each other."

There is no doubt over Chen Shui-bian's contribution to the rise of Taiwan-centric consciousness. "Chen Shui-bian certainly played a role in the shifting of Taiwan society's attitudes toward ethnic identity. The island-wide de-sinicization campaign which he pushed during his presidency, for example, brought about a swift increase in the number of people identifying themselves as Taiwanese, rather than Chinese," said Chang Rong-gong, a political analyst and former ranking KMT official.

According to various public opinion polls, Chen's other political programs, launched as part of his bid for a second term in the March 2004 presidential election and promoted during his time in office, also helped expand the ranks of those identifying themselves as Taiwanese. The measures employed in this campaign included holding Taiwan's first referendum, writing a new constitution, and name rectification for the island.

Still, Chen appeared to have overstated his contribution when he cited "enabling Taiwan-centric consciousness to rise, grow strong and become a mainstream value in society" as one of his major achievements.

Three Natural Factors in the Rise of Taiwan Consciousness

The growing strength of Taiwan-centric consciousness has been a natural and longstanding trend. This trend has resulted from Taiwan's increasing democratization, its long-time divide with the Chinese mainland, and Beijing's sustained hostility toward Taiwan.

According to a United Daily News annual tracking and public opinion survey on the identity issue, the number of people who identified themselves as Taiwanese kept climbing in the 20 years from 1996 when the newspaper first started collecting this kind of data.

In that year, the number of people in Taiwan who saw themselves as Taiwanese stood at 44 percent. By 2006, this figure had risen to 55 percent and by 2016 it had increased further to 73 percent. By comparison, the ratio of those who considered themselves Chinese had dropped to 11 percent from 31 percent 20 years ago.

Below is a brief analysis of how each of the previously raised three factors contributed to the growth of Taiwan-centric consciousness:

First, why growing democratization contributed to the rise of Taiwan-centric consciousness: "This has been the case because practicing democracy has inevitably led to Taiwanization or localization," said former DPP Legislator Hung Ji-chang who, like many others, agreed that democratization was the single most important factor in the growing number of residents identifying with Taiwan.[219]

That's certainly the case. With an invigorated democracy, candidates running for public office had to campaign with policies that addressed issues of concern to their constituencies in Taiwan, if they hoped to win.

In other words, they had to consider things from the perspective of Taiwan and identify with this island when conducting their campaigns. This reversed tradition when public-office contenders were subject to the constraints of the government's one-China policy.

In addition to overstating his contribution, Chen Shui-bian in the same Washington Post interview also misrepresented the significance of the rise of Taiwan-centric consciousness when he said: "Having Taiwan-centric consciousness means identifying with Taiwan and recognizing this sovereign state of Taiwan and the PRC are independent of each other."

This was not entirely true. People who identify with Taiwan or consider themselves Taiwanese do not necessarily support all of Chen's pro-independence views. Otherwise, Chen's party would have won the 2008 legislative elections and the presidential race, instead of being handed a humiliating defeat by voters.

Second, the rise of Taiwan-centric sentiments also has much to do with the longstanding political divide between the mainland and this

---

219 Huang Kuo-liang, Taiwan's Shifting Identification, United Daily News, March 14, 2016.

island.

Taiwan's political divide has a long history dating back to 1949 when Chiang Kai-shek and his government retreated to Taiwan after its defeat at the hands of the communists.

In the first two decades after the KMT government retreated to Taiwan, Chiang Kai-shek's policies were focused on retaking the mainland from the communists. Yet Chiang's "China-centered" policy was gradually revised by his son, Chiang Ching-kuo, after he took power, first as premier (from 1972 to 1978) and then as president (from 1978 until he died in 1988).

Chiang Ching-kuo shifted government priorities to the development of Taiwan. He did so when it was becoming increasingly apparent that there was no immediate prospect of retaking the mainland.

"The younger Chiang understood that whatever the formal slogans might be, the reality was that the ROC government was in Taiwan and was not likely to be leaving soon," observed William H. Gleysteen, Jr., former deputy chief of the U.S. Embassy on Taiwan.[220]

During his years in office, Chiang Ching-kuo concentrated his time and energy on promoting economic development and political reform in Taiwan. His signature "Ten Major Construction Projects" -- including highway and railway systems, an airport and seaport, as well as a petrochemical complex -- helped sustain Taiwan's high economic growth and create the widely hailed "Taiwan economic miracle."

In the final years of his presidency, Chiang Ching-kuo built on

---

220 Chiang Ching-kuo Dies at 77, Ending a Dynasty on Taiwan, the New York Times, January 13, 1988.

those achievements by dismantling martial law and lifting a ban on the formation of new political parties, removing the two most significant impediments to democratic reform.[221]

So it can be said that when Chiang Ching-kuo decided to revise his father's "China-centered" policy and shift emphasis to developing Taiwan, a "Taiwan-centric" concept and strategy had been born amid the island's prolonged political standoff with mainland China.

Chiang Ching-kuo's "Taiwan-centric" strategy was further consolidated by his successor Lee Teng-hui. It was Lee who coined the term "Taiwan First" in handling cross-strait relations. Lee went far beyond adopting the "Taiwan First" posture. During his 12-year tenure as president, Lee consolidated Taiwan's status as a political identity separate from mainland China via a combination of constitutional amendments, executive measures, and Supreme Court interpretations.

The separate political identity of Taiwan was manifested in the highlights of the legal changes as seen below:[222]

First, the ROC government "does not dispute" the fact that Beijing controls mainland China. The point of "does not dispute..." represented a crucial concession on the part of the ROC government, as it amounted to abandoning Taipei's constitutionally prescribed claim of sovereignty over mainland China.

Second, the ROC government acknowledges the fact that it only effectively exercises jurisdiction over Taiwan and its offshore islands

---

221 John F. Copper, A Quiet Revolution: Political Development in the Republic of China, Ethics and Public Policy Center
222 Huang Kuo-liang, Shifting Identity: Who Caused the Tragedy? United Daily News, March 14, 2016.

of Penghu, Kinmen, and Matsu. This acknowledgment was nothing less than a declaration that Taiwan had become a separate entity on its own, rather than a subordinate part of China.

Third, as a central part of the constitutional amendments, the system for selecting the president was changed from indirect to direct elections. This constitutional revision carried rich democratic and political meanings.

As noted earlier, the president had been elected by national assemblymen--those who were selected on the mainland before Chiang Kai-shek withdrew to Taiwan. After the constitutional amendments, the president was elected directly by the residents of Taiwan.

Lee Teng-hui, the last indirectly elected president, also became the first directly elected president under the newly reformed election system, marking a milestone in Taiwan's democratic development.

According to the Chinese-language United Daily News, Lee told CNN in an interview upon his reelection that "Taiwan has become an independent country; it is called the Republic of China."

A look at the CNN news website for what exactly Lee Teng-hui said in the interview found a March 1996 article entitled "Why Beijing Fears Taiwan's Lee Teng-hui." Lee was not directly quoted on the subject in question. Instead, the article began with a quotation from a National Taiwan University professor, Wu Yu-shan.

"If you ask the people of Taiwan whether Taiwan…is a sovereign nation, everyone will say 'Yes,' so Lee has made people feel good. At last, we can say what we are."

Also notable was Lee's "special state-to-state relationship" theory, which he first espoused in July 1999, toward the end of his final term, as a description of the relations between Taiwan and the mainland.

The description made public in an interview with German broadcast media Deutsche Welle, not only infuriated Beijing, which condemned Lee as a "splitter," but also upset Washington, which demanded clarification from Taipei. Lee was pressured to back off from his assertion two months later.

It should be noted that while Lee Teng-hui and Chen Shui-bian both supported independence for Taiwan, their approaches toward that goal varied greatly.

Chen held the view that "with Taiwan and China on the two sides of the Taiwan Strait, each side is a country." What's more, he also believed that Taiwan should "write a new constitution" and seek "name rectification" to become a "normal" country.

Lee Teng-hui, on the other hand, described his position as follows: "Taiwan is already a sovereign country, officially called the Republic of China." Lee based his claim on a series of key constitutional amendments carried out during his presidency.

"In my view, Taiwan already enjoys de jure independence. That is why I have never advocated independence," Lee said in his book My Remaining Life: My Life's Journey and the Road of Taiwan's Democratization."

In sum, be it Chiang Ching-kuo's "Taiwan-centered" strategy, Lee Teng-hui's "special state-to-state relationship" theory, or Chen Shui-bian's "each side is a country" advocacy, they all evolved, in part, from the longstanding political divide between Taiwan and the mainland.

A third major factor in the rise of Taiwan-centric consciousness was Beijing's longstanding military threat to Taiwan -- marked by the large numbers of missiles targeted at this island -- and its unrelenting efforts to isolate Taipei diplomatically and internationally.

Such hostile political and military policies have only served to fuel resentment toward the mainland and spread nationalist feelings in Taiwan, gradually creating a shared sense of security and destiny among the residents.

Nationalism has often been brought up and exploited by politicians in election campaigns. In the 1998 mayoral race in Taipei, for example, then-incumbent Chen Shui-bian drew attention to his opponent Ma Ying-jeou's mainland background, insinuating that as a mainlander, Ma could not fully identify with local issues in Taipei.

Chen's remarks prompted then-president and KMT chairman Lee Teng-hui to step in to defend Ma Ying-jeou. He responded to Chen's charges by coining the "New Taiwanese" concept.

Lee said: "It did not matter whether people were Taiwanese or mainlanders, and that so long as they were committed to Taiwan's continued progress, they should be seen as part of the new people of Taiwan." This formulation took some of the sting out of Chen's attacks on Ma and contributed to the KMT candidate's eventual victory in the election.[223]

---

223 Bruce Dickson and Chao Chien-min, Assessing the Lee Teng-hui Legacy in Taiwan's Politics, Routledge, first published in 2002.

Chapter 11
Chen Shui-bian's Legacy as President

Failing to Separate Political Feuds from Economic Exchanges

In May 2000 when Chen Shui-bian began his first term, he made improving relations with the mainland a top priority of his presidency. Relations between the two sides had long been tense under KMT administrations – part of the political fallout from the Chinese civil war fought on the mainland during the late 1940s.

The primary goal of Chen Shui-bian's mainland policy, as Taiwan's first non-KMT president, was to restore longstanding deadlocked political dialogue with Beijing and normalize trade and economic exchanges across the Taiwan Strait by lifting blanket bans and restrictions imposed during those early years.

The need for Chen to reinstate political dialogue and liberalize economic exchanges with the Chinese mainland was obvious and pressing. The mainland was becoming increasingly important for Taiwan as both an export market and an investment destination. Yet decades-old policies of "no talk" and "no contact" under the former KMT administrations had continued to impede trade and business activities with the mainland.

Although KMT leaders had taken steps to ease exchanges with the mainland, they were far short of what was needed to meet growing demand, particularly from the domestic business community. The most stifling controls in place were those on cross-strait transport, trade, and postal exchanges – known as the "three links."

As a result of these restrictions, travel, cargo, and investment all had to be routed through third locations, such as Hong Kong or Macau.

For Taiwanese and multinational companies doing business across the strait, those detours meant higher costs and lost competitiveness.

Chen Shui-bian was in a position to do something about these problems. Backed by a popular mandate and aided by his non-KMT background, he resolved to liberalize those sectors to allow cross-strait economic activities to be conducted directly. Chen hoped to put these liberalizations in place before the next presidential election in 2004 when he would run for a second term. He wanted to use successes in these key areas to demonstrate to voters his ability to improve relations with Taiwan's longtime foe Beijing.

But by mid-2008 when Chen finished his second term, he had delivered on none of those promises. Strict trade, investment, transport, and travel restrictions still had been kept in place. He did make some minor changes during his eight years in office, but they fell well short of expectations, unable to solve the difficulties faced by companies and individuals doing cross-strait business.

The biggest barrier to the full normalization of relations between Taiwan and the mainland has been the longstanding national sovereignty dispute between the two sides. While such political controversy has persisted for many years, it became even more serious and complicated after Chen Shui-bian and his pro-independence party, the DPP, came to power in 2000.

Beijing maintains that "there is only one China, and that Taiwan is part of China." Chen Shui-bian and his party, on the other hand, held the position that "Taiwan is an independent, sovereign country," separate from China.

Beijing insisted that Chen and his administration had to accept the one-China principle before contact could be resumed between the two sides. Yet for Chen, accepting the one-China principle would amount to sacrificing Taiwan's sovereignty. So he and the DPP firmly refused to accept the PRC's demand.

In the first more than two years of his presidency starting from May 20, 2000, Chen's relations with Beijing could be described essentially as calm and stable, thanks to the well-known "five noes," or the commitment to refrain from pursuing independence.

Launching 'Mini Three Links'

In early 2001, some eight months into his presidency, Chen Shui-bian took the initiative to launch what he called the "mini three links" across the strait. Under this program, a direct shipping route was opened between Taiwan's outlying islands of Kinmen and Matsu and mainland ports in Fujian province.

The willingness of the Chen administration to open the "mini three links" was because these did not involve the main island of Taiwan and were less sensitive in sovereignty terms. The "mini three links" were announced unilaterally by Taipei, without any prior discussion with the mainland side. Beijing, while suspicious of Chen's motives, grudgingly agreed to reciprocal liberalizing measures.

But the "mini three links" could provide only very limited transport services, unable to satisfy the actual needs of travel and trade across the strait. Moreover, passengers and cargo going to and from Taiwan proper still had to pass through the government-designated "mid-point" ports before reaching their final destinations. Such mid-point transport services caused considerable inconvenience for travel and trade.

As a result, calls for the government to fully liberalize the full "three links" remained strong. Yet establishing such direct cross-strait exchanges required Taiwan and the mainland to discuss how to overcome the vexing sovereignty hurdles.

In mid-2002, the Chen administration attempted to authorize private institutions to negotiate full "three links" with the mainland, hoping to model them on an extended air services agreement it had just signed with Hong Kong – which had become a Special Administrative Region of China. Beijing responded positively, saying the mainland side would not require any private groups that were authorized to handle transport negotiations to accept the one-China principle. However, it insisted that any cross-strait air and sea connections had to be treated as "domestic routes."

But the "domestic routes" request was flatly rejected by the Chen administration as "a back-door way to obtain Taipei's indirect acceptance of Beijing's one-China principle."[224]

So even the approach of using unofficial channels failed to help the two sides overcome their differences over the one-China principle. Bilateral relations thus remained deadlocked until Chen Shui-bian left office in May 2008 and transferred power to his successor, Ma Ying-jeou of the KMT.

(Note: Ma Ying-jeou arrived at common ground with the

---

224 David G. Brown, Chen Muddies Cross-Strait Waters, Asian Studies of the John Hopkins School, September 2002.

mainland's leadership on the one-China dispute by returning to a cross-strait agreement reached in 1992. This agreement, which later came to be known as the "92 Consensus," acknowledged there is only one China, but allowed each side to define the meaning of one China. The aim and spirit of the "92 Consensus" was to allow Taiwan and the mainland to set aside their long-held disagreement over sovereignty in order to promote economic and civil exchanges across the strait.)

Missing a Golden Opportunity to Mend PRC Ties

The start of a second term in May 2004 provided Chen Shui-bian with a golden opportunity to repair relations with Beijing after he made significant concessions in his second inaugural address.[225]

The concessions in Chen's 2004 inaugural address included deliberate omissions of his provocative "one country on each side of the strait" slogan and a call to write a controversial new constitution for Taiwan.

Chen also expressed a desire to improve strained relations with the mainland. "If both sides are willing, on the basis of goodwill, to create an environment engendered upon 'peaceful development' and 'freedom of choice,' then in the future, the Republic of China and the People's Republic of China -- or Taiwan and China -- can seek to establish relations in any form whatsoever," he said. "We would not exclude any possibility, so long as there is the consent of the 23 million

---

225 Presidential Office of the Republic of China, President Chen's Inaugural Address: Paving the Way for a Sustainable Taiwan, May 20, 2004.

people of Taiwan..."

Chen's statements won him high praise from the United States. The Bush administration from the White House to the State Department simultaneously welcomed his inaugural remarks as "responsible" and "constructive."

As for Beijing, despite its reservations about Chen Shui-bian's political concessions, it did not flatly reject his peace overtures. At least, the cross-strait atmosphere had become less strained than in the past four years.

So the start of Chen Shui-bian's second term in May 2004 was widely seen as a good opportunity to mend ties with Beijing and downplay politics in the interest of economic exchanges.

But Chen soon infuriated Beijing by launching a series of pro-independence programs. Some of them were new while others were merely updated versions of previous efforts. Chen's new provocations and the mainland's reaction continued to strain cross-strait relations in his second four-year term, increasing the difficulty of loosening restrictions on trade and economic interchanges.

Overall, Chen Shui-bian deserved praise for taking a string of liberalizing steps, mostly in his first term. He did so in order to build a record on cross-strait relations ahead of the 2004 election, in which he would seek a second term.

The first easing measure was the opening in January 2001 of the "mini three links," as mentioned previously. In 2003, he went further to allow regular cross-strait charter flights during the Lunar New Year holiday. The charter flight service was later expanded to other traditional festivals.

Chapter 11
Chen Shui-bian's Legacy as President

With the consent of Beijing, the Chen administration also adopted measures permitting direct remittances between PRC banks and Taiwan's offshore banking units.

Also significantly, Taipei eased restrictions on investments in some designated service industries in the PRC and enacted regulations that made things easier for Taiwan-based multinational firms to employ technical personnel from the PRC.

Yet the most significant of the liberalized measures that Chen introduced in his first term was the easing of his mainland-bound investment policy, described as "active opening and effective management."

This new policy was enacted to replace the "go slow, be patient" rule of Chen's predecessor, President Lee Teng-hui, which set suffocating limits on investments destined for the mainland and became a constant source of complaints from the business community.

Under Chen Shui-bian's less restrictive policy, a NT$50 million cap per project on mainland-bound investment was removed -- an upper limit that had effectively prevented Taiwan companies from implementing any capital-intensive projects on the mainland. The old investment cap deprived local companies of opportunities to expand production or business scale on the mainland. That was seen as hindering the competitiveness of Taiwanese companies.

However, Chen Shui-bian's policy of relaxing investments bound for the mainland underwent a complete reversal at the start of his second term, amid surging anti-China sentiment and growing calls for tighter controls on funds flowing to the mainland.

It's worth noting that the environment in which Chen tightened controls on mainland investment during his second term was somewhat different from that of the "go slow, be patient" era of Lee Teng-hui.

Lee Teng-hui decided to step up controls on investment in the PRC shortly after the 1995-96 military crisis in the Taiwan Strait, triggered by his visit to his alma mater, Cornell University in the United States. The People's Liberation Army conducted a series of intimidating war games and missile tests off Taiwan over a nine-month period. These intimidating military activities collapsed Taiwan's stock and real estate markets, as investors rushed to move their money out of Taiwan to safer places.

Cumulative capital flight incurred during the period was estimated at more than US$20 billion. Taiwan's exports to the mainland, which usually accounted for the bulk of its overseas sales, plunged for the first time, adding to the economic woes already plaguing this island.

The missile crisis and the impact it had on Taiwan's economy reminded Lee Teng-hui of one thing: This island needed to cool its "China trade fever" to avoid the risk of being overly dependent on an economy run by a regime that was still hostile to Taiwan. So Lee instructed his government to regulate investment flows to the mainland, reversing a decade-long liberalization trend of cross-strait exchanges started by the late President Chiang Ching-kuo back in the 1980s.

Yet unlike Lee Teng-hui, Chen Shui-bian decided to resume strict controls on PRC investment for reasons that went far beyond economic security considerations. With a pro-independence president and party having successfully retained governing power for another four years, political ideology came to dominate decision-making in cross-strait exchange policies.

Chen Shui-bian, his fellow DPP politicians, and administration officials now felt it was their responsibility to prevent faster normalization of cross-strait exchanges in the private sector, which they worried could lead to greater economic integration, and ultimately political union with the mainland.

The DPP government reinstated tight controls on cross-strait economic exchanges in a subtle manner. It did not change any particular rules to avoid provoking accusations of flip-flopping on policies. What it did was simply adjust the way the existing "active opening, effective management" policy was implemented. The government quietly shifted the emphasis from "active opening" to "effective management" in regulating Taiwan's mainland-destined investments, thereby slowing the process of screening investment applications.

One high-profile instance of this was the Chen administration's handling of an application filed by Taiwan Semiconductor Manufacturing Co. for a proposed US$898 million investment in the mainland. It took the world's largest producer of custom-made semiconductor chips two full years to get the green light for its proposed 8-inch wafer fabrication plant in Shanghai.

This case and several other similar ones led many critics to the conclusion that the DPP government was indeed using delaying tactics to block big investment projects. They complained that while the government touted the merits of its "active opening, effective management" policy, its actions were indeed focused on "effective management."

Delaying tactics aside, the Chen administration also used various incentives, including subsidized interest on borrowings, to encourage investors to divert projects from China to other countries, such as in Southeast Asia, Latin America, and Africa.

The above-mentioned restrictive measures, however, did little to dampen the enthusiasm of Taiwan companies for cross-strait business. Mainland-bound investment and exports continued to grow at a fast pace.

According to Kerry Brown, a co-author of the study "Investment Across the Taiwan Strait," Taiwan's cumulative investment in the PRC reached US$100 billion in Chen's final years. In annual terms, Taiwan's PRC-bound investment figures for 2007 and 2008 were US$1.7 billion and US$1.8 billion, respectively.[226]

Cross-strait merchandise trade reached US$74.1 billion in the first nine months of 2007, according to the Central News Agency.[227] In that period, Taiwan exported US$53.6 billion worth of products to the mainland and imported US$20.5 billion worth of goods from that market. As these export and import figures showed, Taiwan in the same January to September period continued a long trend of enjoying huge trade surpluses with the mainland.

Two-way travel in the private sector, another vital area in cross-strait exchanges, also had expanded at a rapid pace. Taiwanese made

---

226 Kerry Brown, Justin Hempson-Jones, Jessica Marie Pennisi, Investment Across the Taiwan Strait, Chatham House, November 2010.

227 Luis Huang, Cross-Strait Trade amounts in first three quarters of 2007, Central News Agency, Issued in January 2008.

more than 13 million visits to the mainland over the past decade. And over 250,000 mainland Chinese experts and entrepreneurs traveled to Taiwan during the same period.[228]

The increasing travel, trade, and economic interconnectedness with the PRC put ever-growing pressure on the Chen administration to further accommodate the Taiwan business community by easing restrictions on direct air and sea transport links.

Yet before Ma Ying-jeou of the KMT succeeded Chen Shui-bian as president and liberalized cross-strait exchanges across the board, Taiwan had maintained absolute bans on cross-strait flights and shipping services with the mainland. As noted earlier, these curbs resulted in greater costs in time and money for passenger and cargo traffic, which had to be routed through a third location.

During Chen Shui-bian's eight years in office, calls for removing the transportation restrictions never ceased, but there was no positive response from his administration. Chen and other DPP officials always cited national sovereignty and security considerations as to why the transportation bans could not be lifted.

Chen's Assessment of His Cross-Strait Policy

As his presidency drew to a close, Chen himself provided a general review of his cross-strait economic policy in an interview with The New York Times. The interview was conducted in October 2007, about seven months before he left office. Chen described the state of

---

228 Mainland Affairs Council, Taiwan, January 8, 2008.

economic exchanges with the mainland and explained what he had achieved, what he had failed to do, and why.[229]

Two of the questions put to him by The New York Times were as follows: "You talked in your October 10, 2007, National Day speech about how you thought the 'mini three links' had helped the Taiwanese economy grow. Would 'full three links' then help your stock market, which has lagged behind those in China and Hong Kong; help your manufacturing, which seems to be moving to the mainland; and your tourism industry? Can the Taiwanese economy prosper without 'full three links?'"

To accurately present what President Chen Shui-bian said in reply to the two Times questions, the full text of his answers will be given below:

"Our stock market index is 1,000 points higher than when I took office as President in May 2000. Of course, this is not the whole story, but we cannot be too naïve and so deluded as to think that, with the three links (direct postal, transportation, and commercial links) Taiwan's economy will immediately perk up. This is too simplistic, a case of wishful thinking...

"Rather than imagining that Taiwan's economy would take off after launching the three links under Beijing's one-China principle, should we not take an alternative approach and ask, would not our entire economy be boosted if we could join the United Nations and become a full member? Then, we could freely conduct talks with the

---

229 Transcript of Interview with President Chen Shui-bian of Taiwan, The New York Times, October 18, 2007.

entire world and sign free trade agreements, and we could take part in all of the organizations under the United Nations umbrella, including the IMF and World Bank...

"Taiwan's relationship with China is a country-to-country relationship. Of course, airplanes can fly directly between one country and another, as between Taiwan and the United States or Japan. If Taiwan today were a full member of the U.N., there would of course be nothing strange about direct flights between Taiwan and any city in China. Should we not instead be stressing that only if Taiwan is admitted to the U.N. can it look forward to steady economic growth? (Note: At the time of The New York Times interview, President Chen was in the middle of campaigning for a referendum on whether the government should apply to the United Nations under the name "Taiwan," coming on the heels of his latest U.N. entry bid being rejected by the world body.)

"In fact, during my seven years as President, we have seen an unprecedented intensiveness and closeness of economic relations and business cooperation between Taiwan and China -- including Taiwanese investment in China. This administration launched the 'mini three links' and has expanded it -- something that had not been done before 2000. Moreover, 70 percent of Taiwan's outbound investment goes to China, and 90 percent of Taiwan-based manufacturers' orders are filled by factories in China. So, regarding Taiwan-China economic relations and China-bound investment, the problem is overheating, not any inadequacy...

"Taiwan is an island nation, but we belong to the world and are not cut off from it. So we have to stride out into the world to have a path of survival and a bright future. We know Taiwan cannot afford to isolate itself, but we most certainly cannot put all our resources and economic lifeblood into China...

"In consideration of our national security and national interest, we cannot afford to throw our doors open to a belligerent China that refuses to renounce the use of force against us and is actively scheming to annex us. Therefore, we must adopt a policy of 'active management' in conjunction with 'effective liberalization' in our economic relations with China. Our guiding principle is to move forward pragmatically while maintaining a firm stance [regarding the protection of our national interests]...

"No worthy goal can be achieved overnight. Things must progress in a steady, step-by-step manner. So only after launching the (experimental) mini three links could there be a full three links. Similarly, we already have direct charter flights between Taiwan and China and have expanded them to include four categories [passenger flights on certain holidays as well as special-case cargo flights, ambulance flights, and other humanitarian flights]. We hope, first, to further open up regular direct cargo charter flights, to be followed by regular direct passenger charter flights and, finally by ordinary scheduled flight services. This cannot be done in one swoop...

"Direct transportation is no panacea for enhancing Taiwan's economic development. This applies to the recent promises made by KMT presidential candidate Ma Ying-jeou. If elected, he says, he will open up Taiwan to direct flights between Taiwan and China. In Hualien, he promises to start direct flights from Hualien Airport. In Taitung, it is Taitung Airport. In Taichung, it is Taichung Airport. He wants direct flights everywhere he goes. Can Taiwan accept this?...

"I do not think so. Looking at the matter from the perspective of national security, if we throw all our doors wide open, it would be like giving China the chance to penetrate any locale without meeting with resistance. Could we then maintain the semblance of a nation?...

"If Taiwan is a nation, then Ma Ying-jeou cannot possibly make good his promise within one year after being elected, as he says he will. This cannot happen unless he intends to demote Taiwan to the status of a locale of China, turning it into another special administrative region like Hong Kong or Macau, or a province like Fujian or Jiangsu. If that happened, then, of course, he would have kept his promise. But could the people of Taiwan accept this?"

As Chen Shui-bian remarked in the interview with The New York Times, as quoted above, his initiative to open the "mini three links" early in his presidency indeed was historically significant in cross-strait relations.

But regrettably, he failed to move further to allow the opening of "full three links," which were vitally important to travel and commerce across the strait, only because of his deep-rooted anti-China sentiment and pro-independence ideology.

Chen's assessment that "Taiwan's ties with China are a kind of country-to-country relationship" was only good enough to win praise from the hardline supporters of Taiwan's independence.

But it was not surprising that Beijing had refused to hold talks with Chen's government on air and sea transportation. If it had responded positively, it would have amounted to accepting any cross-strait flights and shipping services as state-to-state or international routes, contradicting its one-China policy.

In the New York Times interview, Chen said: "In consideration of our national security and national interest, we cannot afford to throw our doors open to a belligerent China that refuses to renounce the use of force against us and is actively scheming to annex us."

There indeed was some truth in that statement. But the reality is that Taiwan each year sent the bulk of its exports to the mainland and continued to enjoy huge surpluses in that trade. Under such circumstances, was it feasible or fair for Taiwan to unilaterally keep its doors closed to the mainland on the pretext of protecting its national security and interest? By now, it should be noted that both Taiwan and the mainland had become members of the World Trade Organization, an international body created to promote free trade around the globe.

Douglas Paal, a senior U.S. diplomat who served as the director of the American Institute in Taiwan during most of Chen's presidency, once commented in a speech on Taipei's concerns about "over-dependence" on the PRC market.

"Taiwan must overcome its phobia about economic ties with mainland China," Paal said, adding that these fears were hampering Taiwan's ability to compete effectively in the global economy.[230]

In examining Chen Shui-bian's cross-strait economic policy legacy, these other comments he made in that same New York Times interview also appear to be helpful. He told the newspaper that "70 percent of Taiwan's outbound investment goes to China, and 90 percent

---

230 David G. Brown, 'Chen Muddies Cross-Strait Waters,' the Johns Hopkins School of Advanced International Studies, July-September 2002].

of Taiwan-based manufacturers' orders are filled by factories in China. So, regarding Taiwan-China economic relations and China-bound investment, the problem is overheating."

In some sense, Chen's concerns about overheating were valid. Such heavy reliance on the mainland was unsustainable. However, Chen failed to take any effective measures to address the problem. It was simply not enough for him to continually repeat the refrain: "We most certainly cannot put all our resources and economic lifeblood into China."

Here it was fair to say that by this time Chen Shui-bian still failed to see the root cause of why Taiwan companies had continued to invest huge amounts of money in mainland China and relocate their production there, in defiance of government restrictions and potential punishments.

Put simply, they had done so to stay competitive. Outsourcing production to low-cost countries has long become a universal trend under the pressures of global competition. More and more companies from Germany, the UK, Japan, and the United States, among other major economies, were relocating their processing work to the PRC as their preferred investment destination overseas.

Digby Jones, director general of the Confederation of British Industry, made the following impassioned remarks while addressing a meeting of fellow corporate executives in November 2004 about the need for moving production offshore:

"Offshoring is now part and parcel of doing business in the global economy. This is a survival issue. Anybody who believes that firms have a great deal of choice is naïve. Companies know if they don't do it, somebody else will. If competitors act and they don't respond, they may put their business at risk...Any countries that believe they could fight outsourcing through protectionism live in 'cloud-cuckoo-land'."[231]

However, in Taiwan, President Chen and his ruling party selfishly allowed their political ideologies to outweigh corporate interests by continuing to restrain companies from outsourcing their operations to the PRC to take advantage of lower costs there.

But obviously, the various restrictive rules and regulations enforced over the years were not very successful. The skeptics need only look at the staggering proportion of production outsourced by Taiwan companies to the PRC. As cited by President Chen himself in The New York Times interview, "90 percent of Taiwan-based manufacturers' orders are filled by their factories in China."

Such a high percentage of outsourcing, while unusual, was understandable. Businessmen driven by their need to compete in world markets tended to quietly shift their investments to the mainland, skirting unwelcome government regulations.

The pressure on Taiwan companies to relocate their operations to the mainland could have eased had the Chen government taken measures to lower the cost of production at home, such as opening direct cross-strait transportation services and eliminating unnecessary bureaucracy.

Recent media reports said some Taiwanese companies have

---

231 Larry Elliot, Countries That Fight Outsourcing Are in 'Cloud Cuckoo Land,' The Guardian, Nov. 8.2004.

quietly moved back to this island from mainland China following the 2019 COVID-19 outbreak that prompted widespread lockdowns impacting business activities. The mainland's lingering slow economic growth and its intensifying economic conflict with the United States also appeared to play a role in the latest flow back of investments to Taiwan. More time is needed to tell whether the recent capital inflows are a growing trend. If so, it only proves one fundamental thing: Investors will always move to places where they can operate competitively and profitably.

One other thing also worthy of note here is that Taiwan's longstanding reliance on the mainland market did not weaken its economy or affect its growth and development, as many are concerned. According to the latest International Monetary Fund data, Taiwan is now a highly developed free-market economy. It is the 8th largest in Asia and the 20th largest in the world by purchasing power parity, allowing it to be included in the advanced economies club.

Epilogue

I have long marveled at the complex character of Chen Shui-bian – without doubt, one of Taiwan's most intriguing modern political figures. Chen is a political chameleon, championing different causes throughout his career and appealing to different constituencies as circumstances change. Opinions of the man are sharply divided to this day, and Chen's pro-independence drive, which gained momentum in his second term, was a key factor in this divide.

Chen still has his coterie of admirers, though there are many more detractors, including some of his early comrades in the long struggle to remake Taiwan as a democracy. However, it was the striking contradictions of his character and the confusing mixture of behavior that drew me to the task of recording and analyzing his role in Taiwan's modern history.

In many ways, Chen's assessment of his political contribution is correct -- he did play a vital role in the establishment of a thriving democracy in Taiwan. Without his defeat of the KMT in the 2000 presidential election, Taiwan's journey on the path of democracy might have been sidetracked for a good many years. Chen was hardly the only politician who could claim credit for the island's political transformation from an authoritarian state, but there is no denying that Chen's role was considerable.

As to creating a Taiwan-centric consciousness, Chen's assessment of his performance is only partly accurate. Chen did have an important role in creating the conditions for millions of the island's residents to see themselves as Taiwanese, rather than Chinese, though leaders who preceded him – such as Chiang Ching-kuo and Lee Teng-hui – made major contributions to this too. Chen's push for "name rectification," including a referendum on joining the United Nations under the name "Taiwan," did indeed contribute to this effort. But many would argue that the democratic reforms that Chen and others championed – along with the lengthy political separation of the two regions -- were in reality the main reasons for the development of a very different identity on Taiwan from that of the mainland. The different identity, however, had its limits. Many of those who saw themselves as Taiwanese rather than Chinese, for example, were not supporters of Chen's pro-independence policies.

Chen's version of his legacy also omitted the downside of his controversial presidency. Chen's pro-independence program was implemented with a risky disregard for this island's relationship with critical democratic partners such as the United States. In the end, his actions damaged trust in Washington -- as well as in Beijing.

While Chen initially made modest strides in improving cross-strait ties, putting in place his mini three-links policy, he failed to build on those promising gains. Throughout his eight-year presidency, he tried to maintain tighter controls on investment in the mainland as well as travel and trade across the Taiwan Strait. In the end, his presidency was marred by heightened geopolitical tensions, hampered by his self-imposed ideological obstacles – not to mention Beijing's intransigence.

Most importantly, his venality undermined all of his accomplishments. Once seen as the darling of democracy, even many of his close associates ultimately felt the need to distance themselves from his toxic lack of probity and integrity. In the end, his legacy was also one of political favors, bribe-taking, and funds hidden in overseas bank accounts. His actions aroused the attention of anti-money laundering authorities in countries across the globe -- from Singapore to Switzerland and the United States – to name but a few. Ultimately, his behavior diminished the presidency; it resulted in four criminal convictions (five for his wife) and serious prison sentences for both of them. That is why Chen's story is truly that of a "fall from grace."